T0228686

Handbook of Computational Social Networks

Handbook of Computational Social Networks

Edited by Melva Sawyer

www.statesacademicpress.com

States Academic Press,
109 South 5th Street,
Brooklyn, NY 11249, USA

ISBN: 978-1-63989-256-3

Cataloging-in-Publication Data

Handbook of computational social networks / edited by Melva Sawyer.
    p. cm.
Includes bibliographical references and index.
ISBN 978-1-63989-256-3
1. Online social networks. 2. Computer networks. 3. Human computation.
4. Social networks--Data processing. I. Sawyer, Melva.
QA76.9.C66 H36 2022
006.754--dc23

For information on all States Academic Press publications
visit our website at www.statesacademicpress.com

Contents

Preface

Computational social networks is an academic discipline concerned with the applied, computational, and mathematical aspects of social computing. Computational sociology, culturomics, computational economics, and cliodynamics are certain sub-fields focused on the understanding and investigation of social and behavioral interactions and relationships. Some of the tools used for social analysis include network analysis, social simulation, modelling, and media analysis. This book presents the complex subject of computational social networks in the most comprehensible and easy to understand language. From theories to research to practical applications, case studies related to all contemporary topics of relevance to this field have been included herein. This book will prove to be immensely beneficial to students and researchers in this field.

After months of intensive research and writing, this book is the end result of all who devoted their time and efforts in the initiation and progress of this book. It will surely be a source of reference in enhancing the required knowledge of the new developments in the area. During the course of developing this book, certain measures such as accuracy, authenticity and research focused analytical studies were given preference in order to produce a comprehensive book in the area of study.

This book would not have been possible without the efforts of the authors and the publisher. I extend my sincere thanks to them. Secondly, I express my gratitude to my family and well-wishers. And most importantly, I thank my students for constantly expressing their willingness and curiosity in enhancing their knowledge in the field, which encourages me to take up further research projects for the advancement of the area.

Editor

Real-time topic-aware influence maximization using preprocessing

Wei Chen[1†], Tian Lin[2*†] [iD] and Cheng Yang[3†]

*Correspondence:
lintian06@gmail.com
†Wei Chen, Tian Lin and
Cheng Yang contributed
equally to this work
[2] Institute for Advanced
Study, Tsinghua University,
No. 1 Tsinghua Yuan,
100084 Beijing, China
Full list of author information
is available at the end of the
article

Abstract

Background: Influence maximization is the task of finding a set of seed nodes in a social network such that the influence spread of these seed nodes based on certain influence diffusion model is maximized. Topic-aware influence diffusion models have been recently proposed to address the issue that influence between a pair of users are often topic-dependent and information, ideas, innovations etc. being propagated in networks are typically mixtures of topics.

Methods: In this paper, we focus on the topic-aware influence maximization task. In particular, we study preprocessing methods to avoid redoing influence maximization for each mixture from scratch.

Results: We explore two preprocessing algorithms with theoretical justifications.

Conclusions: Our empirical results on data obtained in a couple of existing studies demonstrate that one of our algorithms stands out as a strong candidate providing microsecond online response time and competitive influence spread, with reasonable preprocessing effort.

Keywords: Influence maximization, Topic-aware influence modeling, Information diffusion

Background

In a social network, information, ideas, rumors, and innovations can be propagated to a large number of people because of the social influence between the connected peers in the network. *Influence maximization* is the task of finding a set of *seed nodes* in a social network such that the influence propagated from the seed nodes can reach the largest number of people in the network. More technically, a social network is modeled as a graph with nodes representing individuals and directed edges representing influence relationships. The network is associated with a stochastic diffusion model (such as independent cascade model and linear threshold model [1]) characterizing the influence propagation dynamics starting from the seed nodes. Influence maximization is to find a set of k seed nodes in the network such that the *influence spread*, defined as the expected number of nodes influenced (or activated) through influence diffusion starting from the seed nodes, is maximized [1, 2].

Influence maximization has a wide range of applications including viral marketing [1, 3, 4], information monitoring and outbreak detection [5], competitive viral marketing and rumor control [6, 7], or even text summarization [8] (by modeling a word influence network). As a result, influence maximization has been extensively studied in the past decade. Research directions include improvements in the efficiency and scalability of influence maximization algorithms [9–11], extensions to other diffusion models and optimization problems [6, 7, 12], and influence model learning from real-world data [13–15].

Most of these works treat diffusions of all information, rumors, ideas, etc. (collectively referred as *items* in this paper) as following the same model with a single set of parameters. In reality, however, influence between a pair of friends may differ depending on the topic. For example, one may be more influential to the other on high-tech gadgets, while the other is more influential on fashion topics, or one researcher is more influential on data mining topics to her peers but less influential on algorithm and theory topics. Recently, Barbieri et al. [16] propose the topic-aware independent cascade (TIC) and linear threshold (TLT) models, in which a diffusion item is a mixture of topics and influence parameters for each item are also mixtures of parameters for individual topics. They provide learning methods to learn influence parameters in the topic-aware models from real-world data. Such topic-mixing models require new thinking in terms of the influence maximization task, which is what we address in this paper.

In this paper, we adopt the models proposed in [16] and study efficient topic-aware influence maximization schemes. One can still apply topic-oblivious influence maximization algorithms in online processing of every diffusion item, but it may not be efficient when there are a large number of items with different topic mixtures or real-time responses are required. Thus, we focus on preprocessing individual topic influence such that when a diffusion item with certain topic mixture comes, the online processing of finding the seed set is fast. To do so, our first step is to collect two datasets in the past studies with available topic-aware influence analysis results on real networks and investigate their properties pertaining to our preprocessing purpose ("Data observation" section). Our data analysis shows that in one network users and their relationships are largely separated by different topics while in the other network they have significant overlaps on different topics. Even with this difference, a common property we find is that in both datasets most top seeds for a topic mixture come from top seeds of the constituent topics, which matches our intuition that influential individuals for a mixed item are usually influential in at least one topic category.

Motivated by our findings from the data analysis, we explore two preprocessing based algorithms ("Preprocessing based algorithms" section). The first algorithm, *Best Topic Selection* (BTS), minimizes online processing by simply using a seed set for one of the constituent topics. Even for such a simple algorithm, we are able to provide a theoretical approximation ratio (when a certain property holds), and thus BTS serves as a baseline for preprocessing algorithms. The second algorithm, *Marginal Influence Sort* (MIS), further uses pre-computed marginal influence of seeds on each topic to avoid slow greedy computation. We provide a theoretical justification showing that MIS can be as good as the offline greedy algorithm when nodes are fully separated by topics.

We then conduct experimental evaluations of these algorithms and comparing them with both the greedy algorithm and a state-of-the-art heuristic algorithm PMIA [10], on the two datasets used in data analysis as well as a third dataset for testing scalability

("Experiments" section). From our results, we see that MIS algorithm stands out as the best candidate for preprocessing based real-time influence maximization: it finishes online processing within a few microseconds and its influence spread either matches or is very close to that of the greedy algorithm.

Our work, together with a recent independent work [17], is one of the first that study topic-aware influence maximization with focus on preprocessing. Comparing to [17], our contributions include: (a) we include data analysis on two real-world datasets with learned influence parameters, which shows different topical influence properties and motivates our algorithm design; (b) we provide theoretical justifications to our algorithms; (c) the use of marginal influence of seeds in individual topics in MIS is novel, and is complementary to the approach in [17]; (d) even though MIS is quite simple, it achieves competitive influence spread within microseconds of online processing time rather than milliseconds needed in [17].

Preliminaries

In this section, we introduce the background and problem definition on the topic-aware influence diffusion models. We focus on the independent cascade model [1] for ease of presentation, but our results also hold for other models parameterized with edge parameters such as the linear threshold model [1].

Independent cascade model

We consider a social network as a directed graph $G = (V, E)$, where each node in V represents a user, and each edge in E represents the relationship between two users. For every edge $(u, v) \in E$, denote its *influence probability* as $p(u, v) \in [0, 1]$, and for all $(u, v) \notin E$ or $u = v$, we assume $p(u, v) = 0$.

The *independent cascade* (IC) model, defined in [1], captures the stochastic process of contagion in discrete time. Initially at time step $t = 0$, a set of nodes $S \subseteq V$ called *seed nodes* are activated. At any time $t \geq 1$, if node u is activated at time $t - 1$, it has one chance of activating each of its inactive outgoing neighbor v with probability $p(u, v)$. A node stays active after it is activated. This process stops when no more nodes are activated. We define *influence spread* of seed set S under influence probability function p, denoted $\sigma(S, p)$, as the expected number of active nodes after the diffusion process ends. As shown in [1], for any fixed p, $\sigma(S, p)$ is monotone [i.e., $\sigma(S, p) \leq \sigma(T, p)$ for any $S \subseteq T$] and submodular [i.e., $\sigma(S \cup \{v\}, p) - \sigma(S, p) \geq \sigma(T \cup \{v\}, p) - \sigma(T, p)$ for any $S \subseteq T$ and $v \in V$] on its seed set parameter. The next lemma further shows that for any fixed S, $\sigma(S, p)$ is monotone in p. For two influence probability functions p and p' on graph $G = (V, E)$, we denote $p \leq p'$ if for any $(u, v) \in E$, $p(u, v) \leq p'(u, v)$. We say that influence spread function $\sigma(S, p)$ is *monotone in p* if for any $p \leq p'$, we have $\sigma(S, p) \leq \sigma(S, p')$.

Lemma 1 *For any fixed seed set $S \subseteq V$, $\sigma(S, p)$ is monotone in p.*

Proof sketch We use the following coupling method. For any edge $(u, v) \in E$, we select a number $x(u, v)$ uniformly at random in $[0, 1]$. Then for any influence probability function p, we select edge (u, v) as a *live edge* if $x(u, v) \leq p(u, v)$ and otherwise it is a *blocked edge*. All live edges form a random *live-edge graph* $G_L(p)$. One can verify that $\sigma(S, p)$ is the expected value of the size of node set reachable from S in random graph $G_L(p)$. Moreover, for p and p' such that $p \leq p'$, one can verify that after fixing the random numbers $x(u, v)'s$, live-edge graph $G_L(p)$ is a subgraph of live-edge graph $G_L(p')$, and thus nodes reachable from S in $G_L(p)$ must be also reachable from S in $G_L(p')$. This implies that $\sigma(S, p) \leq \sigma(S, p')$. $\qquad\qquad\qquad\qquad\qquad\qquad\qquad\qquad\qquad\qquad\qquad\qquad\square$

We remark that using a similar idea as above we could show that influence spread in the linear threshold (LT) model [1] is also monotone in the edge weight parameter.

Algorithm 1 Greedy algorithm.

Require: $G = (V, E)$, p, k.
1: $S_0 = \emptyset$
2: **for** $j = 1, 2, \cdots, k$ **do**
3: $\quad v_j = \text{argmax}_{v \in V \setminus S_{j-1}} MI(v|S_{j-1}, p)$
4: $\quad S_j = S_{j-1} \cup \{v_j\}$
5: **end for**
6: **return** S_k

Influence maximization

Given a graph $G = (V, E)$, an influence probability function p, and a budget k, *influence maximization* is the task of selecting at most k seed nodes such that the influence spread is maximized, i.e., finding set $S^* = S^*(k, p)$ such that

$$S^*(k, p) = \underset{S \subseteq V, |S| \leq k}{\arg \max}\ \sigma(S, p).$$

In [1], Kempe et al. show that the influence maximization problem is NP-hard in both the IC model and the LT model. They propose the greedy approach for influence maximization, as shown in Algorithm 1. Given influence probability function p, the *marginal influence (MI)* of a node v under seed set S is defined as $MI(v|S, p) = \sigma(S \cup \{v\}, p) - \sigma(S, p)$, for any $v \in V$. The greedy algorithm selects k seeds in k iterations, and in the j-th iteration it selects a node v_j with the largest marginal influence under the current seed set S_{j-1} and adds v_j into S_{j-1} to obtain S_j. Kempe et al. use Monte Carlo simulations to obtain accurate estimates on marginal influence $MI(v|S, p)$, and later Chen et al. show that indeed exact computation of influence spread $\sigma(S, p)$ or marginal influence $MI(v|S, p)$ is #P-hard [10]. The monotonicity and submodularity of $\sigma(S, p)$ in S guarantees that the greedy algorithm selects a seed set with approximation ratio $1 - \frac{1}{e} - \varepsilon$, that is, it returns a seed set $S^g = S^g(k, p)$ such that

$$\sigma(S^g, p) \geq \left(1 - \frac{1}{e} - \varepsilon\right)\sigma(S^*, p),$$

for any small $\varepsilon > 0$, where ε accommodates the inaccuracy in Monte Carlo estimations.

Topic-aware independent cascade model and topic-aware influence maximization

Topic-aware independent cascade (TIC) model [16] is an extension of the IC model to incorporate topic mixtures in any diffusion item. Suppose there are d base topics, and we use set notation $[d] = \{1, 2, \ldots, d\}$ to denote topic $1, 2, \ldots, d$. We regard each diffusion item as a distribution of these topics. Thus, any item can be expressed as a vector $I = (\lambda_1, \lambda_2, \ldots, \lambda_d)$ where $\forall i \in [d]$, $\lambda_i \in [0, 1]$ and $\sum_{i \in [d]} \lambda_i = 1$. We also refer $(\lambda_1, \lambda_2, \ldots, \lambda_d)$ as a *topic mixture*. Given a directed social graph $G = (V, E)$, for any topic $i \in [d]$, influence probability on that topic is $p_i : V \times V \rightarrow [0, 1]$, and for all $(u, v) \notin E$ or $u = v$, we assume $p_i(u, v) = 0$. In the TIC model, the influence probability function p for any diffusion item $I = (\lambda_1, \lambda_2, \ldots, \lambda_d)$ is defined as $p(u, v) = \sum_{i \in [d]} \lambda_i p_i(u, v)$, for all $u, v \in V$ (or simply $p = \sum_{i \in [d]} \lambda_i p_i$). Then, the stochastic diffusion process and influence spread $\sigma(S, p)$ are exactly the same as defined in the IC model by using the influence probability p on edges.

Given a social graph G, base topics $[d]$, influence probability function p_i for each base topic i, a budget k and an item $I = (\lambda_1, \lambda_2, \ldots, \lambda_d)$, the *topic-aware influence maximization* is the task of finding optimal seeds $S^* = S^*(k, p) \subseteq V$, where $p = \sum_{i \in [d]} \lambda_i p_i$, to maximize the influence spread, i.e.,

$$S^* = \arg\max_{S \subseteq V, |S| \leq k} \sigma(S, p).$$

Data observation

There are relatively few studies on topic-aware influence analysis. For our study, we are able to obtain datasets from two prior studies, one is on social movie rating network Flixster [16] and the other is on academic collaboration network Arnetminer [14]. In this section, we describe these two datasets, and present statistical observations on these datasets, which will help us in our algorithm design.

Data description

We obtain two real-world datasets, Flixster and Arnetminer, which include influence analysis results from their respective raw data, from the authors of the prior studies [14, 16].

Flixster[1] is an American social movie site for discovering new movies, learning about movies, and meeting others with similar tastes in movies. The raw data in Flixster dataset is the action traces of movie ratings of users. The Flixster network represents users as nodes, and two users u and v are connected by a directed edge (u, v) if they are friends both rating the same movie and v rates the movie shortly later after u does so. The network contains 29,357 nodes, 425,228 directed edges and 10 topics [16]. Barbieri et al. [16] use their proposed TIC model and apply maximum likelihood estimation method on the action traces to obtain influence probabilities on edges for all 10 topics. We found that there are a disproportionate number of edges with influence probabilities higher than 0.99, which is due to the lack of sufficient samplings of propagation events over these edges. We smoothen these influence probability values by changing all the probabilities larger than 0.99 to random numbers according to the probability distribution of all the probabilities smaller than 0.99. We also obtain 11,659 topic mixtures, and demonstrate the distribution of the number of topics in item mixtures in Table 1. We eliminate individual probabilities that are too weak ($\forall i \in [d]$, $\lambda_i < 0.01$). In general, most items are

---

[1] http://www.flixster.com.

on a single topic only, with some two-topic mixtures. Mixtures with three or four topics are already rare and there are no items with five or more topics.

Arnetminer[2] is a free online service used to index and search academic social networks. The Arnetminer network represents authors as nodes and two authors have an edge if they coauthored a paper. The raw data in the Arnetminer dataset is not the action traces but the topic distributions of all nodes and the network structure [14]. Tang et al. apply factor graph analysis to obtain influence probabilities on edges from node topic distributions and the network structure [14]. The resulting network contains 5114 nodes, 34,334 directed edges and 8 topics, and all 8 topics are related to computer science, such as data mining, machine learning, information retrieval, etc. Mixed items propagated in such academic networks could be ideas or papers from related topic mixtures, although there are no raw data of topic mixtures available in Arnetminer.

Table 2 provides statistics for the learned influence probabilities for every topic in Arnetminer and Flixster dataset. Column "nonzero" provides the number of edges having nonzero probabilities on the specific topic. Other columns are mean, standard deviation, 25-, 50-% (median), and 75-% of the probabilities among the nonzero entries. The basic statistics show similar behavior between the two datasets, such as mean probabilities are mostly between 0.1 and 0.2, standard deviations are mostly between 0.1 and 0.3, etc. Comparing among different topics, even though the means and other statistics are similar to one another, the number of nonzero edges may have up to tenfold difference. This indicates that some topics are more likely to propagate than others.

Topic separation on edges and nodes

For the two datasets, we would like to investigate how different topics overlap on edges and nodes. To do so, we define the following coefficients to characterize the properties of a social graph.

Given threshold $\theta \geq 0$, for every topic i, denote edge set $\tau_i(\theta) = \{(u, v) \in E \mid p_i(u, v) > \theta\}$, and node set $v_i(\theta) = \{v \in V \mid \sum_{u:(v,u)\in E} p_i(v, u) + \sum_{u:(u,v)\in E} p_i(u, v) > \theta\}$. For topics i and j, we define *edge overlap coefficient* as $R_{ij}^E(\theta) = \frac{|\tau_i(\theta) \cap \tau_j(\theta)|}{\min\{|\tau_i(\theta)|, |\tau_j(\theta)|\}}$, and *node overlap coefficient* as $R_{ij}^V(\theta) = \frac{|v_i(\theta) \cap v_j(\theta)|}{\min\{|v_i(\theta)|, |v_j(\theta)|\}}$. If θ is small and the overlap coefficient is small, it means that the two topics are fairly separated in the network. In particular, we say that the network is *fully separable* for topics i and j if $R_{ij}^V(0) = 0$, and it is fully separable for all topics if $R_{ij}^V(0) = 0$ for any pair i and j with $i \neq j$. Then we apply the above coefficients to the Flixster and Arnetminer datasets.

Table 3 shows the edge and node overlap coefficients with threshold $\theta = 0.1$ for every pair of topics in the Arnetminer dataset. Correlating with Table 2a, we see that $\theta = 0.1$ is around the mean value for all topics. Thus it is a reasonably small value especially for the node overlap coefficients, which is about aggregated probability of all edges incident to a node. A clear indication in Table 3 is that topic overlap on both edges and nodes are very small in Arnetminer, with most node overlap coefficients less than 5%. We believe that this is because in academic collaboration network, most researchers work on one

---

[2] arnetminer.org.

Table 1 Distribution of topic numbers of mixture items in Flixster

Mixed topics	1	2	3	4	5
Samples	11,285	354	18	2	0
(%)	(96.79)	(3.04)	(0.15)	(0.02)	(0.00)

Table 2 Influence probability statistics

Topic	Nonzero	Mean	Std.	25%	50%	75%
(a) Arnetminer						
1	3355	0.175	0.230	0.023	0.075	0.229
2	13,331	0.093	0.154	0.010	0.031	0.100
3	3821	0.158	0.214	0.020	0.065	0.201
4	1537	0.217	0.243	0.038	0.120	0.316
5	2468	0.197	0.262	0.018	0.080	0.266
6	1236	0.240	0.273	0.034	0.122	0.353
7	4439	0.145	0.222	0.011	0.046	0.177
8	3439	0.162	0.220	0.022	0.069	0.201
(b) Flixster						
1	54,032	0.173	0.215	1.00E−04	0.086	0.264
2	84,322	0.172	0.227	4.36E−05	0.067	0.260
3	231,807	0.089	0.146	1.18E−04	0.024	0.112
4	35,394	0.162	0.226	6.78E−03	0.050	0.250
5	118,125	0.097	0.141	2.45E−03	0.037	0.131
6	37,489	0.090	0.142	6.85E−03	0.033	0.100
7	84,716	0.166	0.230	3.12E−05	0.050	0.250
8	149,140	0.097	0.145	9.01E−04	0.036	0.131
9	152,181	0.103	0.158	2.14E−04	0.032	0.140
10	139,335	0.159	0.235	3.27E−05	0.029	0.250

specific research area, and only a small number of researchers work across different research areas.

Tables 4 and 5 show the edge and node overlap coefficients for the Flixster dataset. Different from the Arnetminer dataset, both edges and nodes have significant overlaps. For edge overlaps, even with threshold $\theta = 0.3$, all topic pairs have edge overlap between 15 and 40%. For node overlap, we test the threshold for both 0.5–5, but the overlap

Table 3 Edge and node overlap coefficients on Arnetminer

–	0.017	0.002	0.000	0.005	0.006	0.000	0.022
0.068	–	0.001	0.004	0.001	0.001	0.002	0.000
0.018	*0.014*	–	0.000	0.000	0.001	0.000	0.000
0.002	*0.029*	*0.000*	–	0.000	0.011	0.017	0.000
0.025	*0.005*	*0.005*	*0.000*	–	0.000	0.000	0.015
0.054	*0.049*	*0.049*	*0.011*	*0.000*	–	0.009	0.001
0.006	*0.025*	*0.003*	*0.017*	*0.007*	*0.063*	–	0.000
0.108	*0.001*	*0.008*	*0.000*	*0.079*	*0.011*	*0.004*	–

The upper triangle represents edge overlap coefficient when $\theta = 0.1$. The entry on row i, column j represents $R^E_{ij}(0.1)$; the lower italic triangle represents node overlap coefficient when $\theta = 0.1$. The entry on row i, column j represents $R^V_{ij}(0.1)$

Table 4 Edge overlap coefficients on Flixster

–	0.33	0.49	0.27	0.36	0.35	0.35	0.42	0.43	0.39
0.22	–	0.48	0.33	0.31	0.41	0.31	0.36	0.38	0.39
0.28	*0.26*	–	0.46	0.50	0.48	0.55	0.50	0.57	0.52
0.15	*0.19*	*0.22*	–	0.33	0.25	0.31	0.37	0.38	0.38
0.20	*0.25*	*0.34*	*0.13*	–	0.52	0.30	0.46	0.45	0.37
0.23	*0.29*	*0.28*	*0.16*	*0.31*	–	0.36	0.50	0.47	0.38
0.25	*0.21*	*0.34*	*0.18*	*0.24*	*0.25*	–	0.37	0.43	0.46
0.21	*0.24*	*0.38*	*0.15*	*0.31*	*0.29*	*0.25*	–	0.44	0.37
0.24	*0.24*	*0.44*	*0.17*	*0.32*	*0.28*	*0.29*	*0.35*	–	0.42
0.28	*0.27*	*0.47*	*0.23*	*0.29*	*0.26*	*0.35*	*0.32*	*0.37*	–

The upper triangle represents edge overlap coefficient when $\theta = 0.1$. The entry on row i, column j represents $R_{ij}^E(0.1)$; the lower italic triangle represents edge overlap coefficient when $\theta = 0.3$. The entry on row i, column j represents $R_{ij}^E(0.3)$

Table 5 Node overlap coefficients on Flixster

–	0.79	0.91	0.68	0.76	0.81	0.77	0.83	0.85	0.87
0.69	–	0.88	0.82	0.76	0.88	0.75	0.74	0.77	0.84
0.83	*0.64*	–	0.93	0.92	0.95	0.91	0.92	0.91	0.87
0.53	*0.67*	*0.75*	–	0.77	0.63	0.78	0.83	0.85	0.89
0.58	*0.70*	*0.87*	*0.50*	–	0.90	0.73	0.84	0.85	0.85
0.76	*0.83*	*0.86*	*0.46*	*0.91*	–	0.86	0.93	0.92	0.91
0.71	*0.53*	*0.72*	*0.62*	*0.72*	*0.78*	–	0.77	0.81	0.88
0.72	*0.57*	*0.82*	*0.60*	*0.85*	*0.89*	*0.59*	–	0.83	0.84
0.74	*0.53*	*0.84*	*0.62*	*0.82*	*0.89*	*0.63*	*0.73*	–	0.83
0.89	*0.74*	*0.81*	*0.83*	*0.88*	*0.89*	*0.82*	*0.82*	*0.84*	–

The upper triangle represents node overlap coefficient when $\theta = 0.5$. The entry on row i, column j represents $R_{ij}^V(0.5)$; the lower italic triangle represents node overlap coefficient when $\theta = 5.0$. The entry on row i, column j represents $R_{ij}^V(5.0)$

coefficients do not significantly change: at $\theta = 5$, most pairs still have above 60% and up to 89% overlap. We think that this could be explained by the nature of Flixster, which is a movie rating site. Most users are interested in multiple categories of movies, and their influence to their friends are also likely to be across multiple categories. It is interesting to see that, even though the per-topic statistics between Arnetminer and Flixster are similar, they show quite different cross-topic overlap behaviors, which can be explained by the nature of the networks. This could be an independent research topic for further investigations on the influence behaviors among different topics.

Table 6 summarizes the edge and node overlap coefficient statistics among all pairs of topics for the two datasets. We can see that Arnetminer network has fairly separate topics on both nodes and edges, while Flixter network have significant topic overlaps. This may be explained by that in an academic network most researchers only work in one research area, but in a movie network many users are interested in more than one type of movies. Therefore, our first observation is:

Observation 1   Topic separation in terms of influence probabilities is network dependent. In the Arnetminer network, topics are mostly separated among different edges and nodes in the network, while in the Flixster network there are significant overlaps on topics among nodes and edges.

Table 6 Overlap coefficient statistics for all topic pairs

	Min	Mean	Max
Arnetminer: R_{ij}^E (0.1)	0	0.0041	0.022
Arnetminer: R_{ij}^V (0.1)	0	0.0236	0.108
Flixster: R_{ij}^E (0.1)	0.25	0.4058	0.57
Flixster: R_{ij}^E (0.3)	0.13	0.2662	0.47
Flixster: R_{ij}^V (0.5)	0.63	0.836	0.95
Flixster: R_{ij}^V (5.0)	0.46	0.734	0.91

Sources of seeds in the mixture

Our second observation is more directly related to influence maximization. We would like to see if seeds selected by the greedy algorithm for a topic mixture are likely coming from top seeds for each individual topic. Intuitively, it seems reasonable to assume that top influencers for a topic mixture are likely from top influencers in their constituent topics.

To check the source of seeds, we randomly generate 50 mixtures of two topics for both Arnetminer and Flixster, and use the greedy algorithm to select seeds for the mixture and the constituent topics. We then check the percentage of seeds in the mixture that is also in the constituent topics. Table 7 shows our test results (Flixster (Dirhilect) is the result using a Dirichlet distribution to generate topic mixtures; see "Experiments" section for more details). Our observation below matches our intuition:

Observation 2 Most seeds for topic mixtures come from the seeds of constituent topics, in both Arnetminer and Flixster networks.

For Arnetminer, it is likely due to the topic separation as observed in Table 3. For Flixster, even though topics have significant overlaps, these overlaps may result in many shared seeds between topics, which would also contribute as top seeds for topic mixtures.

Preprocessing based algorithms

Topic-aware influence maximization can be solved by using existing influence maximization algorithms such as the ones in [1, 10]: when a query on an item $I = (\lambda_1, \lambda_2, \ldots, \lambda_d)$ comes, the algorithm first computes the mixed influence probability function $p = \sum_j \lambda_j p_j$, and then applies existing algorithms using parameter p. This, however, means that for each topic mixture influence maximization has to be carried out from scratch, which could be inefficient in large-scale networks.

Table 7 Percentage of seeds in topic mixture that are also seeds of constituent topics

	Arnetminer	Flixster (random)	Flixster (Dirichlet)
Seeds overlap (%)	94.80	81.16	85.24

Algorithm 2 Best Topic Selection (BTS) Algorithm

Require: $G = (V, E)$, k, $\{p_i \mid i \in [d]\}$, $I = (\lambda_1, \cdots, \lambda_d)$, Λ, $S^g(k, \lambda p_i)$ and $\sigma(S^g(k, \lambda p_i), \lambda p_i)$, $\forall \lambda \in \Lambda, \forall i \in [d]$.
1: $I' = (\underline{\lambda}_1, \cdots, \underline{\lambda}_d)$
2: $i' = \mathrm{argmax}_{i \in D_I^+} \sigma(S^g(k, \underline{\lambda}_i p_i), \underline{\lambda}_i p_i)$
3: **return** $S^g(k, \underline{\lambda}_{i'} p_{i'})$

In this section, motivated by observations made in "Data observation" section, we introduce two preprocessing based algorithms that cover different design choices. The first algorithm Best Topic Selection focuses on minimizing online processing time, and the second one MIS uses pre-computed marginal influence to achieve both fast online processing and competitive influence spread. For convenience, we consider the budget k as fixed in our algorithms, but we could extend the algorithms to consider multiple k values in preprocessing.

Best topic selection (BTS) algorithm

The idea of our first algorithm is to minimize online processing by simply selecting a seed set for one of the constituent topics in the topic mixture that has the best influence performance, and thus we call it Best Topic Selection (BTS) algorithm. More specifically, given an item $I = (\lambda_1, \lambda_2, \ldots, \lambda_d)$, if we have pre-computed the seed set $S_i^g = S^g(k, \lambda p_i)$ via the greedy algorithm for each topic i, then we would simply use the seed set $S_{i'}^g$ that gives the best influence spread, i.e., $i' = \arg\max_{i \in [d]} \sigma(S_i^g, \lambda_i p_i)$. However, in the pre-processing stage, the topic mixture $(\lambda_1, \lambda_2, \ldots, \lambda_d)$ is not guaranteed to be pre-computed exactly. To deal with this issue, we pre-compute influence spread for a number of landmark points for each topic, and use rounding method in online processing to complete seed selection, as we explain in more detail now.

Preprocess stage

Denote constant set $\Lambda = \{\lambda_0^c, \lambda_1^c, \lambda_2^c, \ldots, \lambda_m^c\}$ as a set of *landmarks*, where $0 = \lambda_0^c < \lambda_1^c < \cdots < \lambda_m^c = 1$. For each $\lambda \in \Lambda$ and each topic $i \in [d]$, we pre-compute $S^g(k, \lambda p_i)$ and $\sigma(S^g(k, \lambda p_i), \lambda p_i)$ in the preprocessing stage, and store these values for online processing. In our experiments, we use uniformly selected landmarks and show that they are good enough for influence maximization. More sophisticated landmark selection method may be applied, such as the machine learning based method in [17].

Online stage

We define two rounding notations that return one of the neighboring landmarks in $\Lambda = \{\lambda_0^c, \lambda_1^c, \ldots, \lambda_m^c\}$: for any $\lambda \in [0, 1]$, $\underline{\lambda}$ is denoted as rounding λ down to λ_j^c where $\lambda_j^c \le \lambda < \lambda_{j+1}^c$ and $\lambda_j^c, \lambda_{j+1}^c \in \Lambda$, and $\overline{\lambda}$ as rounding up to λ_{j+1}^c where $\lambda_j^c < \lambda \le \lambda_{j+1}^c$ and $\lambda_j^c, \lambda_{j+1}^c \in \Lambda$. Given $I = (\lambda_1, \lambda_2, \ldots, \lambda_d)$, let $D_I^+ = \{i \in [d] \mid \lambda_i > 0\}$. With the pre-computed $S^g(k, \lambda p_i)$ and $\sigma(S^g(k, \lambda p_i), \lambda p_i)$ for every $\lambda \in \Lambda$ and every topic i, the BTS algorithm is given in Algorithm 2. The algorithm basically rounds down the mixing coefficient on every topic to $(\underline{\lambda}_1, \ldots, \underline{\lambda}_d)$, and then returns the seed set $S^g(k, \underline{\lambda}_{i'} p_{i'})$ that gives the largest influence spread at the round-down landmarks: $i' = \arg\max_{i \in D_I^+} \sigma(S^g(k, \underline{\lambda}_i p_i), \underline{\lambda}_i p_i)$.

BTS is rather simple since it directly outputs a seed set for one of the constituent topics. However, we show below that even such a simple scheme could provide a theoretical approximation guarantee (if the influence spread function is sub-additive as defined below). Thus, we use BTS as a baseline for preprocessing based algorithms.

We say that influence spread function $\sigma(S, p)$ is *c-sub-additive in p* for some constant c if for every set $S \subseteq V$ with $|S| \leq k$ and every mixture $(\lambda_1, \lambda_2, \ldots, \lambda_d)$, $\sigma(S, \sum_{i \in D_I^+} \lambda_i p_i)$ $\leq c \sum_{i \in D_I^+} \sigma(S, \lambda_i p_i)$. The sub-additivity property above means that the influence spread of any seed set S in any topic mixture will not exceed constant times of the sum of the influence spread of the same seed set for each individual topic. It is easy to verify that, when the network is fully separable for all topic pairs, $\sigma(S, p)$ is 1-sub-additive. The only counterexample to the sub-additivity assumption that we could find is a tree structure where even layer edges are for one topic and odd layer edges are for another topic. Such structures are rather artificial, and we believe that for real networks the influence spread is *c-sub-additive in p* with a reasonably small constant c.

We define $\mu_{\max} = \max_{i \in [d], \lambda \in [0,1]} \frac{\sigma(S^g(k, \bar{\lambda} p_i), \bar{\lambda} p_i)}{\sigma(S^g(k, \underline{\lambda} p_i), \underline{\lambda} p_i)}$, which is a value controlled by preprocessing. A fine-grained landmark set Λ could make $\mu_{\max}$ close to 1. The following Theorem 1 guarantees the theoretical approximation ratio of Algorithm 2.

Theorem 1 *If the influence spread function $\sigma(S, p)$ is c-sub-additive in p, Algorithm 2 achieves $\frac{1 - e^{-1}}{c|D_I^+|\mu_{\max}}$ approximation ratio for item $I = (\lambda_1, \lambda_2, \ldots, \lambda_d)$.*

Proof Denote $S^* = S^*(k, p)$, $\overline{S}_i^* = S^*(k, \bar{\lambda}_i p_i)$, $\overline{S}_i^g = S^g(k, \bar{\lambda}_i p_i)$ and $\underline{S}_i^g = S^g(k, \underline{\lambda}_i p_i)$. Since $\sigma(S, p)$ is monotone (Lemma 1) and c-sub-additive in p, it implies $\sigma(S^*, p) = \sigma(S^*, \sum_{i \in D_I^+} \lambda_i p_i) \leq c \sum_{i \in D_I^+} \sigma(S^*, \lambda_i p_i) \leq c \sum_{i \in D_I^+} \sigma(S^*, \bar{\lambda}_i p_i)$. From [1], we know $\sigma(S^*(k, p_0), p_0) \leq \frac{1}{1 - e^{-1}} \sigma(S^g(k, p_0), p_0)$ holds for any p_0 in Algorithm 1. Thus we have, for each $i \in D_I^+$, $\sigma(S^*, \bar{\lambda}_i p_i) \leq \sigma(\overline{S}_i^*, \bar{\lambda}_i p_i) \leq \frac{\sigma(\overline{S}_i^g, \bar{\lambda}_i p_i)}{1 - e^{-1}} \leq \frac{\mu_{\max} \cdot \sigma(\underline{S}_i^g, \underline{\lambda}_i p_i)}{1 - e^{-1}}$. According to line 2 of Algorithm 2, i' satisfies $\sigma(\underline{S}_{i'}^g, \underline{\lambda}_{i'} p_{i'}) = \max_{i \in D_I^+} \sigma(\underline{S}_i^g, \underline{\lambda}_i p_i)$, and $\sigma(\underline{S}_{i'}^g, \underline{\lambda}_{i'} p_{i'}) \leq \sigma(\underline{S}_{i'}^g, \lambda_{i'} p_{i'})$. Thus, connecting all the inequalities, we have $\sigma(S^*, p)$ $\leq \frac{c|D_I^+|\mu_{\max}}{1 - e^{-1}} \sigma(\underline{S}_{i'}^g, \lambda_{i'} p_{i'})$. Therefore, Algorithm 2 achieves approximation ratio of $\frac{1}{c|D_I^+|\mu_{\max}}(1 - \frac{1}{e})$ under the sub-additive assumption. $\qquad\square$

The approximation ratio given in the theorem is a conservative bound for the worst case (e.g., a common setting may be $c = 1$, $\mu_{\max} = 1.5$, $|D_I^+| = 2$). Tighter online bound in our experiment section based on [5] shows that Algorithm 2 performs much better than the worst case scenario.

Marginal influence sort (MIS) algorithm

Our second algorithm derives the seed set from pre-computed seed set of constituent topics, which is based on Observation 2. Moreover, it uses marginal influence information pre-computed to help select seeds from different seed sets. Our idea is partially motivated from Observation 1, especially the observation on Arnetminer dataset, which shows that in some cases the network could be well separated among different topics. Intuitively, if nodes are separable among different topics, and each node v is only pertinent to one topic i, the marginal influence of v would not change much whether it is for a mixed item or the pure topic i. The following lemma makes this intuition precise for the extreme case of fully separable networks.

Lemma 2 *If a network is fully separable among all topics, then for any $v \in V$ and topic $i \in [d]$ such that $\sigma(v, p_i) > 1$, for any item $I = (\lambda_1, \lambda_2, \ldots, \lambda_d)$, for any seed set $S \subseteq V$, we have $MI(v|S, \lambda_i p_i) = MI(v|S, p)$, where $p = \sum_{j \in [d]} \lambda_j p_j$.*

Proof sketch   Let $G_i = (V_i, E_i)$ be the subgraph of G generated by edges (u, w) such that $p_i(u, w) > 0$ and their incident nodes. It is easy to verify that when the network is fully separable among all topics, G_i and G_j are disconnected for any $i \neq j$. In this case, we have (a) for any node v and topic i such that $\sigma(v, p_i) > 1$, $v \in V_i$; (b) for any edge $(u, w) \in E_i$, $p(u, w) = \lambda_i p_i(u, w)$; and (c) $\sigma(S, p') = \sum_{j \in [d]} \sigma(S \cap V_j, p')$ for any p'. With the above property, a simple derivation following the definition of marginal influence will lead to $MI(v|S, \lambda_i p_i) = MI(v|S, p)$.   □

The above lemma suggests that we can use the marginal influence of a node on each topic when dealing with a mixture of topics. Algorithm MIS is based on this idea.

Preprocess stage

Recall the detail of Algorithm 1, given any fixed probability p and budget k, for each iteration $j = 1, 2, \ldots, k$, it calculates v_j to maximize marginal influence $MI(v_j|S_{j-1}, p)$ and let $S_j = S_{j-1} \cup \{v_j\}$ every time, and output $S^g(k, p) = S_k$ as seeds. Let $MI^g(v_j, p) = MI(v_j|S_{j-1}, p)$, if $v_j \in S^g(k, p)$, and 0 otherwise. $MI^g(v_j, p)$ is the marginal influence of v_j according to the greedy selection order. Suppose the landmark set $\Lambda = \{\lambda_0^c, \lambda_1^c, \lambda_2^c, \ldots, \lambda_m^c\}$. For every $\lambda \in \Lambda$, we pre-compute $S^g(k, \lambda p_i)$, for every single topic $i \in [d]$, and cache $MI^g(v, \lambda p_i), \forall v \in S^g(k, \lambda p_i)$ in advance by Algorithm 1.

Online stage

Marginal Influence Sort (MIS) algorithm as described in Algorithm 3. Given an item $I = (\lambda_1, \ldots, \lambda_d)$, the online processing stage first rounding down the mixture to $I' = (\underline{\lambda}_1, \ldots, \underline{\lambda}_d)$, and then use the union $V^g = \cup_{i \in [d], \underline{\lambda}_i > 0} S^g(k, \underline{\lambda}_i p_i)$ as seed candidates. If a node appears in multiple pre-computed seed sets, we add their marginal influence in each set together (line 4). Then we simply sort all nodes in V^g according to their computed marginal influence $f(v)$ and return the top-k nodes as seeds.

Algorithm 3 Marginal Influence Sort (MIS) Algorithm

Require: $G = (V, E)$, k, $\{p_i \,|\, i \in [d]\}$, $I = (\lambda_1, \cdots, \lambda_d)$, Λ, $S^g(k, \lambda p_i)$ and $MI^g(v, \lambda p_i)$, $\forall \lambda \in \Lambda$, $\forall i \in [d]$.

1: $I' = (\underline{\lambda}_1, \cdots, \underline{\lambda}_d)$
2: $V^g = \cup_{i \in [d], \underline{\lambda}_i > 0} S^g(k, \underline{\lambda}_i p_i)$
3: **for** $v \in V^g$ **do**
4:     $f(v) = \sum_{i \in [d], \underline{\lambda}_i > 0} MI^g(v, \underline{\lambda}_i p_i)$
5: **end for**
6: **return** top k nodes with the largest $f(v)$, $\forall v \in V^g$

Although MIS is a heuristic algorithm, it does guarantee the same performance as the original greedy algorithm in fully separable networks when the topic mixtures is from the landmark set, as shown by the theorem below. Note that in a fully separable network, it is reasonable to assume that seeds for one topic comes from the subgraph for that topic, and thus seeds from different topics are disjoint.

Theorem 2 *Suppose $I = (\lambda_1, \lambda_2, \ldots, \lambda_d)$, where each $\lambda_i \in \Lambda$, and $S^g(k, \lambda_1 p_1)$, $\cdots$, $S^g(k, \lambda_d p_d)$ are disjoint. If the network is fully separable for all topics, the seed set calculated by Algorithm 3 is one of the possible sequences generated by Algorithm 1 under the mixed influence probability $p = \sum_{i \in [d]} \lambda_i p_i$.*

Proof sketch Denote $v_1, v_2, \ldots, v_k \in V^g$ as the final seeds selected for the topic mixture in this order, and let $S_0 = \emptyset$ and $S_\ell = S_{\ell-1} \cup \{v_\ell\}$, for $\ell = 1, 2, \ldots, k$. Since the network is fully separable and topic-wise seed sets are disjoint, by Lemma 4.1 we can get that $v_1, v_2, \ldots, v_k$ are selected from topic-wise seeds sets, and $\forall v \in V^g$, $f(v) = MI(v|S_{\ell-1}, p)$. We can prove that $v_\ell = \arg\max_{v \in V \setminus S_{l-1}} MI(v|S_{\ell-1}, p)$, $\forall \ell = 1, 2, \ldots, k$ by induction. It is straightforward to see that $v_1 = \arg\max_{v \in V} MI(v|\emptyset, p)$. Assume it holds for $\ell = j \in \{1, 2, \ldots, k - 1\}$. Then, for $\ell = j + 1$, for a contradiction we suppose that the $(j + 1)$-th seed v' is chosen from $V \setminus V^g$ other than v_{j+1}, i.e., $MI(v'|S_j, p) > MI(v_{j+1}|S_j, p)$. Denote i' such that $\sigma(v', p_{i'}) > 1$. Since budget $k > j$, we can find a node $u \in S^g(k, \lambda_{i'} p_{i'}) \setminus S_j$, such that $MI(u|S_j, \lambda_{i'} p_{i'}) \geq MI(v'|S_j, \lambda_{i'} p_{i'})$, and u is selected before v_{j+1}, which is a contradiction. Therefore, we will conclude that $v_1, v_2, \cdots, v_k$ is one possible sequence from the greedy algorithm. $\square$

The theorem suggests that MIS would work well for networks that are fairly separated among different topics, which are verified by our test results on the Arnetminer dataset. Moreover, even for networks that are not well separated, it is reasonable to assume that the marginal influence of nodes in the mixture is related to the sum of its marginal influence in individual topics, and thus we expect MIS to work also competitively in this case, which is verified by our test results on the Flixster dataset.

Experiments

We test the effectiveness of our algorithms by using a number of real-world datasets, and compare them with state-of-the-art influence maximization algorithms.

Algorithms for comparison

In our experiments, we test our topic-aware preprocessing based algorithms MIS and BTS comprehensively. We also select three classes of algorithms for comparison: (a) Topic-aware algorithms: The topic-aware greedy algorithm (TA-Greedy) and a state-of-the-art fast heuristic algorithm PMIA (TA-PMIA) from [10]; (b) Topic-oblivious algorithms: The topic-oblivious greedy algorithm (TO-Greedy), degree algorithm (TO-Degree) and random algorithm (Random); (c) Simple heuristic algorithms that do not need preprocessing: The topic-aware PageRank algorithm (TA-PageRank) from [18] and WeightedDegree algorithm (TA-WeightedDegree).

The greedy algorithm we use employs lazy evaluation [5] to provide hundreds of time of speedup to the original Monte Carlo based greedy algorithm [1], and also provides the best theoretical guarantee. PMIA is a fast heuristic algorithm for the IC model based on trimming influence propagation to a tree structure and fast recursive computation on

trees, and it achieves thousand fold speedup comparing to optimized greedy approximation algorithms with a small degradation on influence spread [10] (in this paper, we set a
small threshold $\theta = 1/1280$ to alleviate the degradation).

Topic-oblivious algorithms work under previous IC model that does not identify top-
ics, i.e., it takes the fixed mixture $\forall j \in [d], \lambda_j = \frac{1}{d}$. TO-Greedy runs greedy algorithm for
previous IC model and uses the top-k nodes as its seeds. TO-Degree outputs the top-k
nodes with the largest degree based on the original graph. Random simply chooses k
nodes at random.

We also carefully choose two simple heuristic algorithms that do not need preprocessing. TA-PageRank uses the probability of the topic mixture as its transfer probability,
and runs PageRank algorithm to select k nodes with top rankings. The damping factor is
set to 0.85. TA-WeightedDegree uses the degrees weighted by the probability from topic
mixtures, and selects top k nodes with the highest weighted degrees.

Finally, we study the possibility of acceleration for large graphs by comparing PMIA
with greedy algorithm in preprocessing stage. Therefore, we denote MIS and BTS
algorithms, utilizing the seeds and marginal influence from greedy and PMIA, as
MIS[Greedy], BTS[Greedy] and MIS[PMIA], BTS[PMIA], respectively.

Experiment setup

We conduct all the experiments on a computer with 2.4 GHz Intel(R) Xeon(R) E5530
CPU, 2 processors (16 cores), 48G memory, and an operating system of Windows Server
2008 R2 Enterprise (64 bits). The code is written in C++ and compiled by Visual Studio
2010.

We test these algorithms on the Flixster and Arnetminer datasets as we described in
"Data observation" section, which have the advantage that the influence probabilities of
all edges on all topics are learned from real action trace data or node topic distribution
data. To further test the scalability of different algorithms, we use a larger network data
DBLP, which is also used in [10]. DBLP[3] is an academic collaboration network extracted
from the online service, where nodes represent authors and edges represent coauthoring
relationships. It contains 650K nodes and 2 million edges. As DBLP does not have influence probabilities from the real data, we simulate two topics according to the joint distribution of topics 1 and 2 in the Flixster and follow the practice of the TRIVALENCY
model in [10] to rescale it into 0.1, 0.01, or 0.001, standing for strong, medium, and low
influence, respectively.

In terms of topic mixtures, in practice and also supported by our data, an item is usually a mixture of a small number of topics, thus our tests focus on testing topic mixtures
from two topics. First, we test random samples to cover most common mixtures as follows. For these three datasets, we use 50 topic mixtures as testing samples.[4] Each topic
mixture is uniformly selected from all possible two topic mixtures. Second, since we
have the data of real topic mixtures in Flixster dataset, we also test additional cases following the same sampling technique described in "Data description" section of [17]. We
estimate the Dirichlet distribution that maximizes the likelihood over topics learned

---

[3] http://www.DBLP.org.

[4] 50 samples is mainly to fit for the slow greedy algorithm.

Table 8 Running time statistics

	Arnetminer		Flixster		DBLP	
	($\|\Lambda\| = 8 \times 11$)		($\|\Lambda\| = 10 \times 11$)		($\|\Lambda\| = 2 \times 11$)	
	Total	Max	Total	Max	Total	Max
(a) Preprocessing time						
Greedy	8.8 h	1.2 h	26.3 days	3.5 days	$\geq$100 days	$\geq$7 days
PMIA	37 s	7.1 s	2.28 h	12.6 min	9.6 min	4.2 min

	Arnetminer		Flixster		DBLP
			Random	Dirichlet	
(b) Average online response time					
TA-Greedy	9.3 min		1.5 days	20 h	N/A
TA-PMIA	0.52 s		5.5 min	3.8 min	58 s
MIS (μs)	2.85		2.37	3.84	2.09
BTS (μs)	1.20		2.35	1.42	0.49
TA-PageRank (s)	0.15		2.08	2.30	41
TA-WeightedDegree	8.5 ms		29.9 ms	30.7 ms	0.32 s

from the data. After the distribution is learned, we resample 50 topic mixtures for testing.

In the preprocessing stage, we use two algorithms, Greedy and PMIA, to pre-compute seed sets for MIS and BTS, except that for the DBLP dataset, which is too large to run the greedy algorithm, we only run PMIA. Algorithms MIS and BTS need to pre-select landmarks Λ. In our tests, we use 11 equally distant landmarks $\{0, 0.1, 0.2, \ldots, 0.9, 1\}$. Each landmarks can be pre-computed independently, therefore we run them on 16 cores concurrently in different processes.

We choose $k = 50$ seeds in all our tests and compare the influence spread and running time of each algorithm. For the greedy algorithm, we use 10,000 Monte Carlo simulations. We also use 10,000 simulation runs and take the average to obtain the influence spread for each selected seed set.

In addition, we apply offline bound and online bound to estimate influence spread of optimal solutions. Offline bound is the influence spread of any greedy seeds multiplied by factor $1/(1 - e^{-1})$. The online bound is based on Theorem 4 in [5]: for any seed set S, its influence spread plus the sum of top k marginal influence spread of k other nodes is an upper bound on the optimal k seed influence spread. We use the minimum of the upper bounds among the cases of $S = \emptyset$ and S being one of the greedy seed sets selected.

Experiment results

Additional file 1: Figure S1 shows the total influence spread results on Arnetminer with random samples (a); Flixster with random and Dirichlet samples, (b) and (c), respectively; and DBLP with random samples (d). Table 8a shows the preprocessing time based on greedy algorithm and PMIA algorithm on three datasets. Table 8b shows the average online response time of various algorithms in finding 50 seeds (topic-oblivious algorithms always use the same seeds and thus are not reported).

As is shown in Table 8a, we run each landmark concurrently, and count both the total CPU time and the maximum time needed for one landmark. While the total time shows the cumulative preprocessing effort, the maximum time shows the latency when we use parallel preprocessing on multiple cores. The results indicate that the greedy algorithm is suitable for small graphs but infeasible for large graphs like DBLP, while PMIA is a scalable preprocessing solution for large graphs. For this reason, we test two preprocessing techniques and also compare their performance.

For the Arnetminer dataset (Additional file 1: Figure S1), it clearly separates all algorithms into three tiers: the top tier is TA-Greedy, TA-PMIA, MIS[Greedy] and MIS[PMIA]; the middle tier is TA-WeightedDegree, BTS[Greedy], BTS[PMIA] and TA-PageRank; and the lower tier is topic-oblivious algorithms TO-Greedy, TO-Degree and Random. In particular, we measure the gaps of influence spread among different algorithms. We observe that the gap of top tiers are negligible, because TA-PMIA, MIS[Greedy] and MIS[PMIA] are only 0.61, 0.32 and 1.08% smaller than TA-Greedy, respectively; the middle tier algorithms BTS[Greedy], BTS[PMIA], TA-WeightedDegree and TA-PageRank are 4.06, 4.68, 4.67 and 26.84% smaller, respectively; and the lower tier TO-Greedy, TO-Degree and Random have difference of 28.57, 56.75 and 81.48%, respectively. (All percentages reported in this section are averages over influence spread from one seed to 50 seeds.)

The detailed analyses are listed as follows: First, topic-oblivious algorithms does not perform well in topic-aware environment. Based on Observation 1, when topics are separated, algorithms ignoring topic mixtures cannot find influential seeds for all topics, and thus do not have good influence spread. Second, MIS[Greedy] and MIS[PMIA] almost match the influence spread of those of TA-Greedy and TA-PMIA. As indicated from offline and online bounds, MIS[Greedy], BTS[Greedy] are 76.9 and 72.5% of the online bound, which demonstrates their effectiveness is better than their conservative theoretical bounds ($1 - e^{-1} \approx 63.2\%$). The MIS algorithm runs noticeably fast in online processing, finishing 50 seeds selection in just a few microseconds (Table 8b), which is three orders of magnitude faster than the millisecond response time reported in [17], and at least three orders of magnitude faster than any other topic-aware algorithms. This is because it relies on pre-computed marginal influence and only a sorting process is needed online. Third, BTS[Greedy] and BTS[PMIA] are not expected to be better than MIS[Greedy] and MIS[PMIA], since BTS is a baseline algorithm only selecting a seed set from one topic. However, due to the preprocessing stage, we find that it can even perform better than other simple topic-aware heuristic algorithms that have short online response time. In addition, replacing the greedy algorithm with PMIA in the preprocessing stage, MIS and BTS only lose 0.76 and 0.62% in influence spread, indicating that PMIA is a viable choice for preprocessing, which greatly reduces the offline preprocessing time (Table 8a).

What we can conclude from tests on Arnetminer is that, for networks where topics are well separated among nodes and edges such as in academic networks, utilizing preprocessing can greatly save the online processing time. In particular, MIS algorithm is well suited for this environment achieving microsecond response time with very small degradation in seed quality.

For Flixster dataset (Additional file 1: Figure S1), we see that the influence spread of TA-PMIA, MIS[Greedy], MIS[PMIA], BTS[Greedy] and BTS[PMIA] are 1.78, 3.04, 4.58, 3.89 and 5.29% smaller than TA-Greedy for random samples, and 1.41, 1.94, 3.37, 2.31 and 3.59% smaller for Dirichlet samples, respectively. In Flixster, we can see that for networks where topics overlap with one another on nodes, our preprocessing based algorithms can still perform quite well. This is because most seeds of topic mixtures are from the constituent topics (Observation 2). On the other hand, the influence of TA-WeightedDegree, TA-PageRank and TO-Greedy will suffer a noticeable degeneration demonstrated from two curves. In terms of online response time (Table 8b), the result is consistent with the result for Arnetminer: only MIS and BTS can achieve microsecond level online response, and all other topic-aware algorithms need at least milliseconds since they at least need a ranking computation among all nodes in the graph. In addition, TA-PMIA on Flixster is much slower than on Arnetminer, because both the network size and the computed MIA tree size are much larger, indicating that PMIA is not suitable in providing stable online response time. In contrast, the response time of MIS and BTS do not change significantly among different graphs.

In DBLP (Additional file 1: Figure S1), the graph is too large to run greedy algorithm, thus we take TA-PMIA as the baseline algorithm to compare with other algorithms. For different algorithms, the influence spread is close to each other, and our results show that MIS[PMIA] has equal competitive influence spread with TA-PMIA (0.44% slightly larger), while BTS[PMIA], TA-WeightedDegree, TO-Degree and TA-PageRank are 1.33, 1.83, 6.05 and 35.54% smaller than TA-PMIA, respectively. Combining the running time in Table 8, we find that the greedy algorithm is not suitable for preprocessing for large graphs, while PMIA can be used in this case.

To summarize, the greedy algorithm has the best influence spread performance, but is slow and not suitable for large-scale networks or fast response time requirements. PMIA as a fast heuristic can achieve reasonable performance in both influence spread and online processing time, but its response time varies significantly depending on graph size and influence probability parameters, and could take minutes or longer to complete. Our proposed MIS emerges as a strong candidate for fast real-time processing of topic-aware influence maximization task: it achieves microsecond response time, which does not depend on graph size or influence probability parameters, while its influence spread matches or is very close to the best greedy algorithm and outperforms other simple heuristics. Furthermore, in large graphs where greedy is too slow to finish, PMIA is a viable choice for preprocessing, and our MIS using PMIA as the preprocessing algorithm achieves almost the same influence spread as MIS using the greedy algorithm for preprocessing.

Related work

Domingos and Richardson [3, 4] are the first to study influence maximization in an algorithmic framework. Kempe et al. [1] first formulate the discrete influence diffusion models including the independent cascade model and linear threshold model, and provide the first batch of algorithmic results on influence maximization.

A large body of work follows the framework of [1]. One line of research improves on the efficiency and scalability of influence maximization algorithms [9–11, 19]. Others extend the diffusion models and study other related optimization problems [6, 7, 12]. A number of studies propose machine learning methods to learn influence models and parameters [13–15]. A few studies look into the interplay of social influence and topic distributions [14, 20–22]. They focus on inference of social influence from topic distributions or joint inference of influence diffusion and topic distributions. They do not provide a dynamic topic-aware influence diffusion model nor study the influence maximization problem. Barbieri et al. [16] introduce the topic-aware influence diffusion models TIC and TLT as extensions to the IC and LT models. They provide maximum-likelihood based learning method to learn influence parameters in these topic-aware models. We use the their proposed models and their datasets with the learned parameters.

A recent independent work by Aslay et al. [17] is the closest one to our work. Their work focuses on index building in the query space while we use pre-computed marginal influence to help guiding seed selection, and thus the two approaches are complementary. Other differences have been listed in the introduction and will not be repeated here.

Future work

One possible follow-up work is to combine the advantages of our approach and the approach in [17] to further improve the performance. Another direction is to study fast algorithms with stronger theoretical guarantee. An important work is to gather more real-world datasets and conduct a thorough investigation on the topic-wise influence properties of different networks, similar to our preliminary investigation on Arnetminer and Flixster datasets. This could bring more insights to the interplay between topic distributions and influence diffusion, which could guide future algorithm design.

Authors' contributions
All authors participated in the discussion and algorithm design, and thus equally contributed to the work. WC conceived the idea, coordinated the study and helped to draft the manuscript. TL carried out theoretical analysis, and drafted the manuscript. CY implemented the code, and did empirical studies. All authors read and approved the final manuscript.

Author details
[1] Microsoft Research, No. 5 Danling Street, 100080 Beijing, China. [2] Institute for Advanced Study, Tsinghua University, No. 1 Tsinghua Yuan, 100084 Beijing, China. [3] Department of Computer Science and Technology, Tsinghua University, No. 1 Tsinghua Yuan, 100084 Beijing, China.

Acknowledgements
We would like to thank Nicola Barbieri and Jie Tang, the authors of [14, 16], respectively, for providing Flixster and Arnetminer datasets.

Competing interests
The authors declare that they have no competing interests.

References
1. Kempe D, Kleinberg J, Tardos É. Maximizing the spread of influence through a social network. In: Proceedings of the ninth ACM SIGKDD international conference on knowledge discovery and data mining. 2003. p. 137–46.
2. Chen W, Lakshmanan LVS, Castillo C. Information and influence propagation in social networks. San Rafael: Morgan & Claypool Publishers; 2013.
3. Domingos P, Richardson M. Mining the network value of customers. In: KDD'01, New York: ACM; 2001. p. 57–66.
4. Richardson M, Domingos P. Mining knowledge-sharing sites for viral marketing. In: KDD'02. New York: ACM; 2002. p. 61–70.

5. Leskovec J, Krause A, Guestrin C, Faloutsos C, VanBriesen J, Glance N. Cost-effective outbreak detection in networks. In: Proceedings of the 13th ACM SIGKDD international conference on knowledge discovery and data mining. New York: ACM; 2007. p. 420–9.
6. Budak C, Agrawal D, Abbadi AE. Limiting the spread of misinformation in social networks. In: world wide web. 2011. p. 665–74.
7. He X, Song G, Chen W, Jiang Q. Influence blocking maximization in social networks under the competitive linear threshold model. In: Proceedings of the 12th SIAM international conference on data mining. SDM; 2012. p. 463–74.
8. Wang C, Yu X, Li Y, Zhai C, Han J. Content coverage maximization on word networks for hierarchical topic summarization. In: CIKM. 2013. p. 249–58.
9. Chen W, Wang Y, Yang S. Efficient influence maximization in social networks. In: Proceedings of the 15th ACM SIGKDD international conference on knowledge discovery and data mining. New York: ACM; 2009. p. 199–208.
10. Wang C, Chen W, Wang Y. Scalable influence maximization for independent cascade model in large-scale social networks. Data Min Knowl Discov. 2012;25(3):545–76.
11. Goyal A, Lu W, Lakshmanan LV, Simpath. An efficient algorithm for influence maximization under the linear threshold model. In: Data Mining (ICDM), 2011 IEEE 11th International Conference. New Jersey: IEEE; 2011. p. 211–20.
12. Bhagat S, Goyal A, Lakshmanan, LVS. Maximizing product adoption in social networks. In: WSDM. 2012. p. 603–12.
13. Saito K, Nakano R, Kimura M. Prediction of information diffusion probabilities for independent cascade model. In: Knowledge-based intelligent information and engineering systems. Berlin: Springer; 2008. p. 67–75.
14. Tang J, Sun J, Wang C, Yang Z. Social influence analysis in large-scale networks. In: Proceedings of the 15th ACM SIGKDD international conference on knowledge discovery and data mining. New York: ACM; 2009. p. 807–16.
15. Goyal A, Bonchi F, Lakshmanan LV. Learning influence probabilities in social networks. In: Proceedings of the Third ACM international conference on web search and data mining. New York: ACM; 2010. p. 241–50.
16. Barbieri N, Bonchi F, Manco G. Topic-aware social influence propagation models. Knowl Inform Syst. 2013;37(3):555–84.
17. Aslay C, Barbieri N, Bonchi F, Baeza-Yates R. Online topic-aware influence maximization queries. In: EDBT. 2014. p. 295–306.
18. Brin S, Page L. The anatomy of a large-scale hypertextual web search engine. Comp Netw Isdn Syst. 1998;30:107–17.
19. Goyal A, Lu W, Lakshmanan LV. Celf++: optimizing the greedy algorithm for influence maximization in social networks. In: Proceedings of the 20th international conference companion on world wide web. New York: ACM; 2011. p. 47–8.
20. Liu L, Tang J, Han J, Jiang M, Yang S. Mining topic-level influence in heterogeneous networks. In: Proceedings of the 19th ACM international conference on information and knowledge management. New York: ACM; 2010. p. 199–208.
21. Weng J, Lim E-P, Jiang J, He Q. Twitterrank: finding topic-sensitive influential twitterers. In: Proceedings of the Third ACM international conference on web search and data mining. New York: ACM; 2010. p. 261–70.
22. Lin CX, Mei Q, Han J, Jiang Y, Danilevsky M. The joint inference of topic diffusion and evolution in social communities. In: Data mining (ICDM), 2011 IEEE 11th international conference. New Jersey: IEEE; 2011. p. 378–87.

2

Computation and analysis of temporal betweenness in a knowledge mobilization network

Amir Afrasiabi Rad[1], Paola Flocchini[1*] and Joanne Gaudet[2]

*Correspondence:
paola.flocchini@uottawa.ca
[1] School of Electrical
Engineering and Computer
Science, University of Ottawa,
Ottawa, Ontario, Canada
Full list of author information
is available at the end of the
article

Abstract

Background: Highly dynamic social networks, where connectivity continuously changes in time, are becoming more and more pervasive. Knowledge mobilization, which refers to the use of knowledge toward the achievement of goals, is one of the many examples of dynamic social networks. Despite the wide use and extensive study of dynamic networks, their temporal component is often neglected in social network analysis, and statistical measures are usually performed on static network representations. As a result, measures of importance (like betweenness centrality) typically do not reveal the temporal role of the entities involved. Our goal is to contribute to fill this limitation by proposing a form of temporal betweenness measure (foremost betweenness).

Methods: Our method is analytical as well as experimental: we design an algorithm to compute foremost betweenness, and we apply it to a case study to analyze a knowledge mobilization network.

Results: We propose a form of temporal betweenness measure (foremost betweenness) to analyze a knowledge mobilization network and we introduce, for the first time, an algorithm to compute exact foremost betweenness. We then show that this measure, which explicitly takes time into account, allows us to detect centrality roles that were completely hidden in the classical statistical analysis. In particular, we uncover nodes whose static centrality was negligible, but whose temporal role might instead be important to accelerate mobilization flow in the network. We also observe the reverse behavior by detecting nodes with high static centrality, whose role as temporal bridges is instead very low.

Conclusion: In this paper, we focus on a form of temporal betweenness designed to detect accelerators in dynamic networks. By revealing potentially important temporal roles, this study is a first step toward a better understanding of the impact of time in social networks and opens the road to further investigation.

Keywords: Time-varying graphs, Temporal betweenness, Dynamic networks, Temporal analysis, Social networks

Background

Highly dynamic networks are networks where connectivity changes in time and connection patterns display possibly complex dynamics. Such networks are more and more pervasive in everyday life and the study of their properties is the object of extensive investigation in a wide range of very different contexts. Some of these contexts are typically studied in computer science, such as wireless, ad hoc networks, transportation, vehicular networks, satellites, military, and robotic networks (e.g., see [1–6]), while others belong to totally different disciplines. This is the case, for example, of the nervous system, livestock trade, epidemiological networks, and multiple forms of social networks (e.g., see [7–12]). Clearly, while being different in many ways, these domains display common features; a *time-varying graph* (TVG) is a model that formalizes highly dynamic networks encompassing the above contexts into a unique framework and emphasizes their temporal nature [13].

Knowledge mobilization (KM) refers to the use of knowledge toward the achievement of goals [14]. Scientists, for example, use published papers to produce new knowledge in further publications to reach professional goals. In contrast, patient groups can use scientific knowledge to help foster change in patient practices, and corporations can use scientific knowledge to reach financial goals. Recently, researchers have started to analyze knowledge mobilization networks (KMN) using a social network analysis (SNA) approach (e.g., see [15–20]). In particular, [19] proposed a novel approach where a heterogeneous network composed of a main class of actors subdivided into three subtypes (individual human and non-human actors, organizational actors, and non-human mobilization actors) associated according to one relation, knowledge mobilization (a mobilization-network approach). Data covered a 7-year period with static networks for each year. The mobilization network was analyzed using classical SNA measures (e.g., node centrality measures, path length, density) to produce understanding for KM using insights from network structure and actor roles [19].

The KM SNA studies mentioned above, however, lack a fundamental component: in fact, their analysis is based on a static representation of KM networks, incapable of sufficiently accounting for the time of appearance and disappearance of relations between actors beyond static longitudinal analysis. Indeed, incorporating the temporal component into analysis is a challenging task, but it is undoubtedly a critical one, because time is an essential feature of these networks. Temporal analysis of dynamic graphs is in fact an important and extensively studied area of research (e.g., see [21–27]), but there is still much to be discovered. In particular, most temporal studies simply consider network dynamics in successive static snapshots, thus capturing only a partial temporal component by observing how static parameters evolve in time while the network changes. Moreover, very little work has been dedicated to empirically evaluating the usefulness of metrics in time (e.g., see [28, 29]).

In this paper, we represent KMN by TVGs and we propose to analyze them in a truly temporal setting. We design a deterministic algorithm to compute a form of temporal betweenness in time-varying graphs (*foremost betweenness*) that measures centrality of nodes in terms of how often they lie within temporal paths with the earliest arrival. We then provide, for the first time on a real data set, an empirical indication for the effectiveness of foremost betweenness. In particular, we focus on data extracted from [19], here referred to as *Knowledge-Net*. We first consider static snapshots of Knowledge-Net corresponding to the 7 years of its existence, and by studying the classical centrality measures in those time intervals, we provide rudimentary indications of the networks' temporal behavior. To gain a finer temporal understanding, we then concentrate on *temporal betweenness* following a totally different approach. Instead of simply observing the static network over consecutive time intervals, we focus on the TVG that represent Knowledge-Net and we compute foremost betweenness, explicitly and globally taking time into account. We compare the temporal results that we obtain with classical static betweenness measures to gain insights into the impact that time has on the network structure and actor roles. We notice that, while many actors maintain the same role in static and dynamic analysis, some display striking differences. In particular, we observe the emergence of important actors that remained invisible in static analysis, and we advance explanations for these. Results show that the form of temporal betweenness we apply is effective at highlighting the role of nodes whose importance has a temporal nature (e.g., nodes that contribute to mobilization acceleration).

A limitation of our algorithm is its applicability to small networks. In fact, any deterministic solution to the computation of foremost betweenness is inevitably very costly and, when faced with large networks, it is feasible to apply it only on small components. This research opens the road to the design of approximate variations of the algorithm so to make it applicable to larger scenarios, as well as to the study of other temporal measures designed for TVGs.

Time-varying graphs
Definition
Time-varying graphs are graphs whose structure varies over time. Following [13], a time-varying graph (TVG) is defined as a quintuple $\mathcal{G} = (V, E, \mathcal{T}, \rho, \zeta)$, where V is a finite set of nodes and $E \subseteq V \times V$ is a finite set edges. The graph is considered within a finite time span $\mathcal{T} \subseteq \mathbb{T}$, called lifetime of the system. $\rho: E \times \mathcal{T} \to \{0, 1\}$ is the edge presence function, which indicates whether a given edge is available at a given time; $\zeta: E \times \mathcal{T} \to \mathbb{T}$ is the latency function, which indicates the time it takes to cross a given edge if starting at a given date. The model may, of course, be extended by defining the vertex presence function ($\psi: V \times \mathcal{T} \to \{0, 1\}$), and vertex latency function ($\phi: V \times \mathcal{T} \to \{0, 1\}$). The footprint of $\mathcal{G}$ is a static graph composed by the union of all nodes and edges ever appearing during the lifetime $\mathbb{T}$.

Journeys
A journey route R in a TVG $\mathcal{G}$ is a walk in G defined as a sequence of edges $\{e_1, e_2, \ldots, e_k\}$. A journey $\mathcal{J}$, then, is a temporal walk in $\mathcal{G}$ comprising the sequence of ordered pairs $\{(e_1, t_1), (e_2, t_2), \ldots, (e_k, t_k)\}$ if and only if $\rho(e_i, t_i) = 1$ and $t_{i+1} \geq t_i + \zeta(e_i, t_i)$ for all $i < k$. Every journey has a departure ($\mathcal{J}$) and an arrival ($\mathcal{J}$) that refer to journey's starting time t_1 and its finish time $t_k + \zeta(e_k, t_k)$, respectively. Journeys are divided into three classes based on their variations based on the temporal and topological distance [30]. Journeys that have the earliest arrival times are called *foremost* journeys, journeys with the smallest topological distance are referred to as the *shortest* journeys, while the journey that takes the smallest amount of time is called the *fastest*. Moreover, we call *foremost increasing journeys* the ones whose route $\{e_1, e_2, \ldots, e_k\}$ is such that *birth-date*(e_i) $\leq$ *birth-date*(e_{i+1}).

Temporal betweenness
Betweenness is a classic measure of centrality extensively investigated in the context of social network analysis. The betweenness of a node $v \in V$ in a static graph $G = (V, E)$ is defined as follows:

$$B(v) = \sum_{u \neq w \neq v \in V} \frac{|P(u, w, v)|}{|P(u, w)|}, \tag{1}$$

where $|P(u, w)|$ is the number of shortest paths from u to w in G, and $|P(u, w, v)|$ is the number of those passing through v. Even if static betweenness is "atemporal," we denote here by $B(v)^T$ the static betweenness of a node v in a system whose lifetime is T. Typically, vertices with high betweenness centrality direct a greater flow and, thus, have a high load placed on them, which is considered as an indicator for their importance as potential gatekeepers in the network.

While betweenness in static graphs is based on the notion of the shortest path, its temporal version can be extended into three different measures to consider the shortest, foremost, and fastest journeys for a given lifetime T [25].

In this paper, we consider foremost betweenness. Nodes with a high foremost betweenness values do not simply act as gatekeepers of flow, like their static counterparts. In fact, they direct the flow that conveys a message in an *earliest* transmission fashion. In other words, if the message transmission takes the path from foremost between nodes, such nodes provide a means to transmit the message in a more timely manner to all other nodes in the graph compared to the nodes that have lower foremost centrality. Thus, intuitively, they provide some form of "acceleration" in the flow of information.

Foremost betweenness $TB_{\mathcal{F}}^{T}(v)$ for node v with lifetime T is here defined as follows:

$$TB_{\mathcal{F}}^{T}(v) = \frac{n(v)}{n} \sum_{u \neq w \neq v \in V} \frac{|\mathcal{F}^{T}(u, w, v)|}{|\mathcal{F}^{T}(u, w)|}, \tag{2}$$

where $|\mathcal{F}^{T}(u, w)|$ is the number of foremost *journey routes* between u and w during time frame T and $|\mathcal{F}^{T}(u, w, v)|$ is the number of the ones passing through v in the same time frame; n is the total number of nodes, and $n(v)$ is the number of nodes in the connected component to which v belongs. The factor $\frac{n(v)}{n}$ is an adjustment coefficient to take into account possible network disconnections. In fact, it makes the betweenness of a node depend on the actual size of the connected component to which the node belongs, thus avoiding anomalous situations where a node in a very small component could be otherwise perceived as globally central. This would be the case, for example, of the center v of a small component in the shape of a star, where v would have maximum global betweenness while its central role is applied only to a very small portion of the overall network.

Computing foremost betweenness

The computation of betweenness centrality in static graphs can be done quite efficiently. Several approaches exist in the literature (e.g., see [31–35]) proposing either polynomial deterministic solutions or approximate ones for a variety of different graphs. Computing shortest-path betweenness in TVG can also be done in polynomial time, for example by adapting the algorithms described in [26, 30]. The situation is rather different in the case of foremost betweenness, for which no algorithm has been proposed so far. In fact, it is easy to see that there exist TVGs where counting all foremost journeys or journey routes between two vertices is #P-complete, which means that no polynomial-time algorithm is known.

Consider, for example, TVGs where edges always exist (note that a static graph is a particular TVG) and latency is zero. In such a case, any journey between any pair of nodes is a foremost journey. Counting all of them is then equivalent to counting all paths between them, which is a #P-complete problem (see [36]). In general, it is then unavoidable to have worst-case exponential algorithms to compute foremost betweenness in an arbitrary TVG.

In this section, we first focus on foremost betweenness based on journey routes in the general setting (Algorithm 1). We then focus on foremost betweenness for special TVGs with zero latency and instant edges (Algorithm 2), which correspond to the characteristics of the knowledge mobilization network that we analyze in "Knowledge-Net". Note that each solution has the same worst-case time complexity, linear in the number of nodes in all the journey routes in the TVG, which can clearly be exponential. The advantages of the algorithm designed for the special temporal condition of instant edges and zero latency are mainly practical. In fact, the worst-case complexities are the same, but the execution time is better for our particular dataset.

A general algorithm

In this section, we describe an algorithm for counting all journey routes from a given node to all the other nodes in the TVG, passing through any possible intermediate node. This module is at the basis of the computation of foremost betweenness.

1　**Algorithm** COUNTFORMEMOSTJROUTES.
　input : (G, s) : a TVG $G = (V, E)$, $s \in V$
　output: $Count_s[x, y]$, $\forall x, y \in V$: number of foremost journey routes
　　　　　　from s to $y \in V$, passing through $x \in V$

2　**begin**
3　　$Path.push(s, 0), Count_s[., .] \leftarrow 0$
4　　**for** all $w \in Adj(s)$ **do**
5　　　$S.push(s, w, arriv(s, w, 0))$ (* push edge (s, w) with its arrival time *)
6　　**end**
7　　**while** $S \neq \emptyset$ **do**
8　　　$(x, y, t) \leftarrow S.pop()$ (* next candidate edge to visit*)
9　　　**while** $x \neq Path.top()$ **do**
10　　　　$Path.pop()$ (* reflecting possible backtrack *)
11　　　**end**
12　　　Let π be the journey route stored in $Path$
13　　　Let $t_{x,y}$ be the latest possible traversing time of edge (x, y)
14　　　**if** $t_{x,y} \geq arriv(\pi)$ **then**
15　　　　**if** $y \notin Path$ or $y \in Path$ at time $t' < t$ **then**
16　　　　　$Path.push(y, arriv(x, y, t))$ (* visit y *)
17　　　　　**for** each (y, w) such that $t_{y,w} \geq arriv(\pi)$ and either
　　　　　　$w \notin Path$ or $w \in Path$ at time $t' < arriv(y, w, t)$ **do**
18　　　　　　$S.push(y, w, arriv(y, w, t))$ (* update S *)
19　　　　　**end**
20　　　　　**if** $arriv(\pi) = foremost(s, y)$ **then**
21　　　　　　Update $Count_s[z, y]$ for all $z \in Path$
22　　　　　　(* $Path$ contains a foremost journey. Counters are updated*)
23　　　　　**end**
24　　　　**end**
25　　　**end**
26　　**end**
27　**end**

Algorithm 1: Algorithm to count all journey routes from s to all the other nodes.

We start by introducing some notations and functions used in the algorithm. Given an edge (x, y), let function arriv(x, y, t) return the arrival time to y, leaving x at time t. Given a time-stamped journey π, with an abuse of notation, let us indicate by arriv(π) the arrival time at the last node of π. The foremost arrival time in G to any node v from a given source s can be computed using the Algorithm from [30]. Let foremost(s, v) denote such a time.

We are now ready to describe the algorithm. The input of Algorithm COUNTFORMEM-OSTJROUTES is a pair (G, s), where $G = (V, E)$ is a TVG and s is a starting node. The algorithm returns a matrix Count$_s[x, y]$, for all $x, y \in V$ containing the number of foremost journeys from s to y passing through x (note that Count$_s[x, x]$ denotes the number of foremost journeys from s to x).

The counting algorithm is simple and it is based on multiple Depth-First Search (DFS) traversals. It consists of visiting every journey route of G starting from s, incrementing the appropriate counters every time a newly encountered journey is foremost. We remind that a node can reappear more than once in a journey route, with various occurrences corresponding to different times. This means that we need to store the time when a node is visited in the journey route so that, if it is visited again, we can determine whether the subsequent visit corresponds to a later time and thus the node has to be considered again. Note that this is the main difference with respect to a DFS in a static graph, where instead every node is visited exactly once.

To perform the traversal managing multiple visits (corresponding to different traversal times), we use two stacks: *Path* and S, where *Path* contains the nodes corresponding to the journey currently under visit and S contains the edges to be visited. In both *Path* and S, we store also time-stamps, to register the time of the first visit of nodes in *Path* and the time for the future visits of edges in S. If a node happens to be revisited at a later time, in fact, it is treated as a new node.

The traversal starts as a typical DFS, pushing the incident edges of the source s onto stack S with their arrival times in these journeys (lines 4–6). The nodes corresponding to the current journey under visit are kept in the second stack *Path* (these nodes are implicitly marked *visited*), initially containing only the source. When considering the next candidate edge (x, y) to visit (line 8), we may be continuing the current journey (if the top of stack *Path* contains x) or we may have backtracked to some previous nodes (if the top is different from x). In this last case, the content of *Path* is updated to reflect the backtracking (lines 9–11). After visiting a node y (line 16), the DFS continues pushing on S the edges incident to y that are feasible with the current journey under visit (i.e., the edges whose target is not already in *Path*, and whose latest traversal time is greater than or equal to the earliest arrival time at y) (lines 17–19). The *if* clause at line

20 checks whether the discovered journey is foremost and updates the corresponding counters.

In other words, as soon as a journey $\pi = [(x_0, x_1), (x_1, x_2), \dots, (x_{k-1}, x_k)]$ is encountered in the traversal, Count$[x_i, x_k]$, $i \leq k$ is updated only if π is a foremost journey, and, regardless of it being foremost, the traversal continues pushing on the stack the edges incident to x_k that are temporally feasible with π. Whenever backtracking is performed, however, the already visited nodes on the backtracking path are popped from *Path* (thus implicitly remarked *unvisited*) in such a way that they can be revisited as part of different journey routes, not explored yet.

Observations on complexity

The running time of Algorithm CountFormemostJRoutes is linear in the number of nodes belonging to different foremost journeys, because it traverses each one of them. However, depending on the structure of the TVG, such a number could be exponential, thus an overall exponential worst-case complexity.

More precisely, let μ_s be the number of foremost journeys from a source node s to all the other nodes in $\mathcal{G}$, $n(\mu_s)$ be the number of nodes belonging to those journeys, and n the number of nodes of $\mathcal{G}$. Moreover, let μ and $n(\mu)$ be, respectively, the overall number of foremost journeys in $\mathcal{G}$ and the overall number of nodes in those journeys. The algorithm to count all foremost journeys from s to all the other nodes traverses every foremost journey from the source to any other node, and it performs an update for every visited node in each foremost journey that it encounters. Thus, its time complexity is $O(n(\mu_s))$. To compute foremost betweenness, the algorithm has to be repeated for every possible source, thus traversing every possible foremost journey in $\mathcal{G}$ for a total time complexity of $O(n(\mu))$. Since $n(\mu)$ could be exponential in n, we have a worst-case exponential complexity in the size of the network. Note that the high cost is inevitable for any deterministic algorithm to compute foremost betweenness.

Algorithm for KnowledgeNet

Algorithm 1 is applicable to a general TVG. We now consider a very special type of TVG with specific temporal restrictions that correspond to the type of network that we analyze in this paper. One such peculiarity is given by *instant edges* (edges that appear only during a unique time interval). Another characteristic is *zero latency* (i.e., edges that can be traversed instantaneously). Finally, in this setting, we base betweenness computation on increasing journey routes.

```
 1  Algorithm CountAllZeroLatency
        input  : A TVG $G_i$, starting node $s \in V$, and snapshot interval $I$
        output: $Count_s[v, u]$ that records the number of the journeys from
                $s \in V_G$ to all $u \in V_G$ passing through $v \in V_G$ during interval $I$
 2  begin
 3  │   Initialize $Count_s[.,.] \leftarrow 0$
 4  │   $Path.push(s)$
 5  │   for all $w \in Adj(s)$ do
 6  │   │   $S.push(s, w)$
 7  │   end
 8  │   while $S \neq \emptyset$ do
 9  │   │   $(x, y) \leftarrow S.pop()$
10  │   │   while $x \neq Path.top()$ do
11  │   │   │   $Path.pop()$
12  │   │   end
13  │   │   if $y \notin Path$ then
14  │   │   │   $Path.push(y)$
15  │   │   │   if $y$ falls in snapshot interval $I$ then
16  │   │   │   │   for each $(y, w)$ such that $w \notin Path$ do
17  │   │   │   │   │   $S.push(y, w)$
18  │   │   │   │   end
19  │   │   │   │   if path is foremost then
20  │   │   │   │   │   $Count_s[z, y] =$ increment $Count_s[z, y]$ for all $z \in Path$
21  │   │   │   │   end
22  │   │   │   end
23  │   │   else
24  │   │   │   $Count_s[z, y] =$ Special_Count($Count_s[z, x]$,
                $Count_s[z, y]$) for all $z \in Path$
25  │   │   end
26  │   end
27  │   end
28  end
```

Algorithm 2: Counting all foremost journeys in TVGs with zero latency and instant edges.

We then describe a variation of the general algorithm specifically designed for those conditions (instant edges with zero latency), and we compute foremost betweenness applying the foremost betweenness formula restricted to foremost increasing journeys.

Given a TVG $G = (V, E)$, since we assume the presence of instant edges, we can divide time in consecutive intervals $I_1, I_2, \ldots, I_k$ corresponding to k snapshots $G_1, G_2, \ldots G_k$ ($G_i = (V_i, E_i)$), in such a way that $(x, y) \in E_i$ implies that $(x, y) \notin E_j$ for $j \neq i$. Furthermore, we know by $\zeta = 0$ that an edge can be traversed in zero time.

The key idea that can be applied to this very special structure is based on the observation that, given a foremost route $\pi_{x,y}$ from x to y with edges in time intervals I_j, provided that $j > i$ and j appears immediately after i, and given any journey route $\pi'_{s,x}$ from s to x with edges only in I_i, the concatenation of $\pi'_{s,x}$ and $\pi_{x,y}$ is a foremost route from s to y, passing through x.

This observation leads to the design of an algorithm that starts by counting the foremost routes belonging to the last snapshot G_k only, and proceeds backwards using the information already computed. More precisely, when considering snapshot G_i from a source s, the goal is to count all foremost routes involving only edges in $\cup_{j \geq i} E_j$ (i.e., with time intervals in $\cup_{j \geq i} I_j$), and when doing so, all the foremost routes involving only edges strictly in the "future" (i.e., time intervals $\cup_{j > i} I_j$) have been already calculated for any pair of nodes. The already computed information is used when processing snapshot G_i in a dynamic programming fashion.

As for Algorithm 1, the input of Algorithm 2 is a pair: a snapshot G_i and a starting node s. The algorithm returns an array, $Count_s[u, v]$, where $Count_s[u, v]$ for all $u, v \in V$ contains the number of foremost journeys from s to u passing through v counted so far (i.e., considering only edges in $\cup_{j \geq i} E_j$).

The actual counting algorithm on snapshot G_i is a modified version of Algorithm 1, still based on Depth-First Search (DFS) traversal. Lines 2–11 are exactly the same as in Algorithm 1, except that here we do not need to keep track of the arrival time for each edge, as we run Algorithm 2 in a single snapshot and the latency for edges is zero.

In line 13, we examine whether the target of the current edge y has already been visited or not. If it has not been visited already, it either falls in the current snapshot, or it flows into the next snapshot.

In the case where y stays in the current snapshot (lines 15–22), we push its adjacent nodes into the stack S and determine whether the route ending at y is foremost. If a foremost route is discovered at y, we update $Count_s[z, v]$ by incrementing its value for all $z \in Path$ (z being the node that falls on the journey route from s to y).

If instead it is not a foremost route in the current interval (lines 23–25), meaning that y is a node that existed in the "future," a special update is performed using the data already calculated for the "future snapshots."

More precisely, when a journey route (in this case a foremost journey route) from s to x ($s \rightsquigarrow x$) is a prefix of a journey route $x \rightsquigarrow y$ at a later time snapshot, we perform a procedure called SPECIALCOUNT (Algorithm 3). The special count procedure involves aggregating the values of $Count_s[v, x]$ with $Count_x[v', y]$, for all nodes (resp. v, v') occurring in the journey routes between s and x and between x and y (see Algorithm 3). Algorithm 3 simply calculates the product of the number of foremost journeys between two routes $s \rightsquigarrow x$, and $x \rightsquigarrow y$, if they do not share any vertex (lines 4–9). If instead they share some vertex v, the calculation is slightly more complicated: let a be the number of foremost journeys from s to y where v is visited at least once on the route between x and y; let b be the number of foremost journeys from s to y where v is visited at least once on the route between s and x; and let c be the sum of a and b. c represents the number of all foremost journeys from s to y that pass through v. However, c counts the journey route passing through v multiple times if v happened to exist in both $Count_s[v, x]$ and $Count_x[v, y]$, and we need to remove such multiple counting of journeys, which is done along with the update to $Count_s[v, y]$ in line 13.

1 Procedure SPECIALCOUNT.

    input : $Count_s[.,x]$, in G_i, and $Count_x[.,y]$ in $\cup_{j>i} G_j$

    output: $Count_s[v,y]$, $\forall v \in V$: number of foremost journey routes from

              s to $y \in V$, passing through $v \in V$

2 begin

3   **for** *each $v \in U \cup W$ where $U =$ all nodes in $x \rightsquigarrow y$ and*

       $W =$ all nodes in $s \rightsquigarrow x$ **do**

4   **if** $v \in s \rightsquigarrow x$ *and* $v \notin x \rightsquigarrow y$ **then**

5 $Count_s[v,y] += Count_s[v,x] \times Count_x[y,y]$

6   **end**

7   **else if** $v \notin s \rightsquigarrow x$ *and* $v \in x \rightsquigarrow y$ **then**

8 $Count_s[v,y] += Count_s[x,x] \times Count_x[v,y]$

9   **end**

10   **else if** $v \in s \rightsquigarrow x$ *and* $v \in x \rightsquigarrow y$ **then**

11 $a = Count_s[x,x] \times Count_x[v,y]$

12 $b = Count_s[v,x] \times Count_x[y,y]$

13 $Count_s[v,y] += a + b - Count_s[v,x] \times Count_x[v,y]$

14   **end**

15   **end**

16 end

Algorithm 3: The SPECIALCOUNT module.

Observations on Complexity

The worst-case time complexity of Algorithm 2, COUNTALLZEROLATENCY, is the same as the one of the general algorithm, COUNTFORMEMOSTJROUTES. In our network, however, it performed better than Algorithm 1. We try to explain below the reasons for this.

Algorithm 2 has to be executed in anti-chronological order of the different snapshots, starting from the last one, since it uses the previously calculated results in the computation of the new results. This approach is amenable to concurrent computations. In fact, since the graph is divided into independent snapshots, the number of all journeys can be computed separately for each snapshot, and the result of the calculation can be aggregated at the end. This has the advantage of eliminating all the special updates from the first part of the algorithm (while detecting all the journey routes), and deferring them to the second part (when aggregating all the information for the final update). Thus, instead of performing the special count at each level, we can postpone it to the last step of the algorithm, and loop once through all the collected counts with hard-coded intervals in the loop.

While not being advantageous in worst-case scenarios, this strategy results in a more efficient solution from a practical point of view. Still, the algorithm is very costly, even in such a small network (KnowledgeNet has 366 vertices and 750 edges) and it did run in almost a month when implemented in C++ with a machine with 40 cores and 1TB RAM.

Knowledge-Net

Knowledge-Net is a heterogeneous network where nodes represent human and non-human actors (researchers, projects, conference venues, papers, presentations, laboratories) and edges represent knowledge mobilization between two actors. The network was collected for a period of 7 years [19]. Once an entity or a connection is created, it remains in the system for the entire period of the analysis.

Table 1 provides a description of the *Knowledge-Net* dataset. The dataset consists of 366 vertices and 750 edges in 2011. The numbers of entities and connections vary over time starting from only 10 vertices and 14 edges in 2005 and accumulating to the final network year in 2011. *Knowledge-Net* is mainly composed of non-human actors, 272 in total (non-human mobilization actors, NHMA, non-human individual actors, NHIA, and organizational actors, OA), in relation with 94 human actors (HA). Human actors include principle investigators (PI), highly qualified personnel (HQP), and collaborators (CO). It is through mobilization actors (NHMA) that individual, organizational actors and mobilization actors associate and mobilize knowledge to reach goals. For example, scientists mobilize knowledge through articles where not all contributing authors might be in relation with all other authors, yet all relate with the publication [19]. These non-human mobilization actors make up the bulk of the network including conference venues, presentations (invited oral, non-invited oral, and poster), articles, journals, laboratories, research projects, websites, and theses.

According to an interpretation of the *the Actor-Network Theory* [37], the nature/ type/ characteristics of the mobilizer nodes have no interference with their role as a mobilizer. Following this interpretation, we consider that knowledge mobilization is beyond the role and nature of the nodes and we treat KnowledgeNet as a homogeneous network of *knowledge mobilizers*. All nodes of this network have the same function as *knowledge mobilizer* despite the fact that they might be quite different from each other from the view point of nature, type, and/or characteristics.

Classical statistical parameters have been calculated for Knowledge-Net, representing it as a static graph where the time of appearance of nodes and edges did not hold any particular meaning. In doing so, several interesting observations were made regarding the centrality of certain nodes as knowledge mobilizers and the presence of communities [19]. In particular, all actor types increased in number over the 7 years indicating a rise in new mobilization relations over time. Although non-human individual actor absolute numbers remained small (ranging from 3 in 2006 to 15 in 2011), these actors were critical to making visible tacit (non-codified) knowledge mobilization from around the world (mostly laboratory material sharing, including from organizations and universities in the USA, from Norway, and from Canadian universities). Finally, embedded in human individual actor counts were individuals that the laboratory acknowledged in peer-reviewed papers, thus making further tacit and explicit knowledge mobilization visible.

Table 1 *Knowledge-Net* **data set with characteristics of actors and their roles at different times**

Start	Duration		#Nodes		#Edges	Granularity	
2005	7 Years		366		750	1 Year	
Actor type	2005	2006	2007	2008	2009	2010	2011
HIA	3	22	27	46	51	76	94
NHIA	0	3	6	9	9	9	15
NHMA	7	25	43	87	132	194	248
OA	0	5	5	9	9	9	2
Total	10	55	81	151	201	288	366

When representing *Knowledge-Net* as a TVG, we notice that the latency ζ is always zero, as an edge represents a relationship and its creation does not involve any delay; moreover, edges and nodes exist from their creation (their birth-date) to the end of the system lifetime. Let *birth-date(e)* denote the year when edge *e* is created. An example of a small portion of *Knowledge-Net* represented as a TVG is shown in Fig. 1.

We also notice that, due to zero latency, edges spanning only one interval, and to the fact that edges never disappear once created, any shortest journey route in $\mathcal{G}$ is equivalent to a shortest path on the static graph corresponding to its footprint; moreover, the notion of fastest journey does not have much meaning in this context, because on any route corresponding to a journey, there would be a fastest one. On the other hand, the notion of foremost journey, and in particular of foremost increasing journey, is extremely relevant as it describes timely mobilization flow, i.e., flow that arrives at a node as early as possible.

Note that in this setting the computation of foremost betweenness can be performed using Algorithm 2 introduced in the previous section.

Study of KnowledgeNet

Analysis on consecutive snapshots

To provide more clear statistics on the Knowledge-Net dataset and a ground for better understanding of temporal metrics, we first calculated classical statistical measures (e.g., node centrality measures, path length, density) on the seven static graphs, corresponding to the 7 years of study. The average for each value for the graphs is calculated to represent a benchmark on how the rank for each node is compared to others.

The statistical data presented in Table 2 provide valuable information about the graph. The steady decrease in the centrality values (normalized in the [0,1] range) confirms that the network growth is not symmetric, so the centrality values have long tails. According to Hanneman and Riddle [38], we should expect a high value of betweenness in

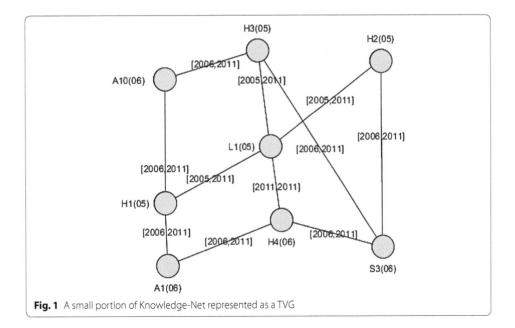

Fig. 1 A small portion of Knowledge-Net represented as a TVG

Table 2 Some static statistical parameters calculated for successive snapshots

	2005	2006	2007	2008	2009	2010	2011
Ave. degree	1.40	1.32	1.63	1.84	1.98	2.02	2.04
Diameter	4	5	5	6	6	6	6
Density	0.31	0.04	0.04	0.02	0.02	0.01	0.01
#Communities	4	3	6	8	8	15	12
Modularity	0.17	0.52	0.46	0.47	0.46	0.54	0.54
Ave. clustering coefficient	0.41	0.06	0.21	0.22	0.20	0.24	0.23
Ave. path length	2.04	3.04	3.06	3.26	3.34	3.46	3.50
Ave. normalized closeness	0.51	0.33	0.33	0.31	0.30	0.29	0.29
Ave. eccentricity	3.10	4.41	4.40	4.70	4.80	4.83	4.83
Ave. betweenness	4.70	58.36	83.53	169.70	234.89	354.23	456.18
Ave. normalized betweenness	0.13	0.03	0.02	0.01	0.01	≈ 0	≈ 0
Ave. page rank	0.10	0.01	0.01	≈ 0	≈ 0	≈ 0	≈ 0
Ave. eigenvector	0.52	0.19	0.15	0.10	0.09	0.07	0.05

dense graphs due to the fact that it is highly possible that a path crosses every node. Meanwhile, when the betweenness values are normalized, they become low if all of the betweenness values are close to each other. Thus, the high value of betweenness (in the range of hundreds), and the low value of its normalized counterpart (close to zero) in Knowledge-Net, indicates that the graph is either dense or is coupled in a way that there is a large number of shortest paths between any two arbitrary vertices. The graph is not dense as it is confirmed by the highest density metric of six. Therefore, the high number of shortest paths in the graphs caused the betweenness for most vertices to be similar and quite low when compared to the ones of nodes with the highest betweenness. Low average path length (highest being 3.50) is a sign that the network presents small-world characteristics and the knowledge mobilization to the whole network is expected to be conducted only in a few hops. Meanwhile, the decreasing graph density (from 0.3 to 0.1) along with the increasing average degree (from 1.4 to 2.04) represents the slow growth in the number of edges compared to the number of nodes. Escalation in the number of communities (by 8 communities) with an increase in graph modularity metrics (from 0.17 to 0.54) shows that the knowledge mobilization actors tend to form communities as time progresses. As the normalized average betweenness decreases steadily, it might be concluded that a few vertices in each community play the role of mediators and create the link between communities.

Apart from these general observations, a static analysis of consecutive snapshots does not provide temporal understanding. For example, it does not reflect which entities engage in knowledge mobilization in a timely fashion, e.g., by facilitating fast mobilization, or slowing mobilization flow.

To tackle some of these questions, we represent *Knowledge-Net* as a TVG and we propose to study it by employing a form of temporal betweenness that makes use of time in an explicit manner.

Foremost betweenness of Knowledge-Net

In this section, we focus on *Knowledge-Net*, and we study $TB_{\mathcal{F}}^{\mathcal{T}}(v)$ for all v. Nodes are ranked according to their betweenness values and their ranks are compared with the ones obtained calculating their static betweenness $B^{\mathcal{T}}(v)$ in the same time frame. Given the different meaning of those two measures, we expect to see the emergence of different behaviors, and, in particular, we hope to be able to detect nodes with important temporal roles that were left undetected in the static analysis.

Foremost Betweenness during the lifetime of the system

Table 3 shows the temporally ranked actors accompanied by their static ranks, and the high-ranked static actors with their temporal ranks, both with lifetime $\mathcal{T} = [2005–2011]$. In our naming convention, an actor named $Xi(yy)$ is of type X, birth-date yy, and it is indexed by i; types are abbreviated as follows: H (human), L (Lab), A (article), C (conference), J (journal), P (project), C (paper citing a publication), I (invited oral presentation), and O (oral presentation). Note that only the nodes whose betweenness has a significant value are considered, in fact betweenness values tend to lose their importance, especially when the differences in the values of two consecutive ranks are very small [34].

Interestingly, the four highest ranked nodes are the same under both measures; in particular, the highest ranked node (L1(05)) corresponds to the main laboratory where the data are collected and it is clearly the most important actor in the network whether considered in a temporal or in a static way. On the other hand, the table reveals several differences worth exploring. From a first look, we see that, while the vertices highest ranked statically appear also among the highest ranked temporal ones, there are some

Table 3 List of the highest ranked actors according to temporal (resp. static) betweenness, accompanied by the corresponding static (resp. temporal) rank in lifetime [2005–2011]

Temporal to static			Static to temporal		
Actor	Temporal rank	Static rank	Actor	Static rank	Temporal rank
L1(05)	1	1	L1(05)	1	1
H1(05)	2	2	H1(05)	2	2
A1(06)	3	3	A1(06)	3	3
A2(08)	4	4	A2(08)	4	4
P1(06)	5	8	A5(08)	5	12
A3(07)	6	9	A4(09)	6	7
A4(09)	7	6	P2(08)	7	9
S1(10)	8	115	P1(06)	8	5
P2(08)	9	7	A3(07)	9	6
J1(06)	10	160	P3(10)	10	17
C1(07)	11	223	A6(11)	11	18
A5(08)	12	5	A8(09)	12	36
I1(09)	13	28	P4(10)	13	22
O1(05)	14	45	P5(11)	14	27
S2(05)	15	46	H2(05)	15	44
I2(05)	16	47	A7(09)	16	21
P3(10)	17	10	A9(10)	17	31
A6(11)	18	11	P5(11)	18	69
C2(10)	19	133	P6(10)	19	23
J2(09)	20	182			
A7(09)	21	16			

nodes with insignificant static betweenness, whose temporal betweenness is extremely high. This is the case, for example, of nodes S1(10) and J1(06).

The case of node S1(10)   To provide some interpretation for this behavior, we observe vertex S1(10) in more detail. This vertex corresponds to a poster presentation at a conference in 2010. We explore two insights. First, although S1(10) has a relatively low degree, it has a great variety of temporal connections. Only three out of ten incident edges of S1(10) are connected to actors that are born on and after 2010, and the rest of the neighbors appear in different times, accounting for at least one neighbor appearing each year for which the data are collected. This helps the node to operate as a temporal bridge between different time instances and to perhaps act as a knowledge mobilization accelerator.

Second, S1(10) is close to the center of the only static community present in [2010–2011] and it is connected to the two most important vertices in the network. The existence of a single dense community, and the proximity to two most productive vertices can explain its negligible static centrality value: while still connecting various vertices S1(10) is not the shortest connector, and its betweenness value is thus low. However, a closer temporal look reveals that it plays an important role as an interaction bridge between all the actors that appear in 2010 and later, and the ones that appear earlier than 2010. This role remained invisible in static analysis and only emerges when we pay attention to the time of appearance of vertices and edges. On the basis of these observations, we can interpret S1(10)'s high temporal betweenness value as providing a fast bridge from vertices created earlier and those appearing later in time. This might indicate reasons for further study of the importance of poster presentations that can blend tacit and explicit knowledge mobilization in human–poster presentation–human relations during conferences, and continue into future mobilization with new non-human actors as was the case for S1(10).

The case of node J1(06)   J1(06), the *Journal of Neurochemistry*, behaves similarly to S1(10) with its high temporal and low static rank. As opposed to S1(10), this node is introduced very early in the network (2006); however, it is only active (i.e., has new incident edges) in 2006 and 2007. It has only three neighbors, A1(06), A3(07), and C1(07), all highly ranked vertices statically (A1(06), A3(07)), or temporally (C1(07)). Since its neighboring vertices are directly connected to each other or in close proximity of two hops, J1(06) fails to act as a static short bridge among graph entities. However, its early introduction and proximity to the most prominent knowledge mobilizers helps it become an important temporal player in the network. This is because temporal journeys overlook geodesic distances and are instead concerned with temporal distances for vertices. These observations might explain the high temporal rank of J1(06) in the knowledge mobilization network.

A finer look at foremost betweenness

A key question is whether the birth-date of a node is an important factor influencing its temporal betweenness. To gain insights, we conducted a finer temporal analysis by considering $TB_{\mathcal{F}}^{\mathcal{T}}$ for all possible birth-dates, i.e., for $\mathcal{T} = [x, 2011]$ $\forall x \in \{2005, 2006, 2007, 2008, 2009, 2010, 2011\}$. This allowed us to observe how temporal betweenness varies depending on the considered birth-date.

Before concentrating on selected vertices (statically or temporally important with at least one interval), and analyzing them in more detail, we briefly describe a temporal community detection mechanism that we employ in analysis.

Detection of temporal communities　According to Tantipathananandh et al. [27], accurately detecting communities in TVGs is an NP-hard and APX-hard task. Tantipathananandh et al. [27] used a heuristic to approximate the community detection for a more efficient algorithm. However, when the number of nodes in a dense graph exceeds double digits, the algorithm becomes computationally unfeasible to run. To the best of our knowledge, the only other work that attacked the community detection problem in TVGs is [39], where the problem is tackled by transforming the TVG into a series of static snapshot graphs with no repeated nodes in snapshots, and by incrementally detecting and adding to communities. While the complexity of the algorithm is not provided, it immediately proves inapplicable to our problem as it (a) works only on series of snapshots with no repetition and (b) includes aging factor in calculations. Thus, we take an approach similar to the one proposed in [27], by only focusing on approximating the communities for the purpose of this research. To do that, we first transform our TVG into a static weighted directed graph (the *journey graph*), which gives a rough indication of the foremost journeys of the actual TVG. We then use the journey graph as input to an existing community detection algorithm, designed for weighted graphs [40]. More precisely, given a TVG $G = (V, E)$, we construct the journey graph of G, $J(G) = (V, E')$ as follows: the nodes of $J(G)$ correspond to the original nodes of G and $(x, y) \in E'$ if there exists at least a foremost journey between x and y in G. The weight associated to edge $(x, y) \in E'$ is equal to the number of foremost journeys between x and y in G. An example of this construction is shown in Fig. 2.

Note that Knowledge-Net, over time, creates only one connected component, but the community analysis of the Knowledge-Net graph results in 14 communities. The largest

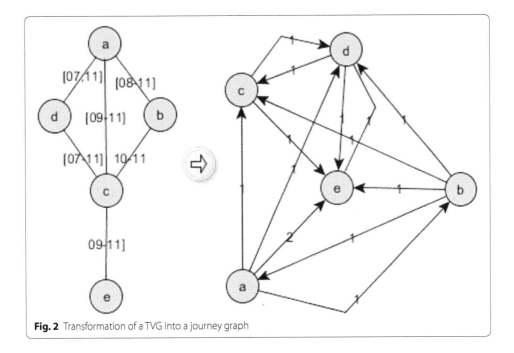

Fig. 2 Transformation of a TVG into a journey graph

community consists of almost 39% of nodes and is centered around L1(05). Given the large number of the nodes belonging to communities and the low number of detected communities, it is clear that some of the central nodes share communities with each other.

The case of node P1(06)   This is a research project led by the principle investigator at L1(05). The project was launched in 2006 and its official institutional and funded elements wrapped up in 2011. Data in Table 3 support that P1(06) has similar temporal and static ranks with regard to its betweenness in lifetime [2005–2011]. One could conclude that the temporal element does not provide additional information on its importance and that the edges that are incident to P(06)-1 convey the same temporal and static flow. However, there is still an unanswered question on whether or not edges act similarly if we start observing the system at different times. Will a vertex keep its importance throughout the system's lifetime?

The result of such analysis is provided in Fig. 3, where $TB_{\mathcal{F}}^{\mathcal{T}}(P1(06))$ is calculated for each birth-date (indicated in the horizontal axis), with all intervals ending in 2011.

While both equally important during the entire lifetime [2005–2011] of the study, this project seems to assume a rather more relevant temporal role when observing the system in a lifetime starting in year 2007 (i.e., $\mathcal{T} = [2007–2011]$), when its static betweenness is instead negligible. This seems to indicate that the temporal flow of edges incident to P1(06) appearing from 2007 on is more significant than the flow of the edges that appeared previously.

With further analysis of P1(06)'s neighborhood in [2007–2011], we can formulate technical explanations for this behavior. First, its direct neighbors also have better temporal betweenness than static betweenness. Moreover, its neighbors belong to various communities, both temporally and statically. However, looking at the graph statically, we see several additional shortest paths that do not pass through P1(06) (thus making it less important in connecting those communities). In contrast, looking at the graph temporally P1(06) acts as a mediator and accelerator between communities. More specifically, we observe that the connections P1(06) creates in 2006 contribute to the merge of different communities that appear only in 2007 and later. When observing within

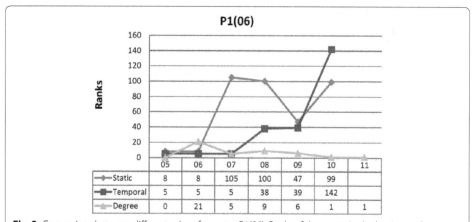

Fig. 3 Comparison between different values for vertex P1(06). Ranks of the vertex in the last interval are not provided as both betweenness values are zero

interval [2006–2011], we then see that P1(06) is quite central from a static point of view, because the appearance of time of edges does not matter, but, when observing it in lifetime [2007–2011], node P1(06) loses this role and becomes statically peripheral because the newer connections relay information in an efficient temporal manner.

In other words, it seems that P1(06) has an important role for knowledge acceleration in the period [2007–2011], a role that was hidden in the static analysis and that does not emerge even from an analysis of consecutive static snapshots. For research funders, revealing a research project's potentially invisible mobilization capacity is relevant. Research projects can thus be understood beyond mobilization outputs and more in terms of networked temporal bridges to broader impact.

The case of node A3(07)   Comparison between different values for vertex A3(07) are shown in Fig. 4, where ranks of the vertex in the last interval are not provided as both betweenness values are zero. The conditions for this node, a paper published in 2007, illustrate a different temporal phenomenon. Node A3(07) has several incident edges in 2007 (similarly to node P1(06)) when both betweenness measures are high. Peering deeper into the temporal communities formed around A3(07) is revealing: up to 2007, this vertex is two steps from vertices that connect two diffrent communities in the static graph. The situation radically changes, however, with the arrival of edges in 2008 that modify the structure of those communities, and push A3(07) to the periphery. The shift is dramatic from a temporal perspective because A3(07) loses its accelerator role where its temporal betweenness becomes negligible, while statically there is only a slight decrease in betweenness. The reason for a dampened decrease in static betweenness is that this vertex is close to the center of the static community, connecting peripheral vertices to the most central nodes of the network (such as L1(05) and H1(05)). It is mainly proximity to these important vertices that sustains A3(07)'s static centrality.

Such temporal insights lend further support to understanding mobilization through a network lens coupled with sensitivity to time. A temporal shift to the periphery for an actor translates into decreased potential for sustained mobilization.

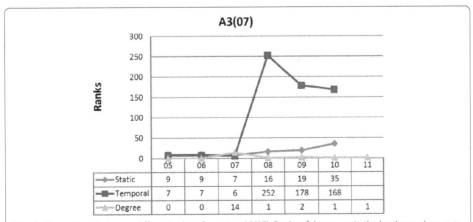

Fig. 4 Comparison between different values for vertex A3(07). Ranks of the vertex in the last interval are not provided as both betweenness values are zero

Invisible rapids and brooks

On the basis of our observations, we define two concepts to differentiate the static and temporal flow of vertices in knowledge mobilization networks. We call *rapids* the nodes with high foremost betweenness, meaning that they can potentially mobilize knowledge in a timelier manner, and *brooks* the ones with insignificant foremost betweenness. Moreover, we call *invisible rapids* those vertices whose temporal betweenness rank is considerably more significant than their static rank (i.e., the ones whose centrality was undetected by static betweenness), and *invisible brooks* the ones whose static betweenness is considerably higher than their temporal betweenness, meaning that these vertices can potentially be effective knowledge mobilizers, yet they are not acting as effectively as others due to slow or non-timely relations.

Invisible rapids and brooks can be present in different lifetimes as their temporal role might be restricted to some time intervals only; for example, as we have seen in the previous section, S1(10) and J1(06) are invisible rapids in $T = [2005-2011]$, P1(06) is an invisible rapid in $T = [2007-2011]$, and A3(07) is an invisible brook in $T = [2008-2011]$. Tables 4 and 5 indicate the major invisible rapids and brooks observed in *Knowledge-Net*.

The presence of a poster presentation, a research project, two journals, and a conference publication among the invisible rapids supports that different types of mobilization actors can impact timely mobilization while not being as effective at creating short paths among entities for knowledge mobilization. In other words, they can play a role of accelerating knowledge mobilization, but to a concentrated group of actors.

As for invisible brooks, we observe a journal (the *Biochemica et Biophysica Acta-Molecular Cell Research* (J3(08)), three papers (C3(11), C4(07), and C5(07)) that cite publications by the main laboratory in the study (L1(05)), a publication (A3(07)) mobilizing knowledge from members of L1(05), and a research assistant who worked on several research projects as an HQP. In comparison with invisible rapids, there is a wider variety in the type of mobilization actors that act as brooks which does not readily lend itself to generalization.

Table 4 Major invisible rapids

Actor	Time	Temp. rank	Stat. rank	Type
P1(06)	[07–11]	5	105	Project
S1(10)	[05–11]	8	115	Poster
	[06–11]	8	113	
	[07–11]	7	115	
	[08–11]	5	104	
J1(06)	[05–11]	10	160	Journal
	[06–11]	10	154	
	[07–11]	10	223	
C1(07)	[05–11]	11	223	Citing publication
	[06–11]	11	220	
J2(09)	[06–11]	17	179	Journal
	[07–11]	16	182	
C2(10)	[05–11]	19	133	Citing poster
	[06–11]	16	132	
	[07–11]	15	133	

Table 5 Major invisible brooks

Actor	Time	Stat. rank	Temp. rank	Type
J3(08)	[08–11]	9	117	Journal
	[09–11]	12	84	
C3(11)	[08–11]	10	191	Citing publication
	[09–11]	15	153	
C4(11)	[08–11]	15	105	Citing publication
H2(05)	[06–11]	16	118	Researcher
	[07–11]	15	134	
A3(07)	[08–11]	16	187	Publication
C5(07)	[08–11]	18	158	Citing publication

Interestingly, we see the presence of journals among invisible rapids and brooks. From our analysis, it seems that journals can hold strikingly opposite roles: on the one hand, they can contribute considerably to more timely mobilization of knowledge while not being very strong bridges between communities, while on the other hand they can play critical roles in bridging network communities, but at a slow pace. A brook, the journal *Biochemica et Biophysica Acta-Molecular Cell Research* (J3(08)), for example, helped mobilize knowledge in two papers for L1(05) (in 2008 and 2009), and is a journal in which a paper (in 2011) citing a L1(05) publication was also published. Given expected variability in potential mobilization for a journal, further research is needed to establish their roles in mobilization, whether these mobilization actors exist at both ends of the spectrum, or they have a neutral role in mobilization of knowledge.

In contrast, the presence of a research project as an invisible rapid might indicate meaningful observations that should be studied further. First, because when public funders invest in research projects as a mobilization actor, an implicit if not explicit measure of success is timely mobilization with potential impact inside and outside of academia [19]. Ranking as a rapid (for a mobilization actor) is one measure that could therefore help funding agencies monitor and detect temporal change in mobilization networks. Second, a research project as rapid might be meaningful because by its very nature a research project can help accelerate mobilization for the full range of mobilization actors, including other research projects. As such, it is not surprising that they can become temporal conduits to knowledge mobilization in all of its forms.

Conclusions

In this paper, we proposed the use of a temporal betweenness measure (foremost betweenness) to analyze a knowledge mobilization network that had been already studied using classical "static" parameters. Our goal was to see the impact on the perceived static central nodes when employing a measure that explicitly takes time into account. We observed interesting differences. In particular, we witnessed the emergence of invisible rapids: nodes whose static centrality was considered negligible, but whose temporal centrality appears relevant. Our interpretation is that nodes with high temporal betweenness contribute to accelerate mobilization flow in the network and, as such, they can remain undetected when the analysis is performed statically. We conclude that foremost betweenness is a crucial tool to understand the temporal role of the actors in a dynamic network, and that the combination of static and temporal betweenness is complementary to provide insights into their importance and centrality.

The algorithm proposed in this paper to compute foremost betweenness constitutes a deterministic solution and its running time can be exponential in the worst case, which makes it applicable only on very small-scale networks. Since counting all foremost journeys in a graph is a #P-complete problem, such a high cost is inevitable for any deterministic solution. An open interesting direction is the design of approximate solutions, feasible for large networks.

Temporal network analysis as performed here is especially pertinent for KM research that must take time into account to understand academic research impact beyond the narrow short-term context of academia. Measures of temporal betweenness, as studied in this paper, can provide researchers and funders with critical tools to more confidently investigate the role of specific mobilization actors for short- and long-term impact within and beyond academia. The same type of analysis could clearly be beneficial when applied to any other temporal context.

In conclusion, we focused here on a form of temporal betweenness designed to detect accelerators. This is only a first step toward understanding temporal dimensions of social networks; other measures are already under investigation.

Authors' contributions

PF has proposed the problem. AAR and PF have discussed and designed together the two algorithms for the computation of foremost betweenness. AAR has implemented the algorithms. JG has provided the knowledge mobilization network data, which she had previously collected for a different study. AAR has conducted the analysis of foremost betweenness for these data. All three co-authors have discussed the results; in particular, JG has provided interpretation in the context of knowledge mobilization. All authors read and approved the final manusript.

Authors' information

Paola Flocchini is Professor at the School of Electrical Engineering and Computer Science. Her work and background are in distributed computing and algorithms. Amir Afrasiabi Rad has recently completed his Ph.D. on temporal analysis of social networks under Prof. Flocchini's supervision. Joanne Gaudet is co-president of an Ottawa-based company. The data collection she performed is from the time when she was a Ph.D. student at the University of Ottawa.

Author details

[1] School of Electrical Engineering and Computer Science, University of Ottawa, Ottawa, Ontario, Canada. [2] Alpen Path Solutions Inc., Ottawa, Ontario, Canada.

Acknowledgements

A preliminary version of this paper appeared in the Proc. of the 2015 IEEE/ACM International Conference on Advances in Social Networks Analysis and Mining, Workshop on Dynamics in Networks, 2015.

Competing interests

The authors declare that they have no competing interests.

Funding

This work was partially supported by the Natural Sciences and Engineering Research Council of Canada (NSERC) under Discovery Grant, and by Dr. Flocchini's University Research Chair.

References

1. Casteigts A, Flocchini P, Mans B, Santoro N. Deterministic computations in time-varying graphs: broadcasting under unstructured mobility. Proceedings of 6th IFIP conference on theoretical computer science. 2010; 111–124.
2. Casteigts A, Flocchini P, Mans B, Santoro N. Measuring temporal lags in delay-tolerant networks. IEEE Trans Comput. 2014;63(2):397–410.

3. Jones EPC, Li L, Schmidtke JK, Ward PAS. Practical routing in delay-tolerant networks. IEEE Trans Mob Comput. 2007;6(8):943–59.

4. Kuhn F, Lynch N, Oshman R. Distributed computation in dynamic networks, Proceedings of 42nd ACM Symposium on theory of computing (STOC). 2010; 513–522.

5. Liu C, Wu J. Scalable routing in cyclic mobile networks. IEEE Trans Parallel Distrib Syst. 2009;20(9):1325–38.

6. Michail O, Chatzigiannakis I, Spirakis P. Distributed computation in dynamic networks. J Parallel Distrib Comput. 2014;74(1):2016–26.

7. Konschake M, Lentz HH, Conraths FJ, Hövel PH, Selhorst T. On the robustness of in-and out-components in a temporal network. PloS ONE. 2013;8(2):e55223.

8. Lentz HHK, Selhorst T, Sokolov IM. Unfolding accessibility provides a macroscopic approach to temporal networks. Phys Rev Lett. 2013;110:118701–6.

9. Mutlu AY, Bernat E, Aviyente S. A signal-processing-based approach to time-varying graph analysis for dynamic brain network identification. Comput Math Methods Med. 2012;2012:451516. doi:10.1155/2012/451516

10. Quattrociocchi W, Conte R, Lodi E. Opinions manipulation: media, power and gossip. Adv Complex Syst. 2011;14(4):567–86.

11. Saba H, Vale VC, Moret MA, Miranda J-G. Spatio-temporal correlation networks of dengue in the state of Bahia. BMC Public Health. 2014;14(1):1085.

12. Saramaki J, Holme P. Temporal networks. Phys Rep. 2012;519(3):97–125.

13. Casteigts A, Flocchini P, Quattrociocchi W, Santoro N. Time-varying graphs and dynamic networks. Int J Parallel Emerg Distrib Syst. 2012;27(5):387–408.

14. Gaudet J. It takes two to tango: knowledge mobilization and ignorance mobilization in science research and innovation. Prometheus. 2013;13(3):169–87.

15. Binz C, Truffer B, Coenen L. Why space matters in technological innovation systems mapping global knowledge dynamics of membrane bioreactor technology. Res Policy. 2014;43(1):138–55.

16. Boland WP, Phillips PWB, Ryan CD, McPhee-Knowles S. Collaboration and the generation of new knowledge in networked innovation systems: a bibliometric analysis. Procedia Soc Behav Sci. 2012;52:15–24.

17. Chan K, Liebowitz J. The synergy of social network analysis and knowledge mapping: a case study. Int J Manag Decis Mak. 2006;7(1):19–35.

18. Eppler MJ. Making knowledge visible through intranet knowledge maps: concepts, elements, cases. Proceedings of 34th Annual Hawaii international conference on system sciences. 2001; 9–19.

19. J. Gaudet. The mobilization-network approach for the social network analysis of knowledge mobilization in science research and innovation. uO Research, (PrePrint). 2014; 1–28.

20. Klenk NL, Dabros A, Hickey GM. Quantifying the research impact of the sustainable forest management network in the social sciences: a bibliometric study. Can J For Res. 2010;40(11):2248–55.

21. Galati A, Vukadinovic V, Olivares M, Mangold S. Analyzing temporal metrics of public transportation for designing scalable delay-tolerant networks. proceedings of 8th ACM Workshop on performance monitoring and measurement of heterogeneous wireless and wired networks. 2013; 37–44.

22. Kossinets G, Kleinberg J, Watts D. The structure of information pathways in a social communication network, Proceedings of 14th international conference on knowledge discovery and data mining (KDD).2008; 435–443.

23. Kostakos V. Temporal graphs. Phys A. 2009;388(6):1007–23.

24. Kim H, Anderson R. Temporal node centrality in complex networks. Phys Rev E. 2012;85(2):026107.

25. Santoro N, Quattrociocchi W, Flocchini P, Casteigts A, Amblard F. Time-varying graphs and social network analysis: temporal indicators and metrics. Proceedings of 3rd social networks and multiagent systems symposium (SNAMAS)

26. Tang J, Musolesi M, Mascolo C, Latora V. Temporal distance metrics for social network analysis. Proceeding of 2nd ACM Workshop on online social networks (WOSN). 2009; 31–36.

27. Tantipathananandh C, Berger-Wolf T, Kempe D. A framework for community identification in dynamic social networks, Proceedings of 13th ACM SIGKDD international Conference on knowledge discovery and data mining. 2007; 717–726.

28. Amblard F, Casteigts A, Flocchini P, Quattrociocchi W, Santoro N. On the temporal analysis of scientific network evolution. International conference on computational aspects of social networks (CASoN). 2011; 169–174.

29. Kossinets G, Watts DJ. Empirical analysis of an evolving social network. Science. 2006;311(5757):88–90.

30. Xuan B, Ferreira A, Jarry A. Computing shortest, fastest, and foremost journeys in dynamic networks. Int J Found Comput Sci. 2003;14(02):267–85.

31. Barthelemy M. Betweenness centrality in large complex networks. Eur Phys J B-Condens Matter Complex Syst. 2004;38(2):163–8.

32. Brandes U. A faster algorithm for betweenness centrality. J Math Sociol. 2001;25:163–77.

33. Brandes U. On variants of shortest-path betweenness centrality and their generic computation. Soc Netw. 2008;30(2):136–45.

34. Freeman LC. A set of measures of centrality based on betweenness. Sociometry. 1977;1:35–41.

35. Newman MEJ. A measure of betweenness centrality based on random walks. Soc Netw. 2005;27(1):39–54.

36. Valiant LG. The complexity of enumeration and reliability problems. SIAM J Comput. 1979;8(3):410–21.

37. Law J. Notes on the theory of the actor-network: ordering, strategy, and heterogeneity. Syst pract. 1992;5(4):379–93.

38. Hanneman R, Riddle M. Introduction to social network methods. Riverside: University of California Riverside; 2005.

39. Chan S, Hui P, Xu K. Community detection of time-varying mobile social networks. Proceedings of international conference on complex sciences. 2009; 1154–1159.

40. Gómez SG, Jensen P, Arenas A. Analysis of community structure in networks of correlated data. Phys Rev E. 2009;80(1):016114.

3

Online network organization of Barcelona en Comú, an emergent movement-party

Pablo Aragón[1,2]* , Helena Gallego[1,2], David Laniado[2], Yana Volkovich[2] and Andreas Kaltenbrunner[1,2]

*Correspondence:
pablo.aragon@upf.edu
[2] Eurecat-Technology
Centre of Catalonia,
Avinguda Diagonal, 177,
08018 Barcelona, Spain
Full list of author information
is available at the end of the
article

Abstract

The emerging grassroots party Barcelona en Comú won the 2015 Barcelona City Council election. This candidacy was devised by activists involved in the Spanish 15M movement to transform citizen outrage into political change. On the one hand, the 15M movement was based on a decentralized structure. On the other hand, political science literature postulates that parties develop oligarchical leadership structures. This tension motivates to examine whether Barcelona en Comú preserved a decentralized structure or adopted a conventional centralized organization. In this study we develop a computational methodology to characterize the online network organization of every party in the election campaign on Twitter. Results on the network of retweets reveal that, while traditional parties are organized in a single cluster, for Barcelona en Comú two well-defined groups co-exist: a centralized cluster led by the candidate and party accounts, and a decentralized cluster with the movement activists. Furthermore, results on the network of replies also shows a dual structure: a cluster around the candidate receiving the largest attention from other parties, and another with the movement activists exhibiting a higher predisposition to dialogue with other parties.

Keywords: Twitter, Politics, Social movements, Political parties, 15M movement, Indignados movement, Spanish elections, Online campaigning

Background

The last decade has seen a global wave of citizen protests: the Arab Spring, the 15M movement in Spain, Occupy Wall Street, #YoSoy132 in Mexico, Occupy Gezi in Turkey, the Brazilian movement #VemPraRua, Occupy Central in Hong Kong, etc. All these movements share common characteristics such as the claim for new models of democracy, the strategic usage of social media (e.g., Twitter), and the occupation of physical public spaces. One of the weaknesses of these movements is their difficulty in accessing institutions and impacting public policies. The 2015 Barcelona City Council election is one of the first cases in which one of these movements has been able to "occupy" the public institutions by building Barcelona en Comú (BeC), a political party that won the elections. BeC was conceived as the confluence of (1) minor and/or emerging parties and, to a large extent, (2) collectives and activists, with no political party affiliation, who played a prominent role in the 15M movement.

The 15M movement, also referred to as #SpanishRevolution or the "Indignados" movement, emerged in May 2011 and has been defined as a "networked social movement of the digital age" [13]. Networked social movements, like the Arab Spring, the 15M, and Occupy Wall Street, are claimed to be "a network of networks, they can afford not to have an identifiable center, and yet ensure coordination functions, as well as deliberation, by interaction between multiple nodes" [13]. Other authors have defined this new model of social movement as a "change from logic of collective action, associated with high levels of organizational resources and the formation of collective identities, to a logic of connective action, based on personalized content sharing across media networks" [7]. There, these can be seen as paradigmatic examples of how the Internet is able to alter the mobilizing structure for collective action [50]. We should note that some voices have refused these theoretical assumptions and argued that "a handful of people control most of the communication flow" and, consequently, the existence of leaders in such movements could not be denied [27]. Empirical studies revealed that the 15M network on Twitter is characterized by its "decentralized structure, based on coalitions of smaller organizations" in spite of "a small core of central users is still critical to trigger chains of messages of high orders of magnitude" [30]. Decentralization has been also observed in [59] in which the 15M network is defined as polycentric.

The 15M network properties (i.e., decentralization, polycentrism) could be perceived as a striking contrast to conventional political organizations, in particular, political parties. The Iron Law of Oligarchy [43] postulates that political parties, like any complex organization, self-generate an elite (i.e., "Who says organization, says oligarchy"). Although some scholars have criticized the idea that organizations will intrinsically build oligarchical leadership structures [18, 37, 55], many political and social theorists have supported that, historically, small minorities hold the most power in political processes [44, 46, 51]. At the interplay between politics and the Internet, different studies have found the frequent presence of elites [19, 57]. Regarding Spanish online politics, a study of the 2011 national election campaign on Twitter revealed that "minor and new parties tend to be more clustered and better connected, which implies a more cohesive community" [5]. Nevertheless, all the diffusion networks of parties in that study were strongly centralized around their candidate and/or party profiles. Later studies analyzed the interactions on Twitter between the 15M nodes and political parties and conclude that networked social movements are *para-institutions*: perceived as institutions but preserving an internal networked organization [52]. However, these conclusions were formulated by analyzing the networks when no elections were held, before institutionalization began. Election campaigns are competitive processes that might favor the centralization of an organization around candidates. Indeed, it has been proved that the network properties of political parties change when elections arrive [23]. Previous hypotheses [58] about Podemos, a member party of the Barcelona en Comú candidacy and as well inspired by the 15M movement, postulate an organization formed by a *front-end* ("spokesmen/spokeswomen who are visible from the media perspective") and a *back-end* ("muscle of the organization, barely visible from the media perspective"). However, there are no empirical validations of this hypothesis.

Given that Barcelona en Comú emerged from the 15M and this networked movement is characterized by a decentralized structure, the first research question of this study is:

RQ1: Has Barcelona en Comú preserved a decentralized structure or has it adopted a conventional centralized organization ruled by an elite?

To answer our first research question, we will analyze the network of retweets in relation to the campaign for the 2015 Barcelona City Council election to (1) identify clusters of political parties and (2) characterize their topology. The identification of the sub-network corresponding to each party will be possible because of the highly divided partisan structure of the retweet network. This assumption relies on previous studies of online polarization in social media in the context of US politics [1, 16]. Online polarization, also known as cyberbalkanization, is a social phenomenon that occurs when Internet users form isolated groups around specific, e.g., political interests. Indeed, this is not only a particular feature of US politics but also a social behavior observed in a diverse range of countries, e.g., Canada [31] and Germany [20]. In Spain, previous studies of Twitter networks in previous elections also showed evidence of polarization, e.g., in the 2010 Catalan election [15] and in the 2011 Spanish elections [11].

We also find of interest to explore the behavior of Barcelona en Comú when discussing with other political parties. The 15M movement, which motivated the emergence of this grassroots party, is characterized by its willingness to expand the practices of deliberative democracy beyond institutions [54]. Indeed, recent studies about the internal communication of Barcelona en Comú have already shown the relevance of discussions in online platforms [10, 32]. In contrast, previous research found little dialogue between the 15M movement and political institutions, with sporadic exceptions with minor and left-wing parties [52]. Given that Barcelona en Comú, as any political party, is expected to discuss with other political parties, the second research question of the study is:

RQ2: Does Barcelona en Comú discuss differently with other political parties than traditional parties do?

The extent of political polarization that can be observed in social media depends on the kind of interaction considered. In the case of the American political blogosphere, a seminal work by Adamic et al. [1] showed that few links connected liberal and conservative blogs, as bloggers mostly refer to ideologically related others. On the contrary in Wikipedia, a platform where users editing the same articles are brought to discuss and pursue consensus, partisan users were observed to be equally likely to interact with others supporting the same or the opposite party [48]. Likewise, in the case of Twitter different results have been observed for retweets and reply networks. Retweeting has been proven as a common mechanism for endorsement [12] which might explain why retweet networks exhibit polarization to a greater extent than reply networks [5, 16]. This is consistent with the results from a study of a Swiss political online platform which concluded that "interactions with positive connotation (supports and likes) revealed significant patterns of polarization with respect to party alignment, unlike the comments layer, which has negligible polarization" [23]. To answer this second question, we will therefore examine the online party discussion networks by analyzing the network of replies and comparing the structure of clusters to the ones from the network of retweets.

This article is organized as follows. In "Methods" section we describe the techniques of our methodology to detect clusters in Twitter networks and to characterize their topology. The dataset of tweets related to the 2015 Barcelona City Council election is described in "Dataset" section. We present in "Online party organization networks" section the results of our methodology using the network of retweets. A similar analysis on the network of replies is shown in "Online party discussion networks" section. In "Discussion" section we discuss the results of the analysis to answer our research questions about the online structure of Barcelona en Comú and the interaction of this new organization towards traditional parties. Finally, we conclude in "Conclusion" section.

Methods

Here we describe the methodology of our study to, given a network, detect the major clusters (i.e., political parties) and characterize their social structures in three dimensions: hierarchical structure, small-world phenomenon, and coreness.

Community detection

Many previous studies have relied on the Louvain method [9] because of its high performance in terms of accuracy, and its efficiency. This method is based on a greedy algorithm that attempts to optimize the modularity of a partition of a given network. Modularity function measures the density of edges inside communities in comparison to edges between communities [49]. Given a network, the modularity value, lying between -1 and 1, is defined as:

$$Q = \frac{1}{2m} \Sigma_{ij} \left[A_{ij} - \frac{d_i d_j}{2m} \right] \delta(c_i, c_j),$$

where A_{ij} is the edge weight between nodes i and j; d_i and d_j are the degrees of the nodes i and j, respectively; m represents the total number of edges in the network; c_i and c_j are the indexes of communities of those nodes; and δ is the Kronecker delta.

The Louvain method follows a two-step approach. First, each node is assigned to its own community. Then, for each node i, the change in modularity is measured for moving i from its own community into the community of each neighbor j:

$$\Delta Q = \left[\frac{S_{in} + w_{i,in}}{2m} - \left(\frac{S_{tot} + d_i}{2m} \right)^2 \right] - \left[\frac{S_{in}}{2m} - \left(\frac{S_{tot}}{2m} \right)^2 - \left(\frac{d_i}{2m} \right)^2 \right],$$

where S_{in} is the sum of all the weights of the intra-edges of the community where i being moved into, S_{tot} is the sum of all the weights of the edges to nodes of the community, d_i is the degree of i, $w_{i,in}$ is the sum of the weights of the edges between i and other nodes in the community, and m is the sum of the weights of all edges in the network. Once this value is measured for all communities that i is linked to, the algorithm sets i into the community that produces the largest increase in modularity. If no increase is possible, i remains in its original community. This process is applied until modularity cannot be increased and a local maximum of modularity is achieved. Then, the method groups the nodes from the same community and builds a new network where nodes are the communities from the previous step. Both steps are repeated until modularity cannot be increased.

N-Louvain method

The Louvain method is a greedy algorithm and has a random component, so each execution produces a different result. To obtain robust results, avoiding dependency on a particular execution of the algorithm, this article introduces the following modification to identify the main clusters of the network in a robust way.

First, it runs N executions of the Louvain algorithm, which produce N different partitions of the network into clusters. To identify each cluster across executions, our method applies the Jaccard index [33] to every pair of clusters c_i and c_j from different executions:

$$J(c_i, c_j) = \frac{|c_i \cap c_j|}{|c_i \cup c_j|}.$$

Thus, clusters across executions are matched if they are the most similar ones. This allows to quantify the occurrences (i.e., executions) of each node in each cluster. Finally, the method assigns to each cluster all the nodes that appear in that cluster in at least a fraction $(1 - \varepsilon)$ of the partitions created, that is to say that ε represents the sensibility level of the algorithm. This procedure allows to validate the results of the community detection algorithm, and to guarantee that all the nodes that are assigned to a cluster do actually belong to it with a given confidence. The remaining nodes, that cannot be assigned in a stable way to any of the main clusters, are left out from all the clusters.

Cluster characterization

Inspired by the social dimensions and corresponding metrics suggested in [23] we propose an extended framework to compare the topology of the intra-network of each cluster.

Hierarchical structure

The hierarchical structure is quantified on the in-degree distribution of each cluster. The in-degree of node i is the total number of edges onto node i. By counting how many nodes have each in-degree value, the in-degree distribution $P(d_{in})$ is equal to the fraction of nodes in the graph with such in-degree d_{in}. The cumulative in-degree distribution $P(x \geq d_{in})$ represents the fraction of nodes in the graph whose in-degree is greater than or equal to d_{in}.

The original framework [23] used an existing method to measure degree centralization defined in [22]. Degree centralization is based on two concepts:

1. How the centrality of the most central node exceeds the centrality of all other nodes.
2. Setting the value as a ratio by comparing to a star network:

$$C_{in} = \frac{\sum_{i=1}^{n}[d_{max}^{in} - d_i^{in}]}{\max \sum_{i=1}^{n}[d_{max}^{in} - d_i^{in}]},$$

where d_i^{in} is the in-degree of node i, d_{max}^{in} is the maximum in-degree of the network, and $\max \sum_{i=1}^{n}[d_{max}^{in} - d_i^{in}]$ is the maximum possible sum of differences for a graph with the same number of nodes (a star network).

The differences of several orders of magnitude between the maximum and average in-degree, which characterize social graphs, make this metric approximately equal to the ratio between the maximum in-degree and the number of nodes:

$$C_{\text{in}} = \frac{\sum_{i=1}^{n}[d_{\text{max}}^{\text{in}} - d_i^{\text{in}}]}{\max \sum_{i=1}^{n}[d_{\text{max}}^{\text{in}} - d_i^{\text{in}}]} \approx \frac{(n-1) \cdot d_{\text{max}}^{\text{in}}}{(n-1) \cdot (n-1)} \approx \frac{d_{\text{max}}^{\text{in}}}{n}.$$

Therefore, to better evaluate the hierarchical structure of graphs, we will also apply the Gini coefficient, a statistical metric to quantify the level of inequality given a distribution [28]. It was initially formulated in Economics to measure the income distribution using the Lorenz curve. The Gini coefficient is equal to

$$G_{\text{in}} = A/(A + B),$$

where A is the area between the line corresponding perfect equality and B is the area under the Lorenz curve. If the Lorenz curve is expressed by the function $y = L(x)$, B is calculated as $B = 1 - 2\int_0^1 L(x)\,dx$ and $A = 1/2 - B$. In the context of network topology, the Gini coefficient is applied to characterize the hierarchical structure of a network based on the inequality of its in-degree distribution.

Small-world phenomenon

The small-world phenomenon states that most nodes of a network are reachable from any other node in a small number of steps and explains information efficiency in social networks. To assess the small-world phenomenon in each cluster, the clustering coefficient and the average path length are computed. Small-world networks tend to have a small average path length and a clustering coefficient significantly higher than expected by random chance [62]. The clustering coefficient measures the extent of nodes to cluster together by calculating the number of triangles in the network. For every node i it sets N_i to be the neighborhood, i.e., $N_i = \{j \in V : (i,j) \in E\}$, and defines the local clustering coefficient as

$$\text{Cl}_i = \frac{2|(j,k) \in E : j, \ k \in N_i|}{k_i(k_i - 1)}.$$

Then, following [62], the clustering coefficient is just the average of the local clustering coefficients: $\text{Cl} = \sum_i \text{Cl}_i/n$, where n is the number of nodes in the network. To calculate the average path length, for every pair of nodes i and j, it sets ℓ_{ij} to be the smallest number of steps among all paths between i and j. This metric is applied to the clusters identified by the new version algorithm for community detection and, by definition, there is always a path between any pair of nodes in every cluster. The average path length is defined as follows:

$$l = \sum_{i \neq j} \ell_{ij}/n(n-1).$$

Coreness

Coreness has been employed in previous literature as a metric of the resilience of a network [24]. The resilience of a social network is the ability of a social group to withstand external stresses. To measure coreness of the intra-network of each cluster the k-core decomposition is applied in order to evaluate the distributions of the nodes within each k-core.

Given a network, a sub-network H induced by the subset of nodes C is defined. H is a k-core of the network if and only if for every node i in C: $\deg_H(i) \geq k$, and H is the maximum sub-graph which fulfills this condition. The degree of the node i in the sub-graph H is denoted as $\deg_H(i)$. A node has k-index equal to k if it belongs to the k-core but not to the $(k+1)$-core. In simple words, k-core decomposition starts with $k = 1$ and removes all nodes with degree equal to 1. The procedure is repeated iteratively until no nodes with degree 1 remain. Next, all removed nodes are assigned k-index to be 1. It continues with the same procedure for $k = 2$ and obtains nodes with indexes equal 2, and so on. The process stops when the last node from the network is removed at the $k_{\max}$ th step. The variable $k_{\max}$ is then the maximum shell index of the graph.

Dataset

Data were collected from Twitter in relation to the campaign for the 2015 Barcelona City Council election (May 1–26, 2015) by the definition of a list of Twitter accounts of the seven main political parties:

- Barcelona en Comú (BeC),[1]
- Convergència i Unió (CiU),[2]
- Ciudadanos (Cs),[3]
- Capgirem Barcelona (CUP),[4]
- Esquerra Republicana de Catalunya (ERC),[5]
- Partit Popular de Catalunya (PP),[6]
- Partit dels Socialistes de Catalunya (PSC).[7]

The lists also include the Twitter accounts of the corresponding candidates for Mayor. For the case of coalitions (CiU, BeC, and CUP) also the party accounts of the parties constituting the coalition were included. The users of the list can be found in Table 1.

It is important to note that the sampling criteria are based on specific accounts instead of hashtags. Some studies have detected differences in the tagging practice of politicians [36]. Previous work has observed that some parties adopt a small set of hashtags during campaigns and some other parties generate new hashtags every day in order to locate them in the list of trending topics. Therefore, sampling messages from a list of campaign hashtags would likely lead to an unbalanced dataset. For this reason, we believe these sampling criteria represent a better approach to capture the communication practices of the communities around parties.

---

[1] https://barcelonaencomu.cat/.

[2] http://www.ciu.cat/.

[3] https://www.ciudadanos-cs.org/.

[4] http://cup.cat/.

[5] http://www.esquerra.cat/.

[6] http://www.ppcatalunya.com/.

[7] http://www.socialistes.cat/.

Table 1 Twitter accounts of the selected political parties and candidates

Political party	Party account(s)	Candidate account
BeC	@bcnencomu	@adacolau
	@icveuiabcn	
	@podem_bcn	
	@equobcn	
	@pconstituentbcn	
CiU	@cdcbarcelona	@xaviertrias
	@uniobcn	
Cs	@cs_bcna	@carinamejias
CUP	@capgirembcn	@mjlecha
	@cupbarcelona	
ERC	@ercbcn	@alfredbosch
PP	@ppbarcelona_	@albertofdezxbcn
PSC	@pscbarcelona	@jaumecollboni

The Twitter streaming API provided 507,597 tweets that (1) were created by, (2) retweeted, or (3) mentioned an account from the list. Figure 1 shows the distribution of the tweets over time, and reveals that the most active dates were the election day (March 24) and the one of the televised debate between candidates (March 21). In contrast, the day preceding the election, known as the reflection day, shows a notable decrease in Twitter activity. This distribution is similar to the one observed in previous studies about Spanish politics on this social network [5].

To detect and characterize the online network organization of political parties, we build a directed weighted graph which comprises a set of nodes (users) and a set of edges (retweets between any pair of users). Each edge in the graph represents that the source user retweeted a message posted by the target user. To exclude anecdotal interactions between users which might not be enough of a signal to infer endorsement [25] and to highlight the structure of the expected clusters, the network only contains the interactions between any pair of nodes that occurred at least 3 times: an edge from user A to user B implies that user A has retweeted at least 3 times user B in the dataset. We considered a threshold of 3 retweets to be strong enough for inferring endorsement, and for

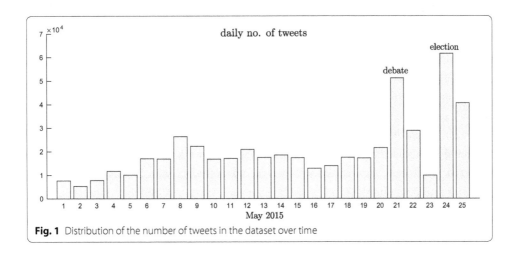

Fig. 1 Distribution of the number of tweets in the dataset over time

filtering out anecdotal interactions without loosing relevant connections. Nodes without edges after this process are removed. The resulting retweet network comprises 6492 nodes and 16,775 edges.

To analyze the discussions between political parties, we built another directed weighted graph, being in this case the edges of the graph replies instead of retweets. Unlike the retweet graph, where the interactions have been filtered by 3, the reply graph is maintaining all the edges. The motivation for this lies in the different nature of replies: while a single retweet could be anecdotal and has a low cost for a user (one click), a reply is a more expensive action involving more cognitive overhead, which makes it a noteworthy interaction already if it happens only once [47]. Indeed, previous work has found that retweeting has a higher likelihood than replying to a tweet [3]. The resulting reply network consists of 21,846 nodes and 44,598 edges.

Online party organization networks

In this section we present the results of detecting and characterizing the major clusters in the network of retweets, i.e., the online party organization networks.

Community detection

To detect the online organization network of each political party, we apply the N-Louvain method. This new version has been designed to detect clusters which only include nodes that are reliably assigned to them. We apply the method by running the Louvain method 100 times and assigning to each cluster only the nodes that fall into that cluster more than 95 times ($N = 100, \varepsilon = 0.05$). By inspecting the results of the 100 executions, a constant presence of eight major clusters, much bigger than the other clusters, is observed. The composition of these clusters is also quite stable: 4973 nodes (82.25%) are assigned to the same cluster in over 95 executions.

We examine the most relevant nodes of every cluster, according to PageRank, and find a single cluster for almost each party: ERC^{rt}, CUP^{rt}, Cs^{rt}, CiU^{rt}, PP^{rt}, and PSC^{rt}. The only exception for such rule is that BeC is composed of two clusters. The manual inspection of the users from these two clusters reveals that one cluster is formed by the official accounts of the party (e.g., @bcnencomu, @ahorapodemos), allied parties (e.g., @ ahoramadrid), the candidate (@adacolau), and a large community of peripheral users. In contrast, the other cluster is composed of activists engaged in the digital communication for the campaign (e.g., @toret, @santidemajo, @galapita), i.e., party activists, many of whom are related to the 15M movement. For this reason, from now on, the analysis distinguishes these clusters as BeC-p^{rt} and BeC-m^{rt}: *party* and *movement*, respectively.

Table 2 shows the top five users with highest PageRank in each cluster, and their role with respect to the corresponding party: *candidate* (the account of the candidate for mayor), *party* (official accounts of parties associated with the candidacy), *activist* (party activists), *institution* (institutional accounts), *media* (accounts of media or journalists). It should be noted that we also considered the category *politician* to distinguish professional politicians from activists; however, no politician with an institutional position was found among the top five users from each cluster. While the topmost relevant users tend to correspond to each party's candidate and official accounts, which is partly caused by the data collection criteria, it is interesting to note the presence of other very

Table 2 Top 5 users for the 8 largest clusters according to their PageRank in the overall network, with their role with respect to the corresponding party

Cluster	User	PageRank	Role
BeC-p	@bcnencomu	0.092	Party
BeC-p	@adacolau	0.029	Candidate
BeC-p	@ahoramadrid	0.009	Allied party
BeC-p	@ahorapodemos	0.009	Party
BeC-p	@isaranjuez	0.002	Activist
BeC-m	@toret	0.014	Activist
BeC-m	@santidemajo	0.005	Activist
BeC-m	@sentitcritic	0.005	Media
BeC-m	@galapita	0.005	Activist
BeC-m	@eloibadia	0.005	Activist
Cs	@carinamejias	0.007	Candidate
Cs	@cs_bcna	0.006	Party
Cs	@ciudadanoscs	0.004	Party
Cs	@soniasi02	0.003	Activist
Cs	@prensacs	0.002	Party
CiU	@xaviertrias	0.012	Candidate
CiU	@ciu	0.004	Party
CiU	@bcn_ajuntament	0.003	Institution
CiU	@cdcbarcelona	0.002	Party
CiU	@uniobcn	0.001	Party
CUP	@cupbarcelona	0.016	Party
CUP	@capgirembcn	0.008	Party
CUP	@albertmartnez	0.005	Media
CUP	@mjlecha	0.002	Candidate
CUP	@simongorjeos	0.003	Media
ERC	@ercbcn	0.016	Party
ERC	@alfredbosch	0.011	Candidate
ERC	@arapolitica	0.007	Media
ERC	@esquerra_erc	0.004	Party
ERC	@directe	0.003	Media
PP	@cati_bcn	0.003	Media
PP	@albertofdezxbcn	0.003	Candidate
PP	@maticatradio	0.002	Media
PP	@ppbarcelona_	0.002	Party
PP	@carmenchusalas	0.001	Activist
PSC	@pscbarcelona	0.003	Party
PSC	@sergifor	0.003	Media
PSC	@jaumecollboni	0.002	Candidate
PSC	@elpaiscat	0.002	Media
PSC	@annatorrasfont	0.001	Media

central nodes in these clusters, including media or institutional accounts (the municipality account, in the cluster of the outgoing mayor's party). BeC-m is the only cluster for which the top users are mostly activists.

The boundaries between ideological online communities are visible in Fig. 2. As one could expect in any polarized scenario, the largest number of retweets occur within the

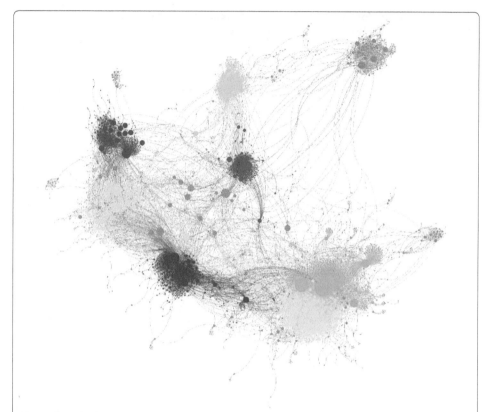

Fig. 2 Network of retweets (giant component). Clusters are represented by color: BeC-p^{rt} (*dark green*); BeC-m^{rt} (*light green*); ERC^{rt} (*yellow*); PSC^{rt} (*red*); CUP^{rt} (*violet*); Cs^{rt} (*orange*); CiU^{rt} (*dark blue*); PP^{rt} (*cyan*). The nodes outside of these clusters are *gray* colored

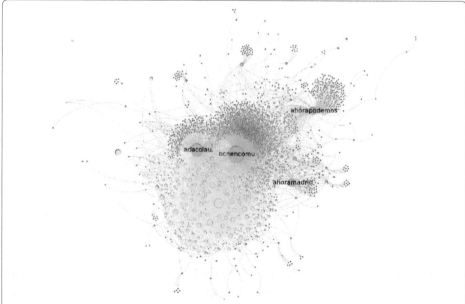

Fig. 3 Sub-network of BeC-p^{rt} (*dark green*) and BeC-m^{rt} (*light green*). For better readability, the labels of public figures are shown

same cluster. There exists, however, a notably large number of links between the two clusters of BeC (BeC-p^{rt}, and BeC-m^{rt}). Figure 3 presents the sub-network formed by the nodes and links of both clusters. To further prove the low levels of interactions between major parties, an interaction matrix A is defined, where $A_{i,j}$ counts all retweets that accounts from cluster i^{rt} made for the tweets from users of cluster j^{rt}. Since the clusters have different sizes, $A_{i,j}$ is normalized by the sum of the all retweets made by the users assigned to cluster i. Figure 4 shows matrix A for all the clusters and confirms that a vast majority of retweets were made between users from the same cluster (main diagonal). This is also true in the case of the two clusters of Barcelona en Comú although there is a presence of communication between movement and party clusters, with a prevalence from the movement to the party (BeC-m$^{rt} \rightarrow$ BeC-p$^{rt} = 0.18$), the largest value out of the main diagonal.

As mentioned above, the new version of the Louvain method proposed in this article only assigns a node to one of the eight largest clusters only if it falls to a particular one of these clusters more than 95 of 100 times. The final inclusion/exclusion of the most relevant nodes to a cluster was manually inspected in order to assess the performance of this new version. For preserving the political preference of non-public users, Table 3 only presents the 20 most relevant nodes which were not assigned to any cluster, their role, and how many times they fall into each cluster over the 100 executions. The results prove that N-Louvain method effectively prevented the inclusion of media accounts in the intra-network of political parties, e.g., @btvnoticies, @elperiodico, @elsmatins, etc. Also, for better readability, when a node falls in different political clusters more than 20% each, we highlight the corresponding values in Table 3. First, we observe that the Catalan pro-independence media outlet @naciodigital and two journalists from that outlet (@bernatff, @jordi_palmer) fell in ERC^{rt} and CUP^{rt}, i.e., clusters of Catalan pro-independence parties. Second, we find that the TV show @puntcattv3 fell in ERC^{rt} and

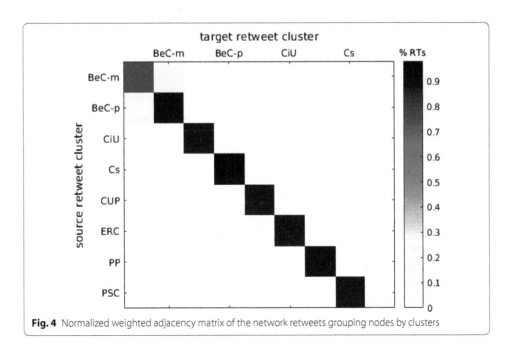

Fig. 4 Normalized weighted adjacency matrix of the network retweets grouping nodes by clusters

Table 3 Most relevant nodes, according to PageRank, which could not be reliably assigned to any of the major clusters indicating the number of executions in each cluster

User	Role	BeC-m^{rt}	BeC-p^{rt}	CiU^{rt}	Cs^{rt}	CUP^{rt}	ERC^{rt}	PP^{rt}	PSC^{rt}	Undef.
@btvnoticies	Media	0	0	0	0	1	0	86	13	0
@elperiodico	Media	0	90	0	3	0	1	0	1	5
@elsmatins	Media	0	0	0	0	0	93	0	7	0
@naciodigital	Media	0	0	1	0	*38*	*61*	0	0	0
@tv3cat	Media	0	0	0	0	3	54	0	19	24
@encampanya	Media	1	0	0	0	36	0	0	0	63
@rocsalafaixa	Citizen	0	0	7	0	1	92	0	0	0
@bernatff	Media	0	0	1	0	*38*	*61*	0	0	0
@jordi_palmer	Media	0	0	1	0	*38*	*61*	0	0	0
@mariamariekke	Citizen	*50*	*50*	0	0	0	0	0	0	0
@puntcattv3	Media	0	0	0	0	0	44	0	56	0
@ramontremosa	Politician	0	0	90	0	0	10	0	0	0
@santimdx5	Media	91	0	0	0	0	0	0	0	9
@mtudela	Media	0	0	7	0	1	92	0	0	0
@pah_bcn	Civic org	89	0	0	0	0	0	0	0	11
@324cat	Media	0	0	0	0	3	52	0	13	32
@terrassaencomu	Party	2	92	0	0	0	0	0	0	6
@sicomtelevision	Media	1	8	0	0	90	0	0	0	1
@xriusenoticies	Media	0	0	*35*	0	0	0	0	*65*	0
@vagadetotes	Civic org	*78*	0	0	0	*22*	0	0	0	0

Values are italics when a node falls in different political clusters more than 20% each

PSC^{rt} and the media outlet @xriusenoticies in CiU^{rt} and PSC^{rt}. Results also show that @mariamariekke, a citizen who created drawings for the BeC campaign, fell between the two clusters of the party (party and movement). Finally, we also find of interest the appearance of civic organizations: *Plataforma de Afectados por la Hipoteca* mostly in BeC-m^{rt} (organization to stop evictions which was co-founded by the candidate of BeC), and Vaga de Totes (feminist labor organization), which lies between the left parties BeC-m^{rt} and CUP^{rt}.

Comparison to the Clique Percolation Method

The design of the N-Louvain method is motivated by the fuzzy community structure of political networks, as one of the campaigns for the 2015 Barcelona City Council election. These networks are usually formed by overlapping communities and the proposed algorithm improves the standard Louvain method by identifying clusters in a more stable way. However, we should note that there are some community detection methods in the state of the art for overlapping communities. In particular, the Clique Percolation Method (CPM) is the most popular one according to [21]. This method is applied on the network of retweets with the CFinder software package[8] to detect k-cliques, i.e., complete (fully connected) sub-graphs of k nodes. Figure 5 presents the number of k-clique graphs obtained through the CPM at every value of k. As expected, the number of

---

[8] http://www.cfinder.org/.

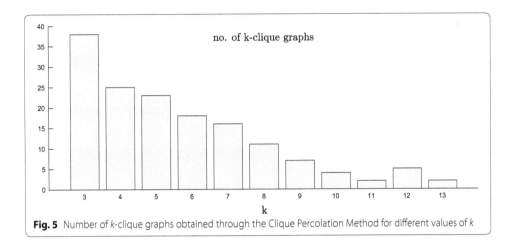

Fig. 5 Number of k-clique graphs obtained through the Clique Percolation Method for different values of k

k-clique graphs tends to decrease as k increases. At its maximum value ($k = 13$), the method only detects two k-clique graphs: one formed by users from BeC and another formed by users from CiU.

While the Louvain method was able to identify every party cluster, CPM at its maximum value only detects two party clusters. This is explained by the different size and structure of the party networks. For this reason, the communities at different values of k have been examined. When $k = 9$, CPM identifies seven k-clique graphs. The inspection of the nodes of each of them reveals that two of them are related to BeC, one is related to a municipal police trade union and the rest are related to each of the political parties CiU, CUP, Cs, and PP. For PSC and ERC, CPM identifies k-clique graphs when $k = 8$ and $k = 7$, respectively. To compare these results with the clusters from the N-Louvain method, Table 4 indicates how many nodes of the each k-clique graph occurred in each cluster, and reveals that:

- All the nodes of the k-clique graphs related to CiU, Cs, CUP, ERC, and PSC are part of the corresponding clusters from the N-Louvain method.
- Only one node from PP k-clique graph was not in PP political cluster.
- The nodes from the k-clique graph related to a trade union of municipal police (GU) were not in a political cluster.

Table 4 Clusters obtained through Clique Percolation Method, k value of k-clique graph, and number of nodes which occur in the clusters obtained through the N-Louvain method

CPM	k	BeC-m[rt]	BeC-p[rt]	CiU[rt]	Cs[rt]	CUP[rt]	ERC[rt]	PP[rt]	PSC[rt]	Undef.
BeC₁	9	*60*	3	0	0	0	0	0	0	2
BeC₂	9	*7*	2	0	0	0	0	0	0	0
CiU	9	0	0	*25*	0	0	0	0	0	0
Cs	9	0	0	0	*10*	0	0	0	0	0
CUP	9	0	0	0	0	*13*	0	0	0	0
ERC	7	0	0	0	0	0	*7*	0	0	0
PP	9	0	0	0	0	0	0	*20*	0	1
PSC	8	0	0	0	0	0	0	0	*18*	0
GU	9	0	0	0	0	0	0	0	0	*11*

The largest number of each row is italics

- The largest BeC k-clique graph (BeC$_1$) is mainly formed by nodes from the BeC movement cluster. The smallest k-clique graph (BeC$_2$) is composed of two nodes from the BeC party cluster and seven nodes from the BeC movement cluster.

Figure 6 presents all these k-clique graphs to better understand their composition. The figure shows an overlap between the two BeC k-clique graphs which is composed of three nodes: @bcnencomu (party account), @adacolau (candidate), and @ciddavid (party member). It is interesting to observe that, although the rest of the nodes of the smallest k-clique graph belongs to the movement cluster, all of them are related to Iniciativa per Catalunya Verds, the main pre-existing party that converged in Barcelona en Comú. In other words, CPM also identifies a k-clique graph related to the institutional elite of BeC and a much larger k-clique graph related to the grassroots elements of BeC.

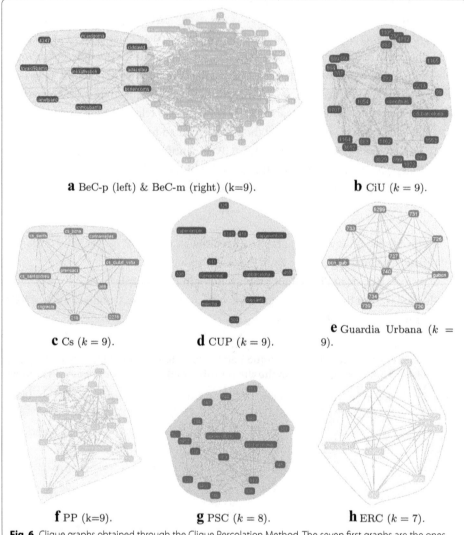

a BeC-p (left) & BeC-m (right) (k=9).   **b** CiU ($k = 9$).

c Cs ($k = 9$).   **d** CUP ($k = 9$).   **e** Guardia Urbana ($k = 9$).

f PP (k=9).   **g** PSC ($k = 8$).   **h** ERC ($k = 7$).

Fig. 6 Clique graphs obtained through the Clique Percolation Method. The seven first graphs are the ones when k equals to 9. The two last graphs are the largest k-clique graphs for PSC ($k = 8$), and ERC ($k = 7$). Accounts of non-public citizens are anonymized by showing a numerical ID in the label

In conclusion, the results from applying CPM are consistent with the ones obtained through the community detection algorithm proposed in this article. However, the N-Louvain method has two substantial advantages over CPM:

- The different size and structure of the political networks make that CPM at the maximum value of k only detects two major clusters. On the other hand, the new method is able to identify every party cluster.
- The clusters obtained through CPM are k-cliques and, therefore, such clusters are dense graphs formed by the core of the party network structure. Social networks are characterized by their heavy-tailed degree distribution so the k-clique graphs exclude the large amount of less active users. Recent studies have proved that these are the nodes which compose the critical periphery in the growth of protest movements [6]. For this reason, the inclusion of these nodes, as the new method does, becomes essential for the following characterization of clusters.

Cluster characterization

The eight clusters detected by the community detection algorithm are then characterized in terms of hierarchical structure, small-world phenomenon, and coreness.

Hierarchical structure

To evaluate the hierarchical structure, the in-degree inequality of each cluster is measured with the Gini coefficient. In-degree centralization, originally suggested in [23], is also computed.

From results in Table 5 a notable divergence between both metrics is seen: the inequality values of CiU^{rt} and PP^{rt} are similar ($G_{in} = 0.893$ and $G_{in} = 0.876$, respectively), but the centralization of PP^{rt} ($C_{in} = 0.378$) is far from the maximum centralization value exhibited by CiU^{rt} ($C_{in} = 0.770$). For Barcelona en Comú, $BeC\text{-}m^{rt}$ emerges as the least inequal and the least centralized structure, while $BeC\text{-}p^{rt}$ forms the most inequal cluster ($G_{in} = 0.995$). The results in Table 5 confirm that the in-degree centralization formulated in [22] is almost equal to the ratio between the maximum in-degree and the number of nodes. In conclusion, this metric is not a good one to capture hierarchical structure for social diffusion graphs, and the Gini coefficient for in-degree inequality represents

Table 5 Inequality based on the Gini coefficient (G_{in}) and centralization (C_{in}) of the in-degree distribution of each cluster in the network of retweets, and ratio between the maximum in-degree and the number of nodes (r)

Cluster	G_{in}	C_{in}	r
BeC-p^{rt}	0.995	0.639	0.639
Cs^{rt}	0.964	0.476	0.480
ERC^{rt}	0.954	0.452	0.454
CUP^{rt}	0.953	0.635	0.636
CiU^{rt}	0.893	0.770	0.774
PP^{rt}	0.876	0.378	0.389
PSC^{rt}	0.818	0.565	0.578
BeC-m^{rt}	0.811	0.290	0.302

a more reliable measure. Finally, the Lorenz curve of the in-degree distribution of the clusters is presented in Fig. 7 to visually validate the different levels of inequality among clusters.

Small-world phenomenon

Broadly speaking, the efficiency of a social network is explained by its small-world phenomenon, i.e., phenomenon of users being linked by a mutual acquaintance. To assess the small-world phenomenon in each party, the average path length and the clustering coefficient are computed.

Table 6 reveals that BeC-m^{rt} has the highest clustering coefficient (Cl = 0.208) closely followed by PP^{rt} and PSC^{rt}, the two smallest clusters by size. On the contrary the clustering coefficient of BeC-p^{rt} is almost 0. This finding is explained by the topology of BeC-p^{rt}, roughly formed by stars whose center nodes are the most visible Twitter accounts of Barcelona en Comú: the party accounts and the candidate.

No remarkable patterns regarding the average path length are observed. It is lower than 3 for the majority of the party clusters with the PSC^{rt} cluster having the lowest value ($l = 2.29$). At the same time ERC^{rt}, CiU^{rt}, and BeC-p^{rt} expose the longest average

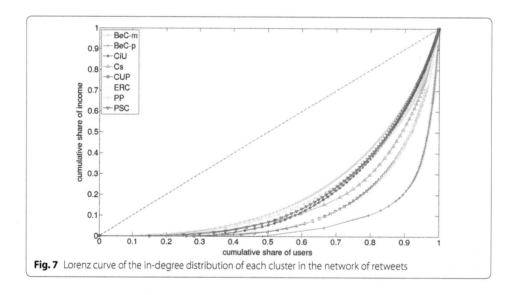

Fig. 7 Lorenz curve of the in-degree distribution of each cluster in the network of retweets

Table 6 Number of nodes (N) and edges (E), clustering coefficient (Cl), and average path length (l) of the intra-network of each cluster in the network of retweets

Cluster	N	E	Cl	l
BeC-m^{rt}	427	2431	0.208	3.35
PP^{rt}	301	1163	0.188	2.73
PSC^{rt}	211	810	0.182	2.29
CiU^{rt}	337	1003	0.114	4.66
Cs^{rt}	352	832	0.073	2.57
CUP^{rt}	635	1422	0.037	2.57
ERC^{rt}	866	1899	0.027	5.43
BeC-p^{rt}	1844	2427	0.002	2.48

path length (5.43, 4.66, 3.35, respectively) that might signal the lower information especially in the case of ERC^{rt}.

Coreness

The coreness of a network is closely related to its social resilience, i.e., the ability of a social group to withstand external stresses [23]. To measure social resilience for a social network, the k-core decomposition of each cluster is performed in order to evaluate the distributions of the nodes within each k-core. The more nodes are in the most inner cores, i.e., the ones with the larger k-indexes, and the larger is the maximal k-index, then the more resilient the cluster is.

Table 7 presents the maximal and average k-indexes for each cluster and Fig. 8 visually shows the corresponding distributions. As in the case of hierarchical structure and small-world phenomenon, BeC-m^{rt} ($k_{max} = 17$, $k_{avg} = 5.90$) and BeC-p^{rt} ($k_{max} = 5$, $k_{avg} = 1.33$) are the highest and lowest values, respectively. In comparison to the other

Table 7 Maximal and average k-index (standard deviation in parentheses) for the intra-network of each cluster in the network of retweets

Cluster	k_{max}	k_{avg}
BeC-m^{rt}	17	5.90 (5.46)
PP^{rt}	12	4.02 (3.99)
PSC^{rt}	11	3.85 (3.55)
CiU^{rt}	13	3.10 (3.44)
ERC^{rt}	8	2.25 (1.85)
Cs^{rt}	10	2.42 (2.42)
CUP^{rt}	10	2.19 (2.22)
BeC-p^{rt}	5	1.33 (0.71)

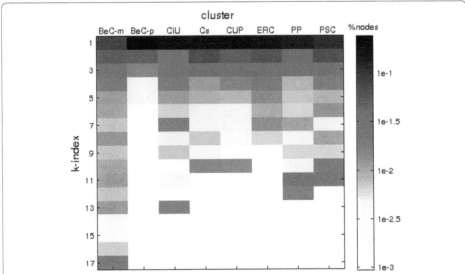

Fig. 8 Distribution of the nodes per cluster (*column*) and k-index (*row*) in the network of retweets. Cells are colored to form a heat map indicating the percentage of nodes (log scale) from each cluster with a given k-index

parties there are clear differences between node distributions for both, BeC-m^{rt} and BeC-p^{rt}, and the rest (the largest concentration of the nodes is in the first k-cores and considerable part is in the most inner cores). Therefore, the movement group of Barcelona en Comú is an online social community with an extreme ability to withstand or recover. At the same time the party group of Barcelona en Comú seems to only focus on the core users.

Online party discussion networks

In this section we present the results of detecting and characterizing the major clusters in the network of replies, i.e., the online party discussion networks.

Community detection

We apply the N-Louvain method on the network of replies. We should note that the network of retweets only contained edges with weight greater or equal to 3 while no threshold was applied for the network of replies. Given that the boundaries between online communities are fuzzier in this network, the method is applied by running the Louvain method 100 times and assigning to each cluster the nodes that fall into that cluster more than 50 times ($N = 100, \varepsilon = 0.5$), instead of 95 times as done for the network of retweets.

The network is presented in Fig. 9. For a better readability of the network, we only show the nodes that were assigned to a cluster with our method. By observing the most relevant node, according to PageRank, we first notice clusters around the leader of a party: CiU^{rp}, Cs^{rp}, PSC^{rp}, ERC^{rp}, PP^{rp}, CUP^{rp}, and Podemos^{rp} (member party of BeC). In

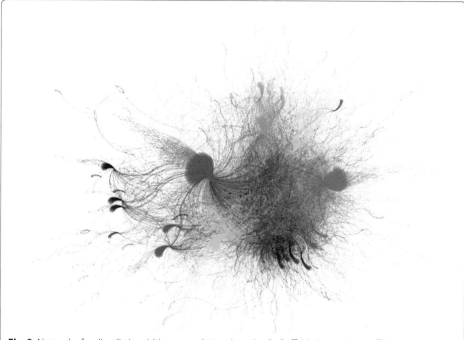

Fig. 9 Network of replies distinguishing party clusters by color: BeC-c^{rp} (*dark green*); BeC-p^{rp} (*light green*); Podemos^{rp} (*purple*); ERC^{rp} (*yellow*); PSC^{rp} (*red*); CUP^{rp} (*violet*); Cs^{rp} (*orange*); CiU^{rp} (*dark blue*); PP^{rp} (*cyan*). *Brown* nodes belong to Ind^{rp}, and *black* nodes belong to either Media-Spa^{rp} (*left*) or Media-Cat^{rp} (*bottom*)

the network of retweets Barcelona en Comú was divided in two clusters: movement and party. In the network of replies we also find two BeC clusters: one around the *candidate* account @adacolau (hereafter BeC-c^{rp}), and another around the *party* account @bcnen-comu (hereafter BeC-c^{rp}). These two clusters are presented separately in Fig. 10.

In addition, the N-Louvain method ($N = 100, \varepsilon = 0.5$) in the network of replies detects other clusters which are worth examining. First, we obtain two clusters which, according to the nodes with highest PageRank, relate to media. This is different from the retweet network where we set $N = 100$ and $\varepsilon = 0.05$ to prevent the inclusion of media accounts in party clusters. We present the two media clusters using different colors in Fig. 11 to show that the main nodes in the red cluster are Spanish media, and the main

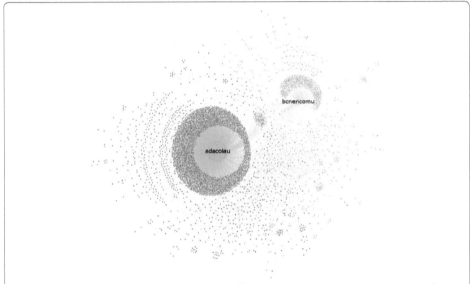

Fig. 10 Sub-network of BeC-c^{rp} (*dark green*) and BeC-p^{rp} (*light green*). For better readability, the label of public users is shown

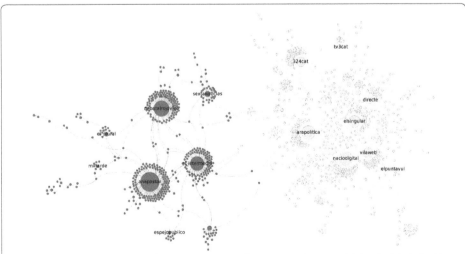

Fig. 11 Sub-network of Media-Spa^{rp} (*red*) and Media-Cat^{rp} (*yellow*). For better readability, the label of public users is shown

nodes in the yellow cluster are Catalan media. For this reason, from now on, the analysis distinguishes these clusters as Media-Spa[rp] and Media-Cat[rp]: Spanish media and Catalan media, respectively. We also observe that few interactions occur between the two clusters. Furthermore, our community detection method finds a large cluster, presented in Fig. 11, formed by users who advocate for the independence of Catalonia (hereafter Ind[rp]).

Comparison to the network of retweets

We now compare replies and retweets between parties. First, we analyze the replies among the clusters of the retweet network. An interaction matrix A is presented in Fig. 12 where, now, an entry $A_{i,j}$ is the number of replies from users from cluster i^{rt} to users from cluster j^{rt}. Although at first sight the vast majority of replies occurs in the main diagonal, like in Fig. 4, it is also evident that users are more likely to interact with users from other parties by replying than by retweeting them. Moreover, we observe behavioral differences between two types of parties. On the one hand, clusters of parties that advocate for a Catalan self-determination referendum (BeC-m[rt], BeC-p[rt], CiU[rt], CUP[rt], ERC[rt]) exhibit a notable amount of inter-party replies. On the other hand, parties against the referendum (PSC[rt], Cs[rt], PP[rt]) show a lower predisposition to dialogue with other parties and, therefore, most of their replies are within their own party.

Looking at each party individually, there are also observable differences. First, it can be seen that BeC-m[rt] and BeC-p[rt], especially the second, receive a higher amount of replies from the other parties than the rest. As previously noted, the parties in favor of a Catalan self-determination referendum interact more with each other; however, they exhibit different patterns: CUP[rt], probably because it is a small party, generates more replies than it receives. It also interacts more with BeC-m[rt], presumably due to their similar grassroots party nature. ERC[rt] gets larger attention from CiU[rt] but the pattern is not symmetrical, as CiU[rt] gets most of its attention from BeC-m[rt] and BeC-p[rt]. It is also

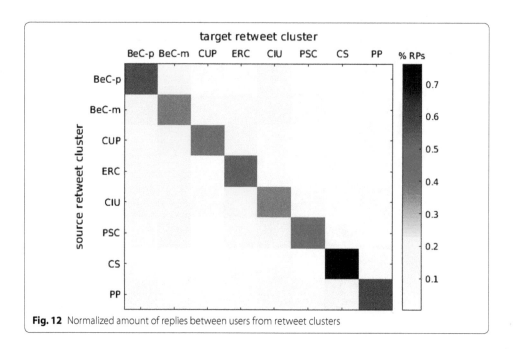

Fig. 12 Normalized amount of replies between users from retweet clusters

interesting to mention that CiU^{rt} is the cluster that has the highest proportion of inter-party interactions. PSC^{rt} follows a different pattern: on the one hand, its users reply to the two BeC clusters, CiU^{rt} and ERC^{rt}, neglecting CUP^{rt}, (Cs^{rt} and PP^{rt}). On the other hand, it receives almost no replies from the other parties. Finally, the right wing parties (Cs^{rt} and PP^{rt}) appear as isolated political communities that do not interact with the other clusters: their proportion of intra-party interactions is the highest (especially Cs), and they write slightly more replies than they receive.

We then compare the clusters from the retweet network to the ones from the reply network. We present in Table 8 how many users from each reply cluster (rows) belong to each retweet cluster (columns); i.e., the party distribution of reply clusters. As expected, the majority of users were assigned to the corresponding cluster in the retweet network, consistent with the diagonal of the adjacency matrix in Fig. 12. It is important to point out the high amount of undefined users. This notorious difference is explained by multiple reasons. First, the retweet network only contains the interactions between any pair of users that occurred at least 3 times. Thus, the retweet network has only 6492 nodes, while the reply network has 21,846. Second, the sensibility level of the N-Louvain method is lower for the retweet network (0.05 vs 0.5), i.e., many users are undefined in the retweet network because they did not fall into the same cluster in more than 95% of the executions. Although the number of undefined users is high, users in retweet clusters might better represent party supporters. Therefore, this comparison becomes a good strategy to have a better understanding of the nature of replies between political parties.

We remark in Table 8 to which cluster of retweets (excluding undefined) the largest number of users of each reply cluster belong (bold values). This allows us to observe interesting patterns. In particular, we notice that most users from BeC-c^{rp} and BeC-p^{rp} are from Barcelona en Comú. When examining the table by columns, we see that users from BeC-m^{rt}, BeC-p^{rt}, CUP^{rt}, and ERC^{rt} appear more frequently in other clusters. This leads us to consider that these users have a higher willingness to dialogue with users from other parties. This is observed particularly in the case of BeC-p^{rt}, as its users occur

Table 8 Number of nodes from each cluster in the reply network (rows) which occur in each cluster in the retweet network (columns)

Cluster	BeC-m^{rt}	BeC-p^{rt}	CiU^{rt}	Cs^{rt}	CUP^{rt}	ERC^{rt}	PP^{rt}	PSC^{rt}	Undef.
BeC-c^{rp}	37	*140*	13	1	14	47	6	3	3259
BeC-p^{rp}	104	*120*	4	0	24	13	0	4	937
CiU^{rp}	27	48	*108*	6	37	17	13	13	1975
Cs^{rp}	2	18	0	*100*	5	16	12	1	925
CUP^{rp}	7	6	0	1	*82*	7	1	1	314
ERC^{rp}	1	6	7	2	9	*113*	0	2	519
Ind^{rp}	14	18	18	1	16	*91*	0	0	807
Media-Cat^{rp}	2	12	6	0	10	*63*	1	4	669
Media-Spa^{rp}	0	*23*	0	1	1	1	1	0	432
Podemos^{rp}	0	*35*	1	0	0	0	1	1	440
PP^{rp}	2	5	5	4	4	6	*80*	4	435
PSC^{rp}	2	4	6	1	5	13	1	*57*	396

The largest number of each row is in italics (undefined users are not considered)

in every reply cluster. However, when examining the table by rows, we see that BeC-c^{rp} and CiU^{rp} are the clusters with more diversity of users, which may indicate that they receive large attention from the others. This is coherent with the fact that the two parties represented the frontrunners in the election, and actually the outgoing and the forthcoming mayors.

Finally, we note that the two media clusters have completely different natures: Media-Cat^{rp} is mainly composed of users from parties advocating for a Catalan self-determination referendum: ERC^{rt}, CUP^{rt}, CiU^{rt}, and both BeC^{rt}. This is expected because Media-Cat^{rp} is formed around Catalan media outlets with higher sensitivity to Catalan political issues. Differently, the party that interacted most with Media-Spa^{rp} is BeC.

Cluster characterization

Finally, we characterize the clusters in the network of replies using the same metrics of the above section. The visualization of Fig. 10 exhibited the star-like structure of both clusters of Barcelona Comú, an effect that is accentuated in BeC-c^{rp}. The results of the metrics present in Table 9 confirm that the Gini coefficient in BeC-c^{rp} ($G_{in} = 0.980$) is higher than in BeC-p^{rp} ($G_{in} = 0.908$). This might be produced by the attention to the candidate of Barcelona en Comú, who finally got elected as Mayor of Barcelona. Also, it is interesting to mention the structure of Ind^{rp}, distinctive from the other clusters. One can observe its decentralized structure in Fig. 13. The metrics bear out this decentralized structure, having this cluster the lower in-degree inequality ($G_{in} = 0.723$), the largest clustering coefficient ($Cl = 0.033$), and the highest maximum and average k-index ($k_{max} = 5$, $k_{avg} = 1.58$). This might be an effect of not being a partisan cluster but one configured around a thematic political discussion. Finally, results also show that the structure of Media-Cat^{rp} ($G_{in} = 0.899$, $Cl = 0.008$, $k_{max} = 4$, $k_{avg} = 1.35$) is more decentralized than the structure of Media-Spa^{rp} ($G_{in} = 0.974$, $Cl = 0.001$, $k_{max} = 2$, $k_{avg} = 1.10$).

Table 9 Number of nodes (N) and edges (E), inequality based on the Gini coefficient (G_{in}) of the in-degree distribution, clustering coefficient (Cl), average path length (l), maximal and average k-index (standard deviation in parentheses) for the intra-network of each cluster in the network of replies

Cluster	N	E	G_{in}	Cl	l	k_{max}	k_{avg}
BeC-c^{rp}	3520	3940	0.980	0.0001	3.28	3	1.11 (0.36)
BeC-p^{rp}	1206	1624	0.908	0.0020	5.19	4	1.30 (0.64)
CiU^{rp}	2244	3446	0.849	0.0009	2.72	4	1.30 (0.60)
Cs^{rp}	1079	1478	0.900	0.0044	3.48	4	1.31 (0.67)
CUP^{rp}	419	528	0.865	0.0052	5.25	3	1.22 (0.49)
ERC^{rp}	659	841	0.927	0.0032	3.36	3	1.24 (0.51)
Ind^{rp}	965	1789	0.724	0.0333	5.37	5	1.58 (0.98)
Media-Cat^{rp}	767	1055	0.899	0.0076	3.57	4	1.35 (0.73)
Media-Spa^{rp}	459	499	0.974	0.0011	1.35	2	1.10 (0.31)
Podemos^{rp}	478	549	0.951	0.0013	1.79	2	1.12 (0.32)
PP^{rp}	545	709	0.876	0.0104	3.26	3	1.27 (0.55)
PSC^{rp}	485	614	0.892	0.0032	2.94	3	1.23 (0.49)

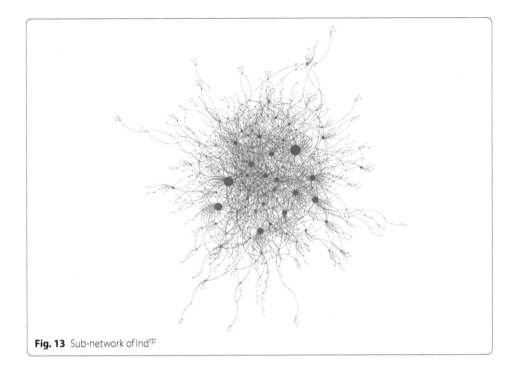

Fig. 13 Sub-network of Ind^{rp}

Discussion

In this study we have proposed and validated a computational methodology to answer two research questions in relation to the Twitter party networks for the 2015 Barcelona City Council election. We discuss in this section the implications of our results.

Institutionalization of a movement

The institutionalization of political parties is a research topic which has attracted much attention from scholars [8, 38, 39, 41, 53, 61]. The analysis of the network of retweets has been designed to answer the first research question that deals with the kind of organizational structure that Barcelona en Comú developed for the election campaign. On the one hand, the cited literature [30, 59] provided evidence of the decentralization of the 15M movement, which inspired the Barcelona en Comú candidacy. On the other hand, many political scientists [43, 44, 46, 51] argued that parties are historically ruled by elites and, therefore, result in centralized organizations. Furthermore, the historical models of political parties reviewed in [34] (i.e., *Caucus parties, Mass parties, Catch-all parties,* and *Cartel parties*) always assumed organization around elites. All of these observations motivated to study whether Barcelona en Comú preserved a decentralized structure, consistent with the decentralization of political power postulated in [14], or adopted a conventional centralized organization.

The results depict a movement-party structure in which the two components form well-defined clusters. In comparison to the clusters of the rest of political parties, the BeC movement community emerges as the least hierarchical, most clustered, and resilient one. In contrast, the BeC party community is the most hierarchical, least clustered, and least resilient one. The centralization of the party cluster points to the candidate and official accounts, the subjects that are commonly associated with the elite. However, unlike the rest of political parties, there is a co-existence of both party and movement clusters. This co-existence is consistent with the hypothesis expressed in [58] when defining Podemos, member party of Barcelona en Comú, as the conjugation of a front-end and a back-end.

This article has provided hints about the characterization of the organization of political parties according to their online diffusion networks. The nature of Barcelona en Comú is similar to the so-called niche parties because this party rejects the traditional class-based orientation of politics, does not fit with classical lines of political division, and is appealing to voters who may cross-cut classical partisan alignments [42]. Although niche parties are the result of institutionalized social movements (e.g., communism, green, nationalism) and differ from mainstream parties, Internet is not found relevant in their process of institutionalization [2]. In contrast, some authors have reported that the Internet played a key role in the organization of the 15M movement for building "a hybrid space between the Internet social networks and the occupied urban space" [13]. According to [59], this hybrid space is the result of *techno-political* practices: "the tactical and strategic use of technological devices (including social networks) for organization, communication and collective action." Are techno-politics the origin of this particular movement-party partition of Barcelona en Comú? Recently, political scientists have postulated the emergence of *cyber parties* "with its origins in developments in media and information and communication technologies" [40]. Although the results of this study cannot ensure that the Internet and social media are the only reason behind this new form of political organization, in this particular context some party activists reported that ICT becomes essential for campaigning [56]. Therefore, a close link between techno-politics and the structure of Barcelona en Comú might exist.

Discussion behaviors

The analysis of the network of replies allows us to answer the second research question about the discussion behavior of Barcelona en Comú. Similar to the network of retweets, the results have depicted another dual structure: one around the candidate and another around the party account, which includes a large amount of 15M activists. Thus, while the candidate cluster received the larger attention from other parties, the party cluster presented a higher willingness to dialogue with other parties. Given that the rest of the parties are mainly organized in a single cluster, this dual structure confirms the different behavior of Barcelona en Comú when discussing with other political parties.

The results have also showed a non-partisan cluster with users associated with the Catalan independence movement. This is consistent with previous research that already indicated that online users do not have a strong preference to discuss with members of the same political party but to discuss around specific topics [23, 48]. In contrast, we have seen that the Spanish parties PP, PSC, and CS have a lower predisposition to dialogue with other parties. This result is of interest given that (1) the independence of Catalonia is a main topic of Spanish politics, and (2) the current Government of Spain is supported by these three parties. In addition, it has been observed that just a few users interacted with both Spanish and Catalan media. On the one hand, this could be an effect of the topics covered by the different types of media, e.g., Catalan issues are expected to be more frequent in Catalan media outlets. On the other hand, this could be also an idiomatic issue, i.e., Catalan native speakers are more likely to interact with media outlets tweeting in Catalan. In general, our analysis depicts the existence of groups of opposing views. Therefore, this scenario could be used to evaluate recent approaches for balancing opposing views to reduce controversy in social media [26].

Contribution of our methodology

The methodology of this article focuses on (1) community detection and (2) cluster characterization. The fuzzy membership of some nodes in certain communities (e.g., media accounts in the party clusters from the retweet network) motivated the modification of a standard community detection algorithm (Louvain method) by setting a sensibility level to parametrize the robustness of the final clusters. In comparison to the standard Louvain method and another community detection algorithm for overlapping communities (Clique Percolation Method), the evaluation proved that the new algorithm identified the political networks in a more stable way. Cluster characterization was inspired by the metrics proposed in [23] to compare political party networks. The original dimensions of this framework were hierarchical structure, information efficiency, and social resilience. The redefinition of these three dimensions and the inclusion of new metrics constitute an improvement of the characterization of political networks:

- *Hierarchical structure* In-degree centralization [22] was originally applied in [23] to measure the hierarchical structure of a network. This metric is based on (1) how the centrality of the most central node exceeds the centrality of all other nodes and (2) the comparison to a star network. Maximum and average in-degree have common differences of several orders of magnitude in social graphs. Therefore, in-degree centralization is approximately equal to the ratio between the maximum in-degree and the number of nodes for social networks with a heavy-tailed in-degree distribution. In other words, the in-degree centralization is not a good metric to capture hierarchical structure for social diffusion graphs, and the Gini coefficient for in-degree inequality represents a more reliable measure of the hierarchical structure of a network.
- *Information efficiency* Information efficiency in social networks is closely related to the *small-world phenomenon*. This article uses the average path length, as the previous framework does [23], and the clustering coefficient to better characterize efficiency in social networks.
- *Social resilience* Previous studies indicated the suitability of the k-core decomposition to measure the resilience of social networks [24]. This framework recommends the term *coreness* which represents a more precise definition of this metric. In addition, showing the distribution of nodes along k-cores does capture resilience better than maximum k-core as done in [23].

Conclusion

In this article we have examined new forms of political organization in social media. The results focus on the Twitter networks of Barcelona en Comú in comparison to the other parties for the 2015 Barcelona municipal elections. The findings rely on a dataset from Twitter but social networks are only a slice of the structure of political organizations and not every party activist has a Twitter account. Furthermore, some experts are skeptical with the digital forms of activism because of the "loss of coherence, morality or even sustainability" [45] and pointed out the rise of a low commitment and feel-good form of activism. Nevertheless, online platforms are playing a key role in political discussion and campaigning, and social media data are leveraging the capacity of revealing patterns of individual and group behaviors [29, 35]. Because of the Internet's potential for increasing debate in political parties [60] and the potential relevance of low commitment online participants for collective action [6], Twitter might be seen as an informative and valuable data source to examine collective behavior and self-organization in social and political contexts.

The results showed that the tension between the decentralization of networked movements and the centralization of political parties led to a movement-party structure: both paradigms co-exist in two well-defined clusters. From this result, future work should investigate the origin of this particular structure by adding longitudinal analyses of the formation of the clusters. Furthermore, it is interesting to note that city council elections were held in every Spanish city in May 2015 and candidacies similar to Barcelona en Comú were built. Indeed, similar organizations (e.g., Ahora Madrid, Zaragoza en Común) obtained the Government of many of the largest Spanish cities. For this reason and because relevant studies on political parties in advanced industrial democracies often ignore the Spanish context [4, 17], future work might apply this framework to examine whether the characteristics observed in Barcelona en Comú are also present in these other Spanish grassroots movement-parties.

Abbreviations

API: Application Programming Interface; BeC: Barcelona en Comú; CiU: Convergència i Unió; Cs: Ciudadanos; CUP: Capgirem Barcelona; ERC: Esquerra Republicana de Catalunya; PP: Partit Popular de Catalunya; PSC: Partit dels Socialistes de Catalunya.

Authors' contributions

PA, HG, DL, YV, and AK made a substantial contribution to this manuscript. All authors read and approved the final manuscript.

Author details

[1] Universitat Pompeu Fabra, Barcelona, Spain. [2] Eurecat-Technology Centre of Catalonia, Avinguda Diagonal, 177, 08018 Barcelona, Spain.

Acknowledgements

We would like to thank DatAnalysis15M Research Network and the #Global-RevExp Forum for their valuable discussions and suggestions that helped to improve this study.

Competing interests

The authors declare that they have no competing interests.

Funding

This work is supported by the EU project D-CENT (FP7 CAPS 610349). The funders had no role in study design, decision to publish, or preparation of the manuscript.

References

1. Adamic LA, Glance N. The political blogosphere and the 2004 us election: divided they blog. In: Proceedings of the 3rd international workshop on link discovery, ACM. 2005. p. 36–43.
2. Adams J, Clark M, Ezrow L, Glasgow G. Are niche parties fundamentally different from mainstream parties? The causes and the electoral consequences of western European parties' policy shifts, 1976–1998. Am J Political Sci. 2006;50(3):513–29.

3. Alhabash S, McAlister AR. Redefining virality in less broad strokes: predicting viral behavioral intentions from motivations and uses of Facebook and Twitter. New Media Soc. 2015;17(8):1317–39.
4. Anstead N, Chadwick A. Parties, election campaigning, and the internet toward a comparative institutional approach. The Routledge handbook of Internet politics 2008;56–71
5. Aragón P, Kappler KE, Kaltenbrunner A, Laniado D, Volkovich Y. Communication dynamics in Twitter during political campaigns: the case of the 2011 Spanish national election. Policy Internet. 2013;5(2):183–206.
6. Barberá P, Wang N, Bonneau R, Jost JT, Nagler J, Tucker J, González-Bailón S. The critical periphery in the growth of social protests. PLoS ONE. 2015;10(11):e0143611.
7. Bennett WL, Segerberg A. The logic of connective action: digital media and the personalization of contentious politics. Inf Commun Soc. 2012;15(5):739–68.
8. Bértoa FC, Mair P. Party system institutionalisation across time in post-communist Europe. Party Gov New Eur. 2012;79:85.
9. Blondel VD, Guillaume JL, Lambiotte R, Lefebvre E. Fast unfolding of communities in large networks. J Stat Mech Theory Exp. 2008;10:P10008.
10. Borge-Holthoefer J, Rivero A, García I, Cauhé E, Ferrer A, Ferrer D, Francos D, Iñiguez D, Pérez MP, Ruiz G, et al. Structural and dynamical patterns on online social networks: the Spanish may 15th movement as a case study. PLoS ONE. 2011;6(8):e23883.
11. Borondo J, Morales A, Losada J, Benito R. Characterizing and modeling an electoral campaign in the context of Twitter: 2011 Spanish presidential election as a case study. Chaos. 2012;22(2):3138.
12. Boyd d, Golder S, Lotan G. Tweet, tweet, retweet: conversational aspects of retweeting on Twitter. In: IEEE system sciences (HICSS). 2010. p. 1–10.
13. Castells M. Networks of outrage and hope: social movements in the Internet age. New York: Wiley; 2013.
14. Chadwick A, Stromer-Galley J. Digital media, power, and democracy in parties and election campaigns: party decline or party renewal? 2016.
15. Congosto ML, Fernández M, Moro E. Twitter y política: información, opinión y¿ predicción? Cuadernos de Comunicación Evoca. 2011;4:11–5.
16. Conover M, Ratkiewicz J, Francisco M, Gonçalves B, Menczer F, Flammini A. Political polarization on Twitter. In: ICWSM. 2011.
17. Dalton RJ. Citizen politics: public opinion and political parties in advanced industrial democracies. Washington: Cq Press; 2013.
18. Edelstein JD, Warner M. Comparative union democracy: organisation and opposition in British and American unions. Piscataway: Transaction Publishers;1979.
19. Farrell H, Drezner DW. The power and politics of blogs. Publ Choice. 2008;134(1–2):15.
20. Feller A, Kuhnert M, Sprenger TO, Welpe IM. Divided they tweet: the network structure of political microbloggers and discussion topics. In: ICWSM. 2011.
21. Fortunato S. Community detection in graphs. Phys Rep. 2010;486(3):75–174.
22. Freeman LC. Centrality in social networks conceptual clarification. Soc Netw. 1979;1(3):215–39.
23. Garcia D, Abisheva A, Schweighofer S, Serdult U, Schweitzer F. Ideological and temporal components of network polarization in online political participatory media. Policy Internet. 2015;7(1):46–79. doi:10.1002/poi3.82.
24. Garcia D, Mavrodiev P, Schweitzer F. Social resilience in online communities: the autopsy of friendster. In: Proceedings of the first ACM conference on online social networks, ACM. 2013. p. 39–50.
25. Garimella K, Morales GDF, Gionis A, Mathioudakis M. Quantifying controversy in social media. arXiv preprint arXiv:1507.05224. 2015.
26. Garimella K, Morales GDF, Gionis A, Mathioudakis M. Balancing opposing views to reduce controversy. arXiv preprint arXiv:1611.00172. 2016.
27. Gerbaudo P. Tweets and the streets: social media and contemporary activism. London: Pluto Press; 2012.
28. Gini C. Variabilità e mutabilità. Reprinted in Memorie di metodologica statistica (Ed. Pizetti E, Salvemini, T). Rome ; 1912:1
29. Golder SA, Macy MW. Digital footprints: opportunities and challenges for online social research. Sociology. 2014;40(1):129.
30. González-Bailón S, Borge-Holthoefer J, Rivero A, Moreno Y. The dynamics of protest recruitment through an online network. Sci Rep. 2011;1:197.
31. Gruzd A, Roy J. Investigating political polarization on Twitter: a canadian perspective. Policy Internet. 2014;6(1):28–45.
32. Haberer M, Peña-López I. Structural conditions for citizen deliberation: a conceptual scheme for the assessment of "new" parties. In: IEEE conference for e-democracy and open government (CeDEM). 2016. p. 115–24.
33. Jaccard P. Etude comparative de la distribution florale dans une portion des Alpes et du Jura. Corbaz: Impr; 1901.
34. Katz RS, Mair P. Changing models of party organization and party democracy the emergence of the cartel party. Party Politics. 1995;1(1):5–28.
35. Lazer D, Pentland AS, Adamic L, Aral S, Barabasi AL, Brewer D, Christakis N, Contractor N, Fowler J, Gutmann M, et al. Life in the network: the coming age of computational social science. Sci (NY). 2009;323(5915):721.
36. Lietz H, Wagner C, Bleier A, Strohmaier M. When politicians talk: assessing online conversational practices of political parties on Twitter. arXiv preprint arXiv:1405.6824. 2014.
37. Lipset SM, Trow MA, Coleman JS, Kerr C. Union democracy: the internal politics of the International Typographical Union. New York: Free Press Glencoe; 1956.
38. Mainwaring S, Scully T, et al. Building democratic institutions: party systems in Latin America. Stanford: Stanford University Press; 1995.
39. Mainwaring S, Torcal M. Party system institutionalization and party system theory after the third wave of democratization. Handb Party Politics. 2006;11(6):204–27.
40. Margetts H. The cyber party. ECPR Joint Sessions. London. 2001.

41. Markowski R. Party system institutionalization in new democracies: Poland—a trend-setter with no followers. Paul G. Lewis (szerk.) party development and democratic change in post-communist Europe. 2001. p. 55–77.
42. Meguid BM. Competition between unequals: the role of mainstream party strategy in niche party success. Am Political Sci Rev. 2005;99(03):347–59.
43. Michels R. Political parties: a sociological study of the oligarchical tendencies of modern democracy. New York: Hearst's International Library Company; 1915.
44. Mills CW. The power elite. Oxford: Oxford University Press; 1999.
45. Morozov E. The net delusion: the dark side of Internet freedom. PublicAffairs. 2012.
46. Mosca G. The ruling class: elementi di scienza politica. 1939.
47. Nagarajan M, Purohit H, Sheth AP. A qualitative examination of topical tweet and retweet practices. ICWSM. 2010;2(010):295–8.
48. Neff JJ, Laniado D, Kappler KE, Volkovich Y, Aragón P, Kaltenbrunner A. Jointly they edit: examining the impact of community identification on political interaction in Wikipedia. PLoS ONE. 2013;8(4):e60584.
49. Newman ME. Analysis of weighted networks. Phys Rev E. 2004;70(5):056131.
50. Norris P. Digital divide: civic engagement, information poverty, and the internet worldwide. Cambridge: Cambridge University Press; 2001.
51. Pareto V, Livingston A, Bongiorno A, Rogers JH, et al. Mind and society.1935.
52. Peña-López I, Congosto M, Aragón P. Spanish indignados and the evolution of the 15 m movement on Twitter: towards networked para-institutions. J Span Cult Stud. 2014;15(1–2):189–216. doi:10.1080/14636204.2014.931678.
53. Randall V, Svåsand L. Party institutionalization in new democracies. Party Politics. 2002;8(1):5–29.
54. Romanos E. El 15 m y la democracia de los movimientos sociales. Books Ideas. 2011;18(11):2011.
55. Rothschild-Whitt J. Conditions facilitating participatory-democratic organizations. Sociol Inq. 1976;46(2):75–86.
56. Sandiumenge L. La guerrilla digital de Colau. 2015. http://districte15.info/la-guerrilla-digital-de-colau/. Accessed 22 July 2015.
57. Shirky C. Power laws, weblogs, and inequality. 2003.
58. Toret J. Una mirada tecnopolítica al primer año de podemos. Seis hipótesis. Teknokultura. 2015;12(1);121–35.
59. Toret J, Calleja-López A, Marín O, Aragón P, Aguilera M, Barandiaran X, Monterde A. Tecnopolítica y 15 m: la potencia de las multitudes conectadas. 2015.
60. Ward S, Gibson R. UK political parties and the internet: prospects for democracy'. 2 (13). Salford: University of Salford; 1997.
61. Ware A. Political parties and party systems, vol. 9. Oxford: Oxford University Press; 1996.
62. Watts DJ, Strogatz SH. Collective dynamics of 'small-world' networks. Nature. 1998;393(6684):440–2.

4

Network partitioning algorithms as cooperative games

Konstantin E. Avrachenkov[1*] ⓘ, Aleksei Y. Kondratev[2,3], Vladimir V. Mazalov[3,4] ⓘ and Dmytro G. Rubanov[1]

*Correspondence:
k.avrachenkov@inria.fr
[1] Inria Sophia Antipolis,
2004 Route des Lucioles,
06902 Valbonne, France
Full list of author information
is available at the end of the
article

Abstract

The paper is devoted to game-theoretic methods for community detection in networks. The traditional methods for detecting community structure are based on selecting dense subgraphs inside the network. Here we propose to use the methods of cooperative game theory that highlight not only the link density but also the mechanisms of cluster formation. Specifically, we suggest two approaches from cooperative game theory: the first approach is based on the Myerson value, whereas the second approach is based on hedonic games. Both approaches allow to detect clusters with various resolutions. However, the tuning of the resolution parameter in the hedonic games approach is particularly intuitive. Furthermore, the modularity-based approach and its generalizations as well as ratio cut and normalized cut methods can be viewed as particular cases of the hedonic games. Finally, for approaches based on potential hedonic games we suggest a very efficient computational scheme using Gibbs sampling.

Keywords: Network partitioning, Community detection, Cooperative game, Myerson value, Hedonic game, Gibbs sampling

Introduction

Community detection in networks is a very important topic which has numerous applications in social network analysis, computer science, telecommunications, and bioinformatics and has attracted the effort of many researchers. In the present work, we consider the framework of crisp community detection or network partitioning, where one would like to partition a network into disjoint sets of nodes. The consideration of overlapping, hierarchical, and local clustering we leave for future research. Even the literature on crisp community detection is huge. We refer to several extensive survey papers [1–6]. Let us just mention main classes of methods for network partitioning. The first very large class is based on spectral elements of the network matrices such as adjacency matrix and Laplacian (see e.g., the surveys [1, 5] and references therein). The second class of methods is based on the use of random walks (see e.g., [7–12] for the most representative works in this research direction). The third class of approaches to network partitioning is based on the optimization of some objective function [13–19], with modularity function [15, 16] as a notable example in this category. Finally, the fourth class, directly related to the present work, is based on the notions from game theory. We recommend to an interested reader a recent survey [4] on the application of game-theoretic techniques to community detection. Most bibliography described in [4] is in fact dedicated to non-cooperative game theory approaches. It appears that the application of the cooperative or coalition games to community detection problem is under-developed and thus with this article we advance this research area.

There are definitely many relations among the above-mentioned classes. In particular, the conditions for minima of the objective functions can often be interpreted in terms of the eigen elements of the network matrices. The eigen elements of the network matrices also characterize the stationary or quasi-stationary state of a random walk on a network. In the present work, we show more connections between the approach based on cooperative games and other approaches.

In essence, all the above-mentioned approaches, with exception of the game theory approach, try to detect dense subgraphs inside the network and do not address the question: what are the natural forces and dynamics behind the formation of network clusters. As noticed in [20], most of traditional clustering methods pursue a top-down approach, whereas typically communities are formed by local interactions in self-organizing fashion, often driven by egocentric decisions. Thus, it is very natural to apply game theory, and in particular, coalition game theory for community detection problem. Also, in most of the above-mentioned methods, the number of communities is a prerequisite parameter. The game theory approach typically does not require a priori knowledge of the number of communities. One more very important benefit in using the methods from game theory is that such methods are naturally distributed and can easily be implemented in clouds and decentralized multi-agent systems.

In the present work, we explore two cooperative game theory approaches to explain possible mechanisms behind cluster formation. Our first approach is based on the Myerson value in cooperative game theory, which particularly emphasizes the value allocation in the context of games with interactions between players constrained by a network. The advantage of the Myerson value is in taking into account the impact of all coalitions. We extend the method developed in [21, 22] to calculate efficiently the Myerson value in a network. A number of network centrality measures based on game-theoretic concepts have been developed, see [22–28] and references therein. It might be interesting to combine node ranking and clustering based on the same approach such as the Myerson value to analyze the network structure. Unfortunately, the computation of the Myerson value is a very difficult problem even for a moderately large number of players. Therefore, we propose the second approach which has efficient computational implementation and can easily be distributed.

The second approach is based on hedonic games [29], which are games explaining well the mechanism behind the formation of coalitions. Both our approaches allow to detect clusters with varying resolutions and thus avoiding the problem of resolution limit [30, 31]. The hedonic game approach is especially well suited to adjust the level of resolution as the limiting cases are given by the grand coalition and sequential maximum clique decomposition, two very natural extreme cases of network partitioning. Furthermore, the modularity-based approaches as well as ratio cut [32] and normalized cut [10, 33] based methods can be cast in the setting of hedonic games. We find that this gives one more, very interesting, interpretation of the modularity-based methods. The advantage of casting the ratio cut and normalized cut in the framework of hedonic games is that we do not need to prespecify the number of clusters as was needed in the original formulations of these methods.

Some hierarchical network partitioning methods based on tree hierarchy, such as [15], cannot produce a clustering on one resolution level with the number of clusters different from the predefined tree shape. Furthermore, the majority of clustering methods require the number of clusters as an input parameter. In contrast, in our approaches we specify the value of the resolution parameter(s) and the method gives a natural number of clusters corresponding to the given resolution parameter(s).

Let us point out major differences between our approaches and approaches suggested in the other works on cooperative game theory for network clustering. In [34], a cooperative game theory approach based on Shapley value has been proposed. However, with the proposed characteristic function, the players tend to form the grand coalition. In the subsequent work [35], a new characteristic function has been proposed, which combines both link-based as well as attribute-based information. The Shapley value associated with that characteristic function is very cumbersome to compute in comparison to the Myerson value for the characteristic function proposed in the first part of our paper. Of course, we admit that the computation of any type of Shapley value is computationally demanding and this is why we propose the second approach which has an efficient, naturally distributed, computational implementation.

The authors of [20] have also proposed to use hedonic games for community detection. They consider only the modularity metric as value function. They have suggested an additional voting mechanism to overcome the resolution problem. Their algorithm is a version of greedy optimization. Our approach is much more general: not only we show that the modularity optimization is a particular case of our approach but we also demonstrate that such known methods as ratio cut and normalized cut are also particular cases of our approach. We also propose a couple of new functions that overcome the resolution problem without a need of additional voting mechanism. Our Gibbs sampling-based algorithm can be used with both fixed and decreasing temperature and hence can be used for local as well as global maxima search. Setting the temperature to a very low value corresponds to the greedy approach.

The authors of [36] in the first part of their paper propose to use the concept of strong Nash equilibrium in addition to the concept of hedonic games. They also define a community as a (λ, γ)-relaxation of the clique. There are several serious problems with their propositions. First of all, the strong Nash equilibrium might not exist (they acknowledge this fact themselves in their work), and such equilibrium is very hard to compute even if it exists. Furthermore, they give two definitions of a maximal (λ, γ)-relaxation of the clique which are contradictory and therefore their algorithm can cycle.

We also note that our approaches based on cooperative games easily work with multigraphs, where several edges (links) are possible between two nodes. A multi-edge has several natural interpretations in the context of social networks. A multi-edge can represent a number of telephone calls; a number of exchanged messages; a number of common friends; or a number of co-occurrences in some social event.

Let us now summarize the main contributions of the paper (we place* in the items, which are new additions to the work in comparison with the conference version [37]):

- First the cooperative game theory approach based on the Myerson value is proposed for network partitioning.
- Then the hedonic coalition formation framework is proposed for network partitioning which has more efficient computational implementation than the approach based on the Myerson value.
- New interpretation in terms of hedonic games is given to modularity, ratio cut, and normalized cut network partitioning methods.*
- Two new network partitioning methods based on potential hedonic games are proposed. (One method is a new addition with respect to the conference paper [37].)* These two methods are especially well suited to find partitions with different levels of resolution; the methods use only one or two parameters. We provide recommendations how to set these parameters.
- For methods constructed on potential hedonic games, we suggest to use a very efficient computational algorithm based on Gibbs sampling.*
- Several numerical evaluations using real* as well as synthetic networks are carried out. These numerical evaluations in particular demonstrate the efficacy of the clustering methods based on potential hedonic games with resolution regularization.

The paper is structured as follows: in the following section, we provide necessary definitions from graph theory, network partitioning, and network games. Then, in "Myerson cooperative game approach" section, we present our first approach based on the Myerson value. The second approach based on the hedonic games is presented in "Hedonic coalition game approach" section. In both "Myerson cooperative game approach and Hedonic coalition game approach" sections, we provide small illustrative examples to explain the essence of the methods. In "Numerical validation" section, we evaluate our methods on a number of real as well as synthetic network examples. Finally, "Conclusion and future research" section provides conclusions and directions for future research.

Preliminaries of graph theory, network partitioning, and network stability

Let $g = (N, E)$ denote an undirected multi-graph consisting of the set of nodes N and the set of edges E. We denote an edge (link) between node i and node j as ij. The interpretation is that if $ij \in E$, then the nodes $i \in N$ and $j \in N$ have a direct connection in network g, while $ij \notin E$, then nodes i and j are not directly connected. Since we generally consider a multi-graph, there could be several edges between a pair of nodes. Multiple edges can be interpreted for instance as a number of telephone calls or as a number of message exchanges in the context of social networks.

We view the nodes of the network as players in a cooperative game. Let $N(g) = \{i : \exists j \text{ such that } ij \in E(g)\}$. For a graph g, a sequence of different nodes $\{i_1, i_2, \ldots, i_k\}$, $k \geq 2$, is a path connecting i_1 and i_k if for all $h = 1, \ldots, k-1$, $i_h i_{h+1} \in g$. The length l of a path is the number of edges in that path, i.e., $l = k - 1$. A path with no repeated nodes is called a *simple path*. Graph g on the set N is connected graph if for any two nodes i and j there exists a path in g connecting i and j.

We refer to a subset of nodes $S \subset N$ as a coalition. The coalition S is connected if any two nodes in S are connected by a path which consists of nodes from S. The graph g' is a (connected) component of g, if for all $i \in N(g')$ and $j \in N(g')$, there exists a path in g' connecting i and j, and for any $i \in N(g')$ and $j \in N(g)$, $ij \in g$ implies that $ij \in g'$. Let $N|g$ be the set of all (connected) components in g and let $g|S$ be the subgraph with the nodes in S.

Let $g - ij$ denote the graph obtained by deleting edge ij from the graph g and $g + ij$ denote the graph obtained by adding edge ij to the graph g.

The result of community detection is a partition of the network (N, E) into subsets (coalitions) $\{S_1, \ldots, S_K\}$ such that $S_k \cap S_l = \emptyset, \forall k, l$ and $S_1 \cup \ldots \cup S_K = N$. This partition is *internally stable* or *Nash stable* if for any player from coalition S_k it is not profitable to join another (possibly empty) coalition S_l. We also say that the partition is *externally stable* if for any player $i \in S_l$ for whom it is beneficial to join a coalition S_k, there exists a player $j \in S_k$ for whom it is not profitable to include there player i. The payoff definition and distribution will be discussed in the following two sections.

Myerson cooperative game approach

In general, a cooperative game of n players is a pair $< N, v >$ where $N = \{1, 2, \ldots, n\}$ is the set of players and $v: 2^N \to R$ is a map prescribing for a coalition $S \in 2^N$ some value $v(S)$ such that $v(\emptyset) = 0$. This function $v(S)$ is the total utility that members of S can jointly attain. Such a function is called the characteristic function of cooperative game. An interested reader can find more details on cooperative games in e.g., [38–40].

Additionally, as in [41], we assume that the cooperation is restricted by a network. The payoff to an individual player is called an imputation. The imputation specifies how the value associated with the network is distributed to the individual players. The imputation in our cooperative game will be based on the Myerson value [21, 22, 41] which was designed to take into account the effect of the network.

The Myerson value [41] is the allocation rule

$$Y(v, g) = (Y_1(v, g), \ldots, Y_n(v, g)),$$

where $Y_i(v, g)$ is the payoff allocated to player i from graph g under the characteristic function v. The Myerson value is uniquely determined by the following two axioms [41]:

Axiom 1 If S is a connected component of g, then the members of the coalition S ought to allocate to themselves the total value $v(S)$ available to them, i.e., $\forall S \in N|g$,

$$\sum_{i \in S} Y_i(v, g) = v(S). \tag{1}$$

Axiom 2 $\forall g$, $\forall ij \in g$ both players i and j obtain equal payoffs after adding or deleting a link ij,

$$Y_i(v, g) - Y_i(v, g - ij) = Y_j(v, g) - Y_j(v, g - ij). \tag{2}$$

Characteristic function (payoff of coalition S) can be defined in different ways. Here we use a general idea from [21, 22, 42, 43], which is based on discounting paths. However, unlike [21, 22, 42, 43], we do not consider shortest paths but rather *simple paths*.

Let us elaborate a bit more on the construction of the characteristic function. Each edge (or direct connection) gives to coalition S the value r, where $0 \leq r \leq 1$. Moreover, players obtain a value from indirect connections. Namely, each *simple* path of length 2 belonging to coalition S gives to this coalition the value r^2, a simple path of length 3 gives to the coalition the value r^3, etc. Set

$$v(i) = 0, \ \forall i \in N.$$

Thus, for any coalition S, we can define the characteristic function as follows:

$$v(S) = a_1(g, S)r + a_2(g, S)r^2 + \cdots = \sum_{k=1}^{\infty} a_k(g, S)r^k, \tag{3}$$

where $a_k(g, S)$ is the number of simple paths of length k in this coalition. Note that we write as infinity the limit of summation only for convenience. Clearly, the length of a simple path is bounded by $n - 1$. The following theorem provides a convenient way to calculate the Myerson value corresponding to the characteristic function (3).

Theorem 1 *Let the characteristic function of a coalition $S \in 2^N$ be defined by Eq. (3). Then the Myerson value of a node i is given by*

$$Y_i(v, g) = \frac{a_1^{(i)}(g, S)}{2}r + \frac{a_2^{(i)}(g, S)}{3}r^2 + \cdots = \sum_{k=1}^{\infty} \frac{a_k^{(i)}(g, S)}{k+1}r^k, \tag{4}$$

where $a_k^{(i)}$ is the number of simple paths of length k containing node i.

Proof We shall prove the theorem by checking directly the Myerson value axioms, i.e., Axioms 1 and 2.

First, we note the following:

$$(k + 1)a_k(g, S) = \sum_{i \in S} a_k^{(i)}(g, S).$$

Since every simple path contains $k + 1$ different nodes, every simple path of the length k is counted $k + 1$ times in the sum $\sum_{i \in S} a_k^{(i)}(g, S)$.

Thus, Axiom 1 is satisfied:

$$\sum_{i \in S} Y_i(v, g) = \sum_{i \in S} \sum_{k=1}^{\infty} \frac{a_k^{(i)}(g, S)}{k+1}r^k = \sum_{i \in S} a_k(g, S)r^k = v(S).$$

For $ij \in g$, let $a_k^{(ij)}(g, S)$ denote the number of paths of length k traversing the edge ij. Then

$$a_k^{(i)}(g, S) - a_k^{(i)}(g - ij, S) = a_k^{(ij)}(g, S) = a_k^{(j)}(g, S) - a_k^{(j)}(g - ij, S).$$

Thus, Axiom 2 is satisfied as well.   □

We can propose the following algorithm for network partitioning based on the Myerson value: Start with a partition of the network $N = \{1, \ldots, n\}$, where each node forms her own coalition. Consider a coalition S_l and a player $i \in S_l$. In the cooperative game with partial cooperation presented by the graph $g|S_l$, we find the Myerson value for player i, $Y_i(g|S_l)$. This is the reward of player i in coalition S_l. Suppose that player i decides to join the coalition S_k. In the new cooperative game with partial cooperation presented by the graph $g|S_k \cup i$, we find the Myerson value $Y_i(g|S_k \cup i)$. So, if for the player $i \in S_l : Y_i(g|S_l) \geq Y_i(g|S_k \cup i)$ then player i has no incentive to join to new coalition S_k, otherwise the player changes the coalition.

The partition $N = \{S_1, \ldots, S_K\}$ is the Nash stable or internally stable if for any player there is no incentive to move from her coalition. Notice that our definition of the characteristic function implies that for any coalition it is always beneficial to accept a new player (of course, for the player herself it might not be profitable to join that coalition). Thus, it is important that in the above algorithm, we consider the internal and not external stability. If one makes moves according to the external stability, then the result will always be the grand coalition.

We would like to note that the above approach also works in the case of multi-graphs, where several edges (links) are possible between two nodes. In such a case, if two paths contain different links between the same pair of nodes, we consider these paths as different.

Example 1   Consider a weighted network of six nodes, $N = \{A, B, C, D, E, F\}$, presented in Fig. 1a. First, we transform this weighted graph to the multi-graph as shown in Fig. 1b.

A natural way of partition of this network is $\{S_1 = \{A, B, C\}, S_2 = \{D, E, F\}\}$. Let us determine under which condition this structure will present the internally stable partition.

Suppose that the characteristic function is defined by (3). To calculate the imputations, we use the formula (4) from Theorem 1. In the coalition S_1, node A participates in 2 simple paths of length 1 $\{\{A, B\}, \{A, C\}\}$ and in 5 simple paths of length 2 $\{\{A, B, C\}, \{A, B, C\}, \{A, C, B\}, \{A, C, B\}, \{B, A, C\}\}$ (note that since the network example is a multi-graph we count twice the paths {A,B,C} and {A,C,B}). Thus, we have

$$Y_A(g|S_1) = \frac{2}{2}r + \frac{5}{3}r^2.$$

In the coalition $S_2 \cup A$, node A participates in 1 simple path of length 1 $\{A, D\}$, in 2 simple paths of length 2 $\{\{A, D, E\}, \{A, D, F\}\}$ and in 4 simple paths of length 3 $\{\{A, D, E, F\}, \{A, D, E, F\}, \{A, D, F, E\}, \{A, D, F, E\}\}$ (again these paths are counted twice for the multi-graph). Thus,

$$Y_A(g|S_2 \cup A) = \frac{1}{2}r + \frac{2}{3}r^2 + \frac{4}{4}r^3.$$

We see that for player A it is not profitable to move from S_1 to $S_2 \cup A$, if

$$\frac{1}{2}r + r^2 - r^3 > 0,$$

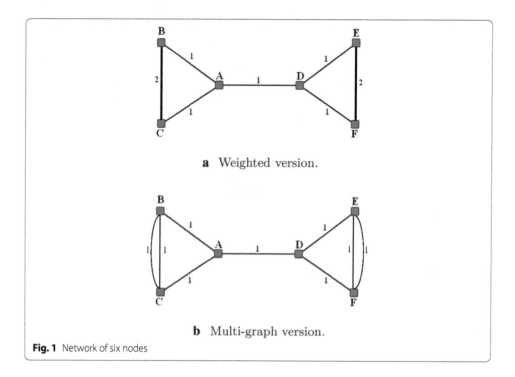

a Weighted version.

b Multi-graph version.

Fig. 1 Network of six nodes

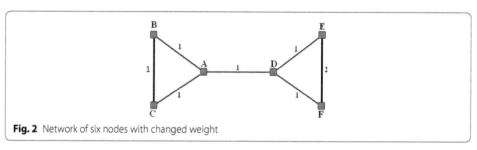

Fig. 2 Network of six nodes with changed weight

which is valid for all r in the interval $(0, 1]$. Therefore, in this partition node, A has no incentive to change the coalition under any choice of r.

Now consider a slightly modified example, where we change the weight 2 on the edge $\{B, C\}$ to weight 1 (see Fig. 2). This change results in the following imputations:

$$Y_A(g|S_1) = \frac{2}{2}r + \frac{3}{3}r^2,$$

and

$$Y_A(g|S_2 \cup A) = \frac{1}{2}r + \frac{2}{3}r^2 + \frac{4}{4}r^3.$$

We see that now $Y_A(g|S_2 \cup A) > Y_A(g|S_1)$, if $r > (1 + \sqrt{19})/6 \approx 0.89$. Thus, if r is sufficiently large, the partition $\{S_1, S_2\}$ becomes internally unstable and the grand coalition becomes the only stable configuration.

In the above example the parameter r can be used to tune the resolution of network partitioning. Resolution scale tuning will be even more natural in the next approach. We shall see that the next approach is also much more computationally efficient than the Myerson value-based approach.

Hedonic coalition game approach

There is another game-theoretic approach for partitioning society into coalitions based on the ground-breaking work [29] on hedonic games.

Assume that the set of players $N = \{1, \ldots, n\}$ is divided into K coalitions by the partition $\Pi = \{S_1, \ldots, S_K\}$. Let $S_\Pi(i)$ denote the coalition $S_k \in \Pi$ such that $i \in S_k$. A hedonic game is defined in terms of player preferences for various coalitions. A player i preferences are represented by a complete, reflexive, and transitive binary relation $\succeq_i$ over the set $\{S \subset N : i \in S\}$. Denote by $\succ_i$ the strict part of this relation.

Let us now apply the framework of hedonic games [29] to network partitioning problem, particularly, specifying the preferences. First, in the next subsection, we consider the case of additively separable preferences and then in "The case of non-additively separable preferences" section, we consider the case of non-additively separable preferences.

The case of additively separable preferences

The preferences are additively separable [29] if there exists a value function $v_i : N \to \mathbb{R}$ such that $v_i(i) = 0$ and

$$S_1 \succeq_i S_2 \Leftrightarrow \sum_{j \in S_1} v_i(j) \geq \sum_{j \in S_2} v_i(j).$$

The preferences $\{v_i, i \in N\}$ are symmetric, if $v_i(j) = v_j(i) = v_{ij} = v_{ji}$ for all $i, j \in N$. The symmetry property defines a very important class of hedonic games.

As in the previous section, the network partition Π is *Nash stable*, if $S_\Pi(i) \succeq_i S_k \cup \{i\}$ for all $i \in N, S_k \in \Pi \cup \{\emptyset\}$. In the Nash-stable partition, there is no player who wants to leave her coalition.

A potential of a coalition partition $\Pi = \{S_1, \ldots, S_K\}$ (see [29]) is

$$P(\Pi) = \sum_{k=1}^{K} P(S_k) = \sum_{k=1}^{K} \sum_{i,j \in S_k} v_{ij}. \tag{5}$$

One natural method for detecting a stable community structure can be based on the following better response type dynamics:

Start with any partition of the network $N = \{S_1, \ldots, S_K\}$. Choose any player i and any coalition S_k different from $S_\Pi(i)$. If $S_k \cup \{i\} \succ_i S_\Pi(i)$, assign node i to the coalition S_k; otherwise, keep the partition unchanged and choose another pair of node-coalition, etc.

Since the game has the potential (5), the above algorithm is guaranteed to converge in a finite number of steps.

Proposition 1 *If players' preferences are additively separable and symmetric ($v_{ii} = 0, v_{ij} = v_{ji}$ for all $i, j \in N$), then the coalition partition Π giving a local maximum of the potential $P(\Pi)$ is the Nash-stable partition.*

One natural way to define a symmetric value function v with a parameter $\alpha \in [0, 1]$ is as follows:

$$
v_{ij} = \begin{cases} 1 - \alpha, & (i,j) \in E, \\ -\alpha, & (i,j) \notin E, \\ 0, & i = j. \end{cases} \tag{6}
$$

For any subgraph $g|S$, denote the number of nodes in S as $n(S)$, and the number of edges in S as $m(S)$. Then, for the value function (6), the potential (5) takes the form

$$
P^\alpha(\Pi) = \sum_{k=1}^{K} \left(m(S_k) - \alpha \frac{n(S_k)(n(S_k) - 1)}{2} \right). \tag{7}
$$

We can characterize the limiting cases $\alpha \to 0$ and $\alpha \to 1$. Towards this goal, let us introduce a special decomposition of the network into cliques. At first, let us find a maximum clique S_1 in the network G (a maximum clique of a graph, is a clique, such that there is no clique with more vertices). Remove all vertices of S_1 from G and consider the new network G'. Let us find a maximum clique S_2 in the network G' and continue this procedure until we derive the partition $\{S_1, ..., S_K\}$ of the network G into cliques. Call this partition the sequential decomposition of the network into maximum cliques.

Proposition 2 *If $\alpha = 0$, the grand coalition partition $N = \{1, \ldots, n\}$ gives the maximum of the potential (7). Whereas if $\alpha \to 1$, the network sequential decomposition into maximum cliques corresponds to a maximum of the potential (7).*

Proof It is immediate to check that for $\alpha = 0$ the grand coalition partition N gives the maximum of the potential (7), and $P^\alpha(N) = m(N)$.

For values of α closed to 1, the partition into maximum cliques $\Pi = \{S_1, \ldots, S_K\}$ gives the maximum of (7). Indeed, assume that a player i from the clique $S_\Pi(i)$ of the size m_1 moves to a clique S_j of the size $m_2 < m_1$. The player $i \in S_\Pi(i)$ and S_j are connected by at most m_2 links. The impact on $P^\alpha(\Pi)$ of this movement is not higher than

$$
m_2(1 - \alpha) - (m_1 - 1)(1 - \alpha) \leq 0.
$$

Now, suppose that player i from the clique $S_\Pi(i)$ moves to a clique S_j of the size $m_2 \geq m_1$. Notice that clique S_j was constructed in the procedure of sequential decomposition before the clique $S_\Pi(i)$. The player $i \in S_\Pi(i)$ is connected with the clique S_j by at most $m_2 - 1$ links. Otherwise, the clique S_j can be increased by adding node i and this contradicts the fact that S_j was a maximum clique at the procedure of decomposition. If i has an incentive to move from $S_\Pi(i)$ to the clique S_j, then for new partition the sum (7) would not be higher than for partition Π by

$$
m_2 - 1 - m_2\alpha - (m_1 - 1)(1 - \alpha) = m_2 - m_1 - \alpha(m_2 - m_1 + 1).
$$

For α close to 1, this impact is negative, so there is no incentive to join the coalition S_j. $\square$

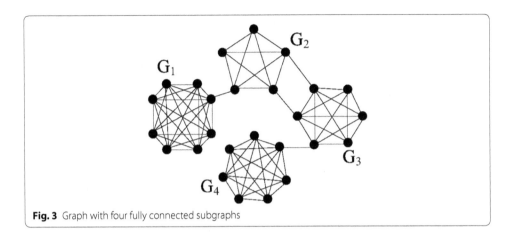

Fig. 3 Graph with four fully connected subgraphs

The grand coalition and the sequential maximum clique decomposition are two extreme partitions into communities. By varying the parameter α we can easily tune the resolution of the community detection algorithm.

Example 2 Consider graph $G = (N, E)$, which consists of $n = 26$ nodes and $m = 78$ edges (see Fig. 3). This graph includes 4 fully connected subgraphs: G_1 with 8 vertices N_1 connected by 28 links, G_2 with 5 vertices N_2 connected by 10 links, G_3 with 6 vertices N_3 connected by 15 links, and G_4 with 7 vertices N_4 connected by 21 links. Subgraph G_1 is connected with G_2 by 1 edge, G_2 with G_3 by 2 edges, and G_3 with G_4 by 1 edge.

Firstly, calculate the potentials (7) for large-scale decompositions of G for any parameter $\alpha \in [0, 1]$. It is easy to check, that $P(N) = 78 - 325\alpha$, $P(\{N_1, N_2 \cup N_3 \cup N_4\}) = 77 - 181\alpha$, $P(\{N_1, N_2 \cup N_3, N_4\}) = 76 - 104\alpha$, $P(\{N_1, N_2, N_3, N_4\}) = 74 - 74\alpha$.

Other coalition partitions give smaller potentials: $P(\{N_1 \cup N_2, N_3 \cup N_4\}) = 76 - 156\alpha < 76 - 104\alpha$, $P(\{N_1 \cup N_2 \cup N_3, N_4\}) = 77 - 192\alpha < 77 - 181\alpha$, $P(\{N_1, N_2, N_3 \cup N_4\}) = 75 - 116\alpha < 76 - 104\alpha$, $P(\{N_1 \cup N_2, N_3, N_4\}) = 75 - 114\alpha < 76 - 104\alpha$.

We solve a sequence of linear inequalities in order to find maximum of the potential for all $\alpha \in [0, 1]$. The result is presented in the table.

Nash-stable coalition partitions in Example 2

α	Coalition partition	Potential
[0, 1/144]	$N_1 \cup N_2 \cup N_3 \cup N_4$	$78 - 325\alpha$
[1/144, 1/77]	$N_1, N_2 \cup N_3 \cup N_4$	$77 - 181\alpha$
[1/77, 1/15]	$N_1, N_2 \cup N_3, N_4$	$76 - 104\alpha$
[1/15, 1]	N_1, N_2, N_3, N_4	$74 - 74\alpha$

Example 1 (ctnd) Note that for the unweighted version of the network example presented in Fig. 1, there are only two stable partitions: $\Pi = N$ for small values of $\alpha \leq 1/9$ and $\Pi = \{\{A, B, C\}, \{D, E, F\}\}$ for $\alpha > 1/9$.

Another natural approach to define a symmetric value function is, roughly speaking, to compare the network under investigation with the configuration random graph model. The configuration random graph model can be viewed as a null model for a network with no community structure. Namely, the following value function can be considered:

$$v_{ij} = \beta_{ij}\left(A_{ij} - \delta\frac{d_i d_j}{2m}\right),\tag{8}$$

where A_{ij} is the number of links between nodes i and j (multi-graph is allowed), d_i and d_j are the degrees of nodes i and j, respectively, $m = \frac{1}{2}\sum_{l\in N} d_l$ is the total number of links in the network, and $\beta_{ij} = \beta_{ji}$ and δ are some parameters.

Note that if $\beta_{ij} = \beta, \forall i,j \in N$, and $\delta = 1$, the potential (7) coincides with the network modularity [15, 16]. If $\beta_{ij} = \beta, \forall i,j \in N$, and $\delta \neq 1$, we obtain the generalized modularity presented first in [18]. The introduction of the non-homogeneous weights was proposed in [19] with the following particularly interesting choice:

$$\beta_{ij} = \frac{2m}{d_i d_j}.$$

The introduction of the resolution parameter δ allows one to obtain clustering with varying granularity as well as to overcome the resolution limit [30].

Thus, we now have an interpretation based on coalition game of the modularity method. Namely, the coalition partition $\Pi = \{S_1, \ldots, S_K\}$ which maximizes the modularity

$$P(\Pi) = \sum_{k=1}^{K} \sum_{i,j\in S_k, i\neq j} \left(A_{ij} - \frac{d_i d_j}{2m}\right)\tag{9}$$

gives the Nash-stable partition of the network in the hedonic game with the value function defined by (8) with $\delta = 1$ and $\beta_{ij} = \beta$.

Example 1 (ctnd) For the network example presented in Fig. 1, we calculate $P(N) = 3/2, P(\{B,C\} \cup \{A,D\} \cup \{E,F\}) = P(\{A,B,C,D\} \cup \{E,F\}) = 7/2$ and $P(\{A,B,C\} \cup \{D,E,F\}) = 5$. Thus, according to the value function (8) with $\delta = 1$ and $\beta_{ij} = \beta$ (modularity value function), $\Pi = \{\{A,B,C\},\{D,E,F\}\}$ is the unique Nash-stable coalition partition.

The case of non-additively separable preferences

Now let us consider a few cases of non-additively separable preferences which still have potentials. First, we consider a slight modification of preference structure (6) which makes it non-additively separable. Namely, define the preference relation as follows:

$$S_1 \succeq_i S_2 \Leftrightarrow \sum_{j\in S_1} v_{ij} - \gamma 1\{S_1 \neq \emptyset\} \geq \sum_{j\in S_2} v_{ij} - \gamma 1\{S_2 \neq \emptyset\},\tag{10}$$

where $1\{\cdot\}$ is the indicator function, giving one if the argument is true, v_{ij} is defined as before in (6), and γ is a parameter representing the cost of coalition creation and allows us to control further the clustering resolution and granularity. As verified in the following proposition, in this case the game also has a potential.

Proposition 3 *The hedonic clustering game defined by the preference relation (10) has the following potential:*

$$P^{\alpha,\gamma}(\Pi) = \sum_{k=1}^{K} \left(m(S_k) - \alpha \frac{n(S_k)(n(S_k) - 1)}{2} \right) - \gamma K. \tag{11}$$

Proof Suppose that partition $\Pi = \{S_1, ..., S_K\}$ maximizes the function (11), possibly locally. Then, if i moves from $S_\Pi(i)$ to S_k, the value of (11) corresponding to the new partition Π' is different from the value corresponding to Π by

$$\sum_{j \in S_k} v_{ij} - \sum_{j \in S_\Pi(i)} v_{ij},$$

note that K is not changing. If i creates its own cluster, then the value of (11) corresponding to Π' is different from that for Π by

$$-\gamma - \sum_{j \in S_\Pi(i)} v_{ij},$$

and in the case $S_\Pi(i) = \{i\}$, the difference is

$$\sum_{j \in S_k} v_{ij} + \gamma.$$

If Π provides a maximum of (11), all these differences are negative. So, according to relation (10), player i indeed has no incentive to move from her coalition $S_\Pi(i)$ to another coalition and the function (11) can be interpreted as a potential. $\square$

Let us provide a few recommendations for the choice of α and γ. Similarly to [18], from the analysis of the mean field model corresponding to a stochastic block model (SBM), one can show that the value of α close to the link density ensures the internal stability of clusters in the mean field model of SBM. Thus, if a network has one main scale, such value of α gives good result. If a network has nested clustering structure, one can vary α to obtain clustering with the needed level of granularity. Again using the mean field model for SBM, one can show that the good value of γ corresponds to the product of α and the smallest size of the cluster we would like to obtain.

We mention that interestingly under a specific choice of parameters the globally optimal partition may contain disconnected clusters. However, such a choice of parameters is typically not natural.

Example 3 Let us consider a graph that consists of a clique of four nodes and two cliques of three nodes connected to it (see Fig. 4).

One can check that for $\alpha = 0.5$ and $\gamma = 5$, the partitioning

$$\tilde{\Pi} = \{\{0, 1, 2, 7, 8, 9\}, \{3, 4, 5, 6\}\}$$

gives the maximum value to the potential $P^{\alpha,\gamma}(\tilde{\Pi}) = -8.5$, while

$$P^{\alpha,\gamma}(\{\{0, 1, 2, 3, 4, 5, 6, 7, 8, 9\}\}) = -18.5,$$
$$P^{\alpha,\gamma}(\{\{0, 1, 2, 3, 4, 5, 6\}, \{7, 8, 9\}\}) = -9,$$
$$P^{\alpha,\gamma}(\{\{0, 1, 2\}, \{3, 4, 5, 6\}, \{7, 8, 9\}\}) = -9.$$

An intuitive interpretation for this choice of parameters is that α is chosen significantly large to encourage splitting of clusters from the grand coalition and γ is also chosen significantly large to penalize the creation of independent clusters.

Next we would like to note that two well-known network partitioning methods: normalized cut [10, 33] and ratio cut [32] can also be viewed as particular instances of potential hedonic clustering games with non-additively separable preferences. Towards this end, let us introduce a few more definitions. Let $S, T \subset N$ be two, possibly overlapping sets of nodes. Then, we define a cut $W(S, T)$ as

$$W(S, T) = \sum_{i \in S, j \in T} 1\{(i, j) \in E\}.$$

Note that an edge is counted twice if its both ends lie in the same set. The volume of a set $S \in N$ is defined as the number of edges between its vertices

$$vol(S) = \frac{1}{2} W(S, S).$$

The normalized cut of a set S is defined by

$$h^{\text{NCUT}}(S) = \frac{W(S, \bar{S})}{W(S, S)} = \frac{1}{2} \frac{W(S, \bar{S})}{vol(S)},$$

where $\bar{S} = N \backslash S$. If $vol(S) = 0$, we define $h^{\text{NCUT}}(S) = +\infty$. One can also define the ratio cut

$$h^{\text{RCUT}}(S) = \frac{W(S, \bar{S})}{|S|}.$$

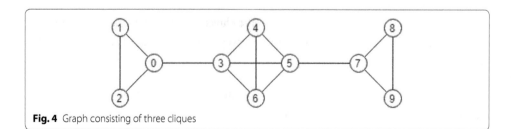

Fig. 4 Graph consisting of three cliques

Similar to the normalized cut, we assign $h^{\text{RCUT}}(S) = +\infty$, if $|S| = 0$, i.e., $S = \emptyset$. Then, the normalized cut [10, 33] and ratio cut [32] network partitioning methods are based on the following potentials

$$P^{\text{NCUT}}(\Pi) = - \sum_{S \in \Pi} h^{\text{NCUT}}(S), \tag{12}$$

$$P^{\text{RCUT}}(\Pi) = - \sum_{S \in \Pi} h^{\text{RCUT}}(S), \tag{13}$$

respectively. Similar to the proof of Proposition 3, one can check that the above potentials correspond to the following preferences: for the normalized cut

$$S_1 \succeq_i S_2 \Leftrightarrow$$
$$\frac{W(S_1 \bigcup\{i\}, \bar{S}_1 \setminus \{i\})}{vol(S_1 \bigcup\{i\})} - \frac{W(S_1, \bar{S}_1 \setminus \{i\})}{vol(S_1)} \leq \frac{W(S_2 \bigcup\{i\}, \bar{S}_2 \setminus \{i\})}{vol(S_2 \bigcup\{i\})} - \frac{W(S_2, \bar{S}_2 \setminus \{i\})}{vol(S_2)} \tag{14}$$

and the ratio cut

$$S_1 \succeq_i S_2 \Leftrightarrow$$
$$\frac{W(S_1 \bigcup\{i\}, \bar{S}_1 \setminus \{i\})}{|S_1| + 1} - \frac{W(S_1, \bar{S}_1 \setminus \{i\})}{|S_1|} \leq \frac{W(S_2 \bigcup\{i\}, \bar{S}_2 \setminus \{i\})}{|S_2| + 1} - \frac{W(S_2, \bar{S}_2 \setminus \{i\})}{|S_2|}, \tag{15}$$

respectively. Thus, two more, well-known network partitioning methods can be cast into our general framework. A very important benefit of such interpretation is that in contrast to the original formulations, we now do not require a priori knowledge of the number of clusters.

Gibbs sampling approach for hedonic games with potential

We note that finding Nash equilibrium in a game with potential is equivalent to finding a maximum of the game's potential. To find a maximum of the game's potential, we can follow the approach based on Gibbs sampling. Let us consider the following Gibbsian distribution over all partitions:

$$\rho(\Pi) = \frac{\exp\left(\beta P(\Pi)\right)}{\sum_{\forall \tilde{\Pi}} \exp\left(\beta P(\tilde{\Pi})\right)}. \tag{16}$$

It is easy to see that as $\beta \to \infty$, the distribution concentrates on the partition corresponding to the maximum of the potential $P(\Pi)$.

Next, denote by Σ the set of indices of the network clusters and by $\Pi_{i \to \sigma}$ the (re)assignment of node i to cluster $\sigma \in \Sigma$ and run the Glauber dynamics [18, 44] according to

$$P_{\Pi \to \Pi'} = \frac{1}{n} \begin{cases} \sum_{i \in N} \frac{\exp\left(\beta P(\Pi)\right)}{\sum_{s \in \Sigma} \exp\left(\beta P(\Pi_{i \to s})\right)}, & \text{if } \Pi' = \Pi, \\ \frac{\exp\left(\beta P(\Pi')\right)}{\sum_{s \in \Sigma} \exp\left(\beta P(\Pi_{i \to s})\right)}, & \text{if } \Pi' = \Pi_{i \to \sigma}, \\ 0, & \text{otherwise,} \end{cases} \tag{17}$$

that is, we choose randomly a node and reassign this node to a new cluster according to the conditional Gibbsian distribution (clearly, it can happen that the node remains in its current cluster). It is well known that the Glauber dynamics corresponds to the reversible Markov chain with the stationary distribution given by (16), see e.g., [44]. One can also cool down the temperature as in simulated annealing [45] in order to find the partition with the global maximum of the potential. We define one iteration as n updates of nodes according to (17). Typically and as will be demonstrated in the next section, if we take a reasonably high inverse temperature β, the process (17) often finds good-quality partition already after 5–10 iterations. The complexity of one iteration is very light in the case of sparse graphs, i.e., $O(|E|)$.

A sample generated by the above-described Glauber dynamics appears to have significant variance. To reduce it, the generalized empirical covariance matrix of several samples can be used, similar to [46] where the standard covariance matrix has been used for the case of two clusters. For one sample, the elements of the generalized covariance matrix are defined as follows:

$$M_{i,j}^{(1)} = \begin{cases} 1, & \text{if } \sigma(i) = \sigma(j), \\ -1, & \text{otherwise.} \end{cases}$$

The empirical generalized covariance matrix of a set of samples is the average of their generalized covariance matrices, i.e.,

$$\hat{M} = \frac{1}{T} \sum_{t=1}^{T} M^{(t)}.$$

An (i, j)th value of the generalized covariance matrix indicates how often the ith and jth nodes appear in the same cluster.

Then, given a generalized covariance matrix one can extract the community structure using threshold-based or PCA-based methods.

Numerical validation

In this section, we validate the proposed approaches on synthetic and real-world networks. As a benchmark, we take a widely used clustering method `sklearn.cluster.spectralclustering` from [47]. The method is based on the eigen elements of the normalized Laplacian and K-means postprocessing and have demonstrated good performance in many previous studies.

If it is available, the ground truth clustering is denoted by Π^{true} and the clustering obtained by an algorithm as Π^{test}. Each time we specify which algorithm we test against the ground truth. We measure the difference between these two partitions by the following function from [48]:

$$\mathcal{E}(\Pi^{\text{true}}, \Pi^{\text{test}}) = 1 - \frac{1}{n} \max_{\pi : \Sigma^{\text{true}} \to \Sigma^{\text{test}}} \sum_{\sigma \in \Sigma^{\text{true}}} n_{\sigma, \pi(\sigma)}. \tag{18}$$

Synthetic network: stochastic block model

We first evaluate various clustering algorithms based on potential hedonic games on stochastic block model (SBM), a synthetic network with known community structure. An SBM with $|\Sigma|$ clusters is represented by a symmetric square matrix P where $p_{\sigma,\sigma}$ is a density of edges inside the cluster σ and $p_{\sigma,\sigma'} = p_{\sigma',\sigma}$ is a density between clusters σ and σ'. Specifically, we use SBM with two communities of 50 and 150 nodes, intra-cluster density $p_{11} = p_{22} = 0.1$ and inter-cluster density $p_{12} = p_{21} = 0.02$. We start from a random coloring and run the process for 100 iterations.

In Fig. 5, we show an example of the Glauber dynamics using NCUT potential (12). For small $\beta = 10$ we observe unstable behavior, while for large $\beta = 500$ the process evolves around a local maximum that provides relatively bad clustering (49 out of 50 nodes of the first community and only 116 out of 150 of the second community are clustered correctly).

Now let us take a closer look at RCUT (13). We discovered that in our example the ground truth partition does not maximize the potential. The process converges fast to a clustering that differs from the ground truth and has larger P^{RCUT} than the ground truth partition. We tested the algorithm on a set of 100 graph instances generated according to the SBM and we show the results in Fig. 6 where we also compare it to the spectral clustering from [47]. One can see that while the Glauber dynamics generally ends up with $P^{\mathrm{RCUT}}(\Pi^{\mathrm{test}}) > P^{\mathrm{RCUT}}(\Pi^{\mathrm{true}})$. The spectral clustering procedure provides a solution that has smaller P^{RCUT} but is closer to the ground truth.

Next let us evaluate the performance of the clustering based on the potential P^{α}, see (7). Empty clusters do not cause any singularities in P^{α} unlike in P^{NCUT} and P^{RCUT}. Hence, the final partition can have less clusters than $|\Sigma|$. Let us at first restrict the number of clusters by setting $\Sigma = \{0, 1\}$. In this context, we have two natural choices for initial coloring of a graph: either, as before, we can choose colors uniformly at random, or we can assign same color to all nodes. We tested both settings on a set of 100 SBM graph instances. The best results are obtained with $\alpha = 0.05$ and $\beta = 10$. If we assign clusters at random at initialization, the process may not converge to a good coloring. Assigning the same initial color to all the nodes leads to better results. Fig. 7a and b shows evolution on the same graph with different initial colorings. The average $\mathcal{E}$ after 20 iterations for random-cluster initialization is 0.033, for single-cluster initialization it is 0.006; while the standard spectral clustering, i.e., the continuous relaxation of the NCUT [33] provides a result with average $\mathcal{E}(\Pi^{\mathrm{true}}, \Pi^{\mathrm{test}}) = 0.025$. We can conclude that the P^{α}-based clustering significantly outperforms the spectral clustering in terms of accuracy. However, it depends on the parameter α that determines the penalty for large clusters. If α is too small, the uniform coloring becomes the ground state, as already indicated in Proposition 2. If α is too large, the obtained clusters will be relatively of the same size but may not represent the real community structure.

We can also try to detect the real number of clusters, if we choose large Σ. Here we can test the case when initially all nodes receive different colors $|\Sigma| = |V|$. We discovered that the final clustering consists of 9 or 10 clusters on average, most of which contain very few nodes. See Fig. 7c for an example of such clustering process.

To prevent the problem described in the previous paragraph, we modify P^{α} to $P^{\alpha,\gamma}$, see Eq. (11), by introducing a penalty term proportional to the number of non-empty

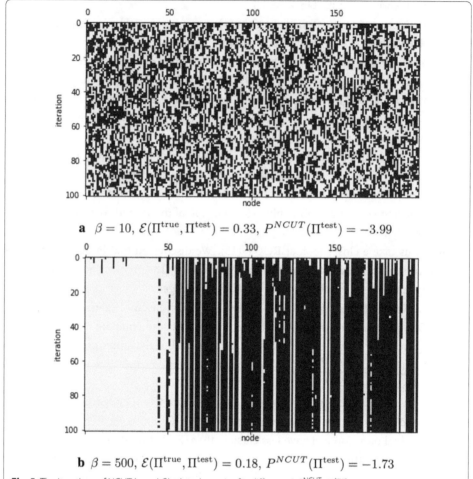

a $\beta = 10$, $\mathcal{E}(\Pi^{\text{true}}, \Pi^{\text{test}}) = 0.33$, $P^{NCUT}(\Pi^{\text{test}}) = -3.99$

b $\beta = 500$, $\mathcal{E}(\Pi^{\text{true}}, \Pi^{\text{test}}) = 0.18$, $P^{NCUT}(\Pi^{\text{test}}) = -1.73$

Fig. 5 The iterations of NCUT-based Glauber dynamics for different β; $P^{NCUT}(\Pi^{\text{true}}) = -1.40$. x-axis corresponds to the node index and y-axis corresponds to the iteration number. Different colors correspond to different clusters

clusters. The potential $P^{\alpha,\gamma}$ depends on parameters α and γ that determine penalties for disparate clusters and for the total number of them, respectively. We tested the respective Glauber dynamics on the same set of random instances of SBM with parameters $\alpha = 0.05$, $\gamma = 5$, $\beta = 10$, and $|\Sigma| = |V| = 200$. We run the process for 20 iterations and averaged the coloring over the last 10 of them. We obtained the following results: 2 clusters were determined in every graph instance and the average $\mathcal{E}(\Pi^{\text{true}}, \Pi^{\text{test}})$ is 0.0057. The average $\mathcal{E}(\Pi^{\text{true}}, \Pi^{\text{test}})$ for the spectral clustering is 0.0252.

In order to validate further the method based on $P^{\alpha,\gamma}$-potential, we tried it on different sets of graphs of different clustering structures with the same algorithm parameters α, γ, and β. On a set of 100 homogeneous Erdős–Rényi random graphs of 200 nodes with edge density 0.1, our algorithm ended up with a uniform coloring on 99 of them and on one graph it finished with 2 clusters where the smaller one contains only two nodes. Given a set of 100 graph instances of SBM with clusters of 50, 150, and 200 nodes, the algorithm correctly determined the number of clusters in each graph and provided on average $\mathcal{E}(\Pi^{\text{true}}, \Pi^{\text{test}}) = 0.006$, while spectral clustering provided on

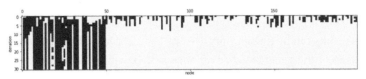

a $\mathcal{E}(\Pi^{\text{true}}, \Pi^{\text{test}}) = 0.085$, $P^{RCUT}(\Pi^{\text{true}}) = -3.307$, $P^{RCUT}(\Pi^{\text{test}}) = -3.085$. x-axis corresponds to the node index and y-axis corresponds to the iteration number. Different colors correspond to different clusters.

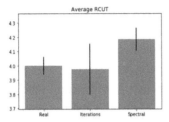

b Average RCUT for ground truth, RCUT-based Glauber dynamics and spectral clustering

c Average $\mathcal{E}(\Pi^{\text{true}}, \Pi^{\text{test}})$ for iterative and spectral clustering

Fig. 6 The iterations of RCUT-based Glauber dynamics for $\beta = 200$ and comparison to the ground truth and spectral clustering

average $\mathcal{E}(\Pi^{\text{true}}, \Pi^{\text{test}}) = 0.026$. On a set of 100 graph instances containing 4 clusters of 50, 100, 150, and 200 nodes, the algorithm after 20 iterations determined 4 clusters in 90 graphs and 3 clusters in 10 graphs. The average $\mathcal{E}(\Pi^{\text{true}}, \Pi^{\text{test}})$ is 0.0335. However, if we increase the number of iterations to 50, we determine correctly 4 clusters for 95 graphs

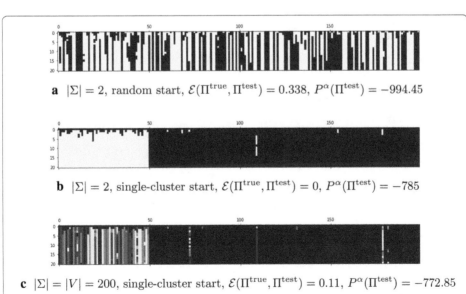

a $|\Sigma| = 2$, random start, $\mathcal{E}(\Pi^{\text{true}}, \Pi^{\text{test}}) = 0.338$, $P^{\alpha}(\Pi^{\text{test}}) = -994.45$

b $|\Sigma| = 2$, single-cluster start, $\mathcal{E}(\Pi^{\text{true}}, \Pi^{\text{test}}) = 0$, $P^{\alpha}(\Pi^{\text{test}}) = -785$

c $|\Sigma| = |V| = 200$, single-cluster start, $\mathcal{E}(\Pi^{\text{true}}, \Pi^{\text{test}}) = 0.11$, $P^{\alpha}(\Pi^{\text{test}}) = -772.85$

Fig. 7 The iterations of hedonic-based process for $\alpha = 0.05$ and $\beta = 10$ for a graph with $P^{\alpha}(\Pi^{\text{true}}) = -785$. x-axis corresponds to the node index and y-axis corresponds to the iteration number. Different colors correspond to different clusters

and 3 clusters for the others. The average $\mathcal{E}(\Pi^{\text{true}}, \Pi^{\text{test}})$ becomes 0.0185. The average $\mathcal{E}(\Pi^{\text{true}}, \Pi^{\text{test}})$ of the spectral clustering on the same set of graphs is 0.0375.

The above results can be further improved by using the generalized covariance matrix. The application of the generalized covariance matrix will be illustrated in some of the following network examples.

Real-world network with ground truth: Karate club

Consider the popular example of the social network from Zachary karate club (see Fig. 8). In his study [49], Zachary observed 34 members of a karate club over a period of 2 years. Due to a disagreement developed between the administrator of the club and the club's instructor there appeared two new clubs associated with the instructor (node 1) and administrator (node 34) of sizes 16 and 18, respectively.

The authors of [15] divide the network into two groups of roughly equal size using modularity and hierarchical clustering tree. They show that this split corresponds almost perfectly with the actual division of the club members following the break-up. Only one node, node 3, is classified incorrectly by the method of [15].

Let us first apply the Myerson value approach to the karate club network. To perform the analytic study, let us start from the ground truth partition [49]

$$R_3 = \{1, 2, 3, 4, 5, 6, 7, 8, 11, 12, 13, 14, 17, 18, 20, 22\} \quad \text{and} \quad L_3 = N \setminus R_3.$$

By using subindex 3, we emphasize the importance of player 3. By enumerating all simple paths and using formula (4), we find the Myerson value for player 3 in coalition R_3

$$Y_3(g|R_3) = \frac{5}{2}r + \frac{41}{3}r^2 + \frac{224}{4}r^3 + \frac{883}{5}r^4 + \frac{2412}{6}r^5 + \frac{4378}{7}r^6 + \frac{5572}{8}r^7 + \\ \frac{6288}{9}r^8 + \frac{6040}{10}r^9 + \frac{3988}{11}r^{10} + \frac{1392}{12}r^{11} + \frac{120}{13}r^{12},$$

and in the coalition $L_3 \cup \{3\}$

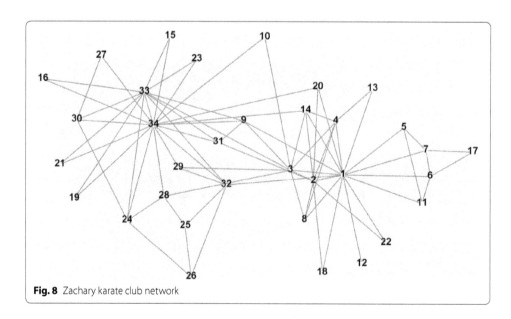

Fig. 8 Zachary karate club network

$$Y_3(g|L_3 \cup \{3\}) = \frac{5}{2}r + \frac{30}{3}r^2 + \frac{190}{4}r^3 + \frac{913}{5}r^4 + \frac{3426}{6}r^5 + \frac{8662}{7}r^6 +$$
$$\frac{17286}{8}r^7 + \frac{29197}{9}r^8 + \frac{40452}{10}r^9 + \frac{40896}{11}r^{10} + \frac{27080}{12}r^{11} +$$
$$\frac{10701}{13}r^{12} + \frac{2209}{14}r^{13} + \frac{150}{15}r^{14}.$$

We have plotted both $Y_3(g|R_3)$ and $Y_3(g|L_3 \cup \{3\})$ as functions of r in Fig. 9. If r is smaller than 0.231, node 3 has no incentive to move from coalition R_3 to coalition L_3. Recall that the modularity-based method of [15] would displace player 3 into the wrong coalition L_3.

It is also interesting to investigate the imputations of the other two border nodes 9 and 10. If we plot the imputations for node 10: $Y_{10}(g|L_3)$ and $Y_{10}(g|R_3 \cup \{10\})$ (see Fig. 10), we observe that as for node 3, for smaller values of r (i.e., for $r < 0.363$), node 10 has no incentive to leave the coalition L_3; whereas for the values of r greater than 0.363, node 10 has incentive to change the coalition.

As it is clear from Fig. 11, node 9 has no incentive to leave the coalition L_3 with any value of r. Thus, we can conclude that the ground truth partition [49] is internally stable according to the Myerson value approach if $r < 0.231$. This has a nice intuitive interpretation. Humans cannot count easily long paths and consequently one needs to apply heavy discounting to mimic humans' decisions.

Let us now apply the hedonic game approach with Glauber dynamics to the karate club network. We started from a random partition into two clusters and run the algorithm using the potential (7) with $\alpha = 0.046$, which corresponds to 1/3 of the edge density, and $\beta = 20$. The algorithm stabilizes after around 5 iterations and the mean error after 10 iterations in 100 runs was 20.0%, which roughly corresponds 7 misclassified nodes. However, the partitioning results differ significantly from run to run.

By applying the spectral clustering algorithm from [47] to Zachary karate club network, we obtain an average error of 25.8%.

To reduce the variance of the Glauber dynamics and hence the clustering error, we computed the empirical generalized covariance matrix $\hat{M}$ for the results of 10

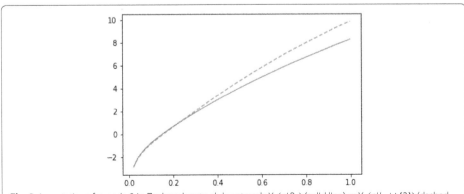

Fig. 9 Imputations for node 3 in Zachary karate club network: $Y_3(g|R_3)$ (solid line) vs $Y_3(g|L_3 \cup \{3\})$ (dashed line) in semilog scale

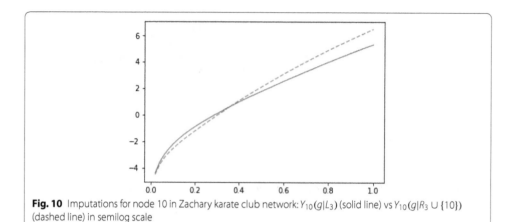

Fig. 10 Imputations for node 10 in Zachary karate club network: $Y_{10}(g|L_3)$ (solid line) vs $Y_{10}(g|R_3 \cup \{10\})$ (dashed line) in semilog scale

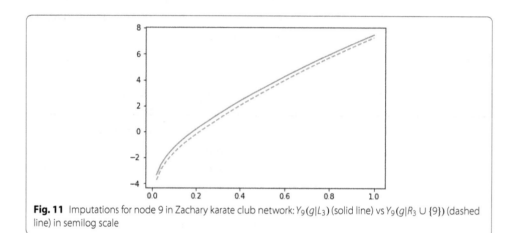

Fig. 11 Imputations for node 9 in Zachary karate club network: $Y_9(g|L_3)$ (solid line) vs $Y_9(g|R_3 \cup \{9\})$ (dashed line) in semilog scale

independent runs of 10 iterations of the Glauber dynamics and then extracted the community structure using the PCA algorithm. Only node 9 was misclassified, which is a border node.

The application of the generalized covariance matrix in addition to the Gibbs sampling really helps to consistently obtain high-quality results.

We would like to note that the application of the generalized covariance matrix to the spectral clustering method from [47] does not improve significantly its results since spectral clustering gives less noisy, however, more biased results compared to the hedonic game approach.

Real-world network with ground truth: Dolphins

Consider now the Dolphins social network from [50]. This network presented in Fig. 12 was constructed from observations of a community of 62 bottle nose Dolphins over a period of 7 years from 1994 to 2001. The nodes in the network represent the Dolphins, and the ties between nodes represent the associations between dolphin pairs occurring more often than expected by chance.

The ground truth partition is presented by two coalitions:

$$L = \{1, 5, 6, 7, 9, 13, 17, 19, 22, 25, 26, 27, 31, 32, 41, 48, 54, 56, 57, 60\}$$

and

$$R = \{0, 2, 3, 4, 8, 10, 11, 12, 14, 15, 16, 18, 20, 21, 23, 24, 28, 29, 30, 33, 34,$$
$$35, 36, 37, 38, 39, 40, 42, 43, 44, 45, 46, 47, 49, 50, 51, 52, 53, 55, 58, 59, 61\}.$$

We studied the Dolphins network using the hedonic game approach with Glauber dynamics in a similar way as we did for Zachary karate club. Note that because of a very large number of simple paths in this network, the application of the Myerson value approach was not feasible. The following parameter values were used: $\alpha = 0.028$, which corresponds to 1/3 of the edge density, and $\beta = 20$. The algorithm stabilizes after around 10 iterations and the mean error after 20 iterations in 100 runs was 24.8%. As with Zachary karate club, the partitioning results differ significantly from run to run.

By applying the spectral clustering algorithm from [47], we obtain an average error of 7.5%.

We computed the empirical generalized covariance matrix $\hat{M}$ of the results of 10 independent runs of 20 iterations of the Glauber dynamics and then extracted the community structure using the PCA algorithm. Then, only one node, node 39, was misclassified. This is a border node connected to only two nodes of different clusters.

In contrast, computing the covariance matrix of 10 results of independent runs of spectral clustering algorithm from [47] led to 4 misclassified nodes: 22, 31, 48, 60.

Real-world network with many clusters and ground truth: Football

The American College Football network [15] represents the games between Division IA Colleges during the regular fall 2000 season (see Fig. 13).

The nodes in the network represent the teams and the links are the games between the teams. There are 115 teams and each team belongs to one of the 12 conferences. The communities in the network are the conferences. So, the ground truth partition is given by 12 coalitions:

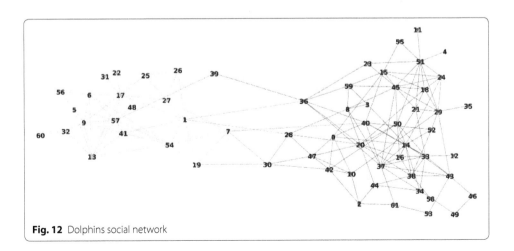

Fig. 12 Dolphins social network

$C_1 = [112, 48, 92, 44, 75, 66, 91, 86, 57, 110]; C_2 = [50, 24, 69, 11, 97, 59, 63];$
$C_3 = [80, 82, 42, 36, 90]; C_4 = [45, 109, 37, 25, 1, 33, 103, 105, 89];$
$C_5 = [9, 4, 104, 0, 93, 16, 41, 23]; C_6 = [5, 74, 3, 98, 10, 40, 84, 81, 52, 102, 107, 72];$
$C_7 = [68, 108, 78, 77, 8, 51, 21, 22, 7, 111]; C_8 = [32, 6, 13, 47, 39, 100, 15, 106, 64, 60, 2];$
$C_9 = [61, 99, 43, 14, 12, 31, 38, 18, 54, 34, 71, 26, 85]; C_{10} = [29, 19, 94, 35, 55, 30, 101, 79];$
$C_{11} = [46, 67, 73, 83, 114, 88, 53, 49, 58, 28]; C_{12} = [62, 65, 95, 17, 70, 56, 113, 27, 87, 20, 76, 96].$

As was the case of the Dolphins network, we could not apply the Myerson value approach to the football network because of the difficulty in enumerating all simple paths. In contrast, the hedonic game approach can easily be applied.

One of the main advantages of the hedonic game approach with $P^{\alpha, \gamma}$ potential (11) is the fact that it does not require the number of clusters as a parameter. Let us test on the football network, which consists of 12 clusters, how the hedonic game approach with $P^{\alpha, \gamma}$ potential can perform without a priori knowledge of the number of clusters.

We set the following parameters of the potential: $\alpha = 0.093$ (edge density), $\gamma = 10$. We run the Glauber dynamics with random initial partition into 20 clusters and the inverse noise $\beta = 10$ for 20 iterations. The clustering dynamics stabilizes after around 10 iterations. We performed 50 independent runs. The average number of detected clusters was 10.22 and the average percentage of misclassified nodes is 13.5%.

As with Zachary and Dolphins networks, we computed the empirical generalized covariance matrix of the clustering results. Since our goal was to determine the clusters without providing its number to the algorithm, we used a simple threshold-based clustering algorithm instead of the PCA algorithm: we build a weighted graph using the generalized covariance matrix as its adjacency matrix and removed the edges with

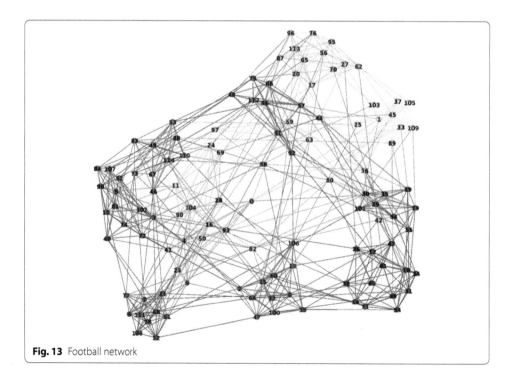

Fig. 13 Football network

weights below 0.5; the connected components of the resulting graph indicate clusters in the original network.

The resulting graph contained 13 connected components, i.e., we identified 13 clusters in the initial network that is quite close to the ground truth value 12. The percentage of the misclassified nodes is 6.9%, which signifies that the generalized covariance matrix improved significantly the quality of the clustering results.

Large real-world network without ground truth: Co-authorships in Math-Net.ru

To test scalability and efficiency of the hedonic game approach, we have chosen to cluster a fairly large social network. We have crawled the site Math-Net.ru, Russian Mathematical Portal, for the co-authorship graph [51]. We further extracted the giant connected component of this co-authorship network, which includes 41,840 authors. We have applied the hedonic game with the potential (7) and run the modified Glauber dynamics using round robin node schedule with random permutation. Twenty iterations of the modified Glauber dynamics run for about 2 min on Intel Core Duo 1.6 GHz processor and 5GB RAM. We have initialized process with a single cluster and restricted the number of clusters to ten. We have again observed stabilization of the modified Glauber dynamics at 15–20 iterations. Recall that one iteration of the modified Glauber dynamics requires $O(|E|)$ operations, which is quite a reasonable cost in the case of sparse networks and which is the case of most real-world networks. We have chosen significantly high value of β, which corresponds to nearly greedy algorithm. First, we have run the modified Glauber dynamics with α corresponding to the average edge density. This has lead to unbalanced clusters, see Table 1. By expecting clusters, we have observed that nearly all academicians (aka leaders of scientific schools) have been clustered to one largest cluster. However, when we have increased α tenfold, the clustering became much more balanced and the academicians have been distributed more evenly among the clusters.

Large synthetic SBM network with ground truth

To continue testing scalability and efficiency of the hedonic game approach and in particular to confirm a rapid convergence of the Glauber dynamics to a good solution, we consider a large stochastic block model graph with known communities. Specifically, we have generated an SBM with two clusters of sizes 50,000 and 150,000 nodes. We have generated the intra-cluster links with probability 0.0002 and the inter-cluster links with probability 0.00005. We run the Glauber dynamics associated with the potential (7), setting $\alpha = 0.0001$ and $\beta = 10$. In a typical run, after 7 iterations, only 97 nodes from the smaller cluster were misclassified to the larger cluster and only 65 nodes from the larger cluster were misclassified to the smaller cluster. It is not

Table 1 Cluster sizes in Math-Net.ru

α	$|S_1|$	$|S_2|$	$|S_3|$	$|S_4|$	$|S_5|$	$|S_6|$	$|S_7|$	$|S_8|$	$|S_9|$	$|S_{10}|$
0.000112	16,457	2820	2820	2820	2821	2821	2820	2821	2820	2820
0.001124	4184	4184	4184	4185	4183	4184	4184	4184	4184	4184

surprising that by the "gravity" effect the larger cluster attracted more nodes. We find that 7 iterations of the Glauber dynamics are not at all a large cost for partitioning 200,000 node network.

Conclusion and future research

We have presented two cooperative game theory-based approaches for network partitioning. The first approach is based on the Myerson value for graph constrained cooperative game, whereas the second approach is based on hedonic games which explain coalition formation. We find the second approach especially interesting as it gives a very natural way to tune the clustering resolution and generalizes the modularity, ratio cut, and normalized cut-based approaches. Within the hedonic games framework, we have proposed two new methods which particularly well regularize clustering resolution and help to adjust the level of granularity. We have shown that normalized cut and ratio cut methods can be modified to avoid the requirement of the number of clusters. All approaches that can be represented as hedonic games with potentials can be very efficiently implemented using Gibbs sampling with Glauber dynamics and generalized covariance matrix. The application of the generalized covariance matrix significantly improves the quality and stability of the clustering results. Our research plans are to test and to compare our methods on more social networks and to study analytically the convergence rate of Gibbs sampling.

Authors' contributions
The contribution of all four authors to the manuscript is quite balanced. All authors read and approved the final manuscript.

Author details
[1] Inria Sophia Antipolis, 2004 Route des Lucioles, 06902 Valbonne, France. [2] Higher School of Economics, 16 Soyuza Pechatnikov St., St. Petersburg 190121, Russia. [3] Institute of Applied Mathematical Research, Karelian Research Center, Russian Academy of Sciences, 11 Pushkinskaya St., Petrozavodsk 185910, Russia. [4] Saint-Petersburg State University, 7/9 Universitetskaya Nab., St. Petersburg 199034, Russia.

Acknowledgements
We would like to thank the editor and the referees for very useful remarks and suggestions that helped to significantly improve the presentation of the results. The work of the first and fourth authors is partly supported by the joint laboratory Inria—Nokia Bell Labs, the joint Inria-UFRJ team THANES and by UCA-JEDI Idex Grant "HGAPHS." The second and the third authors are supported by Russian Fund for Basic Research (Projects 16-51-55006, 16-01-00183). The third author is supported by Russian Science Foundation (Project 17-11-01709).

Competing interests
The authors declare that they have no competing interests.

References
1. Abbe E. Community detection and stochastic block models: recent developments. J Mach Learn Res. 2018;18(177):1–86.
2. Fortunato S. Community detection in graphs. Phys Rep. 2010;486(3):75–174.
3. Fortunato S, Hric D. Community detection in networks: a user guide. Phys Rep. 2016;659:1–44.
4. Jonnalagadda A, Kuppusamy L. A survey on game theoretic models for community detection in social networks. Soc Netw Anal Mining. 2016;6(1):83.
5. Von Luxburg U. A tutorial on spectral clustering. Stat Comput. 2007;17(4):395–416.

6. Schaeffer SE. Graph clustering. Comput Sci Rev. 2007;1(1):27–64.

7. Avrachenkov K, Dobrynin,V, Nemirovsky D, Pham SK, Smirnova E. Pagerank based clustering of hypertext document collections. In: Proceedings of the 31st annual international ACM SIGIR conference on research and development in information retrieval, SIGIR 2008, Singapore, July 20–24; 2008, p. 873–4.

8. Avrachenkov K, Chamie ME, Neglia G. Graph clustering based on mixing time of random walks. In: IEEE international conference on communications, ICC 2014, Sydney, Australia, June 10–14. 2014. p. 4089–94.

9. Dongen S. Performance criteria for graph clustering and Markov cluster experiments. Amsterdam: CWI (Centre for Mathematics and Computer Science); 2000.

10. Meilă M, Shi J. A random walks view of spectral segmentation. In: The 8th international workshop on artifical intelligence and statistics (AISTATS). 2001.

11. Newman ME. A measure of betweenness centrality based on random walks. Soc Netw. 2005;27(1):39–54.

12. Pons P, Latapy M. Computing communities in large networks using random walks. ISCIS. 2005;3733:284–93.

13. Blatt M, Wiseman S, Domany E. Clustering data through an analogy to the potts model. In: Advances in neural information processing systems 8, NIPS, Denver, CO, Nov 27–30. 1995. p. 416–22.

14. Blondel VD, Guillaume J-L, Lambiotte R, Lefebvre E. Fast unfolding of communities in large networks. J Stat Mech. 2008;10:10008.

15. Girvan M, Newman ME. Community structure in social and biological networks. Proc Natl Acad Sci. 2002;99(12):7821–6.

16. Newman ME. Modularity and community structure in networks. Proc Natl Acad Sci. 2006;103(23):8577–82.

17. Raghavan UN, Albert R, Kumara S. Near linear time algorithm to detect community structures in large-scale networks. Phys Rev E. 2007;76(3):036106.

18. Reichardt J, Bornholdt S. Statistical mechanics of community detection. Phys Rev E. 2006;74(1):016110.

19. Waltman L, van Eck NJ, Noyons EC. A unified approach to mapping and clustering of bibliometric networks. J Inform. 2010;4(4):629–35.

20. McSweeney PJ, Mehrotra K, Oh JC. A game theoretic framework for community detection. In: International conference on advances in social networks analysis and mining, ASONAM 2012, Istanbul, Turkey, 26–29 August 2012. p. 227–34.

21. Mazalov VV, Trukhina LI. Generating functions and the myerson vector in communication networks. Discrete Math Appl. 2014;24(5):295–303.

22. Mazalov VV, Avrachenkov K, Trukhina L, Tsynguev BT. Game-theoretic centrality measures for weighted graphs. Fund Inform. 2016;145(3):341–58.

23. Gomez D, González-Arangüena E, Manuel C, Owen G, del Pozo M, Tejada J. Centrality and power in social networks: a game theoretic approach. Math Soc Sci. 2003;46(1):27–54.

24. Suri NR, Narahari Y. Determining the top-k nodes in social networks using the shapley value. In: Proceedings of the 7th international joint conference on autonomous agents and multiagent systems. International foundation for autonomous agents and multiagent systems, Vol. 3, p. 1509–12.

25. Szczepański PL, Michalak T, Rahwan T. A new approach to betweenness centrality based on the shapley value. In: Proceedings of the 11th international conference on autonomous agents and multiagent systems, Vol 1, p. 239–46.

26. Michalak TP, Aadithya KV, Szczepanski PL, Ravindran B, Jennings NR. Efficient computation of the shapley value for game-theoretic network centrality. J Artif Intell Res. 2013;46:607–50.

27. Chen W, Teng S-H. Interplay between social influence and network centrality: a comparative study on shapley centrality and single-node-influence centrality. In: Proceedings of the 26th international conference on World Wide Web. International World Wide Web Conferences Steering Committee. 2017. pp. 967–6.

28. Skibski O, Michalak TP, Rahwan T. Axiomatic characterization of game-theoretic centrality. J Artif Intell Res. 2018;62:33–68.

29. Bogomolnaia A, Jackson MO. The stability of hedonic coalition structures. Games Econ Behav. 2002;38(2):201–30.

30. Fortunato S, Barthélemy M. Resolution limit in community detection. Proc Natl Acad Sci. 2007;104(1):36–41.

31. Leskovec J, Lang KJ, Dasgupta A, Mahoney MW. Community structure in large networks: natural cluster sizes and the absence of large well-defined clusters. Internet Math. 2009;6(1):29–123.

32. Hagen L, Kahng AB. New spectral methods for ratio cut partitioning and clustering. IEEE Trans Comput Aided Design Integ Circuits Syst. 1992;11(9):1074–85.

33. Shi J, Malik J. Normalized cuts and image segmentation. IEEE Trans Pattern Anal Mach Intell. 2000;22(8):888–905.

34. Zhou L, Cheng C, Lü K, Chen H. Using coalitional games to detect communities in social networks. In: International conference on web-age information management. Berlin: Springer; 2013. p. 326–31.

35. Zhou L, Lü K, Cheng C, Chen H. A game theory based approach for community detection in social networks. In: Proceedings Big Data—29th British national conference on databases, BNCOD 2013, Oxford, UK, July 8–10. 2013. p. 268–81.

36. Basu S, Maulik U. Community detection based on strong nash stable graph partition. Soci Netw Anal Mining. 2015;5(1):61.

37. Avrachenkov KE, Kondratev AY, Mazalov VV. Cooperative game theory approaches for network partitioning. In: International computing and combinatorics conference (COCOON/CSoNet). Berlin: Springer; 2017. p. 591–602.

38. Myerson RB. Game Theory. Cambridge: Harvard University Press; 2013.

39. Peleg B, Sudhölter P. Introduction to the theory of cooperative games, vol. 34. Berlin: Springer; 2007.

40. Mazalov V. Mathematical game theory and applications. New York: Wiley; 2014.

41. Myerson RB. Graphs and cooperation in games. Math Operat Res. 1977;2(3):225–9.

42. Jackson MO. Allocation rules for network games. Games Econ Behav. 2005;51(1):128–54.

43. Jackson MO. Social and economic networks. Princeton: Princeton University Press; 2010.

44. Levin DA, Peres Y, Wilmer EL. Markov chains and mixing times. Rhode Island: American Mathematical Soc., Providence; 2009.

45. Hajek B. Cooling schedules for optimal annealing. Math Operat Res. 1988;13(2):311–29.

46. Berthet Q, Rigollet P, Srivastava P. Exact recovery in the ising blockmodel. Ann Stat. 2018;41:1780.

47. Pedregosa F, Varoquaux G, Gramfort A, Michel V, Thirion B, Grisel O, Blondel M, Prettenhofer P, Weiss R, Dubourg V, Vanderplas J, Passos A, Cournapeau D, Brucher M, Perrot M, Duchesnay E. Scikit-learn: machine learning in python. J Mach Learn Res. 2011;12:2825–30.
48. Meilă M, Heckerman D. An experimental comparison of model-based clustering methods. Mach Learn. 2001;42(1–2):9–29.
49. Zachary WW. An information flow model for conflict and fission in small groups. J Anthropol Res. 1977;33(4):452–73.
50. Lusseau D, Schneider K, Boisseau OJ, Haase P, Slooten E, Dawson SM. The bottlenose dolphin community of doubtful sound features a large proportion of long-lasting associations. Behav Ecol Sociobiol. 2003;54(4):396–405.
51. Zhizhchenko AB, Izaak AD. The information system Math-Net.Ru. Application of contemporary technologies in the scientific work of mathematicians. Russian Math Surveys. 2007;62(5):943–966.

5

Influence spreading model used to analyse social networks and detect sub-communities

Vesa Kuikka[*]

*Correspondence:
vesa.kuikka@mil.fi
Finnish Defence
Research Agency, PO
BOX 10, Tykkikentäntie 1,
11311 Riihimäki, Finland

Abstract

A dynamic influence spreading model is presented for computing network central-ity and betweenness measures. Network topology, and possible directed connec-tions and unequal weights of nodes and links, are essential features of the model. The same influence spreading model is used for community detection in social networks and for analysis of network structures. Weaker connections give rise to more sub-communities whereas stronger ties increase the cohesion of a community. The validity of the method is demonstrated with different social networks. Our model takes into account different paths between nodes in the network structure. The dependency of different paths having common links at the beginning of their paths makes the model more realistic compared to classical structural, simulation and random walk models. The influence of all nodes in a network has not been satisfactorily understood. Existing models may underestimate the spreading power of interconnected peripheral nodes as initiators of dynamic processes in social, biological and technical networks.

Keywords: Social networks, Influence spreading, Network dynamics, Influence measure, Network topology, Community detection, Community structure, Closeness centrality, Betweenness centrality

Background

Social influence measures have been developed by using for example local structural characteristics [1, 2] geodesic distances [3] and random walks [4]. Most of these meas-ures don't have exact quantitative interpretations for general network structures and variable sizes of networks. Structural measures take into account local degrees of nodes in the neighbourhood of a source node. Geodesic based measures use distances from a source node. Random walks consider different paths from a source node to a target node but the method still is unsuccessful in combining the contributions from alterna-tive paths to generate an exact quantitative measure.

Models for the process by which influence or ideas propagate through a social net-work have been studied in a number of research articles for example in [5–9]. In a recent article [10] a review of theories for influencer identification in complex networks has been published. Many aspects should be considered when constructing measures for describing and comparing social networks. Several studies propose influence measures for identifying the most influential spreaders or mediators. Obviously when spreading processes are analysed the concept of time should have some kind of role in the model. Some models presented in the literature are static and don't investigate processes evolving dynamically or don't provide justification for how the models describe a steady state or limiting states of a network. Usually network structures are not calculated exactly random walk in a network is an example. One requirement for the theory is a quantitative model with natural interpretations of the variables. This guarantees that the numerical values obtained for all kinds of network topologies and different temporal spreading distributions can be compared with each other. A valid theory and an applicable model are needed to combine the spreading process evolving as a function of time and the structure of a network.

Computational difficulties must be solved in keeping track of various paths and their possible interdependencies. In large networks computing time may set practical constraints for calculations. One requirement for research of large social biological and technical networks is a scalable computing algorithm [11]. Good approximations can be achieved with limited path lengths as the rule of six degrees [12] is valid for many kinds of social networks. Limited path lengths can provide good results in community detection algorithms. In the literature many community detection algorithms take into account only local interactions [13].

Introduction

The aim of this paper is to provide answers to the requirements presented in the previous section. Possible models for describing the temporal spreading process are proposed. A method for modelling the topological structure of a network is presented. Probability theory is used for combining the spreading via all the possible paths from a source node to a target node. Possible dependencies between different paths are taken into account. With these building blocks various problems in social network analysis, and in many other fields of network science, can be solved [14–16].

We present specifications for the most important measures needed to investigate social networks. These are node level ego centric centrality and betweenness measures. Closeness centrality describes node's power to spread influence to other nodes in the network. Betweenness is a measure of the influence of nodes in a network relative to the flow of information between others. Betweenness centrality tends to pick out nodes that play the role of brokers between communities. In addition, an overall network measure, expressed as a function of time that combines different properties of the network, is presented. After all, different measures for different purposes can be constructed. For example, the concept of betweenness can be understood in many ways which makes it impossible to define one absolute betweenness measure.

We demonstrate the method with a real social network documented in the literature and compare the results with the corresponding study published recently. The same network has been investigated in [3] where a comprehensive model suitable for local and global aspects of a social network has been presented. In [3], a model with an adjustable parameter for weighting neighbouring and distant nodes in the network has been used to determine measures for centrality and betweenness.

In many networks a community structure exists, in which network nodes are connected together in groups, between which there are less connections. A number of methods and algorithms have been proposed for detecting communities in social networks, for example published in [17–23]. The research has often been focused on developing different or more efficient algorithms and different implicit or explicit definitions of community [24, 25]. As different definitions of community exist, different algorithms are needed for discovering various kinds of communities.

Some of the algorithms for detecting communities in a network structure are minimum-cut method, hierarchical clustering, Girvan–Newman algorithm, modularity maximization, statistical inference [26], and clique-based methods. Descriptions of the methods can be found for example in [13, 24, 25, 27]. Many classical algorithms for partitioning network nodes into groups are based on matrix and linear algebra methods. Examples are analogues of the Kernighan–Lin algorithm [28] for maximizing modularity and an analogue of the spectral graph partitioning [29, 30] algorithms for community detection. A definition for modularity is the fraction of the edges that fall within the given group minus the expected fraction if edges were distributed at random. The Kernighan–Lin algorithm is based on repeatedly moving, starting from some initial division, the vertices that most increase or least decrease the modularity.

The Louvain method for community detection is a greedy modularity optimization method to extract communities from large networks [31]. For investigation of large-scale biological and social community structures an information theoretic approach has been presented in [32]. Probability flow of random walks on a network is used as a proxy for information flows. There are a number of other greedy or SDP-based (semi-definite programming) approaches for finding communities in large networks [33, 34].

A classification for community discovery methods in complex networks has been presented in [24]. Eight different community discovery methods have been described in the review: feature distance, internal density, bridge detection, diffusion, closeness, structure, link clustering and meta-clustering. Altogether 39 algorithms classified in these eight categories have been described in [24]. One of the methods is more relevant from our perspective: a diffusion community in a complex network is a set of nodes that are grouped together by the propagation of the same property, action or information in the network. In [24] a meta-procedure for detecting a diffusion community has been defined: Perform a diffusion or percolation procedure on the network following a particular set of transmission rules and then group together any nodes that end up in the same state. In this respect, a community can be defined as a set of target nodes influenced by a fixed set of source nodes. In the financial networks literature, a decaying influence model describing propagation of shocks on banking networks has been studied in [35].

Outline

The focus of this paper is to present a new influence spreading model and its applications with examples. Accordingly, the main content of this study is presented in "Theory of social influence measures", "Applications of social influence measures" and "Numerical results and discussion" sections. In addition, the next section introduces classical definitions of closeness centrality and betweenness centrality as well a recent extension of the measures to consider both local and global network structure. Lastly, conclusions provide a short summary of the paper.

The theory is presented in several phases. First, information and influence propagation models are discussed. Next, the influence spreading measure between two nodes of a network is presented with the help of an example network of Dutch students' social network [3, 36]. Then follow definitions of quantities and the general method of combining paths between two nodes of a network. Temporal Spreading of Influence is a sub-model describing time dependence of the spreading process. After this, a high-level algorithm is presented for computing the influence spreading matrix describing the spreading between all nodes of a network.

Applications of the theory of Social Influence Measures are based on the Social Influence Matrix. In this part of the study, definitions of closeness centrality, betweenness centrality and community detection measures are presented.

The model is demonstrated by presenting results for closeness centrality, betweenness centrality and analysis of community structures. Closeness centrality and betweenness centrality measures are illustrated with the Dutch students' social network [3, 36]. Four different networks are used as examples for detecting communities and investigating network structures. As an introduction, an artificial network of the Game of Risk [37] is analysed. Then the 32 Dutch students' social network [36] is investigated introducing more complex structures. Next, an animal social network of dolphins [38] is analysed along with some comments on similarities and differences with respect to human social networks. The scalable version of the algorithm [11] is used for computing the influence spreading matrix for a Facebook social network of 4039 users. The matrix is used as input information for the community detection algorithm.

Geodesic based centrality and betweenness measures

Several measures of centrality and betweenness have been proposed in the literature [1, 39]. Recently, geodesic based centrality and betweenness measures, unifying the local and the global network structure, have been presented [3].

A normalized version of reciprocal closeness centrality [3, 16] is defined by

$$C_C(i) = \frac{\sum_{j \neq i} (g_{ij})^{-1}}{N-1},\tag{1}$$

where the geodesic distance g_{ij} is the distance between ego i and all its others j. N is the total number of nodes in the network. In [3] a generalization of Eq. (1) has been proposed that weights nodes at different distances depending on the value of a gradient parameter δ:

$$C_C^\delta(i) = \frac{\sum_{j \neq i} (g_{ij})^{-\delta}}{N-1},\tag{2}$$

where $\delta \geq 0$.

Classical betweenness centrality measure focuses on the power resulting from being on the shortest path among others. A node with high betweenness centrality is a broker between others in the network. This involves three actors, with the focus on actor i being on the shortest path between actors j and k. Let t_{jk} denote the total number of shortest paths connecting j to k and t_{jik} be the number of shortest paths connecting j to k that pass through i then the betweenness of i [3] is defined by

$$C_B(i) = \sum_{j<k} \left(\frac{t_{jik}}{t_{jk}} \right).$$

Again, in [3] a generalization has been proposed depending on the value of a gradient parameter δ:

$$C_B^\delta(i) = \sum_{j<k} \left(\frac{t_{jik}}{t_{jk}} \right) (g_{jk} - 1)^{-\delta}.$$

Theory of social influence measures

Information and influence propagation models

Different propagation models for influence spreading can be defined depending on the phenomena we are studying. In the context of this paper, two main issues are important. Firstly, a model has to be decided for the time distribution that describes spreading of influence from one node to another. Secondly, propagation can proceed independently of states of mediating nodes, or propagation depends on the states of the nodes along the paths between a source and a target node.

In this paper we use Poisson distribution as the time distribution for propagation between nodes. In the model, it is easy to use any statistical distribution or empirical data instead of Poisson distribution. We have made experiments with a model based on Uniform distribution. This describes, for example, propagation of information via e-mails when users process their e-mails at uniformly distributed time points during a day (or other time unit). This distribution gives comparable results, but not exactly the same, because more spreading occurs at low time values when propagation obeys Uniform instead of Poisson distribution.

The second issue, when the spreading process depends on the states of the intermediate nodes, is more involved. Dependency on static node attributes is a minor addition to the model because the model takes into account nodes and links individually. Dynamic dependency on time dependent states of nodes can be compute-intensive because simulations or iterative algorithms probably are necessary to solve the problem. In this paper, only state independent propagation models are studied. Nodes mediate influence regardless of their own state and states of all the other nodes of the network.

A realistic model for information propagation may be a state dependent variant of the model where propagation events (attempts of influence) occur only for new information (or probability for new information is higher). In other words, information is mediated to neighbouring nodes only in cases when the node is unaware of the information before the propagation event. Nodes are less willing to propagate known information than new information.

Propaganda, or other form of influence, transforms its content during the spreading process. Therefore, recurrent propagation events are more realistic. However, decreasing in amount as a function of path length limits the process. In the model of this paper, this is accomplished with combined effects of time dependency and node (and link) weighting factors. Weighting factors, that are less than one, are realistic when nodes are not fully actively propagating influence. In summary, state dependent and state independent alternatives are the following:

1. Probability of spreading influence depends on the states of nodes. Nodes along the paths between a source and a target typically are less eager to mediate information already known.
2. In the state independent model, propagation occurs independently of nodes' states. The probability to receive and forward influence is determined by the time dependent probability, node weighting factor and link weighting factor.

In our model nodes are assumed to be memoryless. Receiving an attempt to influence node's state and propagating this event forward are assumed to have delays according to the temporal distribution, e.g. Poisson distribution.

1. In summary, the propagation model has the following characteristics: temporal distribution describes node's delays between receiving an influence spreading event and forwarding the event to neighbouring nodes. Links between nodes have no delays.
2. Node weighting factor $w_{N=i}$ for node i describes node i's activity, that is, the probability of forwarding an event of influence to neighbouring nodes. Similarly, link weighting factors $w_{L=i,j}$ are additional factors needed in cases where the influence spreading between nodes i and j are not equal for all the directed links between nodes of the network.
3. The spreading process is assumed to start from one node in the network at time $T = 0$.

Influence spreading measure between two nodes

Example network

In this section, we illustrate mathematical methods of modelling influence spreading measures $C_{s,t}(T)$ between a source node s and a target node t in a small social network at time T. Based on these results, new measures of centrality, betweenness and community detection are defined.

The method aims at solving the requirements explained in the "Background" section. As the recent study in [3] has similarities and many common objectives, we use the same social network of 32 Dutch students [36]. This gives us the possibility to compare the numerical results between the two models. The network is shown in Fig. 1.

Our method takes into account all the possible self-avoiding paths in the network. The generalization including paths allowing nodes to appear several times in a path

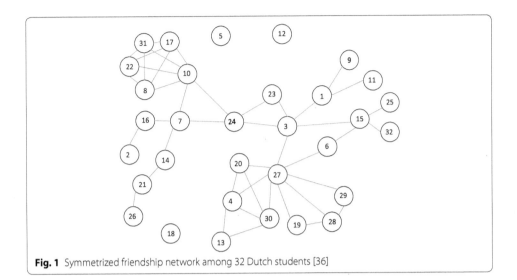

Fig. 1 Symmetrized friendship network among 32 Dutch students [36]

Table 1 The 14 paths from Node 1 to Node 4 of the network in Fig. 1

#	Nodes in a path							
1	1	3	15	6	27	4		
2	1	3	15	6	27	20	4	
3	1	3	15	6	27	20	30	4
4	1	3	15	6	27	20	30	13	4
5	1	3	15	6	27	30	4	
6	1	3	15	6	27	30	13	4
7	1	3	15	6	27	30	20	4
8	1	3	27	4				
9	1	3	27	20	4			
10	1	3	27	20	30	4		
11	1	3	27	20	30	13	4	
12	1	3	27	30	4			
13	1	3	27	30	13	4		
14	1	3	27	30	20	4		

is possible and easy to compute [11]. However, then we must have a limit for path lengths or for the number of possible occurrences on the path. This method requires less computer memory because the list paths need not to be saved in computer memory. For large networks the number of different paths is high and saving memory is important. Self-avoiding paths are suitable for the purposes of presenting the method. Later in this paper, results for a larger social network of 4039 Facebook users will be provided where influence propagation via paths with loops is considered.

As an example, all the self-avoiding paths of the network of Fig. 1 from Node 1 to Node 4 are listed Table 1. As all the paths pass through Node 3, all the 14 paths have dependencies with each other. They have the common link 1–3 from Node 1 to Node

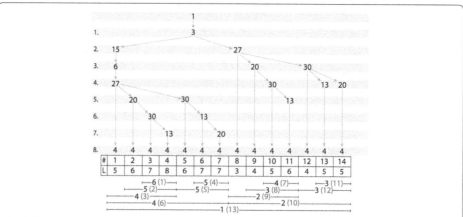

Fig. 2 The 14 paths from Node 1 to Node 4 presented as a hierarchical tree. Nodes of the paths are shown in the tree. The first line (#) indicates the running number of the paths and the second line (L) shows the path lengths. In the lower part of the figure the order of calculation is shown in parenthesis, after a number giving the length of common paths in combing the paths, indicated by the line segments

3. The same procedure of finding common paths at the beginning of different paths originating from a source node to a target node is used iteratively. Figure 2 shows the paths of Table 1 in another format.

To be precise, we present below in Eq. (4) all the steps of computing the probability of influence spreading from Node 1 to Node 4. We denote intermediate steps by subscripts in parentheses. For example, in the first step, $P_{(1)}$ is the combined result of paths 1-3-15-6-27-20-30-4 and 1-3-15-6-27-20-30-13-4 with path lengths 7 and 8 and common path length 6. The steps of the computing algorithm are shown in parenthesis in Fig. 2. The last step in Eq. (4) denoted by $G_{1,4,(1)}$ gives the final result of the influence of Node 1 on Node 4.

In the following, we use the short hand notations $C_6 = $ 1-3-15-6-27-20-30, $B_1 = $ 30-4, and $B_2 = $ 30-13-4 and denote the conditional probabilities by $P_1(B_1|C_6)$ and $P_2(B_2|C_6)$. Also, time variable T is omitted. For example, $P_1(B_1|C_6)$ is the probability that the spreading goes through one link more (path B_1) after the spreading has already propagated through six links (path C_6). The justification for the first equation $P_{(1)}$ follows from the following probabilistic formula:

$$
\begin{aligned}
P_{(1)} &= P_6(C_6)[P_1(B_1|C_6) + P_2(B_2|C_6) - P_1(B_1|C_6)P_2(B_2|C_6)] \\
&= P_6(C_6)P_1(B_1|C_6) + P_6(C_6)P_2(B_2|C_6) - \frac{P_6(C_6)P_1(B_1|C_6)P_6(C_6)P_2(B_2|C_6)}{P_6(C_6)}.
\end{aligned}
\tag{3}
$$

Below, all the intermediate steps of computing the influence of Node 1 on Node 4 are shown. We present only one example of the algorithm as this makes it possible to write the equations for all the connections between all the nodes in a network. We have developed a computer programme for finding all the possible paths and computing the probabilities according to the theory. In the programme, maximum path lengths can be used to limit the computing time. For typical small social networks presented in the literature, there is no need to limit the path lengths. In larger networks the results converge rapidly and a reasonable limit (for example, path lengths between 6 and 10) can be used to get good approximations.

$$
\begin{aligned}
P_{(1)} &= P_7 + P_8 - \frac{P_7 P_8}{P_6} & P_{(2)} &= P_{(1)} + P_6 - \frac{P_{(1)} P_6}{P_5} \\
P_{(3)} &= P_{(2)} + P_5 - \frac{P_{(2)} P_5}{P_4} & P_{(4)} &= P_7 + P_7 - \frac{P_7 P_7}{P_5} \\
P_{(5)} &= P_6 + P_{(4)} - \frac{P_6 P_{(4)}}{P_5} & P_{(6)} &= P_{(3)} + P_{(5)} - \frac{P_{(3)} P_{(5)}}{P_4} \\
P_{(7)} &= P_5 + P_6 - \frac{P_5 P_6}{P_4} & P_{(8)} &= P_4 + P_{(7)} - \frac{P_4 P_{(7)}}{P_3} \\
P_{(9)} &= P_3 + P_{(8)} - \frac{P_3 P_{(8)}}{P_2} & P_{(10)} &= P_{(9)} + P_{(12)} - \frac{P_{(9)} P_{(12)}}{P_2} \\
P_{(11)} &= P_5 + P_5 - \frac{P_5 P_5}{P_3} & P_{(12)} &= P_4 + P_{(11)} - \frac{P_4 P_{(11)}}{P_3} \\
G_{1,4,(1)} &= P_{(13)} = P_{(6)} + P_{(10)} - \frac{P_{(6)} P_{(10)}}{P_1}
\end{aligned}
\tag{4}
$$

In the example of computing the influence of Node 1 on Node 4 all the paths go through Node 3 (link 1–3). If we consider the influence of Node 3 on Node 4, we observe from Fig. 1 that two independent possibilities occur, via links 3–27 and 3–15–6–27. In this particular case, these two contributions are denoted by $G_{3,4,(1)}$ and $G_{3,4,(2)}$. In the following, we denote the number of possible independent contributions by $\mathcal{I}$.

Combining paths between two nodes

Next, we present the general formulation of the theory. In Eq. (5) $G_{n,j,(x)}(w, T)$, $x = 1, \ldots, \mathcal{I}$ describe independent contributions computed with the algorithm. Combining all the independent contributions of Node n on Node j we get:

$$
C_{n,j}(w, T) = 1 - \prod_{x=1}^{\mathcal{I}} \left(1 - G_{n,j,(x)}(w, T)\right), \quad n, j = 1, \ldots, N,
\tag{5}
$$

where $G_{n,j,(x)}(w, T)$ is the probability of spreading from Node n to Node j via Link (x), where (x) denotes an index of the $\mathcal{I}$ links originating form Node n (degree of Node n) at time T. In Eq. (5) node and link weighting factors along the path from Node n to Node j are denoted by vector $w = (w_N, w_L)$ (see Eq. 6), and N is the number of nodes in the network.

Computing $G_{n,j,(x)}(w, T)$ requires searching all the different paths from Node n to Node j with path lengths less than an upper limit $L_{\max}$. Parameter $L_{\max}$ is the maximum path length and it is used to restrict the number of paths and computing time in large networks. Searching the paths is a straightforward task by using the network topology information by following links between the source node and target nodes. The computation is conducted simultaneously from one source node to all the nodes in the network. The algorithm for computing $G_{n,j,(x)}(w, T)$ handles the paths in the descending order of the number of common links at their beginning among the set of paths from Node n to Node j. A simple method would be first to list all the paths and then compute the influence spreading matrix $C_{n,j}(w, T)$, $\quad n, j = 1, \ldots, N$.

The most time consuming task, when computing self-avoiding paths, is keeping track of nodes and rejecting paths where a node appears more than once. This is the reason why the algorithm relaxing the condition of self-avoidance and allowing loops has significantly lower computer running times, essential for large social networks [11].

Weighting factors describe probability of propagating information and opinions. We call this the activity of nodes (or links). Opinion changes in social networks are uncommon when the new ideas are unfamiliar to members of a social network. (To be precise, we should make a difference between influence spreading and opinion spreading. These concepts are related but usually different parameters are needed. Even a different spreading model may be needed, if probability to change opinion is conditional on information or influence spreading events). Technical and biological networks have similar commonalities. Spreading of a computer virus or a biological virus between nodes can have a low probability because of virus protection, vaccination or characteristics of the virus itself.

We illustrate the propagation rules with an example of combining two paths. Also, the effects of node and link weighting factors are shown explicitly. In the algorithm any number of paths can be combined iteratively by using the same method. Combining the effects of different paths between two nodes is computed in the descending order of common path lengths of paths starting from the initial node. Only these common links and nodes are taken into account. If the paths join later or cross each other, they are considered independent events. The probability of influence spreading from Node s to Node t via path of lengths L_1 is

$$C_{s,t}(T) = w_{N=t} W_{L_1} D_{L_1}(T), \tag{6}$$

where

$$W_{L_1} = \prod_{j=0}^{L_1-1} w_{N=I(j)} w_{L=I(j),I(j+1)},$$

where w_N are node weighting factors, w_L are link weighting factors, and $D_L(T)$ is the time dependence of influence spreading process (see $D_L(T)$ in Eq. (8) for Poisson distribution). Function $I(j)$, $j = 0, \ldots, L_1$ maps index j, describing the order of nodes on the path from Node s to Node t, to the unique indexing $\{1, \ldots, N\}$ of all nodes in the network. For example, $s = I(0)$ and $t = I(L_1)$. In our calculations we will use for the first node the activity value of $w_s = 1$. The first node initiates the influence propagation process at time $T = 0$. $D_{L_1}(T)$ is the probability of influence propagation via single path length L_1 during time interval $[0, T]$. Note that in Eq. (6) node and link weights are not included in $D_{L_1}(T)$.

$D_{L_1}(T)$ can be expressed as $D_{L_1}(T) = D_L(T)D_{L_1-L}(T)$, where $D_{L_1-L}(T)$ is the conditional probability of forwarding an influence spreading event via path length $L_1 - L$, given that the event has passed via path length L before that during $[0, T]$. Similarly, W_{L_1} can be expressed as $W_{L_1} = W_L w_m W_{L_1-L}$, where w_m is the node weighting factor of the last node m of the path of length L. Next we assume that influence events can propagate via two routes of lengths L_1 and L_2 with a common path of length L at their beginning. If the paths join later, we assume that they are independent attempts of influence. In the model, we get for the probability of influence spreading via the two routes:

$$C_{s,t}(T) = w_t w_m W_L D_L(T)\big(W_{L_1-L}D_{L_1-L}(T) + W_{L_2-L}D_{L_2-L}(T) - W_{L_1-L}D_{L_1-L}(T)W_{L_2-L}D_{L_2-L}(T)\big)$$
$$= P_{L_1}(T) + P_{L_2}(T) - \frac{P_{L_1}(T)P_{L_2}(T)}{P_L(T)}, \tag{7}$$

where a shorter notation $P_{L_i}(T)$ is used for $w_t W_{L_i} D_{L_i}(T)$ describing the probability of influence propagation over the path of length L_i. In following sections, the algorithm is demonstrated with a more general example of a real-life social network.

At the beginning of this section, Eq. (5) describes non-mutually exclusive events in basic probability theory. It serves as an introduction between commonly known methods of probability and the method of this study for combining probabilities of influence spreading via different paths in a network. In fact, Eq. (5) is the last step in the algorithm with $L = 0$ and $P_L(T) = 1$ in Eq. (7). As a consequence, we could have omitted Eq. (5) because it can be regarded as the last step of the general algorithm.

Temporal spreading distribution

Before we can compute numerically the contributions of different paths of a network, we must have a model for the probabilities $D_L(T)$ of temporal spreading on a chain of nodes. The number of links from a source node to a target node (path length) is denoted by L. Assuming Poisson distribution the probability of at least L events occurring is:

$$D_L(T) = P(K(T) \geq L) = 1 - \sum_{z=0}^{L-1} e^{-\lambda T}\frac{(\lambda T)}{z!}, (D_0 = 1). \tag{8}$$

Here, the interpretation is that the spreading has advanced L or more links in the network at time T. Equation (8) takes into account nodes' delays between receiving an influence spreading event and forwarding the event to neighbouring nodes. When time approaches infinity, nodes' probability of spreading influence approaches one. In Eq. (8), the number of spreading events is denoted by stochastic variable $K(T)$. The intensity parameter of Poisson distribution is denoted by λ. The statistical distribution and its parameters determine the spreading rate in the network. The Poisson distribution is not the only possibility, for example, a model based on Uniform distribution may better describe some other temporal spreading behaviour.

Parameter λ can be estimated from empirical influence propagation data. In most cases, this kind of time dependent information is not available. If empirical data are not available, the intensity parameter could be evaluated by comparing with analyses of other networks with comparable level of development. Values of λ and time T are related in Eq. (8), and also the quantity λT can be estimated. It describes the maturity level of propagation on the network. In practice, evaluating the model parameters is not simple because nodes may have individual characteristics. But if these kind of empirical data are available, the model can be used with different parameters for each node and link of the network. In addition, the stochastic distribution of Eq. (8) can be replaced by an empirical distribution.

Algorithm for computing the influence spreading matrix

An algorithm for computing the values of bidirectional influence measures [11] between all the pairs of nodes in a network is presented. These values make up a $N \times N$ dimensional influence spreading matrix, were N is the number of nodes in the network. The matrix is computed for discrete spreading time values of interest. Closeness centrality, betweenness centrality and community detection measure are defined with the help of the matrix elements. The algorithm for computing the influence spreading matrix $C_{s,t}(T)$, $s,t = 1,\ldots,N$ is described below. Comments in the algorithm below are denoted by '/* */'.

Variables:
G = the nodes in the network
L_{max} = Max path length
C_{prev} = Auxilary list that contains the influence spreading values from the previous iteration of path length
C_{curr} = Influence spreading values to a node in G with different values of T
$model\_values$ = List of values obtained by computing $P(L, T, \lambda)$
$Timesteps$ = List of time values T
$C_{s,t}$ = Influence spreading matrix

Algorithm:

for every node *n* in *G* {

    Assign value 0 to every index used in C_{prev}

    for ($L := L_{max}$; $L \geq 0$; $L := L - 1$) {

        Assign value 0 to every index used in C_{curr}

        for every value in *Timesteps* as *T* {

$$P(L, T, \lambda) := 1 - \sum_{i=0}^{L-1} e^{-1} \frac{(\lambda T)^i}{i!}$$

            Store value of *P(L, T, λ)* in *model_values*

            Store value of *P(L, T, λ)* in $C_{curr}[n][T]$

        }

        for every node *f* in *G* {

            for every neighbour node *t* from *f* {

                w := node & link weight value from *f* to *t*

                /* Update the influence spreading value from node *f* to node *t* for each time step */

                for every *model_values* as *v* and *Timesteps* as *T* {

$$C_{curr}[f][T] := C_{curr}[f][T] + w * C_{prev}[t][T] - \frac{C_{curr}[f][T] * w * Cprev[t][T]}{v}$$

                }

            }

        }

        /* Copy values from C_{curr} to C_{prev} */

        $C_{prev} := C_{curr}$

    }

    Add influence spreading values to $C_{s,t}$, obtained from C_{curr}

}

The applicability of shortest-path-based centralities is limited by the high computational complexity of calculating the shortest paths between all pairs of nodes [10]. A generalization of closeness centrality [40] considers all paths in the network and assigns a larger weight to shorter paths using a tuneable parameter. The method presented in this paper considers all the paths in a network with an additional feature of modelling common links of the paths at the beginning of their routes from a source node to target nodes.

Most of the results of this paper are for self-avoiding paths. A self-avoiding path is a sequence of moves on a path that does not visit the same node more than once. The networks of this paper are selected for illustrative purposes and therefore are small when compared with many modern applications and interests of research.

Table 2 Computing times of the fast algorithm [11] for large social media networks

Social media	Nodes	Links	Computing time
Facebook	4039	88,234	1 min
Twitter	81,306	1,768,149	5 h
Google+	107,614	13,673,453	4 days

With this in mind, a fast algorithm has been developed for analysing large social networks. In [11] large scale social networks of Facebook, Twitter and Google+ have been investigated. Computing times with a PC hardware (Core2 Duo E7503) of closeness centralities for all the nodes in the networks are shown in Table 2.

The algorithm, especially suitable for influence spreading modelling of social networks, allows returns to nodes during the spreading process. The design of the algorithm is based on this property. In fact, disallowing loops would make the algorithm in [11] slower. The value of maximum path length L_{max} can be set to 20 because higher terms are negligible for typical temporal spreading distributions. Lower values are used if they describe the real-world phenomenon by limiting the spreading process to shorter path lengths.

Applications of social influence measures
Definition of closeness centrality measures

In the following we use both normalized and un-normalized versions of centrality and betweenness measures. Normalized measures are divided by the number of nodes N of the network. These measures have a natural interpretation, normalized measures are probabilities and un-normalized measures are expressed in the units of number of nodes.

Equations (9), (10) and (11) are proposed measures for source centrality, target centrality and betweenness correspondingly. Usually, these measures are highly correlated, for example, Eqs. (9) and (10) can be regarded as two different viewpoints of node's centrality in the network. The measure in Eq. (9) has the summation over target nodes instead of the summation over source nodes in Eq. (10). The interpretation of Eq. (9) is a measure of influence of Node n on all other nodes in the network. The measure of Eq. (10) describes the influence of all the nodes of the network on Node m.

$$\frac{C_{n,\cdot}(w, T)}{N} = c_{n,\cdot}(w, T) = \frac{1}{N} \sum_{j=1}^{N} C_{n,j}(w, T) \tag{9}$$

$$\frac{C_{\cdot,m}(w, T)}{N} = c_{\cdot,m}(w, T) = \frac{1}{N} \sum_{i=1}^{N} C_{i,m}(w, T) \tag{10}$$

In Eqs. (9, 10) $C_{i,j}$ is defined in Eq. (5) or equivalently in Eq. (7) and T is time. In the next sections, the measure in Eq. (9) is regarded as the default viewpoint and we denote $C_{n,\cdot}$ by C_n as a short hand notation. From Eqs. (9, 10) a cohesion measure describing the two aspects of these equations can be defined:

$$\frac{C(w, T)}{N} = c(w, T) = \frac{1}{N} \sum_{i=1}^{N} c_{i,\cdot}(w, T) = \frac{1}{N} \sum_{j=1}^{N} c_{\cdot,j}(w, T) \tag{11}$$

Definition of betweenness centrality measures

The idea of defining betweenness measures is based on removing one node form the network. In Eq. (12) Node n is removed from the network and after that the betweenness measure for Node n is calculated in a consistent way with Eqs. (9, 10). We denote $n \notin V$ indicating that Node n is removed from the network. Note that any order of summations in Eq. (12) provides the same results. This is a desirable feature of a betweenness measure. In other words, source nodes and target nodes are in a symmetric position. The measure of Eq. (12) describes the betweenness of Node n in the network.

$$\frac{B_n(w, T)}{N} = \frac{1}{N^2} \sum_{\substack{i = 1 \\ n \notin V}}^{N} \sum_{\substack{j = 1 \\ n \notin V}}^{N} \left(1 - \prod_{x=1}^{\mathcal{J}} \left(1 - G_{i,j,(x)}(w, T)\right)\right) \tag{12}$$

In the definition of Eqs. (9–12) normalization is a question. We have decided to include source nodes with the value of 1.0 in the formulas and as a result of that N is used as a normalization factor. The source node is assumed to be the initiator of influence spreading with probability 1.0.

We can define another measure by dividing Eq. (12) by Eq. (11). This ratio gives the proportional quantity of Eq. (13):

$$R_n(w, T) = \frac{B_n(w, T)}{C(w, T)} \tag{13}$$

Both Eqs. (12) and (13) preserve the same rankings of nodes in the network. The interpretation is that the lowest curve has the highest betweenness. Further, we define a betweenness centrality measure with the help of Eq. (12) as

$$b_n = 1 - R_n(w, T) = \frac{C(w, T) - B_n(w, T)}{C(w, T)}, \tag{14}$$

where $C(w, T)$ is the cohesion measure from Eq. (11) for the whole network. According to Eq. (14) the highest curve has the highest betweenness. In this respect, Eq. (14) is more intuitive and the numerical values from Eq. (14) might be easier to compare with Eqs. (9, 10).

Definition and algorithm for computing a community detection measure

The algorithm for community detection uses the influence measures $C_{s,t}$, $s, t = 1, \ldots, N$ of Eq. (5) [equivalently in Eq. (7)]. The general method can be used also with other centrality measures presented in the literature. The idea in modelling community detection is based on the concept of node's role in the network as a source and a target of influence. Both of these aspects have a role in community formation. Two sub-communities in a social network are detected by searching local maxima of Eq. (15):

$$P(V, \bar{V}) = \sum_{i,t \in V} C_{s,t} + \sum_{i,t \in \bar{V}} C_{s,t}, \tag{15}$$

where V and $\bar{V}$ is the split into two factions of the network of N nodes with $N = N_V + N_{\bar{V}}$. We assume that these roles have equal importance in community formation. The community detection algorithm used in this study searches local maxima of Eq. (15) moving nodes, one at a time, that most increase the measure used for optimizing the division, between these factions.

Similarly, the classical Kernighan–Lin algorithm [28] is based on moving nodes between two factions of a network. However, Kernighan–Lin algorithm searches a community of pre-determined size and provides no sub-structures. In addition, the model of this paper calculates influence between all the nodes of the network as a function of time. Instead, the Kernighan–Lin algorithm is based on modularity maximization of the community and local topology of the network when determining which nodes to exchange between the two factions. Other community detection methods have been reviewed in [13], where strengths and weaknesses of modern methods are pointed out, and directions given to their use.

Typically, social networks with weak interactions between nodes, or social networks in their early development phases, have several local maxima with different compositions. These factions can overlap with each other. In many cases, unions and intersections of the divisions are also local maxima of Eq. (15) with some parameters of the model. If a union or intersection is not identified as a local maximum, these sets of nodes could still be considered as possible sub-groups of the network. In dynamic community building processes sets of nodes divided by different community boundaries may be left as outsiders. This is more probable if the measure of Eq. (15) has a low value or several divisions have almost equal numerical values.

Computing the community detection measure of Eq. (15) can be time consuming for large networks. This is a cost of considering influence spreading globally in the network. Several methods can be used to optimize the algorithm. First, limiting the computation to local nodes is an obvious alternative. Further, if a limited sub-set of the network is of interest, approximations can be computed by considering only the selected sub-set and some neighbouring nodes and structures around it.

The method for community detection consists of two independent main algorithms. The first algorithm is optimized for describing social influence spreading. The scalable version of the algorithm [11] allows loops in the process of influence spreading. The second algorithm uses results of the first algorithm. The input for the second algorithm is $N \times N$ matrix $C_{s,t}$ at time T, and control variables, if the analysis is limited to a specified portion of the network. This is relevant when very large social networks are investigated or a particular set of members of the social network are under investigation. Because the first algorithm is able to deal with large networks up to 100,000 nodes, matrix $C_{s,t}$ is usually computed for the entire network.

The default procedure is to compute $C_{s,t}$ for all the nodes of the network $(s, t = 1, \ldots, N)$ and compute all the communities and sub-communities for the entire network (Step 1 below). From these results analysis and visualization can be focused on different sub-sets of the network (Step 2 below).

1. Compute the influence matrix $C_{s,t}$, $s, t = 1, \ldots, N$. Closeness and betweenness centrality measures are results of this step.

2. Compute the list of communities and sub-communities. Communities and their nested and overlapping structures are analysed.

Next, we present a basic version of the second algorithm for community detection.

1. Randomize values of vector V of N elements. Vector N has elements of zeros and ones.
2. Use $V(n)$, $n = 1,\dots,N$ as the initial state of the network. If $V(n)$ is one, node n belongs to the first faction of the division, and if $V(n)$ is zero n belongs to the complement of the faction.
3. Compute the community detection measure P of Eq. (15). Denote the value of the initial state by P_0.
4. Starting from Node 1 move nodes from one faction to the other. Denote the value of P by P_i for ith move.
5. If the value of P_i is higher than P_{i-1} move the node to the other faction, in other cases don't move the node.
6. After all the nodes of the network have been computed, start from Step 4 again.
7. Repeat Step 6 while the value of P is increasing else a local maximum has been found.
8. Repeat Steps 1–7 until a desired number of local maxima, or no new compositions, are found.
9. Analyse the list of detected communities. The list has the following information for every detected community: the value of P, sizes of the two communities, and the list of nodes for the detected communities. Nested and overlapping structures are discovered from the list of nodes.

A method to optimize the algorithm is to compute the list of communities in two phases. After detecting a desired number of communities with the basic algorithm, nested community structures are considered. In the second phase, in Step 2, the algorithm uses interceptions $C_i - C_j$ of detected communities C_i and their detected sub-communities C_j, where $C_j \in C_i$. The intersections are often sub-communities or they are close to a composition of a sub-community. This makes computing times shorter because Steps 6 and 7 are less iterated.

Secondary effects between the two factions are included when computing the individual influence measure of Eq. (6). A variant of the model, would compute the two factions separately. This may better describe situations of the original social network splitting into two independent networks. The model presented in this paper is proposed for studying existing sub-communities and structures of a social network where interactions between sub-communities are continuous.

Numerical results and discussion

Numerical results for the centrality measure of Eq. (9) and the betweenness measures of Eqs. (12–14) are compared with the results of [3]. The betweenness measures of Eqs. (12–14) are defined with the help of removing one node from a network. This ensures that the closeness centrality and betweenness measures are consistent with each other. The method of community detection measure is also based on the same

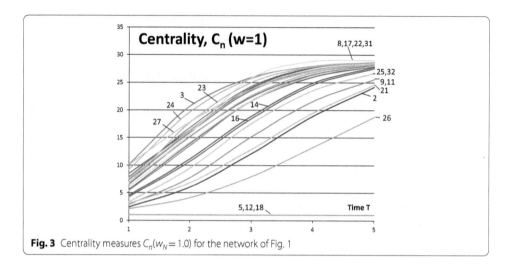

Fig. 3 Centrality measures $C_n(w_N = 1.0)$ for the network of Fig. 1

formulation. Results of analysing community structures of four different networks are presented after the results for closeness centrality and betweenness centrality.

Closeness centrality

First, we investigate the centrality measures C_n of Eq. (9) and, later in the text, compare the results with Eq. (2) in [3]. Figure 3 shows the results of Eq. (9) as a function of time T. In this paper, the convention of value 1.0 is used for the node itself (in [3]) the contribution of the node itself is 0.0). This a matter of convention, the main results presented in this paper remain the same. It is a straight forward task to convert the numerical values between the two conventions. With full activity nodes ($w_N = 1.0$) all the centrality measures C_n start from the value of one and approach the number of nodes in the network $N = 32$ with different rates depending on nodes' positions in the network structure. Exceptions are the isolated nodes whose centrality value from Eq. (9) is constant 1.0.

Table 4 documents the values of centrality measure of Eq. (9) when the weighting factor is $w_N = 1.0$ and Table 5 documents the corresponding results when $w_N = 0.5$. In Table 4 centrality measures are listed when time $T = 1, 3, 5$ and in Table 5 when $T = 1, 3, 10$. The results are shown in the order of node numbers to help comparison with the results in [3]. The right hand side of the tables shows the rankings of nodes. Tables 3 and 4 correspond to Figs. 3 and 4 in the sense that the results of the tables can be found in the figures at the time points T given in the tables.

When $w_N = 1.0$ and time $T = 1$ Nodes 3, 27 and 24 are the most central. Soon after, Node 24 is more central than Node 27. After time $T = 3$ Nodes {8, 17, 22, 31} are the most central nodes. These four nodes are in symmetrical positions in the network (indicated by the curly brackets) and have equal centrality values. These examples show that the most central nodes may change during the influence spreading process. This is a consequence of the network structure. At an early phase of the process Node 27 is more central because the spreading has just started and direct connections from the source node are emphasized. Node 27 has a high degree value of 8. Later Node 24 is more important in a central position between far away parts of the network even if its degree is only 4. The ranking of Node 27 is falling rapidly. Node 10 has similar changes but later

Table 3 Computing times of the community detection algorithm for searching 100 communities or sub-communities

Social media	Nodes	Links	Computing time
Facebook	4039	88,234	1 min
Enron e-mail	36,692	183,831	6 h

Table 4 Results $C_n(w_N = 1.0, T)$ from Eq. (9)

n	$w_N = 1.0$					
	$C_n, T=1$	$C_n, T=3$	$C_n, T=5$	Ranking, $T=1$	Ranking, $T=3$	Ranking, $T=5$
1	0.173	0.677	0.872	3	3	8
2	0.075	0.378	0.756	27	8	17
3	0.317	0.810	0.896	24	17	22
4	0.238	0.744	0.888	10	22	31
5	0.031	0.031	0.031	7	31	24
6	0.204	0.700	0.880	4	24	23
7	0.244	0.759	0.895	30	23	10
8	0.214	0.807	0.906	20	7	3
9	0.089	0.473	0.800	15	10	7
10	0.264	0.751	0.896	8	4	4
11	0.089	0.473	0.800	17	30	30
12	0.031	0.031	0.031	22	27	20
13	0.168	0.678	0.869	31	20	15
14	0.140	0.590	0.868	28	15	27
15	0.215	0.736	0.886	23	28	28
16	0.132	0.576	0.861	6	6	6
17	0.214	0.807	0.906	19	19	19
18	0.031	0.031	0.031	29	29	29
19	0.191	0.678	0.877	1	13	1
20	0.230	0.737	0.888	13	1	13
21	0.095	0.402	0.769	14	14	14
22	0.214	0.807	0.906	16	16	16
23	0.208	0.782	0.896	25	25	25
24	0.287	0.804	0.897	32	32	32
25	0.103	0.548	0.835	21	9	9
26	0.065	0.249	0.586	9	11	11
27	0.315	0.744	0.886	11	21	21
28	0.211	0.707	0.884	2	2	2
29	0.191	0.678	0.877	26	26	26
30	0.238	0.744	0.888	5	5	5
31	0.214	0.807	0.906	12	12	12
32	0.103	0.548	0.835	18	18	18

at time $T = 5$ it is rising again because of the highly connected group of four Nodes {8, 17, 22, 31}.

We may be interested also about the least central nodes. Obviously, the isolate Nodes 5, 12 and 18 are the least central. Nodes 26 and 2 follow in this order. Next Nodes {9, 11} and 21 at time $T = 1$ and Nodes 21 and {9, 11} at times $T = 3, 5$ follow. Again network topology has its implications: Nodes 9 and 11 get benefits from their better connectivity

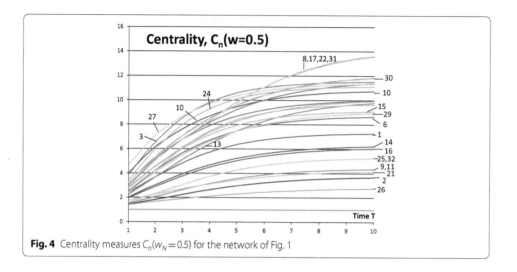

Fig. 4 Centrality measures $C_n(w_N = 0.5)$ for the network of Fig. 1

at later development phases of the influence spreading. Curly brackets indicate that Nodes 9 and 11 are at symmetrical positions in the network structure.

Next, we examine whether less active nodes in the network behave in a similar way. In Fig. 4 the values of the centrality measure of Eq. (9) with node activities $w_N = 0.5$ are shown. The same results and rankings at times $T = 1, 3, 10$ are listed in Table 5. The role of the highly connected group of Nodes {8, 17, 22, 31} is even more emphasized at a later time $T > 6$ but their role is less important at the beginning of the influence spreading process. We make a conclusion that peripheral interconnected nodes' centrality at high values of time (near equilibrium state) is relatively higher for low activity networks than for high activity networks.

Table 6 reiterates some results from Table 1 in [3] in the same format as in Tables 3 and 4 of this paper. Columns show the results of Eq. (2) when $\delta = 5, 1, 0.5$. Nodes at a longer geodesic distance become less important for high values of δ [3]. This is the reason for presenting the results in this order to help comparing with the results of this paper when time T increases. Note that the numerical values cannot be compared directly because of the different definitions of measures in Eqs. (2) and (9).

To compare the results we try to find corresponding columns from the tables. This is not exactly unambiguous because the functional relationship between δ in Eq. (2) and T in Eq. (9) is not known. Probably, no exact functional form exists because the structure of a network can produce complex effects on the functional form. We provide an example how the results can be compared. The results are remarkably similar when the rankings of the most central nodes are compared. However, there are some distinctive differences.

Because development phase of the social network is not known, it is not possible to determine the time value T. We could examine all the possible time values T and compare with the results from Eq. (2) with all the possible values of δ. On the other hand, Eq. (2) is not describing dynamic development of the spreading process. The model of this paper is dynamic and the model of [3] is static. As a consequence, full analysis is not necessary. Instead we give an example that illuminates some similarities and differences of the results. For comparison, we choose one value of δ. Then we

Table 5 Results $C_n(w_N = 0.5, T)$ from Eq. (9)

n	$w_N = 0.5$					
	$C_n, T = 1$	$C_n, T = 3$	$C_n, T = 10$	Ranking, $T = 1$	Ranking, $T = 3$	Ranking, $T = 10$
1	0.074	0.151	0.227	27	27	8
2	0.045	0.070	0.115	10	3	17
3	0.121	0.267	0.359	3	24	22
4	0.101	0.221	0.369	24	10	31
5	0.031	0.031	0.031	4	4	4
6	0.078	0.177	0.270	30	30	30
7	0.098	0.211	0.311	8	20	3
8	0.100	0.211	0.426	17	7	20
9	0.047	0.082	0.136	22	8	27
10	0.125	0.238	0.336	31	17	24
11	0.047	0.082	0.136	7	22	10
12	0.031	0.031	0.031	20	31	7
13	0.069	0.160	0.306	15	28	28
14	0.063	0.124	0.194	28	23	13
15	0.088	0.188	0.284	6	15	23
16	0.061	0.118	0.188	19	6	15
17	0.100	0.211	0.426	29	19	19
18	0.031	0.031	0.031	1	29	29
19	0.076	0.172	0.280	23	13	6
20	0.093	0.212	0.356	13	1	1
21	0.054	0.085	0.130	14	14	14
22	0.100	0.211	0.426	16	16	16
23	0.074	0.190	0.301	21	25	25
24	0.107	0.249	0.347	25	32	32
25	0.050	0.096	0.164	32	21	9
26	0.044	0.059	0.086	9	9	11
27	0.145	0.271	0.354	11	11	21
28	0.085	0.192	0.311	2	2	2
29	0.076	0.172	0.279	26	26	26
30	0.101	0.221	0.369	5	5	5
31	0.100	0.211	0.426	12	12	12
32	0.050	0.096	0.096	18	18	18

search from Tables 3 and 4 time values (columns) that provide roughly the same rankings of the most central nodes and conclude that these time values correspond to the results from Eq. (2) with the value of δ.

The first line in Table 7 shows the ranking results from Eq. (2) [3] with the parameter value of $\delta = 0.5$. Results from Eq. (9) of this paper are shown on the second line with the parameter values of $w_N = 1.0$ and $T = 1$ and on the third line with $w_N = 0.5$ and $T = 3$. These two lines approximately correspond to the first line. It is noticeable that in an active network with $w_N = 1.0$ a shorter development time T, compared with a less active network with $w_N = 0.5$, is required to achieve approximately the same rankings of central nodes in the network. The group of highly interconnected

Table 6 Results of generalized closeness centrality with different from Table 1 in [3]

n	$\delta=5$	$\delta=1$	$\delta=0.5$	Ranking, $\delta=5$	Ranking, $\delta=1$	Ranking, $\delta=0.5$
1	0.103	0.354	0.548	27	27	3
2	0.034	0.227	0.439	10	3	27
3	0.175	0.469	0.635	3	24	24
4	0.135	0.355	0.539	24	10	10
5	0.000	0.000	0.000	7	7	7
6	0.074	0.339	0.534	4	15	15
7	0.138	0.396	0.578	15	23	23
8	0.132	0.327	0.516	30	4	1
9	0.035	0.257	0.469	8	30	4
10	0.199	0.415	0.586	17	1	30
11	0.035	0.257	0.469	22	20	6
12	0.000	0.000	0.000	31	6	20
13	0.067	0.267	0.469	20	28	28
14	0.07	0.305	0.506	1	8	8
15	0.135	0.376	0.561	28	17	17
16	0.069	0.297	0.500	6	22	22
17	0.132	0.327	0.516	19	31	31
18	0.000	0.000	0.000	23	19	19
19	0.072	0.317	0.516	29	29	29
20	0.104	0.339	0.530	14	14	14
21	0.066	0.253	0.456	16	16	16
22	0.132	0.327	0.516	13	13	25
23	0.072	0.359	0.558	21	25	32
24	0.140	0.430	0.609	25	32	13
25	0.036	0.265	0.476	32	9	9
26	0.034	0.199	0.408	9	11	11
27	0.264	0.470	0.623	11	21	21
28	0.103	0.334	0.526	2	2	2
29	0.072	0.317	0.516	26	26	26
30	0.135	0.355	0.539	5	5	5
31	0.132	0.327	0.516	12	12	12
32	0.036	0.265	0.476	18	18	18

Nodes {8, 17, 22, 31} is peripheral in the network structure. These nodes are underestimated in [3] when compared with results of Eq. (9) in Table 7.

Also the parameter value of δ and the time value T are related: high values of δ correspond low values of T. This can be seen when comparing column $T=1$ in Table 5 with column $\delta=5$ in Table 6. Both have the same most influential Nodes {27, 10, 3, 24}. The same comment as above concerning Nodes {8, 17, 22, 31} holds also for $\delta=5$.

Betweenness centrality

Betweenness measures node's role as a broker between others. In Eq. (12), we have presented a new betweenness measure with the help of removing one node from the

Table 7 An example summarized from Tables 3, 4 and 5

Equation (2), $\delta = 0.5$	3	27	24	10	7	15	23	1	4	30	6	20	28	{8, 17, 22, 31}
Equation (9), $w_N = 1.0, T = 1$	3	27	24	10	7	4	30	20	15	{8, 17, 22, 31}	28	23	6	19
Equation (9), $w_N = 0.5, T = 3$	27	3	24	10	4	30	20	7	{8, 17, 22, 31}	28	23	15	6	19

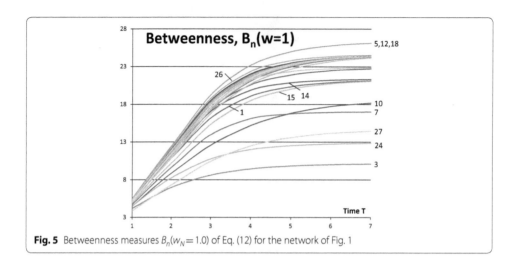

Fig. 5 Betweenness measures $B_n(w_N=1.0)$ of Eq. (12) for the network of Fig. 1

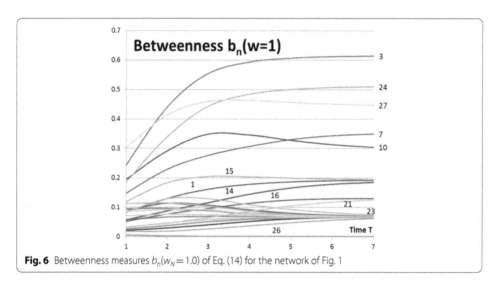

Fig. 6 Betweenness measures $b_n(w_N=1.0)$ of Eq. (14) for the network of Fig. 1

network. An alternative presentation in Eq. (14) is normalized by the value of Eq. (11) describing network structure where all the nodes are present.

Results of Eqs. (12) and (14) for the network of Fig. 1 are shown in Figs. 5 and 6. Network activity is $w_N = 1.0$ in both figures. Notice that the lowest (highest) curves in Fig. 5 (Fig. 6) represent the highest betweenness of nodes. The rankings of betweenness values are the same in both approaches. As can be seen from Figs. 3 and 5 closeness centrality and betweenness centrality describe different characteristics of the network. The most central node is not always the best broker of influence in the network. But in many cases a node can have both of these characteristics at the same time.

Rankings of betweenness values are shown in Figs. 7 and 8 for the activity values of $w_N = 1.0$ and $w_N = 0.5$ correspondingly. Figures 5, 6 and 7 show the same information of betweenness with $w_N = 1.0$ in different formats. From Fig. 1 we can see that Nodes 3, 24 and 27 are nodes having a good location between others. Nodes 10 and 27 have more important roles as brokers at the beginning of the spreading process. They are in a good position as brokers between highly connected peripheral nodes and rest of the network. Figures 7 and 8 highlight the complex behaviour influence spreading processes as

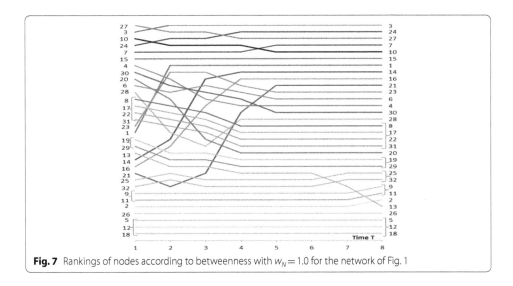

Fig. 7 Rankings of nodes according to betweenness with $w_N = 1.0$ for the network of Fig. 1

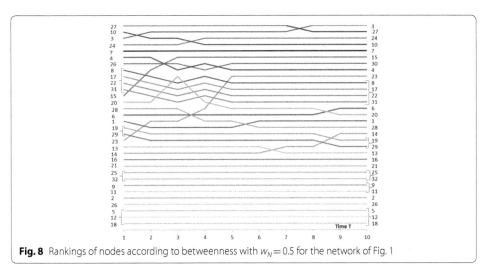

Fig. 8 Rankings of nodes according to betweenness with $w_N = 0.5$ for the network of Fig. 1

a function of time. Betweenness rankings can move in turn up and down depending on the development phase of the process.

Results for community detection

Structure of the territory network of the game of risk

The game of Risk has also been used in the literature [37] as one of test networks for community discovery algorithms. The network is neither a human nor an animal social network that is why real life interpretation for model parameters may not be valid. This network is an example of analysing network structures of general networks, not just social networks and communities. On the other hand, this artificial network turns out to be the simplest of our four example networks. Investigating the social network of 32 Dutch students is analysed after presenting basic ideas with the help of the Game of Risk network structures.

Table 8 The 17 different divisions of the 42 territories of Risk game detected as local maxima of Eq. (15)

R	#	#	Equation (15)	North America (Nodes)									Europe							Asia											
				1	2	3	4	5	6	7	8	9	10	11	12	13	14	15	16	17	18	19	20	21	22	23	24	25	26	27	28
1	38	4	128.0	1	2	3	4	5	6	7	8	9	10	11	12	13	14	15	16	17	18	19	20	21	22	23	24	25	26	27	28
2	4	38	124.4																												
3	33	9	122.8										10	11	12	13	14	15	16	17	18	19	20	21	22	23	24	25	26	27	28
4	34	8	122.3	1	2	3	4	5	6	7	8	9	10	11	12	13	14	15	16	17	18	19	20	21	22	23	24	25	26	27	28
5	13	29	121.1	1	2	3	4	5	6	7	8	9																			
6	29	13	120.6										10	11	12	13	14	15	16	17	18	19	20	21	22	23	24	25	26	27	28
7	25	17	119.0										10	11	12	13	14	15	16	17	18	19	20	21	22	23	24	25	26		
8	6	36	118.2																		18	19	20	21			24	25			
9	10	32	116.3																	17	18	19	20	21			24	25			
10	15	27	116.1	1	2	3	4	5	6	7	8	9									18	19	20	21			24	25			
11	19	23	114.2	1	2	3	4	5	6	7	8	9	10	11							18	19	20	21	22	23	24	25			
12	15	27	114.1																	17	18	19	20	21	22	23	24	25			28
13	23	19	112.5	1	2	3	4	5	6	7	8	9	10	11	12	13	14	15			18	19	20	21			24	25		27	
14	32	10	112.4	1	2	3	4						10	11	12	13	14	15							22	23			26	27	28
15	18	24	112.2															15	16								24	25	26		
16	11	31	112.1															15	16	17	18	19	20	21	22	23	24	25		27	28
17	14	28	110.6										10	11	12	13	14	15	16										26	27	28

Table 8 (continued)

R	#	#	Equation (15)	South America — Nodes				Africa						Australia			
				29	30	31	32	33	34	35	36	37	38	39	40	41	42
1	38	4	128.0	29	30	31	32	33	34	35	36	37	38				42
2	4	38	124.4	29	30	31	32										
3	33	9	122.8	29	30	31	32	33	34	35	36	37	38	39	40	41	42
4	34	8	122.3					33	34	35	36	37	38				
5	13	29	121.1	29	30	31	32										
6	29	13	120.6	29	30	31	32	33	34	35	36	37	38				
7	25	17	119.0					33	34	35	36	37	38				
8	6	36	118.2														
9	10	32	116.3											39	40	41	42
10	15	27	116.1														
11	19	23	114.2											39	40	41	42
12	15	27	114.1											39	40	41	42
13	23	19	112.5	29	30	31	32							39	40	41	42
14	32	10	112.4					33	34	35	36	37	38	39	40	41	42
15	18	24	112.2	29	30	31	32	33	34	35	36	37	38				
16	11	31	112.1														
17	14	28	110.6	29				33	34	35	36	37	38				

The values of the measure in Eq. (15) are shown in the table with the number nodes in the two factions of the network

The title line in the table shows the continents where the 42 territories are located (this information is not used as input in the model)

The board game is played on a political map consistently of six continents which further divide into 43 territories. The territories are connected by boundaries and waterways. The goal of the game is to conquer as much land as possible.

In the model, we presume some reasonable parameter values that provide a number of divisions of the territories network structure. The value of time is $T = 1.0$ and the parameter values are $\lambda = 0.5, w_N = w_L = 1.0, L_{max} = 4$. This choice of parameters provides us 17 different divisions of the 42 territories listed in Table 8. The numbers of territories in the divisions are shown in the column indicated by '#'. The values of the measure of Eq. (15) give the rankings (first column) of the divisions. The results of Table 8 are interpreted in the order of the ranking values.

The first five lines in Table 8 show clearly continents Australia, South America and North America. On lines 1–7 Europe, Africa and Asia are joined together. Not until on line 12 Asia without territory 26, is identified as a division. In addition sub-communities of five {17, 22, 23, 27, 28} and six {18, 19, 20, 21, 24, 25} territories are identified within Asia.

The algorithm, with the parameters used, does not discover Europe and Africa as individual divisions. Node 26 is incorrectly identified to the combined coalition of Europe and Africa. Classifications in the literature have been referenced in [41] where three out of five algorithms, FastQ, LPA and PPC, also misclassify Node 26. Also three algorithms LPA, Infohiermap and PPC extract the same sub-communities of five and six nodes in Asia. Two algorithms, Infohiermap and the active semi-supervised algorithm of [41], identify Europe and Africa and their territories correctly.

When investigating the territory network we observe that Nodes 16 and 26 (see Fig. 9a, b) are critical territories between Europe and Africa. They produce strong interrelations between these continents. Using lower values of the node weighting factors does not change the results as Europe and Africa still appear in the same group in different divisions.

We summarize the results of analysing the artificial Risk game network with the proposed model. Characteristics of human social networks are not assumed to be valid but we can compare the results with other algorithms in the literature. The results are similar, with an exception of two factions of the network identified as

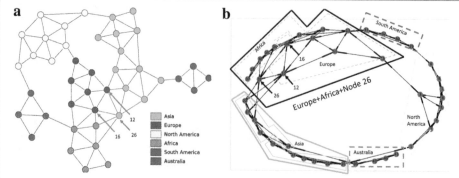

Fig. 9 **a** The network of 42 territories in Risk game where colours indicating the six continents (Wikipedia Commons). **b** The same network automatically generated by a library of Python software package together with the five divisions marked on the network as discovered by the algorithm of this paper. Europe and Africa are identified as one faction by the algorithm

one group. Few other algorithms detect the correct nodes of the two communities although they detect the communities themselves [41]. Some of the algorithms in the literature use supervised or assisted methods which can lead to more accurate results.

In analysing Risk game network we use a tabular form of representing different community structures in the network. This is an illustrative and useful way of detecting communities and sub-communities in a social network. The role of numerical values of the community detection measure of Eq. (15) is highlighted by examining lines of the table in the order of numerical values of the measure.

Community structures of the 32 Dutch students' social network

As the second case for analysing community structures, we use the longitudinal friendship network among 32 Dutch students on the fourth wave of the collected data [36]. Two students are considered to be friends if either or both of them named the other as a friend. A graphical representation of the friendship network is shown in Fig. 1.

The social network is analysed with two different model parameters $w_N = 0.5$ and $w_N = 1.0$ describing strength of the friendship relations. In both cases the parameter values $\lambda = 0.5, T = 1.0, w_L = 1.0$ and $L_{max} = 6$ are used. These parameter values are used for all connections in the network.

Sub-communities detected among the 32 Dutch students' social network are presented in Table 9 and in Fig. 10 for the two values of node weighting factors. The results for $w_N = 0.5$ has 14 different divisions and $w_N = 1.0$ has 6 divisions of the network. The first two columns show the number of nodes in the two factions, the third column shows the label of the division and the fourth column shows the numerical value of the

Table 9 Different divisions into two factions of the social network of Fig. 1

Sub-communities detected among 32 Duch students' social network

$w_N = 0.5$

#	#	D	M	1	2	3	4	5	6	7	8	9	10	11	12	13	14	15	16	17	18	19	20	21	22	23	24	25	26	27	28	29	30	31	32
3	26	A	22.3	1						1		1																								
11	18	B	21.7	1				1	1		1					1		1	1				1	1				1						1	
5	24	C	21.4						1		1								1					1										1	
9	20	D	21.3				1	1						1							1	1							1	1	1	1			
12	17	E	21.3				1	1						1		1					1	1					1		1	1	1	1			1
12	17	F	20.7	1			1	1			1		1	1							1	1							1	1	1	1			
8	21	G	20.6	1						1	1		1	1						1				1								1			
4	25	H	20.6			1								1								1										1			
14	15	I	19.7			1	1	1		1				1					1		1	1		1					1	1	1	1	1		
17	12	J	19.7			1	1	1		1				1		1			1		1	1		1			1		1	1	1	1	1	1	
16	13	K	19.2	1		1	1		1	1				1		1	1		1		1	1		1		1		1				1	1		
12	17	L	19.1	1	1			1									1	1	1					1		1	1	1	1						1
9	20	M	18.9			1			1		1			1						1				1								1	1	1	
12	17	N	18.2	1		1	1			1	1		1	1						1				1								1	1	1	

$w_N = 1.0$

#	#	D	M	1	2	3	4	5	6	7	8	9	10	11	12	13	14	15	16	17	18	19	20	21	22	23	24	25	26	27	28	29	30	31	32
12	17	B	55.2	1				1	1		1					1		1	1				1	1				1		1				1	
5	24	C	53.8						1		1								1					1										1	
13	16	O	53.5			1	1	1						1		1					1	1						1	1	1	1	1			1
9	20	D	53.4				1	1						1							1	1							1	1	1	1			
14	15	P	47.5			1	1	1		1				1					1		1	1		1					1	1	1	1	1		
13	16	Q	47.0	1		1			1		1			1			1			1				1			1		1	1	1				1

Model parameters are $W_N = 0.5$ and $W_N = 1.0$ with $T = 1.0, \lambda = 0.5, W_L = 1.0, L_{max} = 6$

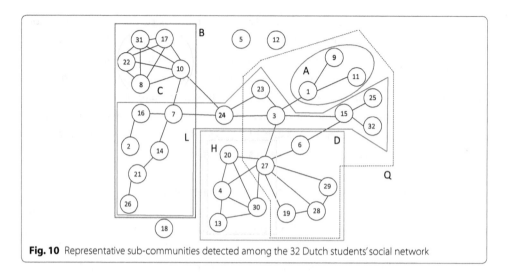

Fig. 10 Representative sub-communities detected among the 32 Dutch students' social network

community detection measure of Eq. (15). The results are presented in descending order of these values. The nodes belonging to one of the two sub-divisions is indicated in the table, the rest of the nodes belong to the second sub-division. Actually only 29 nodes out of the 32 nodes are connected. Nodes 5, 12 and 18 have no connections and they are not included in the sizes of the sub-divisions in Table 9.

For weaker connections of $w_N = 0.5$ (or for low values of spreading time T) the highest value of the local maximum value is $M = 22.3$ for the two factions {1, 9, 11} and {2, 3,..., 8, 10, 12,...32}. This division is not a local maximum for stronger connections of $w_N = 1.0$ at the same time $T = 1.0$. These kinds of weakly connected small sub-groups can exist at an early development phase of friendship relations.

A larger division B, on the left side of Fig. 1, into 11 and 18 nodes can be discovered for both weak $w_N = 0.5$ and strong $w_N = 1.0$ connections. This is also the case for the tightly connected sub-group {8, 10, 17, 22, 31} of division C. The value of the community detection measure for division D is almost as high as for C, even though division O with the four additional nodes ($O = D \cup$ {3, 15, 25, 32}) has a slightly higher value for strongly connected $w_N = 1.0$ network. Almost similar to division O division E ($E = D \cup$ {15, 25, 32}) can be found for weak connections but not for strong connections.

Node 3 is a gateway node with high betweenness values in Figs. 5, 6 and 8. Node 3 is a member of sub-groups in exceptional sub-groups of divisions L and Q. The sub-group of nodes {2, 3, 7, 14, 15, 16, 21, 23, 24, 25, 26, 32} in division L rules out three separate factions A, C, and D. Other examples of unconnected factions can be found in Table 9 in divisions F, G, I, J, K, M, N, and P. In these cases a strongly connected sub-group disconnects the second faction of the division. In this way more than two separate sub-groups can build up as a result of dynamic behaviour of social networks.

In a typical situation sub-groups are nested, for example, $A \subset F, G, N, Q$, $C \subset G, I, J, K, M, N, P$ and $D \subset E, F, I, J, O, P$. Often, sub-groups are unions, for example, $F = A \cup D$, $G = A \cup C$, and $N = A \cup C \cup H$. In many cases, differences of combined sub-groups are stand-alone sub-groups. However, for example, {15, 25, 32} and {2, 7, 14, 16, 21, 26} are not separate sub-groups in any divisions. This can be sensitive to model parameters.

Table 10 Optimal divisions of the dolphin social network

Division	Network	A	B	C	D	E	F
Factions	0 + 62	21 + 41	15 + 47	35 + 27	39 + 23	38 + 24	22 + 40
Eq. (15)	122.2	115.9	114.0	94.9	93.9	92.6	92.5

Community structures of a social network of dolphins

The third dataset we have selected to test the proposed community structure algorithm is the data of dolphin association collected for a research programme [38] of a community of 62 bottlenose dolphins over a period of 7 years. The network describing interactions of dolphins represents one of the real-world networks for which the community structure is already known. The social network has been analysed in [42] with a method published in [43, 44]. Two communities and four sub-communities were detected in the dolphin network. A temporary disappearance of the dolphin denoted by SN100 led to the fission of the dolphin community into two factions.

The animal social network is found to be similar to a human social network in some respects but different in some others such as the level of assortative mixing by degree within the population. Assortative mixing by age but not by vertex is observed in the dolphin social network [42]. Assortative mixing is a bias in favour of connections between network nodes with similar characteristics in complex networks [45]. In the model of this paper this may favour a lower value of maximal path length for the dolphin social network than for human social networks.

In Table 10 factions of nodes producing six local maxima in the values of the measure of Eq. (15) are listed. Boundaries of these divisions are shown in Fig. 11. The highest value is for division A which is the split observed in real life, with one exception of Node SN89, after dolphin SN100 temporarily disappeared from the original dolphin community. Out of the five additional less optimal divisions almost as good division B separates a smaller group of more peripheral 15 nodes. This indicates a mediating role of the six dolphins Beescratch, DN63, Knit, Mus, Notch and Number1.

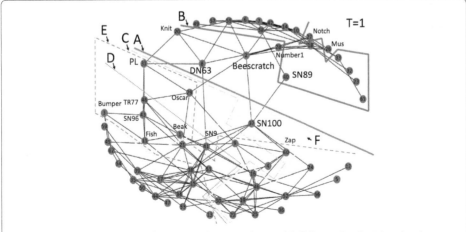

Fig. 11 Communities discovered from the dolphins' social network [42]. Time value $T = 1.0$ and node weighting factors $W_N = 0.5$ are used with model parameter values $\lambda = 0.5, L_{max} = 4$

Division C is an analogous division on the other side of the main spit boundary of dolphin SN100 and a group of 12 closely interconnected dolphins on the right lower part of Fig. 11. These 12 nodes are exactly the nodes identified by [42] as a sub-community in the network. There are also three additional more divisions D, E, and F indicated in Fig. 11.

We have computed also the results with Node SN100 removed from the original network. The results are almost similar. The divisions A and B are the same as in Fig. 11. Division C has one Node Zap moved side. The fourth division of 16 nodes is in the lower left corner of Fig. 11 with dolphin SN9. The fifth and sixth divisions are exactly divisions D and E in Fig. 11.

Betweenness of nodes in the dolphin social network have been studied in [46]. Values of Eq. (12) have been calculated for two different parameter values describing low and high cohesion of the network. The results are very different for these two cases. At early phases of influence spreading different nodes have the highest betweenness, when compared with later phases of the process, because later more nodes have already been affected. At early phases local characteristics and neighbouring nodes are controlling the spreading processes. Node degree is describing centrality in these situations.

In fact, the highest node degrees of the dolphin social network are for dolphins Grin, SN4 and Topless with 12, 11 and 11 node degree values correspondingly. In the low cohesion network, the nine nodes with the highest values of betweenness measure are {Grin, SN4, Topless, Scrabs, SN9, Kringel, Patchpac, Trigger, TR99}.

In the high cohesion network, the eleven nodes with the highest values of betweenness measure are {SN100, Beescratch, SN9, Trigger, SN9, Trigger, SN4, Jet, Scrabs, Stripes, Kringel}. These results are in agreement with the results in [42] identified using the betweenness-based algorithm of [43].

Low cohesion exists at an early phase of influence spreading or when nodes' activities are low, i.e. low node weighting factors. A result of this is that corresponding pairs of time and weighting factor values can be found such that they provide comparable results. In [46] this has been demonstrated in cases of low values of time with high values of weighting factors, and high values of time with low values of weighting factors. Almost identical results are obtained for $T = 1.0, w_N = 1.0$ and $T = 4.5, w_N = 0.5$.

According to the research article [42] the dolphin community has existed quite a long time. On the other hand, the positive assortative mixing by degree was not observed in the study, which is often observed in human social networks. However, a clear statistically significant assortative mixing by sex among the dolphin population has been observed, although the mixing is not as strong as some types of mixing in human societies [42, 45].

We conclude from the results of [42], because of the lack of positive assortative mixing by degree, that relatively low value of $T = 1.0$ is appropriate. The value of $w_N = 0.5$ for node weighting factors are used in Fig. 11. We have made experiments with higher values of weighting factors and higher values of time. In latter development phases of influence spreading local maxima of community detection in Eq. (15) are levelled and fewer sub-communities are discovered. At time $T = 1.0$ with $w_N = 1.0$ only one division is detected which is exactly the same Division A in Fig. 11. Using the method for low and high cohesion circumstances can be regarded as a method to examine a network with diverse resolutions.

We summarize the results of analysing the dolphin social network. The split of the dolphin population into two factions after a temporal disappearance of dolphin SN100 is predicted by the model with the exception of one dolphin SN89. In the literature, sub-communities have been identified using the betweenness-based algorithm in [43]. The proposed model of this study does not predict the same sub-communities but they can be identified by the help of investigating boundaries of different divisions predicted by the model.

There is a question whether the same model parameters are appropriate for dolphin and human social networks. We conclude from the research published in [42] that low values of time T or node weighting factors w_N might be more appropriate for dolphin social networks. The same reasoning applies to maximum path length L used in the model. In the proposed model, the consistent procedure is to use the same parameters for the community detection algorithm and for closeness and betweenness centrality measures.

Community structures of a Facebook social network

In this section we show results for a social network of Facebook. This dataset consists of 'circles' (or lists of friends). The network data have 4039 nodes and 88,234 links between nodes. The data also have nested and overlapping communities. Here, our main focus is on presenting the features of our model and methods for larger social networks. Because of the detailed modelling, where all the nodes are considered, when influence between nodes are calculated, complex phenomena appear which may not be present in very small social networks. We also provide strategies on how to optimize the community detection calculations to minimize computer running times. The Facebook social network is the same as used in [11].

The analysis is conducted with the entire social network data, with loops allowed (except self-loops), maximum path lengths $L_{max} = 6$, node weighting factors $w_N = 0.1$, and link weighting factors $w_L = 1.0$. The community detection measure of Eq. (15) is computed along the paths determined by the 88,234 links between nodes. As a result of the influence spreading process, all the nodes inside the maximum path length L_{max} in a connected graph are influenced by a node and the corresponding elements of the $N \times N$ matrix $C_{s,t}$ have positive values. The full analysis of the network considers all these elements.

All the information for detecting communities and their relations in a network consisting of N nodes is included in one $N \times N$ matrix, which has influence measures of Eq. (6) from N nodes to all the other nodes in the network. Because diagonal elements of the matrix have no effect on the community structure, we set the diagonal elements to zero. We show selected results of detailed structures of the network while the calculations have been conducted using the whole network data. Therefore, the method is global, not local, in this respect. This means that all the interactions have influenced the results, centrality and betweenness measures and community structures.

We have detected 551 sub-structures in the network. Most of these are nested structures inside communities. In large networks, many levels of nested sub-communities can exist. The algorithm provides list of nodes included in the 551 communities and the corresponding values of the community detection measure of Eq. (15). We order the communities by the values of the measure and use the ranking of a community as a unique identifier (in this section only smaller factions of divisions are studied). The analysis should start from important communities, their internal structures and relationships with other communities.

The smaller faction of the division with the highest value of the community detection measure of Eq. (15) consists of the 59 last nodes {3981–4039} of the network data. The value of the un-normalized measure of Eq. (15) is 442,159. This community has also complex sub-structures. Figures 12 and 13 show the overlapping and nested structures among the 59 nodes. Community C_1 and its sub-communities $C_2, \ldots, C_6$ have a significant influence on community structures outside C_1, and in many cases, one or more of $C_1, \ldots, C_6$ are included as sub-sets in these communities.

Nested sub-communities are indicated in Fig. 13 as $C_5 \in C_6 \in C_1$ and $C_4 \in C_3 \in C_2 \in C_1$. Two different divisions of the 59 nodes are shown with dotted lines in Fig. 13 as $C_1 = C_4 + C_6$ and $C_1 = C_3 + C_5$. As can be seen in Fig. 12, three genuine overlapping cases exist: $C_6 - C_5 = S_2$, $C_2 - C_3 = S_8$, and $C_5 - C_2 = S_{32}$. We denote these intersecting sets of nodes by S_2, S_8, and S_{32} because they have not been detected as sub-communities [local maxima of Eq. (15)] and have no community identifier in Fig. 12. However, together the three sets form sub-community C_6, denoted by $C_6 = S_2 + S_8 + S_{32}$. Again, these sets of nodes may appear as sub-communities with lower parameter values. In fact, intersections of detected communities are candidates for new sub-communities.

Figure 14 shows a sample of the analysis of the Facebook social network around the 59 nodes. Sub-communities are marked by their sizes and identifiers [rankings calculated from Eq. (15)]. In the calculations all the 4039 nodes have been considered. This means that the sub-communities and their compositions are probably different if only the nodes in sub-communities shown in Fig. 14 are considered. Figure 14 shows the nested structures of the sub-communities as in Fig. 13. Compositions of the sub-communities (dotted lines in Fig. 13) are not shown in Fig. 14.

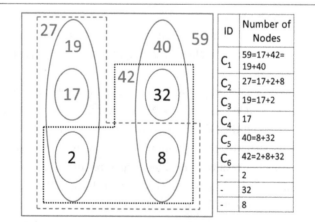

Fig. 12 The five sub-communities $C_2, \ldots, C_6$ detected in community C_1. Numbers of nodes and community identifiers (ID) are shown. The sets of 2, 8 and 32 nodes are not detected as sub-communities with the used model parameters. These sets of nodes are intersections of the detected sub-communities

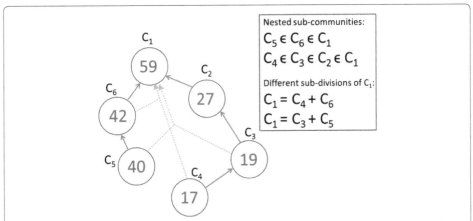

Fig. 13 Nested sub-communities and different divisions of community C_1 are shown with solid and dotted lines correspondingly

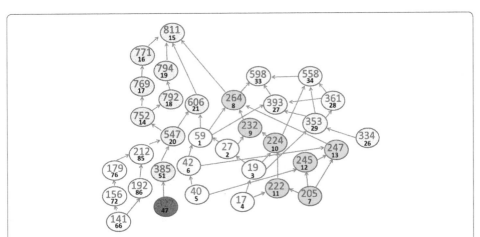

Fig. 14 A sample of community structures in the Facebook social network. Selected sub-communities are shown with information about community sizes and community identifiers (rankings of communities). Arrows indicate nested structures of sub-communities. Analysis has been conducted with the entire network data of the 4039 nodes. Colouring is explained in Fig. 15

In many cases a community has nested structures composed of sub-communities lower in hierarchy like the two examples in Fig. 13. This is a consequence of the fact that influence spreading is considered globally or at least inside the path length L_{max}, if it is not set to infinity. Also, when a nested sub-community is detected inside a community, the other faction S may not be detected as a sub-community. An example is shown in Fig. 12 where $C_3 = S_2 + C_4$. This does not exclude the possibility that S is a constituent of a sub-community on higher levels. An example in Fig. 14 is the sub-community C_8 of 264 nodes composed of sub-community C_9 and a set of 32 nodes S_{32} ($C_8 = S_{32} + C_9$). This is possible because community C_1 and its sub-structures are also nested sub-structures of community C_8 as can been seen in Fig. 14.

Full investigation of a large social network is a major task. In practice, the analysis is started from the most important communities detected from the network. This has been the idea in Figs. 13, 14. Alternatively the analysis is focused on communities, or nodes, of

Rankings

Node	Eq. (9)	Eq. (10)	Eq.(9)&(10)
3438	1435	881	1103
1	1302	1145	1222
3831	2194	1794	2019
687	2403	2049	2304
3522	2628	2567	2599
3981	3664	3585	3681
4031	3939	3933	3934

Fig. 15 Nodes and their rankings with the highest closeness centrality values in sub-communities of Fig. 14. The last column shows the rankings of the average value of Eqs. (9) and (10)

special interest. Different search criteria for the analysed results can be used, for example, node numbers, community identifiers and values of community measures. Nested structures are discovered by comparing the compositions (nodes) of the detected communities. Deep nested hierarchies can exist when some sub-communities extend their influence widely, like C_1 in Figs. 12 and 14.

Closeness centrality rankings of the most important nodes in sub-communities of Fig. 14 are shown in Fig. 15. Rankings of measures of Eq. (9) and (10) are not the same. However, their numerical values typically are close to each other.

Conclusion

We consider a model with one ego initiating the influence spreading process in a social network. This allows us to study different phenomena in structured networks. In practical calculations, the proposed model can also be used for simultaneous source nodes of influence spreading. Dynamic measures for spreading in a social network are used as measures for centrality and betweenness. These measures are functions of network activity and time. Time can be interpreted as the development phase of social relations in a social network. A steady state is reached at high values of time. Therefore, measures describing centrality, betweenness or other characteristics of a network, can be calculated for the steady state or for different development phases of a network.

The proposed model takes into account different paths of the network from a source node to target nodes. Secondly, the dependency of paths is modelled by considering common links at the beginning of the paths. Combining these aspects is the novelty of the model compared to other models in the literature. These features of the model enable many opportunities to study new phenomena in complex networks and to solve existing problems more accurately.

Highly connected peripheral groups have multiple possible paths at the beginning of the spreading process which emphasizes the importance of these nodes as influential spreaders. It is known that initial spreading dynamics is crucial for later development of dynamic processes in a network [47].

We consider networks with a constant structure of nodes and links. Influence is spreading in the network and one node can spread similar influence repeatedly. Results in several recent articles [48–50] indicate that peripheral nodes, which are not highly influential, have more spreading power than most of the existing models predict. Our study provides evidence supporting these statements. Allowing loops (a node is allowed in the same chain of links more than once) further enhance the importance of interconnected peripheral nodes with low connectivity to central core network structures.

Activity of nodes has a nonlinear effect on rankings of the most influential nodes in the network. For example, if nodes' activity is lower, the prominence of peripheral connected nodes is higher. We can say that the activity of nodes is an important aspect and models should take activity as one of the main variables of dynamic social network analysis and influence measures. In the model, activity is described by node and link weighting factors.

A new community detection measure is proposed in this paper. The community detection algorithm can be used to analyse possible sub-communities or closely connected members of the network. The idea in analysing community structures is based on the concept of nodes' role in the network as sources and targets of influence. Both of these aspects have a role in community formation. The algorithm computes local maxima of an influence measure which considers both in- and out-directions of influence. Typically, social networks with weak interactions between nodes or social networks that are at their early development phases have several local maxima with different compositions. These factions can intersect and overlap with each other.

In this paper, we propose a consistent modelling framework for computing powerful influence spreaders and mediators in a social network. The same theory can be used in analysing community structures. The method is discussed and illustrated with several examples and graphical presentations.

Authors' contributions
The author read and approved the final manuscript.

Acknowledgements
The author would like to thank Mr. Matti Syrjänen for writing down the pseudo-code of the algorithm based on the computer programme code developed by Janne Levijoki and Matias Ijäs.

Competing interests
The author declare that he has no competing interests.

Funding
No funding.

References
1. Borgatti SP, Everett MG. A graph-theoretic perspective on centrality. Soc Netw. 2006;28:466–84.
2. Borgatti SP. Identifying sets of key players in a social network. Comput Math Organiz Theor. 2006;12:21–34.
3. Agneessens F, Borgatti SP, Everett MG. Geodesic based centrality: unifying the local and the global. Soc Netw. 2017;49:12–26.
4. Newman MEJ. A measure of betweenness centrality based on random walks. Soc Netw. 2003;27(1):39–54.
5. Malliaros DF, Rossi M-EG, Vazirgiannis M. Locating influential nodes in complex networks. Sci Rep. 2016;6:19307.
6. Gruhl, D, Guha, R, Liben-Nowell, D, Tomkins, A. Information diffusion through blogspace. WWW'04; 2004. p. 491–501.

7. Kempe, D, Kleinberg, J, Tardos, É. Maximizing the spread of influence through a social network. SIGKDD'03 Washington, DC; 2003. p. 137–46.
8. Kempe, D, Kleinberg, J, Tardos, É. Influential nodes in a diffusion model for social networks. In: Proceedings of 32nd international colloquium on automata, languages and programming; 2005. p. 1127–38.
9. Moreno F, Min B, Bo L, Mari R, Makse HA. Collective influence algorithm to find influencers via optimal percolation in massively large social media. Sci Rep. 2016;6:30062.
10. Pei S, Morone F, Makse HA. Theories for influencer identification in complex networks. In: Lehman S, Ahn Y-Y, editors. Sreading dynamics in social systems. Berlin: Springer; 2017.
11. Ijäs, M, Levijoki, J, Kuikka, V. Scalable algorithm for computing influence spreading probabilities in social networks. In: 5th European conference on social media, limerick institute of technology (ECMS 2018), Ireland. 2018.
12. Watts DJ. Six degrees: the science of a connected age. London: W. W. Norton & Company Ltd.; 2004.
13. Fortunato S, Hric D. Community detection in networks: a user guide. Phys Rep. 2016;659(11):1–44.
14. Newman MEJ, Park J. Why social networks are different from other types of networks. Phys Rev E Stat Nonlin Soft Matter. 2003;68:036122.
15. Miller JC, Kiss IZ. Epidemic spread in networks: existing methods and current challenges. Math Model Nat Phenom. 2014;9(2):4–42.
16. Newman MEJ. The structure and function of complex networks. SIAM Rev. 2003;45:167–256.
17. Karrer B, Newman MEJ. Stochastic blockmodels and community structure in networks. Phys Rev E. 2011;83(1):016107.
18. Lai D, Lu H, Nardini C. Enhanced modularity-based community detection by random walk network preprocessing. Phys Rev E. 2010;81(6):066118.
19. Newman MEJ. Detecting community structure in networks. Eur Phys J B. 2004;38(2):321–30.
20. Radicchi F, Castellano C, Cecconi F, Loreto V, Parisi D. Defining and identifying communities in networks. Proc Natl Acad Sci USA. 2004;101(9):2658–63.
21. Shen H-W, Cheng X-Q, Guo J-F. Quantifying and identifying the overlapping community structure in networks. J Stat Mech. 2009;2009:P07042.
22. Thakur GS, Tiwari R, Thai MT, Chen S-S, Dress AWM. Detection of local community structures in complex dynamic networks with random walks. IET Syst Biol. 2009;3(4):266–78.
23. Xiang J, Wang Z-Z, Li H-J, Zhang Y, Li F, Dong L-P, Li J-M, Guo L-J. Community detection based on significance optimization in complex networks. J Stat Mech. 2017;2017:053213.
24. Coscia M, Giannotti F, Pedreschi D. A classification for community discovery methods in complex networks. Stat Anal Data Mining. 2011;4(5):512–46.
25. Lancichinetti A, Fortunato S. Community detection algorithms: a comparative analysis. Phys Rev E. 2009;80:056117.
26. Shuo L, Chai B. Discussion of the community detection algorithm based on statistical inference. Persp Sci. 2016;7:122–5.
27. Newman MEJ. Networks, an introduction. Oxford: Oxford University Press; 2010.
28. Kernighan BW, Lin S. An efficient heuristic procedure for partitioning graphs. Bell Syst Tech J. 1970;49(2):291–307.
29. Fiedler M. Algebraic connectivity of graphs. Czechoslov Math J. 1973;23(98):298–305.
30. Pothen A, Simon H, Liou K-P. Partitioning sparse matrices with eigenvectors of graphs. SIAM J Matrix Anal Appl. 1990;11:430–52.
31. Blondel VD, Guillaume J-L, Lambiotte R, Lefebvre E. Fast unfolding of communities in large networks. J Stat Mech. 2008;10:P10008.
32. Rosvall M, Bergstrom CT. Maps of random walks on complex networks reveal community structure. PNAS. 2008;105(4):1118–23.
33. DasGupta B, Desai D. On the complexity of Newman's community finding approach for biological and social networks. J Comput Syst Sci. 2013;79:50–67.
34. Agarwal G, Kempe D. Modularity-maximizing graph communities via mathematical programming. Eur Phys J B. 2008;66(3):409–18.
35. Berman P, DasGupta B, Kaligounder L, Karpinski M. On the computational complexity of measuring global stability of banking networks. Algorithmica. 2014;70(4):595–647.
36. Van de Bunt GG. Friends by choice. An actor-oriented statistical network model for friendship networks through time. Amsterdam: Thesis Publishers; 1999.
37. https://en.wikipedia.org/wiki/Risk_(game). Accessed 8 Aug 2017.
38. Lusseau D. The emergent properties of a dolphin social network. Proc R Soc Lond B. 2003;270:186–8.
39. Freeman LC. Centrality in social networks: conceptual clarification. Soc Netw. 1979;1:215–39.
40. Katz L. A new status index derived from sociometric analysis. Psychometrica. 1953;18(1):39–42.
41. Cheng J, Leng M, Li L, Zhou H, Chen X. Active semi-supervised community detection based on must-link and cannot-link constraints. PLoS ONE. 2014;9(10):e110088.
42. Lusseau D, Newman MEJ. Identifying the role that individual animals play in their social network. Proc R Soc Lond B (Suppl.). 2004;271:477–81.
43. Girvan M, Newman MEJ. Community structure in social and biological networks. Proc Natl Acad Sci USA. 2002;99(12):7821–6.
44. Newman MEJ, Girvan M. Finding and evaluating community structure in networks. Phys Rev E. 2004;69:026113.
45. Newman MEJ. Mixing patterns in networks. Phys Rev E. 2003;67(2):026126.
46. Kuikka V. Influence spreading model used to community detection in social networks. In: Cherifi C, Cherifi H, Karsai M, Musolesi M, editors. Complex networks & their applications VI. COMPLEX NETWORKS 2017. Studies in computational intelligence, vol. 689. Cham: Springer; 2018. p. 202–15.
47. Zou CC, Towsley D, Gong W. Modeling and simulation study of the propagation and defence of Internet email worm. IEEE Trans Dependable Secure Comput. 2007;4(2):105–18.
48. Šikić M, Lančić A, Antulov-Fantulin N, Štefančić H. Epidemic centrality—is there an underestimated epidemic impact of network peripheral nodes? Eur Phys J B. 2013;2013:86–440.

6

Why continuous discussion can promote the consensus of opinions?

Zhenpeng Li[1*], Xijin Tang[2], Benhui Chen[1], Jian Yang[1] and Peng Su[1]

*Correspondence:
lizhenpeng@amss.ac.cn
[1] Department of Applied
Statistics, Dali University,
Dali 671003, China
Full list of author information
is available at the end of the
article

Abstract

Why group opinions tend to be converged through continued communication, discussion and interactions? Under the framework of the social influence network model, we rigorously prove that the group consensus is almost surely within finite steps. This is a quite certain result, and reflects the real-world common phenomenon. In addition, we give a convergence time lower bound. Although our explanations are purely based on mathematic deduction, it shows that the latent social influence structure is the key factor for the persistence of disagreement and formation of opinions convergence or consensus in the real world social system.

Keywords: Social influence network theory, Random graph, Opinions dynamics

Background

Many social phenomena are embedded within networks of interdependencies, i.e., social networks or social structures. The social structure are constructed by social ties (or social connections) as suggested by Granovetter. Different types of connections might play different roles for the function of network. For example, Granovetter argued that weak ties (individuals are loosely connected in the network) were the necessary condition for spreading to occur across subnetwork within a social system [1]. Burt suggested that structural equivalence is the factor for the adoption of new ideas [2]. In the field of complex networks, researchers focus both the structure and function of social networks, i.e., networks dynamical processes taking place on networks, such as the transmission of disease over human contact and rumors diffusion through internet [3].

Inspired by these researches, instead of discussing spreading or innovation adoption in network, the present research ask how do social networks (different social structures) influence opinions dynamics? i.e., the influence of social network structure on opinions dynamics, we will investigate under what conditions opinions in a group can reach consensus and average consensus.

Here we refer to the network is the pattern of friendship, advice, communication, support or is the form of bargaining, debating and compromising. In the structured social context, individual determines his/her opinions, in accordance with the constraints and possibilities imposed by other's in the network. In other words, individuals are assumed to be responsive to the contextual cues provided by the opinions and behavior of significant others. Through advice, communication, support or bargaining, debating and compromising, consecutively, actors thus establish their own behavior, by appropriately taking into account the opinions and behaviors displayed by their significant others.

In the end, the aggregation of local individual's opinions adjustment contribute to the global group opinions patterns—*polarization or consensus*. In social psychology, during the past decades, group polarization phenomenon has been intensively studied [4–9].

The importance of group polarization is significant as it helps to explain group behavior in a variety of real-life situations. Examples of these situations include public voting, terrorism, and violence. In our former studies, we investigated the group polarization based on Hopfield attractor model, and revealed a very interesting connection between global patterns and local structure balance [10]. Next, we will concentrate on the phenomenon of group opinions convergence and consensus.

Mathematical models are used to describe consensus include DeGroot's classic model [11], Friedkin and Johnsen [12] and Friedkin's extended version [13]. From social psychological point of view, this line of research began with French's formal theory of social power [14], a simple model of collective opinion formation in a network of interpersonal influencing social group. As a step forward, Friedkin presented the social influence network theory based on Latane's social influence theory [15], which considered both cognitive and structural aspects, and focused on the contributions of networks of interpersonal influence to the formation of interpersonal agreements and group consensus.

Over the past few years, models of the convergence of opinion or consensus problem in social systems have been the subjects of a considerable amount of recent attention in the fields such as motion coordination of autonomous agents [16, 17], distributed computation in control theory [16, 18, 19], randomized consensus algorithms [20, 21], and sensor networks about data fusion problems [22–26].

Due to the unpredictability of the environment where the communication between agents occurs, and the random characteristics of influences or interactions among agents in systems (man made or social systems), most of the growing interests in consensus problems (both algorithms and practical applications) are based on probabilistic settings [20].

Recently, the study of opinion dynamics has started to attract the attention of the control community, who with the bulk of motivation have developed about methods to approximate and stabilize consensus, synchronization, and other coherent states. However, comparing with many man-made or engineering systems, social systems do not typically exhibit a consensus of opinions, but rather a persistence of disagreement, i.e., polarization patterns. The ubiquitous group polarization phenomena can be observed from political election to carbon dioxide emissions debate [27]. In a social system, the difficulty in arriving at a collective consensus state roots in the fact that the process of opinion formation can rarely be reduced to accepting or rejecting the consensus of others, as exemplified by Arrow's dilemma of social choice [28]. On the contrary, in most cases individuals construct their options in a complex interpersonal environment or with their prior identities (e.g. prior beliefs, prejudices and social identities etc.), their views are often in a state of disagreement or not easily changed, due to opinion-dependent limitations in the network connectivity and obstinacy of the agents as pointed in Ref.

[29]. This phenomenon shows the complexities of social control in social economic systems.[1]

Consensus as one of the important and regular group opinions dynamic pattern is generally observed in a relative smaller group discussion and barging process. Friedkin and Johnsen's social influence network theory emphasizes that the interpersonal influence social structure (or social influence matrix) is the underling precondition for the group consensus or opinion convergence. In that model, the initial social influence structure of group of actors is assumed to be fixed during the entire process of opinion formation. However, with the evolution of time stamp, considering both stubborn and susceptible effects, the interpersonal influence structure can be regarded as a dynamic recursive process. For this reason, the interpersonal influence structure in their model is also dynamic, as described in "Problem formulation and terminology" section.

In this paper, our aim is to investigate the precondition for consensus formation in a social group based on Friedkin's model. From interpersonal network structure point of view, our investigation presents the conditions for the formation of group opinions convergence and consensus. We investigate the opinions convergence phenomenon over a group of N individuals with a random walk social influence structure, and for any given initial opinions distribution, i.e., the opinions evolution problem with a (time-variant) linear dynamic model driven by random matrices. Our analytic proof provides strict mathematic explanations for the deterministic characterization of the ergodicity, which can be used for studying the consensus over random graphs and the formation of opinion parties. The proof procedures are self-contained and based on ergodic theorem of Markov chain and eigenvalues of random graph, as introduced in Ref. [30].

The rest of the paper arranged as follows. In "Problem formulation and terminology", we will briefly introduce social influence network theory and its mathematical framework. "Random walk on weighted graph'" section present the conditions for a group opinions consensus based on random walk on weighted graph. "The convergence of opinions profile on random graph" section prove that the convergence of group opinions over general weighted and undirected random graph are almost surely. "Numeric simulation" section test the theoretical conclusion by numeric simulation methods. "Conclusions" section is our concluding remarks.

Problem formulation and terminology

Social influence network theory presents a mathematical formalization of the social process of opinions changes that unfold in a social network of interpersonal influences. The spread of influence among individuals in a social network can be naturally modeled under a probabilistic framework. Here, we briefly describe the classical Friedkin and Johnsen's model to illustrate how the opinion dynamics arise in the context of social networks.

Let $W = [w_{ij}]$ is a $N \times N$ matrix of interpersonal influence, i.e., for each i, w_{ij} denotes for the individual j's social influence to i, after normalization W satisfies $\sum_j w_{ij} = 1$. $A = \mathrm{diag}(a_1, a_2, ..., a_N)$ is a $N \times N$ diagonal matrix of individuals susceptibilities to

---

[1] In classical sociological field, social control refers to the occurrence and effectiveness of ongoing efforts in a group to formulate, agree upon and implement collective courses of action.

interpersonal influence on the opinion, and satisfies $a_i = 1 - w_{ii}$. In a group of N persons, with the initial $N \times 1$ opinions vector $y^{(1)}$, the updating opinions vector $y^{(t)}$ in the interpersonal opinions influence system is described by Eq. (1),

$$y^{(t+1)} = AWy^{(t)} + (I - A)y^{(1)} \tag{1}$$

Definition 1 The system (1) reaches the convergence state if, for any initial opinions vector $y^{(1)}$, it holds that $\lim_{t \to \infty} y^{(t)} = y^*$.

Definition 2 The system (1) reaches consensus state if, for any initial opinions vector $y^{(1)}$, and each $1 \leq i, j \leq N$, it holds that $\lim_{t \to \infty} |y_i^{(t)} - y_j^{(t)}| = 0$, where $|.|$ is the symbol of the absolute value. This means that, as a result of the social influence process, in the limit they have the same belief on the subject.

As a consequence of system (1), the opinion profile at time $t \in Z \geq 0$ is equal to

$$y^{(t+1)} = \widehat{W}^t y^{(1)}, \tag{2}$$

where $\widehat{W}^t = (AW)^t + (\Sigma_{k=0}^{t-1}(AW)^k)(I - A)$ is the reduced-form coefficients matrix, discribing the total or net interpersonal effects that transform the initial opinions into equilibrium opinions, and for any entry $\widehat{w}_{ij}^t$ in $\widehat{W}^t$, satisfies $0 \leq \widehat{w}_{ij}^t \leq 1$, $\sum_j \widehat{w}_{ij}^t = 1$. According to Definition 1, under suitable conditions, when $t \to +\infty$ if $I - AW$ is nonsingular, the system (1) arrives at convergence equilibrium opinions profile y^*, where $y^* = \lim_{t \to \infty} y(t) = (I - AW)^{-1}(I - A)y^{(1)}$. When $t \to +\infty$, we have

$$\lim_{t \to \infty} \widehat{W}^t = \lim_{t \to \infty} \left\{ (AW)^t + \sum_{k=0}^{t-1} (AW)^k (I - A) \right\} = (I - AW)^{-1}(I - A) = V. \tag{3}$$

Given large enough time stamp t, and a sufficiently small positive real number ε, V can be approximated by $\widehat{W}^t$. Furthermore, according to the approximation error $||\widehat{W}^t - V|| \leq \varepsilon$ (where $||.||$ denotes the matrix norm), we can obtain the time stamp's upper bound and lower bound as $ln(||V|| - \varepsilon)/ln(||\widehat{W}||) \leq t \leq ln(||V|| + \varepsilon)/ln(||\widehat{W}||)$, where $||\widehat{W}|| = ||AW + I - A||$.

Followed the same lines of the convergence results by Ishii and Tempo [31], and Golub and Jackson [32], by showing the ergodicity property, Frasca et al. proved the convergence result of system (1); [29]. Touri and Nedic studied the ergodicity and consensus problem with a linear discrete-time dynamic model driven by stochastic matrices [33].

It should be noted according to Defintion 1, that equilibrium opinions may settle on the mean of group members' initial opinions, a compromise opinion that differs from the initial ones, or altered opinions that does not form a consensus. When consensus is formed in system (1), i.e., as $t \to +\infty$, $\widehat{W}^t$ will have the form of a stratification of individual contributions as following,

$$\widehat{W}^t = \begin{bmatrix} \widehat{w}_{11}^t & \widehat{w}_{22}^t & \cdots & \widehat{w}_{NN}^t \\ \widehat{w}_{11}^t & \widehat{w}_{22}^t & \cdots & \widehat{w}_{NN}^t \\ \vdots & \vdots & \vdots & \vdots \\ \widehat{w}_{11}^t & \widehat{w}_{22}^t & \cdots & \widehat{w}_{NN}^t \end{bmatrix},$$

which suggests that the initial opinion of each individual makes a particular relative contribution to the emergent consensus.

Random walk on weighted graph

In this section, without the lose of the generality of system (1), we first introduce the weighted adjacency random matrix, the weighted Laplacian and the transition matrix of the random walk, then we present the conditions for a group opinions consensus under the framework of social influence network model. Here we use the canonical graph symbol $G(V, E)$ in which V and E denote vertexes and edges respectively.

A weighted directed graph G is defined as $w : V \times V \longrightarrow R$ such that $w_{ij} \neq 0$, if $\{i, j\} \notin E(G)$ then $w_{ij} = 0$. In the context, the weighted degree d_i of a vertex i is defined as $d_i = \sum_j w_{ij}$, $\mathrm{vol}(G) = \sum_i d_i$ denotes the volume of the graph G. For a general weighted directed graph G, the corresponding random walk is determined by transition probabilities $p_{ij} = Pr(x_{t+1} = j | x_t = i) = w_{ij}/d_i$, which are independent of i. Clearly, for each vertex i satisfies $0 \leq p_{ij} \leq 1$, $\sum_i p_{ij} = 1$, in other words, transition matrix P is row stochastic matrix. In addition if for any $j \in V(G)$ satisfying $\sum_j p_{ij} = 1$, then transition matrix P is named double stochastic matrix.

For any fixed time step t, we define transition matrix P on graph $\widehat{W}^t$ without normalization, with entries $p_{ij} = Pr(x_{t+1} = j | x_t = i) = \widehat{w}_{ij}^t/\widehat{d}_i^t$, where $\widehat{d}_i^t = \sum_j \widehat{w}_{ij}^t$, and matrix L as follows:

$$
L_{ij} = \begin{cases} \widehat{d}_i^t - \widehat{w}_{ii}^t & \text{if } i = j, \\ -\widehat{w}_{ij}^t & \text{if } i \text{ and } j \text{ are adjacent,} \\ 0 & \text{otherwise.} \end{cases} \tag{4}
$$

where $\widehat{w}_{ij}^t \in \widehat{W}^t$ is defined in Equations (2) and (3). Let T denote the diagonal matrix with the (i, i)-th entry having value $\widehat{d}_i^t$ as following

$$
T = \begin{bmatrix} \widehat{d}_1^t & \cdots & \cdots & 0 \\ 0 & \widehat{d}_2^t & \cdots & 0 \\ \vdots & \vdots & \vdots & \vdots \\ 0 & \cdots & \cdots & \widehat{d}_N^t \end{bmatrix}, \tag{5}
$$

we set $T^{-1}(i, i) = 0$ for $\widehat{d}_i^t = 0$, and if $\widehat{d}_i^t = 0$ we say i is an isolated vertex. Then the graph $\widehat{W}^t$'s Laplacian matrix ζ is defined to be the form $\zeta = T^{-1/2}LT^{-1/2}$, and each entry in ζ is listed as following,

$$
\zeta_{ij} = \begin{cases} 1 - \dfrac{\widehat{w}_{ii}^t}{\widehat{d}_i^t} & \text{if } i = j \text{ and } \widehat{d}_i^t \neq 0, \\ -\dfrac{\widehat{w}_{ij}^t}{\sqrt{\widehat{d}_i^t \widehat{d}_j^t}} & \text{if } i \text{ and } j \text{ are adjacent,} \\ 0 & \text{otherwise.} \end{cases} \tag{6}
$$

Obviously, ζ is real number matrix, assume its eigenvalues are all real and non-negative. Let the eigenvalues of ζ be $\{\lambda_i | i = 0 : N - 1\}$ in increasing order of λ_i, such that $0 = \lambda_0 \leq \lambda_1 \leq \dots \leq \lambda_{N-1}$. Then transition matrix P satisfies $P = T^{-1/2}(I - \zeta)T^{1/2}$, and $\mathbf{1}TP = \mathbf{1}T$, where $\mathbf{1}$ is unit vector.

Definition 3   The random walk P^m is said to be irreducibility if for any $i,j \in V$, there exists some t such that $p_{ij}^m > 0$. Definition 3 ensures the graph P^m is strongly connected.

Definition 4   The random walk P^m is aperiodic if the greatest common divisor of the lengths of its simple cycles is 1, i.e., gcd $\{m : p_{ii}^m > 0\} = 1$ for any state i.

Definition 5   The random matrix P is said to be ergodic if there is an unique $n \times 1$ stationary distribution vector π satisfying $\lim_{m \to \infty} P^m (y^{(1)})' = \pi$, where $'$ is the transpose operation.

Definition 6   The random matrix P is convergent if $\lim_{m \to \infty} P^m (y^{(1)})'$ exists, for any initial vectors beliefs $y^{(1)}$.

The social influence exchange among the N agents may be represented by a graph $G(V, E_m)$ with the set E_m of edges given by $E_m = \{(i,j) | p_{ij}^m > 0\}$. But this condition is not sufficient to guarantee consensus of dynamic system (1) as stated in Ref. [24]. This motivates the following stronger version Definition 7, as addressed in Refs. [35, 36].

Definition 7   (Bounded interconnectivity times). There is some $B \geq 1$ such that for each nodes pairs $(i,j) \in E_\infty$, agent j sends his/her social impact to neighbor i at least once at every B consecutive time slots, i.e., the graph $(G(P), E_m \bigcup ... \bigcup E_{(m+B-1)})$ is strongly connected. This condition is equivalent to the requirement that there exists $B \geq 1$ such that $(i,j) \in E_m \bigcup ... \bigcup E_{m+B-1}$ for all $(i,j) \in E_\infty$ and $m \geq 0$.

Definition 5 is the well-known result that aperiodicity is necessary and sufficient for convergence in the case where P is strongly connected. In other words, the necessary conditions for the ergodicity of P are (i) *irreducibility*, (ii) *aperiodicity*, i.e., Definition 5 is equivalent to Definitions 3 and 4. If Definition 5 holds, Definition 6 is satisfied.

If a Markov chain is irreducible and aperiodic, i.e., Definition 3 (or Definition 3's stronger version Definition 7) and Definition 4 are both satisfied, or equivalently Definition 5 holds, then P converges to its corresponding steady distribution. This conclusion is fairly easily verified by adapting theorems on steady-state distributions of Markov chains, such as the proof provided in Ref. [37]. From another alternative, we will prove this result by spectrum graph theorem in the following section.

For above Definitions 3–7, we summarize the associated results in the following Theorem 1, then we emphasize on consensus result proof.

Theorem 1   If P is a random matrix, the following are equivalent:

(i) P is aperiodic and irreducible.

(ii) P is ergodic.

(iii) P is convergent, there is a unique left eigenvector p_s of P corresponding to eigenvalue 1 whose entries sum to 1 such that, for every $y^{(1)}$, $(\lim_{m \to \infty} P^m (y^{(1)})')_i = \pi(i)$, where $\pi(i) = (p_s)' (y^{(1)})'$ for every i.

Both (i) and (ii) in Theorem 1 are the well-known results. Next we focus on the proof of (iii) based on spectral graph theory. Theorem 1 presents the conditions for the formation of opinions convergence.

The convergence of opinions profile on random graph

In this section, with the above Definitions 3, 4 or 7, we prove that the convergence of group opinions over general weighted and undirected random graph are almost surely. In addition, we prove the lower bounds on the convergence time t for random walk P^t to be close to its stationary distribution, given an arbitrary initial distribution and small positive error ϵ. We note that this proof is based on spectrum graph theorem, which is different with Markov chains methods, such as in [20–22, 29].

Proof In a random walk associated with a weighted connected graph G, the transition matrix P satisfies $\mathbf{1}TP = \mathbf{1}T$, where $\mathbf{1}$ is the vector with all elements are scalar 1. Therefore, the stationary distribution is exactly $\pi = \mathbf{1}T/\text{vol}(G)$. We show that for any initial opinions profile distribution $y^{(1)}$, when m is large enough, $P^m y^{(1)}$ converges to the stationary distribution π in the sense of L_2 or Euclidean norm. We write $y^{(1)}T^{-1/2} = \sum_i a_i e_i$, where e_i denotes the orthonormal eigenfunction associated with λ_i. Because $e_0 = \mathbf{1}T^{1/2}/\sqrt{\text{vol}(G)}$ and $<y^{(1)}, \mathbf{1}> = 1$, $||.||$ represents the L^2 norm, we have $a_0 = \frac{<y^{(1)}T^{-1/2}, \mathbf{1}T^{1/2}>}{||\mathbf{1}T^{1/2}||} = \frac{1}{\sqrt{\text{vol}(G)}}$. We then have

$$||y^{(1)}P^m - \pi|| = ||y^{(1)}P^m - \mathbf{1}T/\text{vol}(G)|| = ||y^{(1)}P^m - a_0 e_0 T^{1/2}||$$

$$= ||y^{(1)}T^{-1/2}(I - \zeta)^m T^{1/2} - a_0 e_0 T^{1/2}|| = ||\sum_{i \neq 0}(1 - \lambda_i)^m a_i e_i T^{1/2}||$$

$$\leq (1 - \lambda')^m \frac{\max_j \sqrt{\widehat{d_j^t}}}{\min_j \sqrt{\widehat{d_j^t}}} \leq e^{-m\lambda'} \frac{\max_j \sqrt{\widehat{d_j^t}}}{\min_j \sqrt{\widehat{d_j^t}}} \tag{7}$$

where

$$\lambda' = \begin{cases} \lambda_1, & \text{if } 1 - \lambda_1 \geq \lambda_{N-1} - 1 \\ 2 - \lambda_{N-1}, & \text{else.} \end{cases}$$

Given any $\epsilon > 0$, for Eq. (7) we have

$$e^{-m\lambda'} \frac{\max_j \sqrt{\widehat{d_j^t}}}{\min_j \sqrt{\widehat{d_j^t}}} \leq \epsilon, \tag{8}$$

then we have $\frac{\max_j \sqrt{\widehat{d_j^t}}}{\epsilon \min_j \sqrt{\widehat{d_j^t}}} \leq e^{m\lambda'}$, so $m \geq \frac{1}{\lambda'} \log\left(\frac{\max_j \sqrt{\widehat{d_j^t}}}{\epsilon \min_j \sqrt{\widehat{d_j^t}}}\right)$.

With the symmetry of transition probability P^m, we easily check that $||y^{(1)}P^m - \pi'|| = ||(y^{(1)}P^m - \pi')'|| = ||(y^{(1)}P^m)' - \pi|| = ||(P^m)'(y^{(1)})' - \pi|| = ||P^m(y^{(1)})' - \pi||$.

With this we conclude that after $m \geq \lceil \frac{1}{\lambda'} \log(\frac{\max_j \sqrt{\widehat{d_j^t}}}{\epsilon \min_j \sqrt{\widehat{d_j^t}}}) \rceil$ steps, the L_2 distance between $P^m(y^{(1)})'$ and its stationary distribution π' is at most ϵ. Thus, P^m converges to a matrix with all of whose rows are equal to the positive vector $\pi' = (\pi_1, \pi_2, ..., \pi_N)'$, when a consensus is formed in Friedkin and Johnsen's model. Accordingly, we have $(\lim_{m\to\infty} y^{(m)})_i = \sum_{i=1}^{N} \pi_i y_i^{(1)}$ almost surely with ε approximating error corresponding to t updating steps.

In the herding example, there is consensus (of sorts), while which could lead to the wrong outcome or misunderstandings (misdirections) for the whole social group, such the "Mob phenomenon" of French revolution described by *Gustave LeBon*. In this case, group consensus is equivalent to the unwisdom of crowds. If group consensus to be emerged at certain slot m^*, such that $y^{(m^*)} = \frac{1}{N}\sum_{i=1}^{N} y_j^{(1)}$, for each j in a social group, we say that the society is wise, i.e., each individual arrives the group average initial opinions profile.

One special case of the above theorem is when P is a double random matrix. With this condition, the matrix has vector $\mathbf{1}$ as their common left eigenvector at all times, and, therefore, all the entries of the state vector converge to $(1/N)(\mathbf{1}^T y^{(1)})\mathbf{1} = (1/N)\sum_{j=1}^{N} y_j^{(1)}\mathbf{1}$, in other words, the mean of the initial N individual's opinion profile, with probability 1. This special case is addressed in Ref. [38], we say this group is a wise social group, as introduced in Ref. [32].

Numeric simulation

In this section, we aim to test the theoretical conclusion by numeric simulation methods. We consider the a group (with 34 individuals) discussion processes, and assume that (a) each member is presented with an issue on which opinions could range from -10 to 10 uniformly, (b) independently form an initial opinion on the issue. We fix time $t = 1$, and generate random initial interpersonal influence matrix W, with entries between 0 and 7. After realization of W, we calculate $max_j(\widehat{d}_j^t) = 48$, and $min_j(\widehat{d}_j^t) = 3$. Then following the same theoretical line, we construct P^t for $t = 1$, compute (4–6) and have $\{\lambda_i | i = 0 : N - 1\}$. According to inequality (7), based on $\{\lambda_i | i = 0 : N - 1\}$ we have

$\lambda' = 0.1101$. Given $\epsilon = 0.01$, according to (8) we have $m \geq \frac{1}{\lambda'}log(\frac{max_j\sqrt{\widehat{d}_j^t}}{\epsilon min_j\sqrt{\widehat{d}_j^t}}) = 54.4184$.

The result means that after $m > 54$ rounds of discussion and negotiation, the group reaches consensus steady state with preestablished error $\epsilon = 0.01$. Figure 1 illustrates the

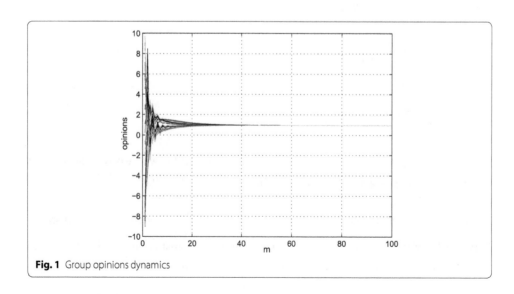

Fig. 1 Group opinions dynamics

group opinions dynamic processes, we can see that after $m > 50$ the difference among members approximate to zero.

Next, we continue simulate Friedkin and Johnsen's model (1) based on the following assumptions:

A1. Prototype group: where group numbers do not know each other, so each one put equal weight on other individuals;

A2. Group in evolution: where group numbers have already known each other, so each one might put unequal weight on different individuals according to his/her prior judgements.

Under these two assumptions, we try to find the connection between the behavior of agents and how long the group reaches consensus. Here, we refer to the individuals behaviors as individuals susceptibilities to interpersonal influence on the opinions, or individuals is open minded to take others opinions into account. It is obviously that the diagonals of matrix A represent the *susceptible level* (SL) as an parameter measure to describe individuals' open minded level. Since $I-A$ is the diagonal of W, i.e., $SL = a_i = 1 - w_{ii}, i = 1, \ldots, N$, where $SL = 0$ means that an agent only looks at his opinion (stubborn or egoistic behavior) and $SL = 1$ means that he does not look at his opinion at all, but takes all other opinions into account (open minded or altruistic behavior).

Under assumption A1, since an agent does not know all the other, that is why he equally takes all other opinion into account. In our simulation, we set equal influence weight for each individual (however with small weights if the group size is larger). Under A2, in order to describe each individual might exert different effects on other individuals, we randomly assign $w_{ij} \in [0, 1], i \neq j$. Figure 2 show the connection between *susceptible level* (SL) and how long it takes to reach consensus, within *Prototype group/Group in evolution*.

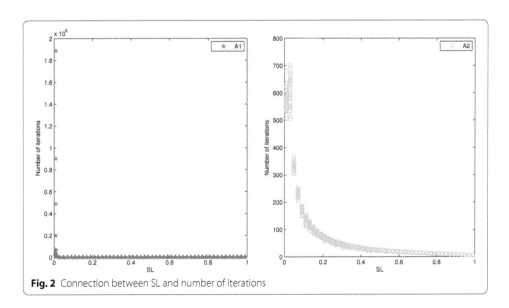

Fig. 2 Connection between SL and number of iterations

The Fig. 2 also illustrates, under both assumption A1 and A2, if SL = 0, according to (1) which means that every agent sticks on his opinion, completely without taking care of any other opinion, infinite iterations are needed to reach consensus, means that no consensus will be reached. For a group of very stubborn agent (SL close to 0, but SL ≠ 0 which means that every agent sticks on his opinion taking less care of any other opinion), the group needs more time to reach consensus. However, carefully examine we observe the dominant difference between A1 and A2: (1) when SL = 0, both group under assumptions A1 and A2 need enough time to reach consensus, but group A2 needs less convergence time than that of group A1. (2) for *Prototype group* if SL just a little greater than zero, then the group could rapidly toward consensus. However, for a *group in evolution*, because each individual imposes different influence weights on others (this means the group is heterogeneous comparing with *Prototype group*), with the continuously increasing of SL, the number of iterations needed to reach consensus (group consensus time) shows smoothing decaying characteristic.

Conclusions

In this study, from random walk aspects, we investigate the well-known Friedkin and Johnsen's model. We define a weighted random walk P based on the social influence matrix. If P satisfies ergodicity, i.e., aperiodic and irreducible, Friedkin and Johnsen's model converges to the stable consensus. Furthermore, we prove the lower bounds on the convergence time m for random walk P^m to be close to its consensus state, given an arbitrary initial opinions profiles and a small achieved convergence tolerance ϵ. We also verify the theoretical result by numeric simulation. Finally, under both *Prototype group* and *Group in evolution* assumptions, we simulate how long the group takes to reach a steady consensus state. We find that with the increasing of *susceptible level* (SL) both *Prototype group* and *Group in evolution* demonstrate opinions convergent characteristics, however, *Prototype group* rapidly tends to consensus if *susceptible level* (SL) bigger than 0.

We hope this study succeeds in providing a rigorous framework to explain and understand group consensus phenomenon. The next work will further consider influence of opinion leaders on population differentiation and the role of the convergence and the control of polarization in Internet group opinions. In addition, because the topology of networks could also be a key factor when opinions spreads among individuals, the networks model in this study may be replaced by small-world, scale free, regular networks, or interdependent network.

Since this paper mainly focuses on the group opinions dynamics over the networked social influence structure, that might ignore the case as social influence mostly follows either independent cascade or linear threshold model. We will combine the cascade or threshold effect into the social influence network model in our future study.

Authors' contributions
Conceived and designed the experiments: ZL, XT. Performed the experiments: ZL, BC. Contributed simulation tools: JY, PS. Wrote the paper: ZL, JY. All authors read and approved the final manuscript.

Author details
[1] Department of Applied Statistics, Dali University, Dali 671003, China. [2] Academy of Mathematics and Systems Sciences, Chinese Academy of Sciences, Beijing 100190, China.

Acknowledgements
The authors thank reviewers' helpful suggestions. This research was supported by National Natural Science Foundation of China under Grant Nos.71171187,71661001, 61473284,61462003, 71462001,11661030 and Scientific Research Foundation of Yunnan Provincial Education Department under Grant No. 2015Y386,2014Z137.

Competing interests
The authors declare that they have no competing interests.

References
1. Mark G. The strength of weak ties. Am J Sociol. 1973;78:1360–80.
2. Burt RS. Innovation as a structural interest: Rethinking the impact of network position on innovation adoption. Soc Netw. 1980;2(4):327–55.
3. Newman MEJ. Complex systems: a survey. Am J Phys. 2011;79:800–10.
4. Stoner JA. A comparison of individual and group decision involving risk. Master's thesis, Massachusetts Institute of Technology, 1961.
5. Myers DG, Lamm H. The group polarization phenomenon. Psychol Bull. 1976;83(4):602.
6. Mackie DM. Social identification effects in group polarization. J Personal Soc Psychol. 1986;50:720–8.
7. Moscovici S, et al. Studies in group decision II: differences of positions differences of opinion and group polarization. Eur J. 1972;2:385–99.
8. Sunstein CR. The law of group polarization. University of Chicago Law School. John M. Olin Law and Economics Working Paper, 1999;91.
9. Friedkin NE. Choice shift and group polarization. Am Sociol Rev. 1999;64(6):856–75.
10. Li Z, Tang X. Group polarization: connecting, influence and balance, a simulation study based on hopfield modeling. In: PRICAI 2012: trends in artificial intelligence. Berlin: Springer; 2012; p. 710–721.
11. DeGroot MH. Reaching a consensus. J Am Stat Assoc. 1974;69(345):118–21.
12. Friedkin NE, Johnsen EC. Social influence networks and opinion change. In: Lawler EJ, Macy MW editos. Advances in Group Processes. 1999;16:1–29.
13. Friedkin NE. A formal theory of reflected appraisals in the evolution of power. Admin Sci Q. 2011;56(4):501–29.
14. French J. A formal theory of social power. Psychol Rev. 1956;63:181–94.
15. Latane B. The psychology of social impact. Am Psychol. 1981;36:343–56.
16. Jadbabaie A, Lin J, Morse AS. Coordination of groups of mobile autonomous agents using nearest neighbor rules. IEEE Trans Autom Control. 2003;48(6):988–1001.
17. Blondel V, Hendrickx JM, Olshevsky A, et al. Convergence in multiagent coordination, consensus, and flocking. The 44th IEEE conference on decision and control and the European control conference 2005, 2996–3000
18. Olfati-Saber R, Murray RM. Consensus problems in networks of agents with switching topology and time-delays. IEEE Trans Autom Control. 2004;49(9):1520–33.
19. Moreau L. Stability of multiagent systems with time-dependent communication links. IEEE Trans Autom Control. 2005;50(2):169–82.
20. Fagnani F, Zampieri S. Randomized consensus algorithms over large scale networks. IEEE J Sel Areas Commun. 2008;26(4):634–49.
21. Tsitsiklis JN. Problems in decentralized decision making and computation. Ph.D. Dissertation, Massachusetts Institute of Technology. 1985.
22. Kempe D, Dobra A, Gehrke J. Gossip-based computation of aggregate information. In: Proceedings of the 44th annual IEEE symposium on foundations of computer science, IEEE. 2003. p. 482–91.
23. Intanagonwiwat C, Govindan R, Estrin D. Directed diffusion: a scalable and robust communication paradigm for sensor networks. In: Proceedings of the 6th annual international conference on mobile computing and networking. ACM. 2000. p. 56–67.
24. Zhao J, Govindan R, Estrin D. Computing aggregates for monitoring wireless sensor networks. In: Proceedings of the first IEEE international workshop on sensor network protocols and applications, IEEE. 2003; p. 139–48.
25. Xiao L, Boyd S, Lall S: A scheme for robust distributed sensor fusion based on average consensus. The 4th international symposium on information processing in sensor networks, IEEE. 2005, p. 63–70.
26. Dimakis AG, Sarwate AD, Wainwright MJ: Geographic gossip: efficient aggregation for sensor networks. In: Proceedings of the 5th international conference on information processing in sensor networks. ACM. 2006, p. 69–76.
27. Galam S. From 2000 Bush–Gore to 2006 Italian elections: voting at fifty-fifty and the contrarian effect. Qual Quant. 2007;41(4):579–89.
28. Arrow KJ. Social choice and individual values. New York: Wiley; 1951.
29. Frasca P, Ravazzi C, Tempo R, et al. Gossips and prejudices: Ergodic randomized dynamics in social networks. arXiv:1304.2268. 2013.
30. Chung FRK. Spectral Graph Theory, Vol. 92. American Mathematical Society; 1997.
31. Ishii H, Tempo R. Distributed randomized algorithms for the PageRank computation. IEEE Trans Autom Control. 2010;55(9):1987–2002.
32. Golub B, Jackson MO. Naïve learning in social networks and the wisdom of crowds. Am Econ J Microecon. 2010;2(1):112–149.
33. Touri B, Nedic A. On ergodicity, infinite flow, and consensus in random models. IEEE Trans Autom Control. 2011;56(7):1593–605.
34. Bertsekas D, Tsitsiklis JN: Parallel and Distributed Computation: Numerical Methods,Prentice Hall, 1989.
35. Nedic A, Ozdaglar A. Distributed subgradient methods for multi-agent optimization. IEEE Trans Autom Control. 2009;54(1):48–61.
36. Olshevsky A, Tsitsiklis JN. Convergence speed in distributed consensus and averaging. SIAM J Control Optim. 2009;48(1):33–55.

7

Distribution and dependence of extremes in network sampling processes

Konstantin Avrachenkov[1], Natalia M. Markovich[2] and Jithin K. Sreedharan[1*]

*Correspondence:
jithin.sreedharan@inria.fr
[1] INRIA Sophia Antipolis 2004, route des Lucioles - BP 93, 06902 Sophia Antipolis Cedex, France
Full list of author information is available at the end of the article

Abstract

We explore the dependence structure in the sampled sequence of complex networks. We consider randomized algorithms to sample the nodes and study extremal properties in any associated stationary sequence of characteristics of interest like node degrees, number of followers, or income of the nodes in online social networks, which satisfy two mixing conditions. Several useful extremes of the sampled sequence like the kth largest value, clusters of exceedances over a threshold, and first hitting time of a large value are investigated. We abstract the dependence and the statistics of extremes into a single parameter that appears in extreme value theory called extremal index (EI). In this work, we derive this parameter analytically and also estimate it empirically. We propose the use of EI as a parameter to compare different sampling procedures. As a specific example, degree correlations between neighboring nodes are studied in detail with three prominent random walks as sampling techniques.

Keywords: Network sampling; Extreme value theory; Extremal index; Random walks on graph

Introduction

Data from real complex networks shows that correlations exist in various forms, for instance the existence of social relationships and interests in social networks. Degree correlations between neighbors, correlations in income, followers of users, and number of likes of specific pages in social networks are some examples, to name a few. These kind of correlations have several implications in network structure. For example, degree-degree correlation manifests itself in assortativity or disassortativity of the network [1].

We consider very large complex networks where it is impractical to have a complete picture *a priori*. Crawling or sampling techniques can be employed in practice to explore such networks by making the use of application programming interface (API) calls or HTML scrapping. We look into randomized sampling techniques which generate stationary samples. As an example, random walk-based algorithms are in use in many cases because of several advantages offered by them [2, 3].

We focus on the extremal properties in the correlated and stationary sequence of characteristics of interest $X_1, \ldots, X_n$ which is a function of the node sequence, the one actually generated by sampling algorithms. The characteristics of interest, for instance, can be node degrees, node income, number of followers of the node in online social networks (OSN), etc. Among the properties, clusters of exceedances of such sequences over high thresholds are studied in particular. The cluster of exceedances is roughly defined as the consecutive exceedances of $\{X_n\}$ over the threshold $\{u_n\}$ between two consecutive non-exceedances. For more rigorous definitions, see [4–6]. It is important to investigate stochastic nature of extremes since it allows us to collect statistics or opinions more effectively in the clustered (network sampling) process.

The dependence structure of sampled sequence exceeding sufficiently high thresholds is measured using a parameter called extremal index (EI), θ. It is defined in extremal value theory as follows.

Definition 1. *([7], p. 53)* The stationary sequence $\{X_n\}_{n\geq 1}$, with F as the marginal distribution function and $M_n = \max\{X_1, ..., X_n\}$, is said to have the extremal index $\theta \in [0, 1]$ if for each $0 < \tau < \infty$ there is a sequence of real numbers (thresholds) $u_n = u_n(\tau)$ such that

$$\lim_{n\to\infty} n(1 - F(u_n)) = \tau \text{ and} \tag{1}$$

$$\lim_{n\to\infty} P\{M_n \leq u_n\} = e^{-\theta\tau}. \tag{2}$$

The maxima M_n is related to EI more clearly as ([4], p. 381)[1]

$$P\{M_n \leq u_n\} = F^{n\theta}(u_n) + o(1). \tag{3}$$

When $\{X_n\}_{n\geq 1}$ is independent and identically distributed (i.i.d.) (for instance, in uniform independent node sampling), $\theta = 1$ and point processes of exceedances over threshold u_n converges weakly to homogeneous Poisson process with rate τ as $n \to \infty$ ([4], chapter 5). But when $0 \leq \theta < 1$, point processes of exceedances converges weakly to compound Poisson process with rate $\theta\tau$ and this implies that exceedances of high threshold values u_n tend to occur in clusters for dependent data ([4], chapter 10).

EI has many useful interpretations and applications like

- Finding distribution of order statistics of the sampled sequence. These can be used to find quantiles and predict the kth largest value which arise with a certain probability. Specifically for the distribution of maxima, Eq. 3 is available and the quantile of maxima is proportional to EI. Hence in case of samples with lower EI, lower values of maxima can be expected. When sampled sequence is the sequence of node degrees, these give many useful results.
- Close relation to the distribution and expectation of the size of clusters of exceedances (see for e.g. [4, 6]).
- Characterization of the first hitting time of the sampled sequence to (u_n, ∞). Thus in case of applications where the aim is to detect large values of samples quickly, without actually employing sampling (which might be very costly), we can compare different sampling procedures by EI: smaller EI leads to longer waiting of the first hitting time.

These interpretations are explained later in the paper. The network topology as well as the sampling method determine the stationary distribution of the characteristics of interest under a sampling technique and is reflected on the EI.

Our contributions

The main contributions in this work are as follows. We associated extremal value theory of stationary sequences to sampling of large complex networks, and we study the extremal and clustering properties of the sampling process due to dependencies. In order to facilitate a painless future study of correlations and clusters of samples in large networks, we propose to abstract the extremal properties into a single and handy parameter, EI. For any general stationary samples meeting two mixing conditions, we find that knowledge of bivariate distribution or bivariate copula is sufficient to compute EI analytically and thereby deriving many extremal properties. Several useful applications of EI (first hitting time, order statistics, and mean cluster size) to analyze large graphs, known only through sampled sequences, are proposed. Degree correlations are explained in detail with a random graph model for which joint degree distribution exists for neighbor nodes. Three different random walk-based algorithms that are widely discussed in literature (see [2] and the references therein) are then revised for degree state space, and EI is calculated when the joint degree distribution is bivariate Pareto. We establish a general lower bound for EI in PageRank processes irrespective of the degree correlation model. Finally, using two estimation techniques, EI is numerically computed for a synthetic graph with neighbor degrees correlated and for two real networks (Enron email network and DBLP network).

The paper is organized as follows. In section "Calculation of extremal index (EI)", methods to derive EI are presented. Section "Degree correlations" considers the case of degree correlations. In section "Description of the configuration model with degree-degree correlation", the graph model and correlated graph generation technique are presented. Section "Description of random walk-based sampling processes" explains the different types of random walks studied and derives associated transition kernels and joint degree distributions. EI is calculated for different sampling techniques later in section "Extremal index for bivariate Pareto degree correlation". In section "Applications of extremal index in network sampling processes", we provide several applications of EI in graph sampling techniques. In section "Estimation of extremal index and numerical results", we estimate EI and perform numerical comparisons. Finally, section "Conclusions" concludes the paper.

A shorter version of this work has appeared in [8].

Calculation of extremal index (EI)

We consider networks represented by an undirected graph G with N vertices and M edges. Since the networks under consideration are huge, we assume it is impossible to describe them completely, i.e., no adjacency matrix is given beforehand. Assume any randomized sampling procedure is employed and let the sampled sequence $\{X_i\}$ be any general sequence.

This section explains a way to calculate EI from the bivariate joint distribution if the sampled sequence admits two mixing conditions.

Condition $(D(u_n))$.

$$\left| P(X_{i_1} \leq u_n, \ldots, X_{i_p} \leq u_n, X_{j_1} \leq u_n, \ldots, X_{j_q} \leq u_n) \right.$$
$$\left. -P(X_{i_1} \leq u_n, \ldots, X_{i_p} \leq u_n)P(X_{j_1} \leq u_n, \ldots, X_{j_q} \leq u_n) \right| \leq \alpha_{n,l_n},$$

where $\alpha_{n,l_n} \to 0$ for some sequence $l_n = o(n)$ as $n \to \infty$, for any integers $i_1 \leq \ldots < i_p < j_1 < \ldots \leq j_q$ with $j_1 - i_p > l_n$.

Condition $(D''(u_n))$.

$$\lim_{n\to\infty} n \sum_{m=3}^{r_n} P(X_1 > u_n \geq X_2, X_m > u_n) = 0,$$

where $(n/r_n)\alpha_{n,l_n} \to 0$ and $l_n/r_n \to 0$ with α_{n,l_n}, l_n as in Condition $D(u_n)$ and r_n as $o(n)$.

Let $C(u,v)$ be a bivariate copula [9] ($[0,1]^2 \to [0,1]$) and $\underline{1} \cdot \nabla C(u,v)$ is its directional derivative along the direction $(1,1)$. Using Sklar's theorem ([9], p. 18), with F as the marginal stationary distribution function of the sampling process, the copula is given by

$$C(u,v) = P(X_1 \leq F^{-1}(u), X_2 \leq F^{-1}(v)),$$

where F^{-1} denotes the inverse function of F. This representation is unique if the stationary distribution $F(x)$ is continuous.

Theorem 1. *If the sampled sequence is stationary and satisfies conditions $D(u_n)$ and $D''(u_n)$, and the limits in Eqs. 1 and 2 take place, then the extremal index is given by*

$$\theta = \underline{1} \cdot \nabla C(1,1) - 1, \tag{4}$$

and $0 \leq \theta \leq 1$.

Proof. For a stationary sequence $\{X_n\}$ holding conditions $D(u_n)$ and $D''(u_n)$, if the limits in Eqs. 1 and 2 take place, $\theta = \lim_{n\to\infty} P(X_2 \leq u_n | X_1 > u_n)$ [10]. Then, we have

$$\begin{aligned}
\theta &= \lim_{n\to\infty} \frac{P(X_2 \leq u_n, X_1 > u_n)}{P(X_1 > u_n)} \\
&= \lim_{n\to\infty} \frac{P(X_2 \leq u_n) - P(X_1 \leq u_n, X_2 \leq u_n)}{P(X_1 > u_n)} \\
&= \lim_{n\to\infty} \frac{P(X_2 \leq u_n) - C\big(P(X_1 \leq u_n), P(X_2 \leq u_n)\big)}{1 - P(X_1 \leq u_n)} \\
&= \lim_{x\to 1} \frac{x - C(x,x)}{1 - x} \\
&= \underline{1} \cdot \nabla C(1,1) - 1,
\end{aligned}$$

which completes the proof. $\qquad\square$

Remark 1. *Condition $D''(u_n)$ can be made weaker to $D^{(k)}(u_n)$ presented in [11],*

$$\lim_{n\to\infty} nP\left(X_1 > u_n \geq \max_{2\leq i\leq k} X_i, \max_{k+1\leq j\leq r_n} X_j > u_n\right) = 0,$$

where r_n is defined as in $D''(u_n)$. For the stationary sequence, $D^{(2)}(u_n)$ is identical to $D''(u_n)$. If we assume $D^{(k)}$ is satisfied for some $k \geq 2$ along with $D(u_n)$, then following the proof of Theorem 1, EI can be derived as

$$\theta = \underline{1} \cdot \nabla C_k(1,\dots,1) - \underline{1} \cdot \nabla C_{k-1}(1,\dots,1),$$

where $C_k(x_1,\dots,x_k)$ represents the copula of k-dimensional vector $(x_1,\dots,x_k)$, C_{k-1} is its $(k-1)$th marginal, $C_{k-1}(x) = C_{k-1}(x_1,\dots,x_{k-1},1)$, and $\underline{1} \cdot \nabla C_k(x_1,\dots,x_k)$ denotes the directional derivative of $C_k(x_1,\dots,x_k)$ along the k-dimensional vector $(1,1,\dots,1)$.

In some cases, it is easy to work with the joint tail distribution. Survival copula $\widehat{C}(\cdot, \cdot)$ which corresponds to

$$P(X_1 > x, X_2 > x) = \widehat{C}(\overline{F}(x), \overline{F}(x)),$$

with $\overline{F}(x) = 1 - F(x)$, can also be used to calculate θ. It is related to copula as $\widehat{C}(u, u) = C(1 - u, 1 - u) + 2u - 1$ ([9], p. 32). Hence, $\theta = \underline{1} \cdot \nabla C(1, 1) - 1 = 1 - \underline{1} \cdot \nabla \widehat{C}(0, 0)$.

Lower tail dependence function of survival copula is defined as [12]

$$\lambda(u_1, u_2) = \lim_{t \to 0^+} \frac{\widehat{C}(tu_1, tu_2)}{t}.$$

Hence, $\underline{1} \cdot \nabla \widehat{C}(0, 0) = \lambda(1, 1)$. λ can be calculated for different copula families. In particular, if $\widehat{C}$ is a bivariate Archimedean copula, then it can be represented as $\widehat{C}(u_1, u_2) = \psi\left(\psi^{-1}(u_1) + \psi^{-1}(u_2)\right)$, where ψ is the generator function and ψ^{-1} is its inverse with $\psi : [0, \infty] \to [0, 1]$ meeting several other conditions. If ψ is a regularly varying distribution with index $-\beta$, $\beta > 0$, then $\lambda(x_1, x_2) = \left(x_1^{-\beta^{-1}} + x_2^{-\beta^{-1}}\right)^{-\beta}$ and (X_1, X_2) has a bivariate regularly varying distribution [12]. Therefore, for Archimedean copula family, EI is given by

$$\theta = 1 - 1/2^\beta. \tag{5}$$

As an example, bivariate Pareto distribution of the form $P(X_1 > x_1, X_2 > x_2) = (1 + x_1 + x_2)^{-\gamma}$, $\gamma > 0$ has Archimedean copula with generator function $\psi(x) = (1 + x)^{-\gamma}$. This gives $\theta = 1 - 1/2^\gamma$. Bivariate exponential distribution of the form

$$P(X_1 > x_1, X_2 > x_2) = 1 - e^{-x_1} - e^{-x_2} + e^{-(x_1 + x_2 + \eta x_1 x_2)},$$

$0 \leq \eta \leq 1$, also admits Archimedean copula.

Check of conditions $D(u_n)$ and $D''(u_n)$ for functions of Markov samples

If the sampling technique is assumed to be based on a Markov chain and the sampled sequence is a measurable function of stationary Markov samples, then such a sequence is stationary and [13] proved that another mixing condition $\text{AIM}(u_n)$ which implies $D(u_n)$ is satisfied. Condition $D''(u_n)$ allows clusters with consecutive exceedances and eliminates the possibility of clusters with upcrossing of the threshold u_n ($X_i \leq u_n < X_{i+1}$). Hence in those cases, where it is tedious to check the condition $D''(u_n)$ theoretically, we can use numerical procedures to measure ratio of number of consecutive exceedances to number of exceedances and the ratio of number of upcrossings to number of consecutive exceedances in small intervals. Such an example is provided in section "Extremal index for bivariate Pareto degree correlation".

Remark 2. *The EI derived in [14] has the same expression as in Eq. 4. But [14] assumes $\{X_n\}$ is sampled from a first-order Markov chain. We relax the Markov property requirement to D and D'' conditions, and the example below demonstrates a hidden Markov chain that can satisfy D and D''.*

Let us consider a hidden Markov chain with the observations $\{X_k\}_{k \geq 1}$ and the underlying homogeneous Markov chain as $\{Y_k\}_{k \geq 1}$ in stationarity. The underlying Markov chain is finite state space, but the conditional distributions of the observations $P(X_k \leq x | Y_k = y) = F_y(x)$ have infinite support and condition Eq. 1 holds for $F_y(x)$.

Proposition 1. *When condition Eq. 1 holds for $F_y(x)$, the observation sequence $\{X_k\}_{k \geq 1}$ of the hidden Markov chain satisfies Condition D''.*

Proof. Let the transition probability matrix of $\{Y_k\}_{k \geq 1}$ be P (with $P(Y_2 = j | Y_1 = i) = P_{ij}$) and the stationary distribution be π (with $P(Y_1 = i) = \pi_i$). We have,

$$P(X_1 > u_n \geq X_2, X_m > u_n)$$
$$= \sum_{i,j,k} P(Y_1 = i, Y_2 = j, Y_m = k) P(X_1 > u_n \geq X_2, X_m > u_n | Y_1, Y_2, Y_m)$$
$$= \sum_{i,j,k} \pi_i P_{ij} P_{jk}^{(m-2)} P_i(X_1 > u_n) P_j(X_2 \leq u_n) P_k(X_m > u_n)$$
$$\sim \sum_{i,j,k} \pi_i P_{ij} P_{jk}^{(m-2)} \frac{\tau}{n} \left(1 - \frac{\tau}{n}\right) \frac{\tau}{n}, \quad n \to \infty.$$

Thus

$$\lim_{n \to \infty} n \sum_{m=3}^{r_n} P(X_1 > u_n \geq X_2, X_m > u_n) = 0,$$

since $r_n = o(n)$, which completes the proof. $\qquad\square$

Proposition 1 essentially tells that if the graph is explored by a Markov chain-based sampling algorithm and the samples are taken as any measurable functions of the underlying Markov chain, satisfying Condition (1) then Condition D'' holds. Measurable functions, for example, can represent various attributes of the nodes such as income or frequency of messages in social networks.

Degree correlations

The techniques established in section "Calculation of extremal index (EI)" are very general, applicable to any sampling techniques and any sequence of samples which satisfy certain conditions. In this section, we illustrate the calculation of EI for dependencies among degrees. We revise different sampling techniques. We denote the sampled sequence $\{X_i\}$ as $\{D_i\}$ in this section, since the sampled degree sequence will be a case study in this section.

Description of the configuration model with degree-degree correlation

To test the proposed approaches and the derived formulas, we use a synthetically generated configuration type random graph with a given joint degree-degree probability distribution, which takes into account correlation in degrees between neighbor nodes. The dependence structure in the graph is described by the joint degree-degree probability density function $f(d_1, d_2)$ with d_1 and d_2 indicating the degrees of adjacent nodes or equivalently by the corresponding tail distribution function $\overline{F}(d_1, d_2) = P(D_1 \geq d_1, D_2 \geq d_2)$ with D_1 and D_2 representing the degree random variables (see e.g., [1, 15, 16]).

The probability that a randomly chosen edge has the end vertices with degrees $d_1 \leq d \leq d_1 + \Delta(d_1)$ and $d_2 \leq d \leq d_2 + \Delta(d_2)$ is $(2 - \delta_{d_1 d_2}) f(d_1, d_2) \Delta(d_1) \Delta(d_2)$. Here $\delta_{d_1 d_2} = 1$ if $d_1 = d_2$, otherwise $\delta_{d_1 d_2} = 0$. The multiplying factor 2 appears on the above expression when $d_1 \neq d_2$ because of the symmetry in $f(d_1, d_2)$, $f(d_1, d_2) = f(d_2, d_1)$ due to the undirected nature of the underlying graph and the fact that both $f(d_1, d_2)$ and $f(d_2, d_1)$ contribute to the edge probability under consideration.

The degree density $f_d(d_1)$ can be related to the marginal of $f(d_1, d_2)$ as follows:

$$f(d_1) = \int_{d_2} f(d_1, d_2) d(d_2) \approx \frac{d_1 f_d(d_1)}{E[D]}, \tag{6}$$

where $E[D]$ denotes the mean node degree,

$$E[D] = \left[\int \int \left(\frac{f(d_1, d_2)}{d_1} \right) d(d_1) d(d_2) \right]^{-1}.$$

$f(.)$ can be interpreted as the degree density of a vertex reached by following a randomly chosen edge. The approximation for $f(d_1)$ is obtained as follows: in the right-hand side (R.H.S.) of Eq. 6, roughly, $d_1 f_d(d_1) N$ is the number of half edges from nodes with degree around d_1 and $E[D] N$ is the total number of half edges. For discrete distributions, Eq. 6 becomes equality.

From the above description, it can be noted that the knowledge of $f(d_1, d_2)$ is sufficient to describe this random graph model and for its generation.

Most of the results in this paper are derived assuming continuous probability distributions for $f(d_1, d_2)$ and $f_d(d_1)$ because an easy and unique way to calculate EI exists for continuous distributions in our setup (more details in section "Calculation of extremal index (EI)"). Also the EI might not exist for many discrete valued distributions [7].

Random graph generation

A random graph with bivariate joint degree-degree distribution can be generated as follows ([17]):

1. Degree sequence is generated according to the degree distribution, $f_d(d) = \frac{f(d)E[D]}{d}$
2. An uncorrelated random graph is generated with the generated degree sequence using configuration model ([1, 18])
3. Metropolis dynamics is now applied on the generated graph: choose two edges randomly (denoted by the vertex pairs (v_1, w_1) and (v_2, w_2)) and measure the degrees, (j_1, k_1) and (j_2, k_2), that correspond to these vertex pairs and generated a random number, y, according to uniform distribution in $[0, 1]$. If $y \le \min(1, (f(j_1, j_2) f(k_1, k_2)) / (f(j_1, k_1) f(j_2, k_2)))$, then remove the selected edges and construct news ones as (v_1, v_2) and (w_1, w_2). Otherwise, keep the selected edges intact. This dynamics will generate an instance of the random graph with the required joint degree-degree distribution. Run Metropolis dynamics well enough to mix the generating process.

As an example, we shall often use the following bivariate Pareto model for the joint degree-degree tail function of the graph,

$$\bar{F}(d_1, d_2) = \left(1 + \frac{d_1 - \mu}{\sigma} + \frac{d_2 - \mu}{\sigma} \right)^{-\gamma}, \tag{7}$$

where σ, μ, and γ are positive values. The use of the bivariate Pareto distribution can be justified by the statistical analysis in [19].

Description of random walk-based sampling processes

In this section, we explain three different random walk-based algorithms for exploring the network. They have been extensively studied in previous works [2, 3, 20] where they are formulated with vertex set as the state space of the underlying Markov chain on graph. The walker in these algorithms, after reaching each node, moves to another node randomly by following the transition kernel of the Markov chain. However, the quantity of interest is generally a measurable function of the Markov chain. As a case study, let us again take the degree sequence. We use $f_{\mathscr{X}}$ and $P_{\mathscr{X}}$ to represent the probability density function and probability measure under the algorithm $\mathscr{X}$ with the exception that f_d represents the probability density function of degrees.

Random walk (RW)

In a random walk, the next node to visit is chosen uniformly among the neighbors of the current node. Let $V_1, V_2, \ldots$ be the nodes crawled by the RW and $D_1, D_2, \ldots$ be the degree sequence corresponding to the sequence $V_1, V_2, \ldots$.

Theorem 2. *The following relation holds in the stationary regime*

$$f_{\mathrm{RW}}(d_1, d_2) = f(d_1, d_2), \tag{8}$$

where $f(d_1, d_2)$ is the joint degree-degree distribution and $f_{\mathrm{RW}}(d_1, d_2)$ is the bi-variate joint distribution of the degree sequences generated by the standard random walk.

Proof. We note that the sequence $\{(V_i, V_{i+1})\}_{i \geq 1}$ also forms a Markov chain. With the assumption that the graph is connected, the ergodicity holds for any function g, i.e.,

$$\frac{1}{T} \sum_{i=1}^{T} g(V_i, V_{i+1}) \to \mathrm{E}_\pi \left[g(V_\xi, V_{\xi+1}) \right], \quad T \to \infty,$$

where E_π is the expectation under stationary distribution π of $\{(V_i, V_{i+1})\}$ (which is uniform over edges) and $(V_\xi, V_{\xi+1})$ indicates a randomly picked edge. The ergodicity can then be extended to functions of the degree sequence $\{(D_i, D_{i+1})\}$ corresponding to $\{(V_i, V_{i+1})\}$, and in particular

$$\frac{1}{T} \sum_{i=1}^{T} \mathbf{1}\{D_i = d_1, D_{i+1} = d_2\} \to \mathrm{E}_\pi \left[\mathbf{1}\{D_\xi = d_1, D_{\xi+1} = d_2\} \right], \quad T \to \infty$$

$$= \frac{1}{M} \sum_{(p,q) \in E} \mathbf{1}\{D_p = d_1, D_q = d_2\}$$

$$= f(d_1, d_2), \tag{9}$$

where $\mathbf{1}\{\mathcal{A}\}$ denotes the indicator function for the event $\mathcal{A}$. L.H.S. of (9) is an estimator of $f_{\mathrm{RW}}(d_1, d_2)$. This means that when the RW is in stationary regime $\mathrm{E}[\mathbf{1}\{D_i = d_1, D_{i+1} = d_2\}] = \mathrm{E}_\pi[\mathbf{1}\{D_\xi = d_1, D_{\xi+1} = d_2\}]$ and hence Eq. 8 holds. $\qquad\square$

PageRank (PR)

Using Eq. 6, we can approximate the degree sequence by a random walk on degree space with the following transition kernel:

$$f_{\mathrm{RW}}(d_{t+1}|d_t) = \frac{\mathrm{E}[D] f(d_t, d_{t+1})}{d_t f_d(d_t)}, \tag{10}$$

where the present node has degree d_t and the next node is with degree d_{t+1}. The above relation holds with equality for discrete degree distribution, but some care needs to be taken if one uses continuous version for the degree distributions.

If the standard random walk on the vertex set is in the stationary regime, its stationary distribution (probability of staying at a particular vertex i) is proportional to the degree (see e.g., [20]) and is given by $d_i/2M$, M being the number of edges. Then in the standard random walk on degree set, the stationary distribution of staying at any node with degree around d_1 can be approximated as $Nf_d(d_1)(d_1/2M)$, with N as the number of nodes. Thus

$$f_{\mathrm{RW}}(d_1) = \frac{d_1}{\mathrm{E}[D]}f_d(d_1).$$

Check of the approximation

We provide comparison of simulated values and theoretical values of transition kernel of RW in Fig. 1. To be specific, we use the bivariate Pareto distribution given (7). In the figure, N is 5,000. $\mu = 10$, $\gamma = 1.2$ and $\sigma = 15$. These choices of parameters provide $E[D] = 21.0052$. At each instant Metropolis dynamics will choose two edges and it has run 200,000 times (provides sufficient mixing). The figure shows satisfactory fitting of the approximation.

PageRank is a modification of the random walk which with a fixed probability $1 - c$ samples a random node with uniform distribution and with a probability c, it follows the random walk transition [3]. Its evolution on degree state space can be described as follows:

$$\begin{aligned}
f_{PR}(d_{t+1}|d_t) &= c\,f_{RW}(d_{t+1}|d_t) + (1-c)\frac{1}{N}Nf_d(d_{t+1}) \\
&= c\,f_{RW}(d_{t+1}|d_t) + (1-c)f_d(d_{t+1}).
\end{aligned} \tag{11}$$

Here the $1/N$ corresponds to the uniform sampling on vertex set and $\frac{1}{N}Nf_d(d_{t+1})$ indicates the net probability of jumping to all the nodes with degree around d_{t+1}.

Consistency with PageRank value distribution

We make a consistency check of the approximation derived for transition kernel by studying tail behavior of degree distribution and PageRank value distribution. It is known that

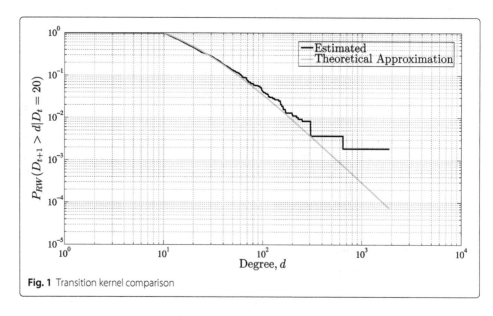

Fig. 1 Transition kernel comparison

under some strict conditions, for a directed graph, PageRank and Indegree have same tail exponents [21]. In our formulation in terms of degrees, for *uncorrelated* and undirected graph, PageRank for a given degree d, $\mathrm{PR}(d)$, can be approximated from the basic definition as,

$$\mathrm{PR}(d) = f_{\mathrm{PR}}(d) = c\, f_{\mathrm{RW}}(d) + (1 - c)\, f_d(d).$$

This is a deterministic quantity. We are interested in the distribution of the random variable $\mathrm{PR}(D)$, PageRank of a randomly chosen degree class D. PageRank $\mathrm{PR}(d)$ is also the long term proportion or probability that PageRank process ends in a degree class with degree d. This can be scaled suitably to provide a rank-type information. Its tail distribution is

$$P(\mathrm{PR}(D) > x) = P\left(c.f_{\mathrm{RW}}(D) + (1 - c).f_d(D) > x\right),$$

where $D \sim f_d(.)$. The PageRank of any vertex inside the degree class d is $\mathrm{PR}(d)/(Nf_d(d))$. The distribution of PageRank of a randomly chosen vertex i, $P(\mathrm{PR}(i) > x)$ after appropriate scaling for comparison with degree distribution is $P(N.\mathrm{PR}(i) > \hat{d})$, where $\hat{d} = Nx$. Now

$$
\begin{aligned}
P(N.\mathrm{PR}(i) > \hat{d}) &= P\left(N\frac{PR(D)}{Nf_d(D)} > \hat{d}\right) \\
&= P\left(D > \frac{E[D]}{c}\left[\hat{d} - (1 - c)\right]\right).
\end{aligned}
$$

This of the form $P(D > A\hat{d} + B)$ with A and B as appropriate constants and hence will have the same exponent of degree distribution tail when the graph is *uncorrelated*.

There is no convenient expression for the stationary distribution of PageRank, to the best of our knowledge, and it is difficult to come up with an easy to handle expression for the joint distribution. Therefore, along with other advantages, we consider another modification of the standard random walk.

Random walk with jumps (RWJ)

RW sampling leads to many practical issues like the possibility to get stuck in a disconnected component, biased estimators etc. RWJ overcomes such problems [2].

In this algorithm, we follow random walk on a modified graph which is a superposition of the original graph and complete graph on same vertex set of the original graph with weight α/N on each artificially added edge, $\alpha \in [0, \infty]$ being a design parameter [2]. The algorithm can be shown to be equivalent to select $c = \alpha/(d_t + \alpha)$ in the PageRank algorithm, where d_t is the degree of the present node. The larger the node's degree, the less likely is the artificial jump of the process. This modification makes the underlying Markov chain time reversible, significantly reduces mixing time, improves estimation error, and leads to a closed form expression for stationary distribution.

Before proceeding to formulate the next theorem, we recall that the degree distribution $f_d(d_1)$ is different from the marginal of $f(d_1, d_2), f(d_1)$.

Theorem 3. *The following relation holds in the stationary regime*

$$f_{\mathrm{RWJ}}(d_1, d_2) = \frac{E[D]}{E[D] + \alpha} f(d_1, d_2) + \frac{\alpha}{E[D] + \alpha} f_d(d_1) f_d(d_2), \tag{12}$$

where $f(d_1, d_2)$ is the joint degree-degree distribution, $f_d(d_1)$ is the degree distribution, and $f_{RWJ}(d_1, d_2)$ is the bi-variate joint distribution of the degree sequences generated by the random walk with jumps.

Proof. On the similar lines in the analysis of RW, $f_{RWJ}(d_1, d_2)$ can be calculated as follows. The stationary distribution, $f_{RWJ}(p)$, for node p (on the vertex set) is $(d_p + \alpha)/(2M + N\alpha)$. The transition probability from node p to node q, $f_{RWJ}(q|p)$, is $(\alpha/N + 1)/(d_p + \alpha)$ when there is a link from p to q, and when there is no link, it is $(\alpha/N)/(d_p + \alpha)$ [2]. Then, the joint distribution between nodes is given by

$$f_{RWJ}(p, q) = f_{RWJ}(q|p)f_{RWJ}(p) = \begin{cases} \frac{\frac{\alpha}{N} + 1}{2M + N\alpha} & \text{if } p \text{ has link to } q, \\ \frac{\frac{\alpha}{N}}{2M + N\alpha} & \text{if } p \text{ does not have link to } q. \end{cases}$$

Therefore

$$\begin{aligned} f_{RWJ}(d_1, d_2) \\ &= \mathrm{E}_\pi\left[\mathbf{1}\left\{D_\xi = d_1, D_{\xi+1} = d_2\right\}\right] \\ &\overset{(a)}{=} 2\frac{\frac{\alpha}{N} + 1}{2M + N\alpha}\sum_{(p,q)\in E}\mathbf{1}\left\{D_p = d_1, D_q = d_2\right\} \\ &\qquad + 2\frac{\frac{\alpha}{N}}{2M + N\alpha}\sum_{(p,q)\notin E}\mathbf{1}\left\{D_p = d_1, D_q = d_2\right\} \\ &\overset{(b)}{=} 2\frac{\frac{\alpha}{N} + 1}{2M + N\alpha}Mf(d_1, d_2) \\ &\qquad + 2\frac{\frac{\alpha}{N}}{2M + N\alpha}\left(\frac{1}{2}\sum_{p\in V}\mathbf{1}\{D_p = d_1\}\sum_{q\in V}\mathbf{1}\{D_q = d_2\} - Mf(d_1, d_2)\right) \\ &= \frac{\mathrm{E}[D]}{\mathrm{E}[D] + \alpha}f(d_1, d_2) + \frac{\alpha}{\mathrm{E}[D] + \alpha}f_d(d_1)f_d(d_2). \end{aligned}$$

Here $\mathrm{E}[D] = 2M/N$. The multiplying factor 2 is introduced in (a) because of the symmetry in the joint distribution $f_{RWJ}(p, q)$ over the nodes, terms outside the summation in the R.H.S. The factor $1/2$ in R.H.S. in (b) is to take into account the fact that only half of the combinations of (p, q) is needed. $\qquad\square$

We also have the following. The stationary distribution on degree set by collecting all the nodes with same degree is

$$\begin{aligned} f_{RWJ}(d_1) &= \left(\frac{d_1 + \alpha}{2M + N\alpha}\right)Nf_d(d_1) \\ &= \frac{(d_1 + \alpha)f_d(d_1)}{\mathrm{E}[D] + \alpha}. \end{aligned} \qquad (13)$$

Moreover, the associated tail distribution has a simple form,

$$f_{RWJ}(D_{t+1} > d_{t+1}, D_t > d_t) = \frac{\mathrm{E}[D]\overline{F}(d_{t+1}, d_t) + \alpha\overline{F}_d(d_{t+1})\overline{F}_d(d_t)}{\mathrm{E}[D] + \alpha}. \qquad (14)$$

Remark 3. Characterizing Markov chain-based sampling in terms of degree evolution has some advantages.

- In the different random walk algorithms considered on the vertex set, all the nodes with same degree have same stationary distribution. This also implies that it is more natural to formulate the random walk evolution in terms of degree.
- For uncorrelated networks, $f_{RW}(d_1, d_2) = f_{RW}(d_1)f_{RW}(d_2)$, $f_{PR}(d_1, d_2) = f_{PR}(d_1)f_{PR}(d_2)$ and $f_{RWJ}(d_1, d_2) = f_{RWJ}(d_1)f_{RWJ}(d_2)$.

Extremal index for bivariate Pareto degree correlation

As explained in the "Introduction" section, EI is an important parameter in characterizing dependence and extremal properties in a stationary sequence. We assume that we have waited sufficiently long that the underlying Markov chain of the three different graph sampling algorithms are in stationary regime now. Here, we derive EI of RW and RWJ for the model with degree correlation among neighbors as bivariate Pareto (7).

The two mixing conditions $D(u_n)$ and $D''(u_n)$ introduced in section "Calculation of extremal index (EI)" are needed for our EI analysis. Condition $D(u_n)$ is satisfied as explained in section "Check of conditions $D(u_n)$ and $D''(u_n)$ for functions of Markov samples." An empirical evaluation of $D''(u_n)$ is provided in section "Check of condition D''."

EI for random walk sampling

We use the expression for EI given in Theorem 1. As $f_{RW}(x, y)$ is same as $f(x, y)$, we have,

$$\widehat{C}(u, u) = P(D_1 > \bar{F}^{-1}(u), D_2 > \bar{F}^{-1}(u))$$
$$= \left(1 + 2(u^{-1/\gamma} - 1)\right)^{-\gamma}$$
$$\underline{1} \cdot \nabla \widehat{C}(u, u) = 2(2 - u^{1/\gamma})^{-(\gamma+1)}.$$

Thus $\theta = 1 - \underline{1} \cdot \nabla \widehat{C}(0, 0) = 1 - 1/2^{\gamma}$. For $\gamma = 1$, we get $\theta = 1/2$. In this case, we can also use expression obtained in Eq. 5.

EI for random walk with jumps sampling

Although it is possible to derive EI as in RW case above, we provide an alternative way to avoid the calculation of tail distribution of degrees and inverse of RWJ marginal (with respect to the bivariate Pareto degree correlation). We assume the existence of EI in the following proposition.

Proposition 2. *When the bivariate joint degree distribution of neighboring nodes are Pareto distributed as given by Eq. 7 and random walk with jumps is employed for sampling, the EI is given by*

$$\theta = 1 - \frac{E[D]}{E[D] + \alpha} 2^{-\gamma}, \tag{15}$$

where $E[D]$ is the expected degree, α is the parameter of the random walk with jumps, and γ is the tail index of the bivariate Pareto distribution.

Proof. Under the assumption of D'',

$$\theta = \lim_{n \to \infty} \frac{P(D_2 \le u_n, D_1 > u_n)}{P(D_1 > u_n)} = \lim_{n \to \infty} \frac{P(D_1 \ge u_n) - P(D_2 \ge u_n, D_1 \ge u_n)}{P(D_1 > u_n)} \tag{16}$$

Now using the Condition 1 on the marginal and joint tail distribution of RWJ in Eq. 14, we can write[2]

$$\frac{P(D_1 \geq u_n) - P(D_2 \geq u_n, D_1 \geq u_n)}{P(D_1 > u_n)}$$

$$= \frac{\tau/n + o(1/n) - \frac{E[D]}{E[D]+\alpha} P_{\mathrm{RW}}(D_2 \geq u_n, D_1 \geq u_n) - \frac{\alpha}{E[D]+\alpha} O(\tau/n) O(\tau/n)}{\tau/n + o(1/n)}$$

The asymptotics in the last term of the numerator is due to the following:

$$\overline{F}_{\mathrm{RWJ}}(u_n) = \frac{E[D]}{E[D]+\alpha} \overline{F}(u_n) + \frac{\alpha}{E[D]+\alpha} \overline{F}_d(u_n) = \tau/n + o(1/n),$$

and hence $\overline{F}_d(u_n) = O(\tau/n)$. Therefore, Eq. 16 becomes

$$\theta = 1 - \frac{E[D]}{E[D]+\alpha} \lim_{n\to\infty} P_{\mathrm{RW}}(D_2 \geq u_n, D_1 \geq u_n) n/\tau$$

Then in the case of the bivariate Pareto distribution in Eq. 7, we obtain Eq. 15.   □

Lower bound of EI of the PageRank

We obtain the following lower bound for EI in the PageRank processes.

Proposition 3. *For the stationary PageRank process on degree state space Eq. 10 with EI θ, irrespective of the degree correlation structure in the underlying graph, the EI is bounded by*

$$\theta \geq (1 - c),$$

where c is the damping factor in the PageRank algorithm.

Proof. From [13], with another mixing condition $\mathrm{AIM}(u_n)$ which is satisfied for functions of stationary Markov samples (e.g., degree samples) the following representation of EI holds,

$$\lim_{n\to\infty} P\{M_{1,p_n} \leq u_n | D_1 > u_n\} \leq \theta, \tag{17}$$

where $\{p_n\}$ is an increasing sequence of positive integers, $p_n = o(n)$ as $n \to \infty$ and $M_{1,p_n} = \max\{D_2, ..., D_{p_n}\}$. Let $\mathcal{A}$ be the event that the node corresponding to D_2 is selected uniformly among all the nodes, not following random walk from the node for D_1. Then, $P_{\mathrm{PR}}(\mathcal{A}) = 1 - c$. Now, with Eq. 11,

$$
\begin{aligned}
P_{\mathrm{PR}}(M_{1,p_n} \leq u_n | D_1 > u_n) &\geq P_{\mathrm{PR}}(M_{1,p_n} \leq u_n, \mathcal{A} | D_1 > u_n) \\
&= P_{\mathrm{PR}}(\mathcal{A} | D_1 > u_n) P_{\mathrm{PR}}(M_{1,p_n} \leq u_n | \mathcal{A}, D_1 > u_n) \\
&\overset{(i)}{=} (1-c) P_{\mathrm{PR}}(M_{1,p_n} \leq u_n), \\
&\overset{(ii)}{=} (1-c) P_{\mathrm{PR}}^{(p_n-1)\theta}(D_1 \leq u_n) + o(1) \\
&\geq (1-c) P_{\mathrm{PR}}^{(p_n-1)}(D_1 \leq u_n) + o(1) \\
&\overset{(iii)}{\sim} (1-c)(1 - \tau/n)^{p_n-1},
\end{aligned}
\tag{18}
$$

where $\{p_n\}$ is the same sequence as in Eq. 17 and (*i*) follows mainly from the observation that conditioned on $\mathcal{A}$, $\{M_{1,p_n} \leq u_n\}$ is independent of $\{D_1 > u_n\}$, and (*ii*) and (*iii*) result from the limits in Eqs. 3 and 1, respectively.

Assuming $p_n - 1 = n^{1/2}$ and since $(1 - \tau/n)^{p_n-1} \sim e^{-\tau/\sqrt{n}} \to 1$ as $n \to \infty$, from Eqs. 17 and 18,

$$\theta \geq 1 - c.$$

The PageRank transition kernel (Eq. 11) on the degree state space does not depend upon the random graph model in section "Description of the configuration model with degree-degree correlation". Hence, the derived lower bound of EI is useful for any degree correlation model.   □

Applications of extremal index in network sampling processes

This section provides several applications of EI in inferring the sampled sequence. This emphasizes that the analytical calculation and estimation of EI are practically relevant.

The limit of the point process of exceedances, $N_n(.)$, which counts the times, normalized by n, at which $\{X_i\}_{i=1}^n$ exceeds a threshold u_n provides many applications of EI. A cluster is considered to be formed by the exceedances in a block of size r_n $(r_n = o(n))$ in n with cluster size $\xi_n = \sum_{i=1}^{r_n} 1(X_i > u_n)$ when there is at least one exceedance within r_n. The point process N_n converges weakly to a compound poisson process (CP) with rate $\theta\tau$ and i.i.d. distribution as the limiting distribution of cluster size, under Condition 1 and a mixing condition, and the points of exceedances in CP correspond to the clusters (see [4], Section 10.3 for details). We also call this kind of clusters as blocks of exceedances.

The applications below require a choice of the threshold sequence $\{u_n\}$ satisfying Eq. 1. For practical purposes, if a single threshold u is demanded for the sampling budget B, we can fix $u = \max\{u_1, \ldots, u_B\}$.

The applications in this section are explained with the assumption that the sampled sequence is the sequence of node degrees. But the following techniques are very general and can be extended to any sampled sequence satisfying conditions $D(u_n)$ and $D''(u_n)$.

Order statistics of the sampled degrees

The order statistics $X_{n-k,n}$, $(n - k)$th maxima is related to $N_n(.)$ and thus to θ by

$$P(X_{n-k,n} \leq u_n) = P(N_n((0, 1]) \leq k),$$

where we apply the result of convergence of N_n to CP ([4], Section 10.3.1).

Distribution of maxima

The distribution of the maxima of the sampled degree sequences can be derived as Eq. 3 when $n \to \infty$.

Hence if the EI of the underlying process is known then from Eq. 3, one can approximate the $(1 - \eta)$th quantile x_η of the maximal degree M_n as

$$P\{M_n \leq x_\eta\} = F^{n\theta}(x_\eta) = P^{n\theta}\{X_1 \leq x_\eta\} = 1 - \eta,$$

i.e.,

$$x_\eta \approx F^{-1}\left((1 - \eta)^{1/(n\theta)}\right). \tag{19}$$

In other words, quantiles can be used to find the maxima of the degree sequence with certain probability.

If the sampling procedures have same marginal distribution, with calculation of EI, it is possible to predict how much large values can be achieved. Lower EI indicates lower value for x_η and higher represents high x_η.

For the random walk example in section "EI for random walk sampling" for the degree correlation model, with the use of Eq. 19, we get the $(1 - \eta)$th quantile of the maxima M_n

$$x_\eta \approx \mu + \sigma \left(\left(1 - (1 - \eta)^{1/(n\theta)}\right)^{-1/\gamma} - 1 \right).$$

The following example demonstrates the effect of neglecting correlations on the prediction of the largest degree node. The largest degree, with the assumption of Pareto distribution for the degree distribution, can be approximated as $KN^{1/\delta}$ with $K \approx 1$, N as the number of nodes and γ as the tail index of complementary distribution function of degrees [22]. For Twitter graph (recorded in 2012), $\delta = 1.124$ for out-degree distribution and $N = 537,523,432$ [23]. This gives the largest degree prediction as 59,453,030. But the actual largest out-degree is 22,717,037. This difference is because the analysis in [22] assumes i.i.d. samples and does not take into account the degree correlation. With the knowledge of EI, correlation can be taken into account as in Eq. 3. In the following section, we derive an expression for such a case.

Estimation of largest degree when the marginals are Pareto distributed

It is known that many social networks have the degree asymptotically distributed as Pareto [18]. We find that in these cases, the marginal distribution of degrees of the random walk based methods also follow Pareto distribution (though we have derived only for the model with degree correlations among neighbors, see section "Degree correlations".)

Proposition 4. *For any stationary sequence with marginal distribution following Pareto distribution $\bar{F}(x) = Cx^{-\delta}$, the largest value, approximated as the median of the extreme value distribution, is given by*

$$M_n \approx (n\theta)^{1/\delta} \left(\frac{C}{\log 2} \right)^{1/\delta}.$$

Proof. From extreme value theory [4], it is known that when $\{X_i, i \geq 1\}$ are i.i.d.,

$$\lim_{n \to \infty} P\left(\frac{M_n - b_n}{a_n} \leq x \right) = H_\gamma(x), \tag{20}$$

where $H_\gamma(x)$ is the extreme value distribution with index γ and $\{a_n\}$ and $\{b_n\}$ are appropriately chosen deterministic sequences. When $\{X_i, i \geq 1\}$ are stationary with EI θ, the limiting distribution becomes $H'_{\gamma'}(x)$ and it differs from $H_\gamma(x)$ only through parameters. $H_\gamma(x) = \exp(-t(x))$ with $t(x) = \left(1 + \left(\frac{x-\mu}{\sigma}\right)\gamma\right)^{-1/\gamma}$. With the normalizing constants ($\mu = 0$ and $\sigma = 1$), $H'_{\gamma'}$ has the same shape as H_γ with parameters $\gamma' = \gamma$, $\sigma' = \theta^\gamma$ and $\mu' = (\theta^\gamma - 1)/\gamma$ ([4], Section 10.2.3).

For Pareto case, $\bar{F}(x) = Cx^{-\delta}$, $\gamma = 1/\delta$, $a_n = \gamma C^\gamma n^\gamma$, and $b_n = C^\gamma n^\gamma$. From Eq. 20, for large n, M_n is stochastically equivalent to $a_n \chi + b_n$, where χ is a random variable with distribution $H'_{\gamma'}$. It is observed in [22] that median of χ is an appropriate choice for the estimation of M_n. Median of $\chi = \mu' + \sigma' \left(\frac{(\log 2)^{-\gamma'} - 1}{\gamma'} \right) = (\theta^\gamma (\log 2)^{-\gamma} - 1)\gamma^{-1}$. Hence,

$$M_n \approx a_n \left(\frac{\theta^\gamma (\log 2)^{-\gamma}}{\gamma} - 1 \right) + b_n$$

$$= (n\theta)^{1/\delta} \left(\frac{C}{\log 2} \right)^{1/\delta}$$

$\square$

Relation to first hitting time and interpretations

Extremal index also gives information about the first time $\{X_n\}$ hits (u_n, ∞). Let T_n be this time epoch. As N_n converges to compound poisson process, it can be observed that T_n/n is asymptotically an exponential random variable with rate $\theta\tau$, i.e., $\lim_{n\to\infty} P(T_n/n > x) = \exp(-\theta\tau x)$. Therefore, $\lim_{n\to\infty} E(T_n/n) = 1/(\theta\tau)$. Thus, the smaller EI is, the longer it will take to hit the extreme levels as compared to independent sampling. This property is particularly useful to compare different sampling procedures. It can also be used in quick detection of high degree nodes [22, 24].

Relation to mean cluster size

If Condition $D''(u_n)$ is satisfied along with $D(u_n)$, asymptotically, a run of the consecutive exceedances following an upcrossing is observed, i.e., $\{X_n\}$ crosses the threshold u_n at a time epoch and stays above u_n for some more time before crossing u_n downwards and stays below it for some time until next upcrossing of u_n happens. This is called cluster of exceedances and is more practically relevant than blocks of exceedances at the starting of this section and is shown in [10] that these two definitions clusters are asymptotically equivalent resulting in similar cluster size distribution.

The expected value of cluster of exceedances converges to inverse of EI ([4], p. 384), i.e.,

$$\theta^{-1} = \lim_{n\to\infty} \sum_{j\geq 1} j\pi_n(j),$$

where $\{\pi_n(j), j \geq 1\}$ is the distribution of size of cluster of exceedances with n samples. Asymptotical cluster size distribution and its mean are derived in [6].

Estimation of extremal index and numerical results

This section introduces two estimators for EI. Two types of networks are presented: synthetic correlated graph and real networks (Enron email network and DBLP network (http://dblp.uni-trier.de/)). For the synthetic graph, we compare the estimated EI to its theoretical value. For the real network, we calculate EI using the two estimators.

We take $\{X_i\}$ as the degree sequence and use RW, PR, and RWJ as the sampling techniques. The methods mentioned in the following are general and are not specific to degree sequence or random walk technique.

Empirical copula-based estimator

We have tried different estimators for EI available in literature [4, 14] and found that the idea of estimating copula and then finding value of its derivative at $(1, 1)$ works without the need to choose and optimize several parameters found in other estimators. We assume that $\{X_i\}$ satisfies $D(u_n)$ and $D''(u_n)$, and we use Eq. 4 for calculation of EI. Copula $C(u, v)$ is estimated empirically by

$$C_n(u,v) = \frac{1}{n} \sum_{k=1}^{n} \mathbb{I}\left(\frac{R_{i_k}^X}{n+1} \leq u, \frac{R_{i_k}^Y}{n+1} \leq v\right),$$

with $R_{i_k}^X$ indicates rank of the element X_{i_k} in $\{X_{i_k}, 1 \leq k \leq n\}$ and $R_{i_k}^Y$ is defined respectively. The sequence $\{X_{i_k}\}$ is chosen from the original sequence $\{X_i\}$ in such a way that X_{i_k} and $X_{i_{k+1}}$ are sufficiently apart to make them independent to a certain extent and $Y_{i_k} = X_{i_k+1}$. The large sample distribution of $C_n(u,v)$ is normal and centered at copula $C(u,v)$. Now, to get θ, we use linear least squares error fitting to find the slope at $(1,1)$ or use cubic spline interpolation for better results.

Intervals estimator

This estimator does not assume any conditions on $\{X_i\}$ but has the parameter u to choose appropriately. Let $N = \sum_{i=1}^{n} 1(X_i > u)$ be the number of exceedances of u at time epochs $1 \leq S_1 < \ldots < S_N \leq n$ and let the interexceedance times be $T_i = S_{i+1} - S_i$. Then intervals estimator is defined as ([4], p. 391),

$$\hat{\theta}_n(u) = \begin{cases} \min(1, \hat{\theta}_n^1(u)), \text{ if } \max T_i : 1 \leq i \leq N-1 \leq 2, \\ \min(1, \hat{\theta}_n^2(u)), \text{ if } \max T_i : 1 \leq i \leq N-1 > 2, \end{cases}$$

where

$$\hat{\theta}_n^1(u) = \frac{2\left(\sum_{i=1}^{N-1} T_i\right)^2}{(N-1)\sum_{i=1}^{N-1} T_i^2},$$

and

$$\hat{\theta}_n^2(u) = \frac{2\left(\sum_{i=1}^{N-1}(T_i - 1)\right)^2}{(N-1)\sum_{i=1}^{N-1}(T_i - 1)(T_i - 2)}.$$

We choose u as δ percentage quantile thresholds, i.e., δ percentage of $\{X_i, 1 \leq i \leq n\}$ falls below u,

$$k_\delta = \min\left\{k : \sum_{i=1}^{n} \frac{1\{X_i \leq X_k\}}{n} \geq \frac{\delta}{100}, 1 \leq k \leq n\right\}, \qquad u = X_{k_\delta}.$$

We plot θ_n vs δ for the intervals estimator in the following sections. The EI is usually selected as the value corresponding to the stability interval in this plot.

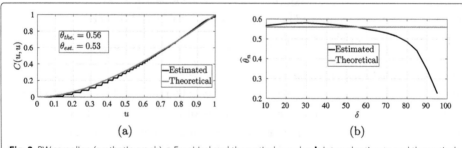

Fig. 2 RW sampling (synthetic graph). **a** Empirical and theoretical copulas. **b** Interval estimate and theoretical value

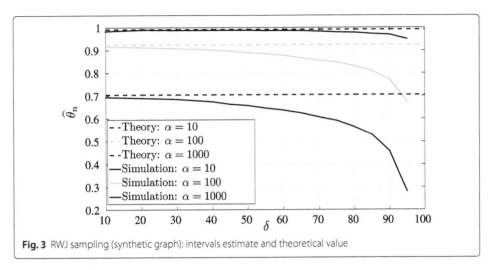

Fig. 3 RWJ sampling (synthetic graph): intervals estimate and theoretical value

Synthetic graph

The simulations in the section follow the bivariate Pareto model and parameters introduced in Eq. 7. We use the same set of parameters as for Fig. 1, and the graph is generated according to the Metropolis technique in section "Random graph generation".

For the RW case, Fig. 2a shows copula estimator, and theoretical copula-based on the continuous distribution in Eq. 7, and is given by

$$C(u, u) = \left(1 + 2((1 - u)^{-1/\gamma} - 1)\right)^{-\gamma} + 2u - 1.$$

Though we take quantized values for degree sequence, it is found that the copula estimated matches with theoretical copula. The value of EI is then obtained after cubic interpolation and numerical differentiation of copula estimator at point $(1, 1)$. For the theoretical copula, EI is $1 - 1/2^\gamma$, where $\gamma = 1.2$. Figure 2b displays the comparison between the theoretical value of EI and intervals estimate.

For the RWJ algorithm, Fig. 3 shows the interval estimate and theoretical value for different α. We used Eq. 15 for theoretical calculation. The small difference in theory and simulation results is due to the assumption of continuous degrees in the analysis, but the practical usage requires quantized version. Here $\alpha = 0$ case corresponds to RW sampling.

Figure 4 displays the interval estimate of EI with PR sampling. It can be seen that the lower bound proposed in Proposition 3 gets tighter as c decreases. When $c = 1$, PR sampling becomes RW sampling.

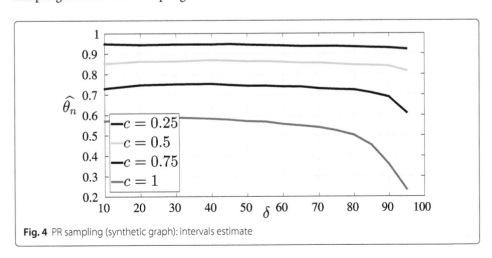

Fig. 4 PR sampling (synthetic graph): intervals estimate

Table 1 Test of Condition D'' in the synthetic graph

	r_{up} (%)	$r_{cluster}$ (%)
RW	4	89
PR	7	91
RWJ	5	86

Check of condition D''

The mixing conditions $D(u_n)$ and $D''(u_n)$ need to be satisfied for using the theory in section "Calculation of extremal index (EI)". Though intervals estimator does not require them, these conditions will provide the representation by Eq. 4. Condition $D(u_n)$ works in this case as explained in previous sections and for $D''(u_n)$, we do the following empirical test. We collect samples for each of the techniques RW, PR, and RWJ with parameters given in respective figures. Intervals are taken of duration $5, 10, 15,$ and 20 time samples. The ratio of number of upcrossings to number of exceedances r_{up} and ratio of number consecutive exceedances to number of exceedances $r_{cluster}$ are calculated in Table 1. These proportions are averaged over 2000 occurrences of each of these intervals and over all the different intervals. The statistics in the table indicates strong occurrence of Condition $D''(u_n)$. We have also observed that the changes in the parameters does not affect this inference.

Real network

We consider two real-world networks: Enron email network and DBLP network. The data is collected from [25]. Both the networks satisfy the check for Condition $D''(u_n)$ reasonably well.

For the RW sampling, Fig. 5a shows the empirical copula, and it also mentions corresponding EI. Intervals estimator is presented in Fig. 5b. After observing plateaux in the plots, we took EI as 0.25 and 0.2 for DBLP and Enron email graphs, respectively.

In case of RWJ sampling, Fig. 6a, b presents the intervals estimator for email-Enron and DBLP graphs, respectively.

Conclusions

In this work, we have associated extreme value theory of stationary sequences to sampling of large networks. We show that for any general stationary samples (function of node samples) meeting two mixing conditions, the knowledge of bivariate distribution or bivariate copula is sufficient to derive many of its extremal properties. The parameter

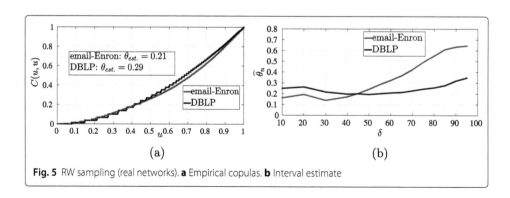

(a)   (b)

Fig. 5 RW sampling (real networks). **a** Empirical copulas. **b** Interval estimate

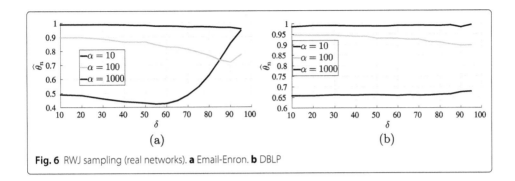

Fig. 6 RWJ sampling (real networks). **a** Email-Enron. **b** DBLP

extremal index (EI) encapsulates this relation. We relate EI to many relevant extremes in networks like order statistics, first hitting time, and mean cluster size. In particular, we model dependence in degrees of adjacent nodes and examine random walk-based degree sampling. Finally, we have obtained estimates of EI for a synthetic graph with degree correlations and find a good match with the theory. We also calculate EI for two real-world networks. In future, we plan to investigate the relation between assortativity coefficient and EI and intends to study in detail the EI in real networks.

Endnotes
[1]$F^k(.)$ kth power of $F(.)$ throughout the paper except when $k = -1$ where it denotes the inverse function.

[2]$\sim$' stands for asymptotically equal, i.e., $f(x) \sim g(x) \Leftrightarrow f(x)/g(x) \rightarrow 1$ as $x \rightarrow a, x \in M$ where the functions $f(x)$ and $g(x)$ are defined on some set M, and a is a limit point of M. $f(x) = o(g(x))$ means $\lim_{x \rightarrow a} f(x)/g(x) = 0$. Also $f(x) = O(g(x))$ indicates that there exist $\delta > 0$ and $M > 0$ such that $|f(x)| \leq M|g(x)|$ for $|x - a| < \delta$.

Competing interests
The authors declare that they have no competing interests.

Authors' contributions
The contribution of all three authors to the manuscript is quite balanced. All authors read and approved the final manuscript.

Acknowledgements
The work of the first and third authors is partly supported by ADR "Network Science" of the Alcatel-Lucent Inria joint lab. The second author was partly supported by the Russian Foundation for Basic Research, grant 13-08-00744 A, and Campus France—Russian Embassy bilateral exchange programme.
The authors are thankful to Remco van der Hofstad for helpful suggestions during the preparation of this manuscript.

Author details
[1]INRIA Sophia Antipolis 2004, route des Lucioles - BP 93, 06902 Sophia Antipolis Cedex, France. [2]Institute of Control Sciences, Russian Academy of Sciences, Moscow, Russia.

References
1. Barrat, A, Barthelemy, M, Vespignani, A: Dynamical Processes on Complex Networks. Cambridge University Press, New York (2008)
2. Avrachenkov, K, Ribeiro, B, Towsley, D: Improving random walk estimation accuracy with uniform restarts. In: LNCS, pp. 98–109. Springer, Berlin Heidelberg, (2010)
3. Brin, S, Page, L: The anatomy of a large-scale hypertextual web search engine. Comput. Netw. ISDN Syst. **30**(1), 107–117 (1998)
4. Beirlant, J, Goegebeur, Y, Teugels, J, Segers, J: Statistics of Extremes: Theory and Applications. Wiley, Chichester, West Sussex (2004)
5. Ferro, CAT, Segers, J: Inference for clusters of extreme values. J. R. Stat. Soc. Ser. B. **65**, 545–556 (2003)
6. Markovich, NM: Modeling clusters of extreme values. Extremes. **17**(1), 97–125 (2014)
7. Leadbetter, MR, Lindgren, G, Rootzén, H: Extremes and Related Properties of Random Sequences and Processes, Vol. 21. Springer, New York (1983)

8. Avrachenkov, K, M. Markovich, N, Sreedharan, JK: Distribution and dependence of extremes in network sampling processes. In: Third International IEEE Workshop on Complex Networks and Their Applications. IEEE, Marrakesh, Morocco, (2014)
9. Nelsen, RB: An Introduction to Copulas. 2nd edn. Springer, New York (2007)
10. Leadbetter, MR, Nandagopalan, S: On exceedance point processes for stationary sequences under mild oscillation restrictions. In: Extreme Value Theory. Lecture Notes in Statistics, pp. 69–80. Springer, New York, (1989)
11. Chernick, MR, Hsing, T, McCormick, WP: Calculating the extremal index for a class of stationary sequences. Adv. Appl. Probab. **23**(4), 835–850 (1991)
12. Weng, C, Zhang, Y: Characterization of multivariate heavy-tailed distribution families via copula. J. Multivar. Anal. **106**(0), 178–186 (2012)
13. O'Brien, GL: Extreme values for stationary and Markov sequences. Ann. Probab. **15**(1), 281–291 (1987)
14. Ferreira, A, Ferreira, H: Extremal functions, extremal index and Markov chains. Technical report, Notas e comunicações CEAUL (December 2007)
15. Boguna, M, Pastor-Satorras, R, Vespignani, A: Epidemic spreading in complex networks with degree correlations. Stat. Mech. Complex Netw. Lect. Notes Physica. **625**, 127–147 (2003)
16. Goltsev, AV, Dorogovtsev, SN, Mendes, JFF: Percolation on correlated networks. Phys. Rev. E. **78**, 051105 (2008)
17. Newman, ME: Assortative mixing in networks. Phys. Rev. Lett. **89**(20), 208701 (2002)
18. Van Der Hofstad, R: Random graphs and complex networks Vol. i. (2014). Available on http://www.win.tue.nl/~rhofstad/NotesRGCN.pdf, accessed on 23 December 2014
19. Zhukovskiy, M, Vinogradov, D, Pritykin, Y, Ostroumova, L, Grechnikov, E, Gusev, G, Serdyukov, P, Raigorodskii, A: Empirical validation of the Buckley-Osthus model for the web host graph: degree and edge distributions. In: Proceedings of the 21st ACM International Conference on Information and Knowledge Management, pp. 1577–1581. ACM, Sheraton, Maui Hawaii, (2012)
20. Lovász, L: Random walks on graphs: a survey. Combinatorics, Paul erdos is eighty. **2**(1), 1–46 (1993)
21. Litvak, N, Scheinhardt, W. R, Volkovich, Y: In-degree and PageRank: why do they follow similar power laws?. Internet Math. **4**(2-3), 175–198 (2007)
22. Avrachenkov, K, Litvak, N, Sokol, M, Towsley, D: Quick detection of nodes with large degrees. In: Algorithms and Models for the Web Graph. Lecture Notes in Computer Science, pp. 54–65. Springer, Berlin Heidelberg, (2012)
23. Gabielkov, M, Rao, A, Legout, A: Studying social networks at scale: macroscopic anatomy of the twitter social graph. SIGMETRICS Perform. Eval. Rev. **42**(1), 277–288 (2014)
24. Avrachenkov, K, Litvak, N, Prokhorenkova, L. O, Suyargulova, E: Quick detection of high-degree entities in large directed networks. In: Proceedings of IEEE ICDM, (2014)
25. Stanford Large Network Dataset Collection. (2014). https://snap.stanford.edu/data/index.html, accessed on 11 December 2014

8

Co-evolutionary dynamics in social networks: a case study of Twitter

Demetris Antoniades[1]* and Constantine Dovrolis[2]

*Correspondence:
danton@cs.ucy.ac.cy
[1] Department of Computer Science,
University of Cyprus, Nicosia, Cyprus
Full list of author information is
available at the end of the article

Abstract

Complex networks often exhibit co-evolutionary dynamics, meaning that the network topology and the state of nodes or links are coupled, affecting each other in overlapping time scales. We focus on the co-evolutionary dynamics of online social networks, and on Twitter in particular. Monitoring the activity of thousands of Twitter users in real-time, and tracking their followers and tweets/retweets, we propose a method to infer new retweet-driven follower relations. The formation of such relations is much more likely than the exogenous creation of new followers in the absence of any retweets. We identify the most significant factors (reciprocity and the number of retweets that a potential new follower receives) and propose a simple probabilistic model of this effect. We also discuss the implications of such co-evolutionary dynamics on the topology and function of a social network. Finally, we briefly consider a second instance of co-evolutionary dynamics on Twitter, namely the possibility that a user removes a follower link after receiving a tweet or retweet from the corresponding followee.

Keywords: Online social networks; Complex networks; Co-evolution

Introduction

Online social networks (OSNs), such as Twitter and Facebook, have changed how individuals interact with society, how information flows between actors, and how people influence each other. These are all complex dynamic processes that are now widely studied empirically and in a large scale, thanks to the availability of data from OSNs. Most OSN studies focus on one of the following two aspects of network dynamics. Dynamics *on* networks refer to changes in the state of network nodes or links considering a static topology [1, 2]. Dynamics *of* networks, on the other hand, refer to changes in the topology of a network, without explicitly modeling its underlying causes [3]. As noted by Gross and Blasius in [4], however, real OSNs typically exhibit both types of dynamics, forming an adaptive, or co-evolutionary, system in which the network topology and the state of nodes/links affect each other through a (rather poorly understood) feedback loop.

Dynamic processes in OSNs, such as information diffusion or influence, are obviously affected by the underlying network topology, but they also have the power to affect that topology. For instance, users may decide to add or drop a "friendship" or "follower" relation depending on what the potential "friend" or "followee" has recently said or done in the context of that OSN. Previous empirical or modeling OSN studies often choose to ignore such co-evolutionary dynamics, mostly for simplicity, assuming a static network topology, or assuming that the topology and node/link states are decoupled and evolve in separate time scales [5].

In this paper, we focus on co-evolutionary dynamics in the context of Twitter. Twitter users create *follower–followee* relations with each other. A directed link from a user R to a user S, denoted by $R \rightarrow S$, means that R is a follower of S, receiving S's tweets; S is referred to as a followee of R. R can choose to propagate a tweet of S to her own followers, denoted by $F(R)$, creating a *retweet*. When a follower $L \in F(R)$ receives a retweet of S through R, L can choose to add S to her followers. We call this sequence a *Tweet-Retweet-Follow* (TRF) event, and refer to its three main actors as *Speaker S*, *Repeater R*, and *Listener L*. TRF events represent a clear case of co-evolutionary dynamics: information propagation (tweet-retweet) causes a topology change (new follower).

Figure 1 shows this sequence of events for the simplest TRF case in which $R \rightarrow S$ and $L \rightarrow R$. In general, the Repeater R may not be a follower of S but she may receive S's tweet through a cascade of retweets. Additionally, the Listener L may receive multiple retweets of S from the same or from different Repeaters. The contributions of this study are as follows:

1. We propose a measurement approach to detect TRF events, based on near real-time monitoring of a Speaker's activity and followers.
2. We show that the formation of new follower relations through TRF events is orders of magnitude more likely than the exogenous arrival of new followers in the absence of any retweets.
3. We identify the most significant factors for the likelihood of a TRF event: reciprocity (i.e., is Speaker S already following Listener L?), number of received retweets (i.e., how many retweets of S were received at L during a given time interval Δ), and of course the interval Δ itself.
4. We propose a simple but accurate two-parameter model to capture the probability of TRF events.
5. We discuss the implications of TRF events in the structure and function of social networks.
6. We briefly consider a second instance of co-evolutionary dynamics on Twitter, namely the possibility that a user removes a follower link after receiving a tweet or retweet from the corresponding followee.

This paper is an extended version of work published in [6]. We extend our previous work by examining a second instance of co-evolutionary dynamics on Twitter, namely the possibility of an unfollow event to occur.

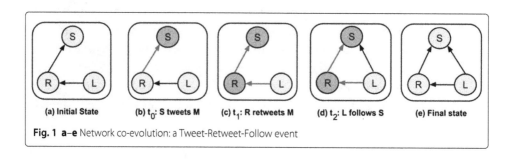

(a) Initial State   (b) t_0: S tweets M   (c) t_1: R retweets M   (d) t_2: L follows S   (e) Final state

Fig. 1 a–e Network co-evolution: a Tweet-Retweet-Follow event

Related work

Preferential attachment [7] is a common way to think about the formation of new ties in a social network. It is based on the idea that it is more likely for well-connected people to attract new ties. Subsequent research provided a deeper understanding by exploring mechanisms such as user similarity [8, 9] (homophily) and directed closure [10–12]. For instance, Romero and Kleinberg [12] studied the *directed closure process* in Twitter. This process states that there is an increased likelihood for a node A to follow a node C if there already exists a direct path of length two from C to A. They showed that this process is taking place at a significantly higher rate than what would be expected by chance, but this rate also varies significantly among different users. Here, we identify TRF events as a plausible mechanism for the emergence of directed closure. Further, we examine the factors that affect the probability of closure, offering a plausible explanation for the high variability across users.

Golder and Yardi conducted a user study to identify structural predictors for tie formation in Twitter. Their results show that lack of transitivity has a negative effect in link prediction [10]. Hopcroft et al. examined the question: "when you follow a particular user, how likely will she follow you back?" [8]. They showed that geographic distance and homophily are good predictors of follow-back ("reciprocal") relations. Our work confirms that reciprocity amplifies significantly the likelihood of TRF events.

Muchnik et al. examined the correlation between a user's degree and activity, and found that activity has a causal increasing effect on degree [13]. Our analysis is related, showing that the number of retweets of a user S that user L receives increases the probability that L will follow S. Leskovec et al. studied network evolution of four social networks and observed that most edges are local, "closing triangles" in particular [11]. Gallos et al. examined the formation and evolution of social networks and analyzed how reciprocity and social balance affect what we refer to as TRF probability [14].

Information diffusion on Twitter has also received significant attention. Several events have shown the major role that Twitter plays in amplifying and spreading information across the globe [15, 16]. Romero et al. [17] analyzed ways in which socially sensitive topics, including politics, propagate on Twitter and reported that such topics are more likely to spread after multiple exposures than others. Myers et al. [18] examined how information reaches a user in Twitter. By analyzing URL mentions, they discovered that information tends to "jump" across the network (probably because users discover this information from external sources).

The literature on co-evolutionary dynamics has relied mostly on abstract models so far, without sufficient empirical validation. For instance, Kosma and Barrat examined how the topology of an adaptive network of interacting agents and of the agents' opinions can influence each other [19]. When agents rewire their links in a way that depends on the opinions of their neighbors, the result can be either a large number of small clusters, making global consensus difficult, or a highly connected but polarized network. Shaw and Schwartz [20] examined the effects of vaccination in static versus adaptive networks. Interestingly, they show that vaccination is much more effective in adaptive networks, and that two orders of magnitude less vaccine resources are needed in adaptive networks. Volz and Mayers studied epidemics in dynamic contact networks and showed that the rate at which contacts are initiated and terminated affects the disease reproductive ratio [21]. They concluded that static approximations of dynamic networks can be inadequate. Rocha et al. simulated epidemics in an empirical spatio-temporal network of sexual contacts [22], showing that dynamic network effects accelerate epidemic outbreaks. Perra et al. studied the effect of time-varying networks in random walks and search processes [23]. The behavior of both processes was found to be "strikingly different" compared to their behavior in static networks.

The most relevant prior work, by Weng et al., analyzed the complete graph and activity of *Yahoo! Meme*,[1] to identify the effect of information diffusion on the evolution of the underlying network [24]. They show that information diffusion causes about 24 % of the new links, and that the likelihood of a new link from a user X to a user Y increases with the number of Y's posts seen by X. More recently, Myers and Leskovec showed that Twitter users gain or loose bursts of followers soon after their tweet activity event [25]. These bursts increase both the density of connections between a user's followers and the similarity of a user with her followers. Similarly to our work, they show that 21 % of all new follows are formed by users who recently saw a retweet of the target user.

Data collection

This section explains the data collection process in detail.

To identify TRF events, we need to observe the appearance of a new follower link from an arbitrary Listener L to a monitored Speaker S, shortly after L has received a retweet of S through a Repeater R. This requires information about both the time of the retweet(s) as well as the time the new follower link has appeared. The Twitter API, though extended in functionality, does not provide information about the creation time of follower relations. Furthermore, existing link creation time inference methods [26] are not applicable in our study because they cannot be used in real time. To retrieve (near) real-time timing, we have implemented a Twitter data retrieval system that periodically checks for new followers and retweets in a given set of Speakers. An overview of our data collection process is shown in Fig. 2. We explain each step of the process in the following paragraphs.

Selection of active Speakers

We obtain a number of active Twitter users as potential Speakers through a stratified sampling method. It has been reported that about 25 % of Twitter users have never posted

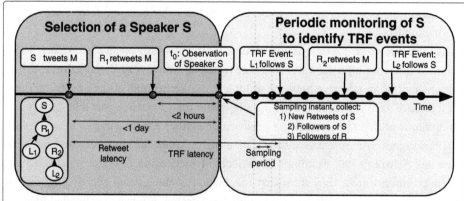

Fig. 2 Speaker selection and monitoring process timeline. Our data collection process consists of two phases. In the first, we select a number of Speakers (active Twitter users that have been recently retweeted). In the second phase, we periodically monitor the Twitter activity of each Speaker (posts and changes in their set of followers) to identify TRF events

any messages [27] and that most users check their Twitter feeds rarely [28]. A random user selection process would most likely visit a number of users without recent posts, wasting a large number of our limited Twitter API calls. The adopted sampling method ensures that we monitor users that have recently posted a tweet. Specifically, we crawl the Twitter search page [29] based on a single-character search selected at random from the set of $[1 - 9A - Za - z]$. The search returns the latest 20 tweets containing the search term. We identify the users that posted these tweets and add them to our monitored Speakers set. For each selected Speaker, we also collect information about their "join time", number of followees, followers and posted tweets. For each observed tweet, we collect the time it was posted and the posted message. Note that the collected tweets are not limited to the English language (as long as they include at least one numeric digit or English character).

Given this set of monitored Speakers, we look for any retweets of their tweets posted during the last 2 h. We only consider retweets that are flagged as such by the Twitter API. For each retweet, we retrieve the set of followers, set of followees of the Speaker and the Repeater R at the time instant we first observed that retweet. Additionally, we collect the set of followers and followees of the Repeater at that time.

Monitoring of Speakers

The previous process results in a number of possible TRF events, whenever a follower of a Repeater receives a retweet of a monitored Speaker. To identify new followers, we need to examine any changes in the Speaker's followers before and after the retweet. To do so, we retrieve the set of followers of the Speaker periodically, approximately every 5 min. We identify a TRF event when the set of followers of S gains a new member (Listener L) that was previously seen in the set of followers of R. At that point, we log the time L was seen to follow S and calculate *TRF latency* as the time difference between the time R retweeted S and the time L followed S. If L received multiple retweets of S (as the same tweet from multiple Repeaters, multiple tweets from the same Repeater, or multiple tweets from multiple Repeaters), we assign the TRF event to the most recent retweet of S received by L. The intuition here is that the most recent tweets will appear at the top of L's inbox and they are more likely to be read than older retweets. At this point we also collect the set of followers and followees of the Listener.

Every 5 min, we also update the set of monitored Speakers as follows. If a selected Speaker has not posted any tweets during the last 24 h, we stop monitoring that user and select a new Speaker using our sampling method. The reason is that most new follower relations tend to occur within few hours from the time a Speaker has been active [30, 31].

Data collection system

Due to the complexity and the real-time nature of our data collection process, we need a large Twitter API request throughput. We used Twitter's API 1.0, which limits users to 350 API requests per hour. To increase this request throughput, we use a large number of distributed hosts, provided by PlanetLab, as proxies for accessing Twitter [32]. Our collection process is coordinated by a "dispatcher" application located at Georgia Tech. The dispatcher decides what data are required at any point in time and instructs a number of "workers" to request that data from Twitter. Each worker is assigned a single Planetlab host that routes API requests to Twitter. When a worker runs out of requests, it deactivates itself and notifies the dispatcher. At that point, the dispatcher generates a new worker, providing it with a fresh request workload.

We divide the data collection process to small independent processes, each of them requiring the smallest possible number of requests. In this way, we partition different parts of the Speaker monitoring process to a number of workers, speeding up the collection process. For instance, when requesting an update for a Speaker, the retrieval of tweets, retweets and follower sets are executed through different Planetlab hosts. Further, we limit the number of concurrently monitored Speakers to 500 to avoid overloading both Twitter and our collection system.

Bot-filtering

A major concern for any Twitter dataset is to avoid bots. Such accounts act differently than most regular Twitter users, biasing the analysis. To identify and remove bot accounts from our dataset, we revisited each account 3 months after the initial data collection to check which of those accounts have been suspended by Twitter. This practice has been used by Thomas et al. [33] as "ground truth" for the Twitter bot detection problem. Further, it has been reported that only few bots survive Twitter's policies for more than a week [34]. In our data, about 1 % of the observed users were suspended by Twitter (uniformly distributed across Speakers, Repeaters, and Listeners), accounting for roughly 10 % of the observed TRF events.[2]

Collected data

Dataset-1

To estimate the exogenous and endogenous probabilities (Section "Endogenous versus exogenous link creation") we use a small-scale dataset (compared to the dataset used in the rest of the paper). Specifically, we monitor 200 unique Twitter users (Speakers) for a period of 10 days. For each Speaker, we collect periodically (every 30 min) her Twitter timeline, tweets and retweets, along with the list of her followers. We also collect the followers of every follower of the 200 monitored Speakers. Based on this dataset, we can observe all Tweet-Retweet (TR) events for every monitored Speaker over the course of 10 days, and so we can ask whether a Speaker has gained one or more new followers among the set of Listeners of her retweets.

Dataset-2

In the rest of the paper, we use a larger dataset. This dataset was collected during 1 week, from September 19 to September 25, 2012. During this time period, we collected about 300 GBytes of raw Twitter data. In this dataset we monitored 4746 Speakers that posted 386,980 tweets. These messages were retweeted 146,867 times by 83,860 distinct Repeaters. Twitter allows users that are not following a Speaker to retweet her messages. For this reason, in Dataset-2, we do not require that the Repeaters are followers of the Speaker. After removing bot accounts, we end up with 7451 observed TRF events. This figure represents 17 % of the new follower links observed in our dataset.

Endogenous versus exogenous link creation

A user also gains new followers due to exogenous factors, such as Twitter's "Who to follow" service [35]. Here, we compare the likelihood with which a user gains new followers when there are no recent retweets of her messages (exogenous link creation) compared to the case that she gains new followers when at least one of her messages has been recently retweeted (endogenous link creation).

We focus here on potential new followers L of S that were already following a follower of S. That is, we only examine three-actor relations in which $L \to R$ and $R \to S$. We then ask *"is it more likely that L will follow S (L → S) when L received a retweet of S through R (TRF event) or when L did not receive any retweet from her followees that follow S (TF event)?"* Fig. 3a illustrates the TRF and TF events. Note that the difference between endogenous (TRF) and exogenous (TF) events is the retweet of S from R; the local structure and the activity of S remain the same in both cases.

We estimate the probability $P_{EXO}(\Delta)$ of exogenous new followers as follows. Consider a tweet of Speaker S at time t_s. Suppose that this tweet is not retweeted by any of the followers of S in the period $[t_s, t_s + \Delta]$. Let $\Phi(S, t_s)$ be the set of followers of followers of S that are not directly following S at t_s, i.e., $\Phi(S, t_s) = \{X : X \notin F(S, t_s), X \in F(Y, t_s), Y \in F(S, t_S)\}$. What is the fraction of these users that follow S by time $t_s + \Delta$?

$$P_{EXO}(\Delta) = \frac{|L : L \in \Phi(S, t_s), L \in F(S, t_s + \Delta)|}{|\Phi(S, t_s)|} \tag{1}$$

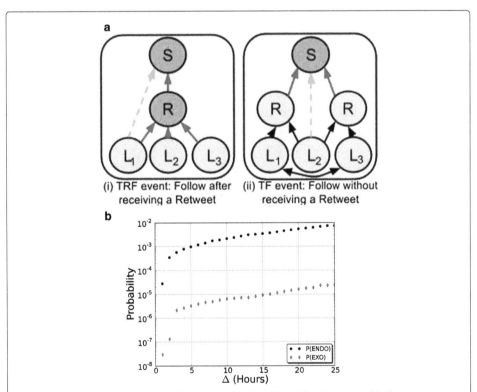

Fig. 3 a Controlling for the structural relation between S, R and L and for the activity of S allows us to compare the likelihood of a new follower L when L received a retweet of S (*i*) compared to the case that L did not receive a retweet of S (*ii*). The *arrow direction* shows who follows whom. *Orange nodes* represent tweet or retweet activity. *Red edges* show the extent of information propagation. *Green dashed edges* show new follower links. **b** Probability that a Speaker S gains at least one new follower L within an interval Δ from the time of a tweet (TF) or retweet (TRF) of S. The Listener L is not a follower of S at the time of the tweet (TF) or retweet (TRF)

Similarly, we estimate the probability $P_{\text{ENDO}}(\Delta)$ of endogenous new followers as follows. Consider again a tweet of Speaker S at time t_s but suppose that this message has been retweeted by a specific follower of S, referred to as Repeater R, at time $t_r > t_s$. Let $\Phi_R(S, t_r)$ be the subset of $\Phi(S, t_r)$ that includes only followers of R. What is the fraction of these users that follow S by time $t_r + \Delta$?

$$P_{\text{ENDO}}(\Delta) = \frac{|L : L \in \Phi_R(S, t_r), L \in F(S, t_r + \Delta)|}{|\Phi_R(S, t_r)|} \tag{2}$$

In a small-scale dataset (Dataset-1), we observed 4945 new followers for the 200 monitored Speakers over 10 days. TRF events accounted for 42 % of these new links. This shows that TRF events are rather infrequent, compared to tweets and retweets, but they are responsible for a large percentage of the new links in Twitter.

Figure 3b compares the two probabilities for increasing values of Δ, averaged across all TF and TRF events in our dataset. We omit confidence intervals because they are too narrow. Note that the probability of endogenous new followers is consistently much higher than the probability of exogenous new followers. Especially for short Δ (up to 2 h), P_{ENDO} is three orders of magnitude higher than P_{EXO}. The difference drops to two orders of magnitude and remains stable even for values of Δ larger than 24 h.

Please note that the previous comparison does not prove causality: *we cannot be certain whether a user L decided to follow S because she received a retweet of S*. However, if L had not received that retweet, it would be 100–1000 times less likely that she would follow S within a given time interval.

Figure 3b shows that P_{ENDO} increases significantly as Δ increases to about 24 h. After that point, P_{ENDO} saturates to a value that is about 10^{-2}. It can be argued that this underestimates the actual TRF probability. The reason is that a large fraction of Twitter users are either completely inactive or they do not visit Twitter often. Recent statistics report that only 20 % of registered users visit Twitter at least once per month [36]. Additionally, a report from Pew Internet [37] in 2010 reported that only 36 % of Twitter users check their inbox at least once a day.

TRF characteristics

The previous analysis verifies our initial intuition that the likelihood with which a user L follows a user S greatly increases when L receives a retweet of S. Furthermore, this likelihood is also affected by the length of the interval between the retweet and the time L observed of that retweet. We now give a more precise definition of Tweet-Retweet-Follow events. We say that a Tweet-Retweet-Follow event between users S, R, and L, where R might not be a direct follower of S, occurs when we observe the following sequence of events:

1. S tweets a message M at time t_s,
2.   A user R retweets M at some time $t_r > t_s$,
3.   A user L, who is a follower of R (i.e. $L \rightarrow R$) at t_r but not a follower of S, follows S by time t_l, where $t_l \in [t_r, t_r + \Delta]$.

We collected a larger dataset (Dataset-2) that we use to analyze and model TRF events. In this dataset, we observe 7451 TRF events, which represent 17 % of the observed new follower relations.

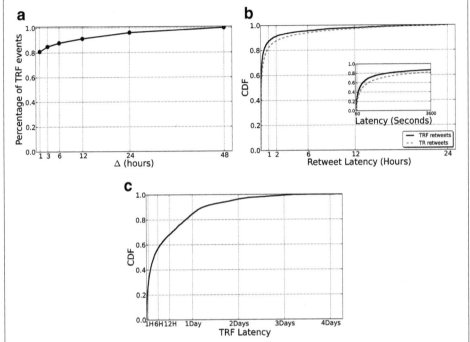

Fig. 4 a Percentage of identified TRF events as function of Δ. **b** Retweet latency for all observed retweets. We plot separately retweets that lead to a TRF event, and retweets that do not (TR retweets). **c** Delay between the time of a retweet of Speaker S and the time the Listener L follows S

Δ is the only parameter in this definition, and it affects the likelihood of TRF events. Figure 4a shows the percentage of identified TRF events as a function of the parameter Δ. As expected, the number of TRF events increases with Δ but most of them occur within 24 h from the corresponding retweet.

Retweet latency

Figure 4b distinguishes between retweets that resulted in at least one TRF event (TRF retweets) and retweets that did not result in a TRF event (TR retweets). The analysis of these retweet events shows that more than 90 % of them occur in less than an hour from the corresponding tweet; we refer to this time interval as *retweet latency*. This result supports the idea that "retweeting users" tend to act soon after new information becomes available.

TRF latency

We observe new $L \to S$ relations even 4 days after L has received a retweet of S, as shown in Fig. 4c. However, more than 80 % of the TRF events occur in less than 24 h after the retweet. Unless stated otherwise, in the rest of this paper we set $\Delta = 24$ h.

TRF probability

For each monitored Speaker, we collect at each sampling instant her list of followers $F(S)$, tweets, retweets, Repeaters and the set of followers for each Repeater $F(R)$. We then identify the set of *Tweet-Retweet (TR) events* for each retweet of Speaker S: $TR(S, R, L, t_r, I_\Delta)$. A TR event denotes that Listener L received a message of S at time t_r through a retweet by Repeater R. The indicator variable I_Δ is 1 if L followed S during a time period of length Δ after t_r.

We could define the TRF probability as the fraction of TR events for which $I_\Delta = 1$. This calculation, however, does not consider that a Listener may receive multiple retweets (of the same or different tweets) of that Speaker. It would not be realistic to assume that the Listener will decide whether to follow the Speaker immediately after each retweet. Typically, users do not read each tweet immediately when it is generated, nor they have an infinite attention span that would allow them to consider all tweets in their inbox [31]. It is more reasonable to expect that each time a user opens her inbox she reads several recent tweets at the same time. So, we assume that a Listener decides whether to follow a Speaker based on a group of received retweets that were recently received.

Specifically, we group TR events into *Retweet Groups (RG)* as follows. Each RG is represented as $RG(S, L, t_r, n, I_\Delta)$, where S and L are the Speaker and Listener, respectively, t_r is the timestamp of the first retweet in that group, and n is the number of retweets of S received by L during the time window $< t_r, t_r + \Delta >$. Note that these retweets may be generated by different Repeaters. The indicator variable I_Δ is 1 if L followed S by the end of the previous time interval. If L followed S at time $t_r \leq t \leq t_r + \Delta$, the corresponding RG includes only those retweets received by L before t; any subsequent retweets are ignored because L already follows S.

Based on this Retweet Grouping method, we calculate the TRF probability $P_{\text{TRF}}(\Delta)$ as the fraction of RGs for which $I_\Delta = 1$.

Factors that affect the TRF probability

We now examine a number of factors that may affect the TRF probability. The small magnitude of the TRF probability makes the identification of important factors more challenging [38]; the following results, however, are given with satisfactory statistical significance (see p values in Table 1).

Table 1 lists the structural and informational factors (features) we consider.[3] We use logistic regression to analyze how these features correlate with the TRF probability. Based

Table 1 List of examined factors

Factor	Description	Odds ratio	95 % CI
Structural features			
$|F(S)|$	Number of followers of S	1.000***	[1.000, 1.000]
$|F'(S)|$	Number of followees of S	0.999***	[0.999, 0.999]
AGE(S)	Number of days since S joined Twitter	0.998***	[0.998, 0.998]
$S \rightarrow L$	Reciprocity: whether the Speaker was following the Listener at the time of the TR event	27.344***	[25.663, 29.136]
Informational features			
$|ST(S)|$	Total number of tweets of S	1.000***	[1.000, 1.000]
$A_{\text{rate}}(S)$	Rate of S tweets per day	0.989***	[0.988, 0.991]
Tweets(S, L, Δ)	Number of distinct tweets of S received by L during period Δ	2.010***	[1.781, 2.270]
Retweets(S, L, Δ)	Number of distinct retweets of S received by L during period Δ	1.603***	[1.371, 1.873]
Repeaters(S, L, Δ)	Number of Repeaters R that L received tweets of S from during period Δ	2.076***	[1.889, 2.282]

*$p < 0.1$; **$p < 0.05$; ***$p < 0.01$

on (3), we estimate the correlation coefficient κ_i for each factor X_i. κ_i denotes the effect of X_i to the "odds" of TRF events,

$$ln \left(\frac{P_{TRF}}{1 - P_{TRF}} \right) = \kappa_0 + \sum_{i=1}^{n} \kappa_i X_i \tag{3}$$

Table 1 shows the odds ratio and the corresponding 95 % confidence interval for each feature. An odds ratio ρ represents a $\rho \times P_{TRF}$ increase in the TRF probability for every unit increase of the corresponding feature. Thus, odds ratios close to 1 suggest that those features have no major effect on the TRF probability. Table 1 shows that all odds ratios are statistically significant ($p < 0.01$).

The "Twitter age" of the Speaker, the number of followers and followees (factors that were previously shown to correlate with Twitter activity) as well as the tweeting [28, 39] and retweeting [40] rate of the Speaker, show no correlation with the TRF probability. Similar results are obtained when examining the age and number of followers or followees of the Listener. We have also examined a number of aggregated informational features, namely the Speaker's overall activity and her daily tweeting activity. Both features show no significant correlation with the TRF probability.

Reciprocity

A structural feature that examines the reverse relation between S and L, i.e., *whether S was already following L when L received one or more retweets of S*, has a large effect on the TRF probability. Reciprocity increases the probability that L will follow S by 27.3 times compared to the base TRF probability. Previous work has shown *reciprocity* to be a dominant characteristic of several online social networks such as Twitter [28], Flickr [41], and Yahoo 360 [42].

In 44 % of the observed TRF events, S was following L prior to the formation of the reverse link. Figure 5 shows $P_{TRF}(\Delta)$ independent of reciprocity (solid line), when reciprocity is present (dashed line), and when reciprocity is not present (dotted line). When reciprocity is present, the TRF probability, denoted by $P_{TRF}(\Delta, \leftrightarrow)$, is one order of magnitude larger than the probability without reciprocity, denoted by $P_{TRF}(\Delta, \rightarrow)$. For $\Delta > 3$ h, $P_{TRF}(\Delta, \leftrightarrow)$ further increases and gradually becomes up to two orders of magnitude larger.

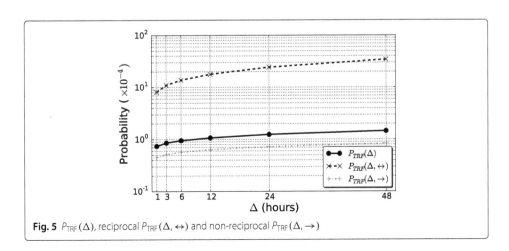

Fig. 5 $P_{TRF}(\Delta)$, reciprocal $P_{TRF}(\Delta, \leftrightarrow)$ and non-reciprocal $P_{TRF}(\Delta, \rightarrow)$

The large quantitative effect of reciprocity on the TRF probability implies that there may be different reasons for the formation of a link from L to S in that case. The existence of the reverse link, $S \to L$, could imply that these two users have some prior relation. They may know each other in other social contexts (online or offline) or they may belong to similar interest groups. In such cases, the retweet of S can make L aware of the existence and activity of S in the Twitter network.

Number of tweets and repeaters

Earlier social influence studies showed that the probability that an individual adopts a new behavior increases with the number of her ties already engaging in that behavior [1, 17, 43–45]. Similarly, we examine whether the number of tweets and retweets of S received by L affects the TRF probability. It turns out that P_{TRF} increases with both the number of distinct tweets of S that L receives (odds ratio = 2.01), and with the number of distinct Repeaters that L received retweets from (odds ratio = 2.08).

For simplicity, we choose to aggregate the number of distinct Repeaters and the number of distinct tweets of S that L received into a single parameter: the total number n of retweets (potentially not distinct) of S that were received by L in a time period of length Δ. This new factor has high correlation with the TRF probability (odds ratio = 1.25, $p < 0.001$). Figure 6 (left) shows the TRF probability in the absence of reciprocity ($L \to S$) while Fig. 6 (right) shows the TRF probability in the presence of reciprocity ($L \leftrightarrow S$), as a function of n.

TRF model

We now construct a simple model for the probability of TRF events. The objective of this exercise is to create a parsimonious probabilistic model that can be used in analytical or computational studies of co-evolutionary dynamics in social networks.

The model considers two independent mechanisms behind each TRF event: How many retweets n of Speaker S did the Listener L receive? And, did L actually observe (i.e., read) this group of retweets? The simplest approach is to assume, first, that the n received retweets are either observed as a group with probability p or they are completely missed, and second, that each observed retweet causes a TRF event independently and with the same probability q. Then, the probability of a TRF event after receiving at most n retweets is

$$P_{TRF}(n) = p \times \left(1 - (1-q)^n\right) \tag{4}$$

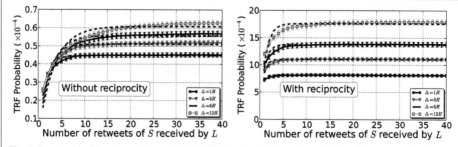

Fig. 6 Empirical (*solid*) and model-based (*dashed*) TRF probability $P_{TRF}(\to, n)$ (*left*) and $P_{TRF}(\leftrightarrow, n)$ (*right*) as a function of the number n of received retweets of S at L, for four different values of Δ

Table 2 Estimated value of the two model parameters p and $p \times q$

Δ (h)	p	$p \times q$	p	$p \times q$
	Without reciprocity		With reciprocity	
1	0.5×10^{-4}	0.12×10^{-4}	8.1×10^{-4}	7.2×10^{-4}
3	0.5×10^{-4}	0.13×10^{-4}	11.0×10^{-4}	8.5×10^{-4}
6	0.6×10^{-4}	0.14×10^{-4}	13.0×10^{-4}	9.3×10^{-4}
12	0.6×10^{-4}	0.15×10^{-4}	17.6×10^{-4}	9.3×10^{-4}
24	0.7×10^{-4}	0.16×10^{-4}	24.0×10^{-4}	10.2×10^{-4}
48	0.8×10^{-4}	0.16×10^{-4}	33.1×10^{-4}	10.2×10^{-4}

Thus, the probability of a TRF event after only one received retweet is $p \times q$. For a large number of received retweets, the TRF probability tends to the observation probability p.

As shown in Fig. 6 (left), the measured TRF probability $P_{\text{TRF}}(\rightarrow, n)$ without reciprocity seems to "saturate" after n exceeds about 10–20 retweets. The same trend is observed in the case of reciprocity (Fig. 6 (right)), but the saturation appears earlier (after around 5–10 retweets). The model of (4) captures the dependency with n quite well. The parameters p and q depend on reciprocity as well as on the time window Δ, as shown in Table 2. Reciprocity increases significantly both the observation probability p and the probability $p \times q$ that a single received retweet will cause a TRF event. As expected, increasing the observation time window Δ increases the observation probability. The effect of Δ on the probability $p \times q$ is weaker, especially when there is no reciprocity.

We further examined the accuracy of the proposed model through a cross-validation approach. We split the dataset in two equal parts, one for parameterizing the model and another for testing that model. Figure 7 shows this comparison for different values of Δ.

Implications of TRF events

Most prior work in online social networks focused either on the exogenous evolution of the topology (dynamics of networks) or on influence and information diffusion on static networks (dynamics on networks), ignoring the potential coupling between these two dynamics. We now discuss how TRF events may gradually transform the structure of a social network. We consider two fundamentally different network topologies, and discuss the implications of TRF events from the information diffusion perspective.

Effect on topologies with directed cycles

The left graph of Fig. 8a shows a weakly connected network, which may be a subset of the Twitter topology. A directed cycle exists between some of its nodes, namely $A \rightarrow B \rightarrow$

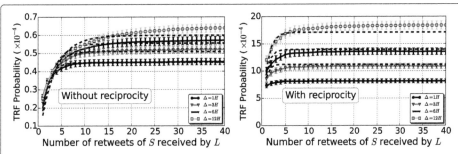

Fig. 7 Cross-validation of the proposed model. Half of the observed TRF events are used to parameterize the model of Eq. 4 (*dashed lines*), while the other half is used to estimate the TRF probability empirically (*solid lines*)

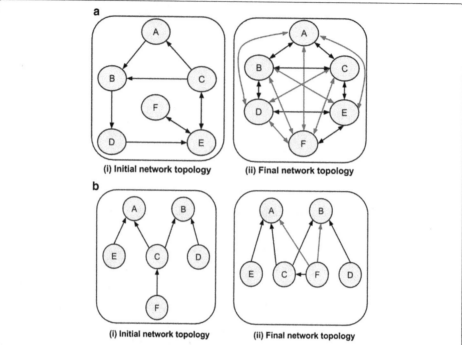

Fig. 8 a An initial network that includes a directed cycle. A sequence of TRF events can transform this cycle to a clique, meaning that the corresponding users gradually form a tightly knit community. **b** A hierarchical initial network. A sequence of TRF events can transform this multi-layer hierarchy into a two-layer hierarchy in which each sink node is directly followed by a set of other nodes (its "sphere of influence"), while each non-sink node follows at least one sink node

$D \rightarrow E \leftrightarrow C \rightarrow A$. Let us focus on the largest directed cycle in this network, i.e., in its largest strongly connected component (SCC). The ties of the participating nodes may also include links to or from nodes out of this cycle, such as the $E \leftrightarrow F$ relation.

Suppose that A posts a tweet at some point in time and C decides to retweet it. Node E will receive that retweet and may follow A (TRF event). It is easy to see that, after a sufficiently large number of TRF events, the nodes of this directed cycle will form a fully connected directed graph, as shown in the right graph of Fig. 8a (red edges denote connections created through TRF events), in which everyone is following all others. This transformation can only take place when a cycle already exists in the initial network; TRF events *cannot* create directed cycles. So, when an initial network includes a directed cycle, a sequence of TRF events may transform that cycle into a clique in which everyone can generate information that all others receive directly from the source.

Effect on hierarchical topologies

The left graph of Fig. 8b shows a hierarchical weakly connected directed network. Again, this network may be a subset of the Twitter topology. This network contains no directed cycles, but a number of sink nodes (i.e., nodes with no outgoing edges; A and B in this example).

User F may receive a retweet of A and B through C, and she may then decide to follow them. After a sequence of TRF events, this network can then reach the topological equilibrium shown in the right graph of Fig. 8b, in which no new links can be added through

TRF events. More generally, suppose that $F'(X) = \{X_1, \ldots, X_n\}$ is the set of followees of X. The set of Speakers that X may receive a retweet from can be defined recursively as $F'_U(X) = F'(X) \cup (F'_U(X_1) \cup \ldots F'_U(X_n))$; if user X does not have any followees then $F'_U(X)$ is the empty set. It is easy to see that, after a sufficiently large number of TRF events, a multi-layer hierarchical network will converge to a two-layer hierarchy in which every non-sink user X follows *all* users in $F'_U(X)$. Then, an initial sink node X will be followed directly by all users that had a directed path towards X in the initial network. A consequence of TRF events in such hierarchical networks is the emergence of some highly influential users that were the sink nodes in the initial network. Further, non-sink nodes will be partitioned, with the users in each partition following a distinct set of sink nodes.

The previous two topologies are obvious extremes. In practice, a given weakly connected subset of Twitter users may contain groups of nodes that form directed cycles as well as nodes that do not belong in any directed cycle. An interesting question then is: *given a weakly connected directed social network, what fraction of its nodes belong to the longest directed cycle (i.e., largest SCC) in that network?* If this fraction is large, the network resembles the example of Fig. 8a, while if it is close to zero the network is similar to the example of Fig. 8b.

We investigated the previous question based on samples of the actual Twitter topology, at least as it was measured by Kwak et al. [28] in 2010.[4]

We collected weakly connected network samples using the *Random-Walk* [46] and *Snowball* (Breadth-First-Search) [47] sampling methods. The largest SCC was determined with Tarjan's algorithm [48].

In the case of moderately large samples, between 1000 to 1,000,000 nodes, *the largest SCC contained consistently more than 90 % of the nodes.* This result suggests that the Twitter topology is closer to the network of Fig. 8a than to the network of Fig. 8b. The creation of such large cliques, however, may require a very long time, and it may also be impractical for a user to follow thousands of other users. Consequently, we are more interested in smaller samples, including only tens or hundreds of Twitter users.

Figure 9 shows the percentage of Twitter users that are included in the SCC of small network samples, in the range of 10–1000 nodes. Each point is the average

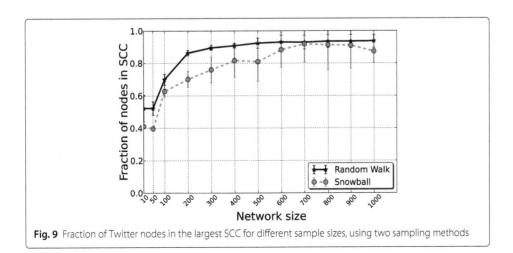

Fig. 9 Fraction of Twitter nodes in the largest SCC for different sample sizes, using two sampling methods

of 1000 samples of that size, and the error bars represent 95 % confidence intervals. Independent of the sampling method, the SCC typically includes the majority of the nodes even for samples of few tens of users. The SCC percentage increases to about 80–90 % for networks with more than 200–400 users. These results imply that co-evolutionary dynamics, and the TRF mechanism in particular, have the potential to gradually create very dense communities of users in which everyone is following almost everyone else, as long as the involved users are active, tweeting and retweeting information.

Unfollow events

TRF events can be considered as only one instance of co-evolutionary dynamics in social networks. More such mechanisms may exist however. For instance, a sequence of one or more tweets from a Speaker S received by a follower L may cause L to remove the link to S; we refer to this as an *endogenous unfollow* event. On the other hand, *exogenous unfollow* events occur when L removes the link to S for reasons that are unrelated to S's tweeting activity. In the rest of this section, we briefly investigate unfollow events. Unfortunately, we are not able to distinguish between endogenous and exogenous unfollow events. Instead, we simply examine the timing of unfollow events relative to the Speaker's last tweet and analyze statistically the effect of various structural and informational features on the probability of unfollow events.

Kwak et al. showed through data analysis and user interviews that unfollow events are highly correlated with the tweeting activity of the Speaker [49]. Additionally, Kivran-Swaine et al. [50] showed that structural properties of two individuals significantly affect the probability that they will be connected in the future.

Unfollow data

We monitor a set of Speakers selected as described in Section "Data collection". One difference is that we collect periodically only the set of followers of S; we do not collect retweets, repeaters and their followers. A follower L of S is said to unfollow S at a sampling instant t_{k+1} if L is in $F(S, t_k)$ but not in $F(S, t_{k+1})$. As in the case of TRF events, the sampling period is about 5 min.

Additionally, we download the total activity of each monitored Speaker during the data collection period (1 week). This activity includes the original tweets posted by the Speaker as well as tweets of others that were retweeted by the Speaker. We also log the time of the tweet or retweet, and the initiator of that post in the case of a retweet.

This "unfollow dataset" includes 3648 monitored Speakers, while the initial number of followers (before any unfollow events) is 4,055,327 (3,609,649 distinct users). During the 1-week data collection period, we observed 5325 unfollow events (0.13 % of the total number of followers)) from 5220 Listeners to 983 Speakers.

Figure 10 shows the CDF of the latency between the time L unfollowed S ($L \nrightarrow S$) and the last activity of S received by L before the unfollow event. Almost 60 % of the unfollow events occur during the first hour after S has posted some content, and almost 100 % of the unfollow events occur within a day. This observation suggests that many unfollow events may be endogenous. We cannot distinguish between endogenous and exogenous unfollow events strictly based on this latency, however, especially when the Speaker tweets at a high frequency (say, several times per day).

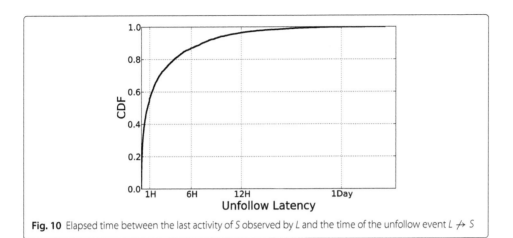

Fig. 10 Elapsed time between the last activity of S observed by L and the time of the unfollow event $L \nrightarrow S$

Unfollow probability

How likely is for a Listener L to unfollow Speaker S during a time period Δ after receiving a tweet (or retweet) from S? We define the probability of an unfollow event similar to the TRF probability. We first identify all *Activity events* (A) for each post of each Speaker S. An Activity event is denoted by $A(S, L, t_a, I_R, I_\Delta)$ and it means that follower L of S ($L \in F(S)$) received a tweet or retweet from S at time t_a. The indicator variable I_R is 1 if the message was a retweet, and 0 if it was an original tweet of S. The indicator variable I_Δ is 1 if L unfollowed S during a time period of length Δ after t_a.

We group such Activity events to *Activity Groups* (AG) of the form $AG(S, L, t_a, n, n_t, n_r, I_\Delta)$. n, n_t, n_r denote the total number of posts, tweets, and retweets of S received by L during the time window $< t_a, t_a + \Delta >$. The grouping method is similar to the clustering of TR events in RG. We then calculate the probability of an unfollow event $P_{UNF}(\Delta)$ as the fraction of AGs for which $I_\Delta = 1$. Figure 11 shows the unfollow probability P_{UNF} as a function of Δ.

Using the multivariate logistic regression model of Eq. 3, we estimate the correlation between a number of features and the unfollow probability. We use features similar to those described in Table 1, but excluding any Repeater-related features. The "number

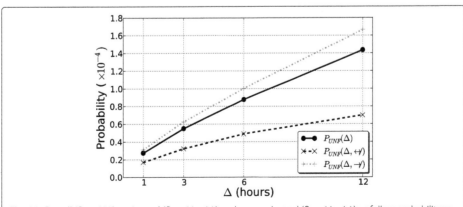

Fig. 11 Overall ($P_{UNF}(\Delta)$), reciprocal ($P_{UNF}(\Delta, \nleftrightarrow)$) and non-reciprocal ($P_{UNF}(\Delta, \nrightarrow)$) unfollow probability as a function of Δ

Table 3 Odds ratio and its 95 % confidence interval for each feature of the multivariate logistic regression model for P_{UNF}

	Odds ratio	95 % CI
Structural features		
$\|F(S)\|$	0.999***	[0.999, 0.999]
$\|F'(S)\|$	1.000***	[1.000, 1.000]
AGE(S)	0.998***	[0.998, 0.998]
$S \rightarrow L$	0.302***	[0.261, 0.348]
Informational features		
ST(S)	1.000***	[1.000, 1.000]
$A_{\mathrm{rate}}(S)$	0.972***	[0.967, 0.978]
Tweets(S, L, Δ)	1.041***	[1.025, 1.057]
Retweets(S, L, Δ)	1.026	[0.992, 1.006]

*$p < 0.1$; **$p < 0.05$; ***$p < 0.01$

of tweets" and "number of retweets" refer to the number of original posts by S and the number of posts forwarded by S, respectively.

Table 3 shows the resulting odds ratios and the corresponding 95 % confidence intervals for each feature. Note that most of the features have limited or no effect on the unfollow probability; most of the structural features return an odds value close to 1. As the number of tweets increases, P_{UNF} slightly increases, implying that unfollow events may be more likely for Speakers that tweet too frequently. However, this effect is not sufficiently strong.

Only the reciprocity factor seems to significantly affect P_{UNF}. In the presence of reciprocity, meaning that the Speaker S follows the Listener L, it is about 70 % less likely for L to unfollow S. In only 18 % of the observed unfollow events S followed L. Figure 11 shows P_{UNF} conditioned on the presence of reciprocity ($P_{\mathrm{UNF}}(\Delta, \nleftrightarrow)$) or conditioned on the absence of reciprocity ($P_{\mathrm{UNF}}(\Delta, \nrightarrow)$). Note that it is at least twice more likely for L to unfollow S when their relationship is not reciprocal. As discussed in the case of TRF events, reciprocal relations may represent a connection between two users outside the context of Twitter, or a stronger degree of homophily between them.

The small percentage of unfollow events in reciprocal relations may be explained as follows: Kwak et al. [49] claim that some users follow back all new followers as a courtesy. After a while, however, the former may decide that they are not interested in the posts of their new followers and unfollow them.

Kwak et al. showed that people often appreciate receiving acknowledgments from other users (in the form of replies or tweets of the same content/hashtag). Such activity often decreases the likelihood of unfollow events [51, 52]. Hutto et al. have found that the content of someone's tweets significantly impacts the number of followers of that user [53]. Their results show that expressing negative sentiment has an adverse effect on the follower count, whereas expressing positive sentiment helps to increase the latter. This prior work has focused on a small number of snapshots that are few months apart. We plan to leverage our near real-time data collection system to monitor unfollow events and their dependence on the actual content of tweets in smaller time scales.

Conclusions

Most prior work in online social networks focused either on the exogenous evolution of the topology (dynamics of network) or on influence and information diffusion on static networks (dynamics on network), ignoring the potential coupling between these two dynamics. In this paper, we considered co-evolutionary dynamics in the specific case of the Twitter online social network. Most of our study focused on the addition of new links through the so-called Tweet-Retweet-Follow events. We showed that it is much more likely for a user to get a new follower if her tweets are retweeted than in the case where her tweets are not retweeted. We showed that TRF events, although infrequent compared to tweets or retweets, occur in practice and they are responsible for a significant fraction (about 20 %) of the new edges in Twitter. Through (near) real-time monitoring of many Twitter users, we showed how to identify TRF events and investigated their temporal and statistical characteristics. More than 80 % of TRF events occur in less than 24 h after the corresponding retweet. The main factors that affect the probability of a TRF event are reciprocity and the total number of retweets received by the Listener. Based on these findings, we have proposed a simple probabilistic model for the probability of TRF events. We have also discussed how TRF events can affect the structure of the underlying social network. TRF events tend to transform directed cycles into cliques, creating closely knit communities of users in which everyone is following everyone else. The analysis of samples from the 2010 Twitter topology shows that weakly connected groups of more than 200–400 users contain large directed cycles that include more than 80–90 % of the users. Finally, we have argued that TRF events are not the only form of co-evolutionary dynamics in Twitter. Users may also break existing relations (unfollow others) based on the tweeting activity of the latter. An analysis of this effect shows that 60 % of the unfollow events occur during the first hour after the Speaker has posted some content. Also, a reciprocal relation (a link from the Speaker to the Listener) greatly decreases the likelihood of an unfollow event in the opposite direction. In future work, we plan to explore additional types of co-evolutionary dynamics and to quantify their effect. Such events include the creation of new follower relations after a "reply" or "mention" user action.

Endnotes
[1] http://en.wikipedia.org/wiki/Yahoo!_Meme
[2] Exploring the impact of bots on the evolution of the Twitter topology is an interesting area for future work.
[3] Features such as the number of common friends between S and L are not examined because they would require additional data that we have not collected.
[4] http://an.kaist.ac.kr/traces/WWW2010.html

Competing interests
The authors declare that they have no competing interests.

Authors' contributions
Both authors designed the research, data collection and experiments. Demetris Antoniades carried out the data collection and executed the experiments. Both authors contributed to the writing of the manuscript. Both authors read and approved the final manuscript.

Acknowledgements
This material is based upon work supported in part by the Defense Advanced Research Projects Agency (DARPA) under Contract No. W911NF-12-1-0043. Any opinions, findings, and conclusions or recommendations expressed in this material are those of the authors and do not necessarily reflect the views of DARPA or the U.S. Government. The views and conclusions contained in this document are those of the authors and should not be interpreted as representing the official policies, either expressly or implied, of the Defense Advanced Research Projects Agency or the U.S. Government.

Author details
[1] Department of Computer Science, University of Cyprus, Nicosia, Cyprus. [2] College of Computing, Georgia Institute of Technology, Atlanta, Georgia, USA.

References

1. Bakshy, E, Karrer, B, Adamic, LA: Social influence and the diffusion of user-created content. In: Proc. of the tenth ACM conference on Electronic commerce, pp. 325–334, (2009)
2. Vespignani, A: Modelling dynamical processes in complex socio-technical systems. Nat. Physics. **8**(1), 32–39 (2011)
3. Leskovec, J, Kleinberg, J, Faloutsos, C: Graphs over time: densification laws, shrinking diameters and possible explanations. In: Proc. of the eleventh ACM SIGKDD international conference on Knowledge discovery in data mining, pp. 177–187. ACM, New York, NY, USA, (2005)
4. Gross, T, Blasius, B: Adaptive coevolutionary networks: a review. J. R. Society Interface. **5**(20), 259–271 (2008)
5. Leskovec, J, McGlohon, M, Faloutsos, C, Glance, NS, Hurst, M: Patterns of cascading behavior in large blog graphs. In: Proc. of SIAM SDM 2007. SIAM, (2007)
6. Antoniades, D, Dovrolis, C: Co-evolutionary dynamics in social networks: A case study of Twitter. In: Proc. of the Third IEEE International Workshop on Complex Networks and their Applications, (2014)
7. Barabási, A-L, Albert, R: Emergence of scaling in random networks. Science. **286**(5439), 509–512 (1999)
8. Hopcroft, J, Lou, T, Tang, J: Who will follow you back?: reciprocal relationship prediction. In: Proc. of the 20th ACM international conference on Information and knowledge management, pp. 1137–1146. ACM, (2011)
9. Papadopoulos, F, Kitsak, M, Serrano, MÁ, Boguñá, M, Krioukov, D: Popularity versus similarity in growing networks. Nature. **489**(7417), 537–540 (2012)
10. Golder, SA, Yardi, S: Structural predictors of tie formation in Twitter: Transitivity and mutuality. In: Social Computing (SocialCom), 2010 IEEE Second International Conference on, pp. 88–95. IEEE, (2010)
11. Leskovec, J, Backstrom, L, Kumar, R, Tomkins, A: Microscopic evolution of social networks. In: Proc. of the 14th ACM SIGKDD International Conference on Knowledge Discovery and Data Mining, pp. 462–470, (2008)
12. Romero, DM, Kleinberg, J: The directed closure process in hybrid social-information networks, with an analysis of link formation on Twitter. In: Proc. of the 4th International AAAI Conference on Weblogs and Social Media, pp. 138–145, (2010)
13. Muchnik, L, Pei, S, Parra, LC, Reis, SD, Jr. Andrade, JS, Havlin, S, Makse, HA: Origins of power-law degree distribution in the heterogeneity of human activity in social networks. Scientific reports. **3** (2013)
14. Gallos, LK, Rybski, D, Liljeros, F, Havlin, S, Makse, HA: How people interact in evolving online affiliation networks. Phys. Rev. X. **2**, 031014 (2012)
15. Lotan, G, Graeff, E, Ananny, M, Gaffney, D, Pearce, I, Boyd, D: The revolutions were tweeted: Information flows during the Tunisian and Egyptian revolutions. Int. J. Commun. **5**, 1375–1405 (2011)
16. Starbird, K, Palen, L: (How) will the revolution be retweeted?: information diffusion and the 2011 Egyptian uprising. In: Proc. of the acm 2012 conference on computer supported cooperative work, pp. 7–16. ACM, (2012)
17. Romero, DM, Meeder, B, Kleinberg, JM: Differences in the mechanics of information diffusion across topics: idioms, political hashtags, and complex contagion on Twitter. In: Proc. of the 20th International Conference on World Wide Web, pp. 695–704, (2011)
18. Myers, SA, Zhu, C, Leskovec, J: Information diffusion and external influence in networks. In: Proc. of the 18th ACM SIGKDD international conference on Knowledge discovery and data mining, pp. 33–41. ACM, (2012)
19. Kozma, B, Barrat, A: Consensus formation on adaptive networks. Physical Review E. **77**(1), 016102 (2008)
20. Shaw, LB, Schwartz, IB: Enhanced vaccine control of epidemics in adaptive networks. Phys. Rev. E. **81**, 046120 (2010)
21. Volz, E, Meyers, LA: Epidemic thresholds in dynamic contact networks. J. R. Soc. Inter. **6**(32), 233–241 (2009)
22. Rocha, LE, Liljeros, F, Holme, P: Simulated epidemics in an empirical spatiotemporal network of 50,185 sexual contacts. PLoS Comput. Biol. **7**(3), e1001109 (2011)
23. Perra, N, Baronchelli, A, Mocanu, D, Gonçalves, B, Pastor-Satorras, R, Vespignani, A: Random walks and search in time-varying networks. Phys. Rev. Lett. **109**, 238701 (2012)
24. Weng, L, Ratkiewicz, J, Perra, N, Gonçalves, B, Castillo, C, Bonchi, F, Schifanella, R, Menczer, F, Flammini, A: The role of information diffusion in the evolution of social networks. In: Proc. of the 19th ACM SIGKDD international conference on Knowledge discovery and data mining KDD '13, pp. 356–364. ACM, New York, NY, USA, (2013)
25. Myers, SA, Leskovec, J: The bursty dynamics of the Twitter information network. In: Proc. of the 23rd international conference on World wide web, pp. 913–924. International World Wide Web Conferences Steering Committee, (2014)
26. Meeder, B, Karrer, B, Sayedi, A, Ravi, R, Borgs, C, Chayes, J: We know who you followed last summer: inferring social link creation times in Twitter. In: Proc. of the 20th international conference on World wide web, pp. 517–526. ACM, (2011)
27. An Exhaustive Study of Twitter Users Across the World (2012). http://www.beevolve.com/twitter-statistics/.
28. Kwak, H, Lee, C, Park, H, Moon, S: What is Twitter, a social network or a news media? In: Proc. of the 19th International Conference on World Wide Web, pp. 591–600, (2010)
29. Twitter search. http://search.twitter.com.
30. Antoniades, D, Polakis, I, Kontaxis, G, Athanasopoulos, E, Ioannidis, S, Markatos, EP, Karagiannis, T: we. b: The web of short URLs. In: Proc. of the 20th international conference on World wide web, pp. 715–724. ACM, (2011)
31. Weng, L, Flammini, A, Vespignani, A, Menczer, F: Competition among memes in a world with limited attention. Sci. Rep. **2** (2012)
32. Chun, B, Culler, D, Roscoe, T, Bavier, A, Peterson, L, Wawrzoniak, M, Bowman, M: Planetlab: an overlay testbed for broad-coverage services. ACM. SIGCOMM. CCR. **33**(3), 3–12 (2003)
33. Thomas, K, Grier, C, Song, D, Paxson, V: Suspended accounts in retrospect: An analysis of Twitter spam. In: Proc. of the 2011 ACM SIGCOMM conference on Internet measurement conference, pp. 243–258. ACM, (2011)
34. Sridharan, V, Shankar, V, Gupta, M: Twitter games: how successful spammers pick targets. In: Proc. of the 28th Annual Computer Security Applications Conference, pp. 389–398. ACM, (2012)
35. Gupta, P, Goel, A, Lin, J, Sharma, A, Wang, D, Zadeh, R: WTF: The who to follow service at Twitter. In: Proc. of the 22nd international conference on World Wide Web, pp. 505–514. International World Wide Web Conferences Steering Committee, (2013)

36. statisticbrain.com: Twitter Statistics (2013). http://www.statisticbrain.com/twitter-statistics/
37. Aaron, S, Lee, R: 8 % of online Americans use Twitter (2010). http://www.pewinternet.org/Reports/2010/Twitter-Update-2010.aspx
38. He, H, Garcia, EA: Learning from imbalanced data. Knowl. Data Eng. IEEE Trans. **21**(9), 1263–1284 (2009)
39. Huberman, B, Romero, D, Wu, F: Social networks that matter: Twitter under the microscope (2008). Available at SSRN: http://ssrn.com/abstract=1313405 or http://dx.doi.org/10.2139/ssrn.1313405
40. Suh, B, Hong, L, Pirolli, P, Chi, E: Want to be retweeted? large scale analytics on factors impacting retweet in Twitter network. In: Social Computing (SocialCom), 2010 IEEE Second International Conference on, pp. 177–184. IEEE, (2010)
41. Cha, M, Mislove, A, Gummadi, KP: A measurement driven analysis of information propagation in the Flickr social network. In: Proc. of the 18th international conference on World wide web, pp. 721–730. ACM, (2009)
42. Kumar, R, Novak, J, Tomkins, A: Structure and Evolution of Online Social Networks. In: Yu, PS, Han, J, Faloutsos, C (eds.) Link Mining: Models, Algorithms, and Applications, pp. 337–357. Springer, New York, (2010)
43. Backstrom, L, Huttenlocher, D, Kleinberg, J, Lan, X: Group formation in large social networks: membership, growth, and evolution. In: Proc. of the 12th ACM SIGKDD international conference on Knowledge discovery and data mining, pp. 44–54. ACM, (2006)
44. Hodas, NO, Lerman, K: How visibility and divided attention constrain social contagion. In: Proc. of the 2012 ASE/IEEE International Conference on Social Computing and 2012 ASE/IEEE International Conference on Privacy, Security, Risk and Trust. IEEE Computer Society, (2012)
45. Feng, L, Hu, Y, Li, B, Stanley, HE, Havlin, S, Braunstein, LA: Competing for Attention in Social Media under Information Overload Conditions. PLoS ONE. **10**(7), e0126090 (2015)
46. Leskovec, J, Faloutsos, C: Sampling from large graphs. In: Proc. of the 12th ACM SIGKDD international conference on Knowledge discovery and data mining KDD '06, pp. 631–636. ACM, New York, NY, USA, (2006)
47. Goodman, LA: Snowball sampling. Annals Math. Stat. **32**(1), 148–170 (1961)
48. Tarjan, R: Depth-first search and linear graph algorithms. SIAM Journal Comput. **1**(2), 146–160 (1972)
49. Kwak, H, Chun, H, Moon, S: Fragile online relationship: a first look at unfollow dynamics in Twitter. In: Proc. of the 2011 annual conference on Human factors in computing systems CHI '13, pp. 1091–1100. ACM, (2011)
50. Kivran-Swaine, F, Govindan, P, Naaman, M: The impact of network structure on breaking ties in online social networks: unfollowing on Twitter. In: Proc. of the SIGCHI Conference on Human Factors in Computing Systems CHI '11, pp. 1101–1104. ACM, New York, NY, USA, (2011)
51. Kwak, H, Moon, S, Lee, W: More of a receiver than a giver: Why do people unfollow in Twitter? In: Proc. of AAAI ICWSM 2012, (2012)
52. Xu, B, Huang, Y, Kwak, H, Contractor, N: Structures of broken ties: exploring unfollow behavior on Twitter. In: Proc. of the 2013 conference on Computer supported cooperative work, pp. 871–876. ACM, New York, NY, USA, (2013)
53. Hutto, C, Yardi, S, Gilbert, E: A longitudinal study of follow predictors on Twitter. In: Proc. of the SIGCHI Conference on Human Factors in Computing Systems, pp. 821–830. ACM, New York, NY, USA, (2013)

9

A study on the influential neighbors to maximize information diffusion in online social networks

Hyoungshick Kim[1]*, Konstantin Beznosov[2] and Eiko Yoneki[3]

*Correspondence:
hyoung@skku.edu
[1] Department of Computer Science and Engineering, Sungkyunkwan University, Suwon, Korea
Full list of author information is available at the end of the article

Abstract

The problem of spreading information is a topic of considerable recent interest, but the traditional influence maximization problem is inadequate for a typical viral marketer who cannot access the entire network topology. To fix this flawed assumption that the marketer can control any arbitrary k nodes in a network, we have developed a decentralized version of the influential maximization problem by influencing k neighbors rather than arbitrary users in the entire network. We present several practical strategies and evaluate their performance with a real dataset collected from Twitter during the 2010 UK election campaign. Our experimental results show that information can be efficiently propagated in online social networks using neighbors with a high propagation rate rather than those with a high number of neighbors. To examine the importance of using real propagation rates, we additionally performed an experiment under the same conditions except the use of synthetic propagation rates, which is widely used in studying the influence maximization problem and found that their results were significantly different from real-world experiences.

Keywords: Information diffusion; Information dissemination; Online social networks; Viral marketing

Introduction

In the field of social network analysis, a fundamental problem is to develop an epidemiological model for finding an efficient way to spread information through the model. It seems natural that many people are often influenced by their friends' opinions or recommendations. This is called the 'word of mouth' effect and has for long been recognized as a powerful force affecting product recommendation [1].

Recent advances in the network theory have provided us with the mathematical and computational tools to understand them better. For example, in the *Independent Cascade* (IC) model proposed by Goldenberg et al. [2], (1) some non-empty set of nodes are initially *activated* (or influenced); (2) at each successive step, the influence is propagated by activated nodes, independently activating their inactive neighbors based on the *propagation probabilities* of the adjacent edges. Here, activated nodes mean the nodes that have adopted the information or have been infected. This models how a piece of information will likely be spread through a network over time. It enables us to investigate what sort of information diffusion scheme might be the most effective one under certain conditions.

This model is also highly relevant to security. For example, cyberstalkers might be interested in spreading rumors, gossips, news, or pictures through social networks to damage their victims' (e.g., celebrity, political party, company, or country) reputation. The same model works in social media campaign where spammers and propagandists want to share their advertisements on online social networks; fake accounts with automated bots are often used to amplify advertising campaigns in social media [3-5].

Thus far, however, the models and analytic tools used to analyze epidemics have been somewhat limited. Most previous studies [6,7] aimed to analyze the process of information diffusion by choosing a set of arbitrary k nodes in a network as the initially activated nodes from a bird's eye perspective based on the full control of the entire network, which may indeed be unacceptable in many real-life applications since there is no such central entity (except the online social network service provider itself).

From the point of view of an individual user (e.g., viral marketer) who wants to efficiently spread a piece of information (or a rumor) through a network, a more reasonable epidemiological model would not assume the knowledge of the entire network topology. Kim and Yoneki [8] recently introduced the problem called Influential Neighbor Selection (INS) where a spreader s spreads a piece of information through carefully chosen k neighbors of hers instead of a set of any arbitrary k nodes in a network. Under this model, each user can only communicate with the user's immediate neighbors and has no knowledge of the global network topology except for her own connections. However, their work has two limitations: (1) it was simply assumed to use a constant propagation rate, despite variations in user propagation rates in practice. For example, in real-world online social network services such as Twitter or Facebook, each user has a distinct propagation rate for her neighbors on spreading information according to the user's reputation and/or role, such as opinion formers, leaders, or followers [9]; (2) their experimental results were limited to undirected graphs with parameter values chosen in a somewhat *ad hoc* manner.

Recently, Kim [10] extended this model by introducing several parameters (*user propagation weight*, *content interestingness*, and *decay factor*) to provide a more general and practical information diffusion model. This gives much finer granularity than the previous model [8]. However, their experiments still depended on synthetic parameters that might significantly affect the information diffusion process.

With a real dataset (Twitter users and messages related to the 2010 UK election campaign), we revisited the INS problem and evaluated the performance of four spreading schemes from the simple random neighbor selection to a sophisticated neighbor selection scheme using both the 'number of friends' and 'user propagation rate' each neighbor has. To measure the performance of these schemes, we used the conventional *Independent Cascade* (IC) model [2], which is widely used for the analysis of information diffusion [2,7,11].

In particular, we demonstrated the importance of using real propagation rates by comparing the simulation results with those using the randomly assigned synthetic parameters which were often used in studying the influence maximization problem. Our comparison results show that their results were significantly different, which indicate that the use of such synthetic propagation rates might be undesirable to understand the characteristics of information diffusion on a real-world social network (e.g., Twitter).

We also performed a simulation with various parameters. Our experimental results suggest that the scheme to select neighbors who wrote popular posts produced the best overall results, even without consideration of the 'number of friends'. Moreover, we found that the information diffusion speed of some schemes (e.g., random neighbor selection) in the previous study [10] was quite exaggerated and thus contributed to the reduction of the performance gap between information diffusion schemes. For example, we observed that the random selection scheme is not practically effective even with a high number k initially activated nodes; this is quite different from previous studies [8,10], which showed that the random selection scheme achieved reasonable performance when $k \geq 3$.

The rest of this paper is organized as follows. Related work is discussed in Section 'Related work'. In Section 'Influential neighbor selection problem', we formally define the INS problem and notations. Then, we present the four reasonable neighbor selection schemes in Section 'Neighbor selection schemes'. In Section 'Experimental results', we evaluate their performance through simulation with a real dataset collected from Twitter and recommend the best neighbor selection scheme with various conditions. We conclude in Section 'Conclusions'.

Related work

Influential maximization (IM) problem has recently received increasing attention, given the growing popularity of online social networks, such as Facebook and Twitter, which have provided great opportunities for the diffusion of information, opinions, and adoption of new products.

The IM problem was originally introduced for marketing purposes by Domingos and Richardson [6]: The goal is to find a set of k initially activated nodes with the maximum number of activated nodes after the time step t. Kempe et al. [7] formulated this problem under two basic stochastic influence cascade models: the *Independent Cascade* (IC) model [2] and the *Linear Threshold* (LT) model [7]. In the IC model, each edge has a propagation probability and influence is propagated by activated nodes independently activating their inactive neighbors based on the edge propagation probabilities. In the LT model, each edge has a weight, each node has a threshold chosen uniformly at random, and a node becomes activated, if the weighted sum of its activated neighbors exceeds its threshold. Kempe et al. [7] showed that the optimization problem of selecting the most influential nodes in a graph is NP hard for both models and also proposed a greedy algorithm that provides a good approximation ratio of 63% of the optimal solution. However, their greedy algorithm relies on the Monte Carlo simulation on influence cascade to estimate the influence spread, which makes the algorithm slow and not scalable.

A number of papers in recent years have tried to overcome the inefficiency of this greedy algorithm by improving the original algorithm [12,13] or proposing new algorithms [13-15]. Leskovec et al. [12] proposed the *cost-effective lazy forward* (CELF) scheme in selecting new seeds to reduce the number of influence spread evaluations, but it is still slow and not scalable to large graphs, as demonstrated in [15]. Kimura and Saito [14] proposed shortest-path-based heuristic algorithms to evaluate the influence spread. Chen et al. [13] proposed two faster greedy algorithms called *MixedGreedy* and *DegreeDiscount* for the IC model where the propagation probabilities on all edges are the same; MixedGreedy removes the edges that have no contribution for propagating influence, which can reduce the computation on the unnecessary edges; DegreeDiscount assumes that the influence spread increases with node degree. Chen et al. [15] proposed the *Maximum Influence Arborescence* (MIA) heuristic based on local tree structures to reduce computation costs. Wang et al. [16] proposed a community-based greedy algorithm for identifying the most influential nodes. The main idea is to divide a social network into communities and estimate the influence spread in each community instead of the whole network topology.

As a variant of the conventional IM problem, Kim and Yoneki [8] introduced the problem called *Influential neighbor selection* (INS) to select the most influential neighbors of a node, rather than the most influential arbitrary nodes in a network. Kim [10] extended this epidemiological model by introducing several parameters (*user propagation weight*, *content interestingness*, and *decay factor*) to provide a more general and practical information diffusion model. However, they still used synthetic parameters that might significantly affect the information diffusion process. More recently, Kim et al. [10] found that the information diffusion speed of some schemes (e.g., propagation weight and random) in the previous study [17] was quite overestimated. In this paper, we extend their work by analyzing the effects of real propagation rates compared with the synthetic propagation rates.

Many studies noted that the levels of information-sharing activity varied greatly between users in social networks. Romero et al. [18] argued that a majority of Twitter users might be passive, not engaging in creating and sharing information. Cha et al. [9] found that users with many followers do not necessarily influence in terms of spawning retweets or mentions – the Spearman's rank correlation coefficient between the 'ranking by followers' and 'ranking by retweets' for all users was 0.549. Zhou et al. [19] showed that in Twitter, the content of a tweet might be an important factor in determining the 'retweet rate' – the mean retweet rate was 0.0136 but standard deviation was as high as 0.0501. Also, they observed that cascades tend to be wide and not too deep suggesting that the retweet rate may decay as the cascades spread away from the source – the mean of decay factors was about 0.2.

Influential neighbor selection problem

We begin with the definition of the *Independent Cascade* (IC) model [2] and then introduce the *Influential Neighbor Selection* (INS) problem, which will be used in the rest of the paper.

We model an *influence network* as a directed graph $G = (V, E)$ consisting of a set of nodes V and a set of ordered pairs of nodes E called the edge set, representing the communication channels between node pairs. A directed edge (u, v) from node u to node v of G is associated with a *propagation probability* $\lambda_{u,v}$, which is the probability that v is activated by u through the edge in the next time step if u is activated. Here, v is said to be a *neighbor* (or successor) of node u. For node $u \in V$, we use $N(u)$ to denote the set of u's neighbors. The *outdegree* of node u is denoted as $d(u) = |N(u)|$, which could be used simply in estimating the node u's influence on information propagation.

In the IC model [2], we assume that the time during which a network is observed is finite; without loss of generality, the time period is divided into fixed discrete steps $\{1, \ldots, t\}$. Let $S_i \subseteq V$ be the set of nodes that are activated at the time step i. We consider the dynamic process of information diffusion starting from the set of nodes $S_0 \subseteq V$ that are initially activated until the time step t as follows: At each time step i where $1 \leq i \leq t$, every node $u \in S_{i-1}$ activates its inactivated neighbors $v \in V \setminus S_{i-1}$ with a propagation probability $\lambda_{u,v}$. The process ends after the time step t with S_t. A conventional *Influential Maximization* (IM) problem is to find a set S_0 consisting of k nodes to maximize $|S_t|$.

The *Influential Neighbor Selection* (INS) problem [8] is a variant of the IM problem: Given a spreader $s \in V$ and a budget constraint k, we aim to maximize the number of activated nodes in a network after the time step t by selecting s's $\min(k, d(s))$ neighbors only (rather than any subset of k nodes), as the set of nodes $S_0 \subseteq V$ that are initially activated. Compared to the conventional IM problem, the INS problem has three additional requirements: (1) each node only communicates with its immediate neighbors; (2) each node has no knowledge about the entire network topology except for its own connections; and (3) each message size is bounded to $O(\log|V|)$ bits (more intuitively, each message can only contain the node identity and some constant values of the node properties).

However, the initial INS problem in [8] – every edge has the same propagation probability – is too simple to correctly reflect the characteristics of the information diffusion process in real-world situations. Clearly, in the most popular online social network services such as Twitter or Facebook, each user has a different propagation rate for her neighbors on spreading information in a network according to the user's reputation or role such as opinion formers, leaders, or followers [9]. Figure 1 shows an example of the INS problem where each user has a different propagation rate. In this figure, a number in each node indicates the node's propagation rate. Here, for example, the node g's propagation rate is 0.4. Given this graph with the spreader node s, when $k = 1$, we might choose g as an initially activated node to maximize the number of activated nodes in the future; however, when every edge has the same propagation probability, the optimal choice might be either f rather than g.

We used the three important parameters (user propagation weight ω, content interestingness ϕ, and decay factor γ) to establish a more general and practical information propagation model. The details are as follows:

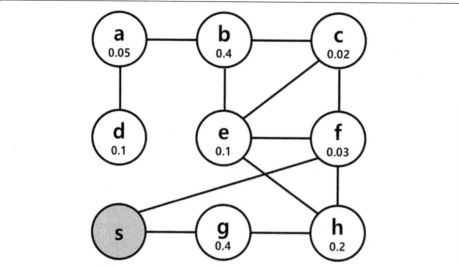

Figure 1 An example of the INS problem. Each node's propagation rate is provided as a number in the node. With the spreader node s, when $k = 1$, we should choose g as an initially activated node to maximize $|S_t|$; however, when every edge has the same propagation probability, the optimal choice might be either f rather than g.

The user propagation weight ω represents each user's average propagation rate to her neighbors. Given a user u, $\omega(u)$ is defined as $\tau(u)/(\rho(u)/d(u))$ where $\tau(u)$ and $\rho(u)$ are the number of u's posts shared by u's neighbors and the number of u's all posts, respectively. For example, if a user u with 1,000 neighbors wrote 10 posts and gets 100 shares, $\omega(u)$ is $100/(10 \cdot 1000) = 0.01$.

The content interestingness $\phi(r)$ of information r represents a measure to determine how much users want to share the information r with their neighbors. Naturally, higher content interestingness ϕ of a piece of information may facilitate higher propagation for the information through a network. Previous studies [19,20] showed that propagation probability λ can be greatly changed with the content of information (i.e., content interestingness ϕ).

The decay factor γ at hop N represents the ratio between the propagation probability at hop N and the propagation probability at hop $N - 1$. In practice, the propagation probability might decay exponentially as the cascades spread away from the information source. Here, one possible explanation would be that the freshness of the information would drop as the time goes on.

With these parameters, given an edge $(u, v) \in E$, a spreader $s \in V$ and a piece of information r, $\lambda(u, v, s, r)$ is finally defined as follows [10]:

$$\lambda(u, v, s, r) = \min \left\{ \omega(u) \cdot \phi(r) \cdot \gamma^{\delta(u,s,r)-1}, 1 \right\} \tag{1}$$

where $\delta(u, s, r)$ is the number of times the information r is to be relayed from s to u.

For example, when $\phi(r) = 0.0136$, $\delta(u, s, r) = 3$, and $\gamma = 0.2$, a user u with $\omega(u) = 1$ would activate his (or her) neighbor v with the probability of about 0.0005 ($\approx 1 \cdot 0.0136 \cdot (0.2)^2$).

In this paper, we also use these parameters and the propagation probability equation. We particularly performed experiments with a real dataset (Twitter users and messages related to the 2010 UK election campaign) instead of using randomly generated synthetic parameters to provide more realistic simulation results than the previous study [10] which was not capable of considering the correlation between the number of neighbors and the propagation rate that might significantly affect the information diffusion process.

Neighbor selection schemes

For the INS problem described in Section 'Influential neighbor selection problem,' we basically use a greedy strategy to select the influential neighbors.

Assume that a spreader $s \in V$ wants to spread a piece of information r through the network $G = (V, E)$ by sharing r with its $\min(k, d(s))$ neighbors at the initial step. Node s first tries to assess the influence of information diffusion for each neighbor $v \in N(s)$, respectively, by collecting the information about v. We note that the neighbors' influence should be estimated based on s's local information only, rather than the whole network. Since online social networks, such as Facebook, typically provide APIs to obtain the neighborhood information about the user, s can automatically collect the information about her own neighbors. After estimating the neighbors' influences, s selects the top $\min(k, d(s))$ nodes with the highest influence values from $N(s)$; that is, for the IC model in Section 'Influential neighbor selection problem', these nodes are selected as the set of initially activated nodes $S_0 \subseteq V$.

For the purpose of influence estimation, we test the following four selection schemes based on the 'number of friends' and 'user propagation weight' each user has:

- Random selection: Pick $\min(k, d(s))$ nodes randomly from $N(s)$. This scheme is very simple and easy to implement – the spreader s does not need any knowledge of the network topology.

- Degree selection: Pick the $\min(k, d(s))$ highest degree nodes from $N(s)$. This scheme requires the degree knowledge of neighbors.

- Propagation-weight selection: Pick the $\min(k, d(s))$ highest user propagation weight nodes from $N(s)$. This scheme requires the user propagation weight knowledge of the nodes. To calculate $\omega(v)$ for s's neighbor $v \in N(s)$, the information about $\tau(v)$, $\rho(v)$ and $d(v)$ is required where $\tau(v)$ and $\rho(v)$ are the number of v's posts shared by v's neighbors and the number of v's all posts, respectively.

- Hybrid selection: Pick the $\min(k, d(s))$ nodes $v \in V$ with the highest *weighted* node degree $\omega d(v)$ which is defined as $\omega d(v) = \omega(v) \cdot d(v)$. At the first glance, this scheme requires the knowledge of both the degree and the user propagation weight of neighbors. In fact, however, this scheme can be simply implemented without the knowledge about node degree since $\omega(v) \cdot d(v)$ is calculated as $\tau(v)/\rho(v)$; $d(v)$ is automatically canceled in the calculation.

The algorithm of those schemes is commonly specified as follows:

1: **procedure** SELECT-k-NEIGHBORS$(G, s, k,$ SCHEME$)$
2:   $S_0 \leftarrow \emptyset$ ▷ initialize the set of initially activated nodes S_0
3:   $N \leftarrow$ Find-Neighbor-Set(s) ▷ find the node s's neighbors
4:   $m \leftarrow \min(k, |N|)$ ▷ calculate $\min(k, d(s))$ to determine the number of selecting neighbors (i.e., $|N| = d(s)$)
5:   **switch** SCHEME **do**
6:     **case** Random
7:       $Q \leftarrow$ Random-Shuffle(N) ▷ construct a queue Q with m elements randomly drawn from N
8:     **case** Degree
9:       $Q \leftarrow$ Construct-Max-Queue(N) ▷ construct a max-priority queue Q where the key is the node degree $d(v)$ for $v \in N$
10:    **case** Propagation
11:      $Q \leftarrow$ Construct-Max-Queue(N) ▷ construct a max-priority queue Q where the key is the node propagation weight $\omega(v)$ for $v \in N$
12:    **case** Hybrid
13:      $Q \leftarrow$ Construct-Max-Queue(N) ▷ construct a max-priority queue Q where the key is the weighted node degree $\omega d(v)$ for $v \in N$
14:    **for** $i \leftarrow 1, m$ **do**
15:      $v \leftarrow$ Extract-Max(Q) ▷ get a node v with the maximum key (i.e., the promising candidate in each greedy scheme except for Random)
16:      Insert(S_0, v) ▷ insert the selected node v into the set of initially activated nodes S_0
17:    **end for**
18: **end procedure**

The proposed algorithm runs in $O(|N| + m \log |N|)$ time – the maximum-priority queue Q can be constructed bottom-up in $O(|N|)$; the priority queue operations (extract-max) can be performed in $O(\log |N|)$ in each of m iterations. In practice, the term of '$m \log |N|$' can be simply ignored since m is less than or equal to a constant k. That is, these schemes can efficiently be performed.

Furthermore, we note that these schemes seem to be the most reasonable and promising for the INS problem since we cannot calculate network centrality metrics, such as closeness and betweenness [21], which require the knowledge of the entire network topology. Here, we do not consider the other metrics (e.g., [22]) to estimate node centrality based on localized information alone since the previous work [8] already showed that these metrics are ineffective for the INS problem compared with node degree.

The communication costs of all these schemes are $O(d(s))$ since the spreader s can obtain $d(v)$, $\omega(v)$, or $\omega d(v)$ through only direct communications with each neighbor $v \in N(s)$.

Experimental results

In this section, we analyze the performance of the selection schemes presented in Section 'Neighbor selection schemes.' Our goal was to find the best neighbor selection scheme to maximize information diffusion in Twitter through the experiments.

For experiments, we used the Twitter dataset [23] related to the 2010 UK general election between the 5th and 12th of May since this dataset reflects typical behavior of information diffusion in a political campaign.

To remove insignificant test cases, we filtered out users who did not either write any posts or had any followers and constructed the Twitter follower graph for those users. In this graph, each node represents a Twitter user and each edge represents a follow relation as a directed edge going from the followed user to the follower; when a user u follows another user v, we added an edge from v to u with a weight of $\omega(v)$ from the point of view of information flow. Unlike previous studies that used network topology alone [8] or synthetic datasets [10], we used real propagation rate $\omega(u)$ for each node u calculated from the Twitter messages. That is, from the collected tweets, we counted the number of tweets produced by u and the number of u's tweets shared (i.e., retweeted) by u's neighbors, respectively, to calculate the user u's propagation rate with those numbers.

The constructed graph consists of 45,179 nodes and 1,938,734 edges representing a sub-network of Twitter. This graph has the following properties: (1) its average degree is 42.91; (2) its number of strongly connected components is 4,559; and (3) the number of weakly connected components is 18 (i.e., this graph is divided into 18 disconnected components).

We used the IC model described in Section 'Influential neighbor selection problem' to evaluate the performance of the schemes presented in Section 'Neighbor selection schemes', with varying the number of initially activated neighbors k. The propagation probability $\lambda(u, v, s, r)$ on an edge $(u, v) \in E$ was defined with the spreader $s \in V$ and a piece of information r described in Section 'Influential neighbor selection problem'.

In each simulation run, we randomly picked a spreader with a piece of information r and then selected its k neighbors according to a selection criterion presented in Section 'Neighbor selection schemes', where the content interestingness $\phi(r)$ was randomly drawn from the normal distribution with the mean of 0.0136 and the standard deviation of 0.0501, according to real data [19]. We also set the decay factor $\gamma = 0.2$ according to the mean of decay factors observed in the same dataset.

For evaluation, we observed the changes in the number of activated nodes during the 200th time steps. With a fixed k, we repeated this 500 times to minimize the bias of the test samples (randomly selected spreaders); we measured the ratio of the average number of activated nodes per test sample to the total number of nodes in the network. To establish a fair comparison, the parameter values were the same for all selection schemes in the ith run. Figure 2 shows how these values are changed over time t with $k = 1, 3, 5$, or 7 under the IC model.

From this figure, we can see that the hybrid selection scheme outperformed the other selection schemes: When $k = 1$, in the hybrid selection scheme, the ratio of the average number of activated nodes to the total number of nodes were over 0.002 (i.e., 2%) while the ratios were below 0.002 in degree and propagation-weight selection schemes. As k increased to 7, the gap between hybrid and other selection schemes was rather reduced but still seemed significant. This shows that we can effectively spread information using the hybrid scheme, even without consideration of the 'number of friends' information since the node degree is not needed to use the hybrid scheme. Interestingly, the degree selection was slightly better than the propagation-weight selection when $k = 3, 5$, or 7, while these schemes produced almost the same results when $k = 1$.

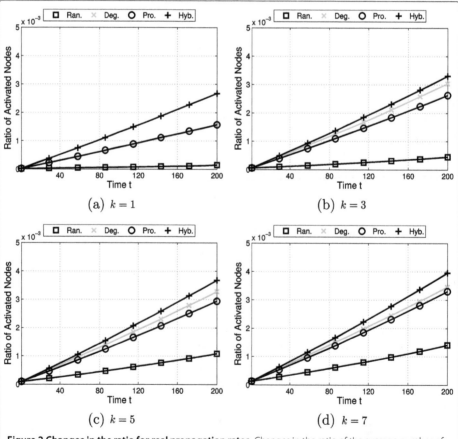

Figure 2 Changes in the ratio for real propagation rates. Changes in the ratio of the average number of activated nodes to the total number of nodes in the network over time t for the *real* propagation rates.

Paired one-tailed t-tests with $\alpha = 0.01$ were used to compare the performance of the neighbor selection schemes in a statistically significant manner. We tested whether the distributions of the numbers of the activated nodes between schemes after the final time step (i.e., the 200th) were statistically different. The test results show that the performance of all the schemes appeared to be significantly different, except for the comparison of `propagation`-weight and `degree` when $k = 1$ ($p = 0.5202$).

To examine the influence of real propagation rate, we performed additional experiments using the above Twitter datasets, except the use of synthetic propagation rate parameters. As for synthetic propagation rates, the distribution of nodes' propagation rates were obtained by randomly shuffling the associations between nodes and propagation rates (i.e., we randomly permute user propagation rates and sequentially assign them to users) while keeping the network topology. Figure 3 shows how the numbers of activated nodes were changed over time t with $k = 1, 3, 5$, or 7 for the cases of using synthetic propagation rates. Since the resulting numbers with *synthetic* propagation rates are quite different from those with *real* propagation rates, we used a different y-axis scale for clarity.

Unlike the cases of using *real* propagation rates, we can see that the `propagation`-weight scheme is significantly better than the `degree` scheme. Moreover, the performance of the `propagation`-weight scheme is almost similar to that of the `hybrid` scheme – this trend appears to be totally different from the cases of using *real* propagation rates but similar to the results presented in Kim et al. [10] which also used

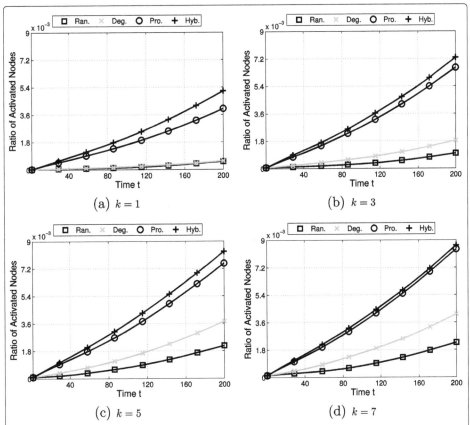

Figure 3 Changes in the ratio for synthetic propagation rates. Changes in the ratio of the average number of activated nodes to the total number of nodes in the network over time *t* for the *synthetic* propagation rates.

synthetic parameters for experiments. This implies that there exists the reciprocal relationship between the node degree and propagation rate in a real-world social network. To show this, we calculate the Spearman correlation coefficient between the degree ranking of nodes and their propagation rate ranking. The computed rank correlation is 0.1936 ($P < 0.0001$), which indicates there exists a weak correlation between them.

We discuss how the performance of the proposed neighbor selection schemes may change with the number of initially activated nodes k. To accelerate the speed of information diffusion, a possible straightforward approach is to increase the number of initially activated neighbors k. Probably, we can imagine that even the naive `random` selection scheme can also be used to efficiently disseminate a piece of information if k increases sufficiently.

To demonstrate the effects of k, we analyzed the ratio of the average number of activated nodes after the 50th, 100th, 150th, and 200th time steps, respectively, with k ranging from 1 to 7. The experimental results are shown in Figure 4.

Unsurprisingly, the effects of k were rather limited for the process of early stage – in all selection strategies, the number of activated nodes were not greatly increased until the 50th step. After around that time, however, the performance of all selection schemes overall was improved as k increased. The ratios of activated nodes, except the `random`

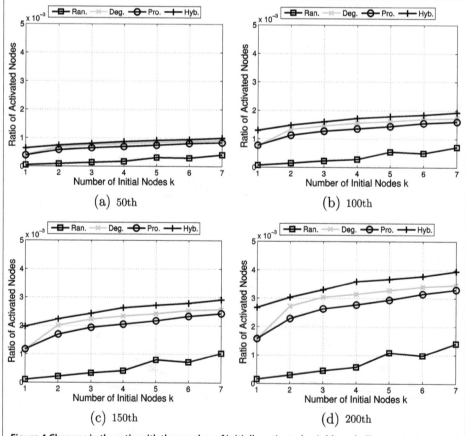

Figure 4 Changes in the ratio with the number of initially activated neighbors k. Changes in the ratio of the average number of activated nodes to the total number of nodes in the network with the number of initially activated neighbors k.

selection scheme, show almost a similar pattern – the curves commonly had gentle slopes. Although the `random` selection scheme was relatively highly affected by k, the average number of activated nodes in the `random` selection scheme was still below 0.002 after the 200th time step even for $k = 7$. We can also see that the performance gaps between the schemes still existed with k. Even when the time step is 50th, the `hybrid`, `degree`, and `propagation`-weight selection schemes were significantly better than the `random` selection scheme. Moreover, after the 200th time steps, the performance gaps between selection schemes are clearly shown. We note that although the number of the initial activated nodes is really important, selection scheme is also important to accelerate the diffusion of information through the network. The performance of the `hybrid` selection scheme, when $k = 4$, was better than the other schemes even when $k = 7$.

We now move to the discussion on the performance of neighbor selection schemes when the content interestingness ϕ changes by fixing $k = 1$. We analyzed the ratio of the average number of activated nodes after the 50th, 100th, 150th, and 200th time steps, respectively, with mean of $\phi(r)$ ranging from 0.01 to 0.05 (and standard deviation 0.0501). The experimental results are shown in Figure 5.

Overall, the performance of all selection schemes except the `random` selection was improved and that of the `hybrid` selection scheme was particularly increased among those schemes with $\phi(r)$ compared with the other schemes. Therefore, the `hybrid`

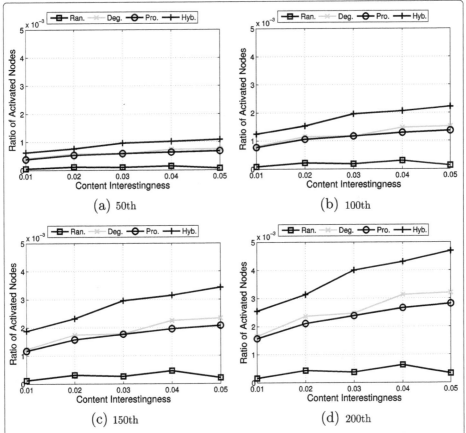

Figure 5 Changes in the ratio with the content interestingness $\phi(r)$. Changes in the ratio of the average number of activated nodes to the total number of nodes in the network with the content interestingness $\phi(r)$.

selection scheme is still recommendable even for contents with a high $\phi(r)$. We note that the performance of the random selection was not significantly affected by $\phi(r)$.

Finally, we discuss the effects of the decay factor γ presented in Section 'Influential neighbor selection problem'. To demonstrate the effects of γ, we analyzed the ratio of the average number of activated nodes after the 50th, 100th, 150th, and 200th time steps, respectively, with $k = 1$ and γ ranging from 0.2 to 1. The experimental results are shown in Figure 6. We use a different y-axis scale on this figure since the numbers of activated nodes were greatly increased with γ.

Although the effects of γ were rather limited for the process of early stage within the 100th time step, after the 150th time step, the performance of all selection schemes except the random selection generally improved and the gaps between the schemes grew with γ.

Thus our suggestion is to use the hybrid selection scheme even with a large decay factor γ. Interestingly, we can also observe two different patterns in Figure 6: one is for the hybrid and degree selection schemes, which tends to increase quickly when $\gamma = 0.6$, and the other one is for the propagation-weight and random selection schemes, which tends to increase relatively slowly.

Conclusions

Given the increasing popularity of online social networks, it is of growing interest to investigate the characteristics of epidemic spreading, in order to accelerate or mitigate it. Kim and Yoneki [8] introduced the optimization problem to find *influential neighbors* for

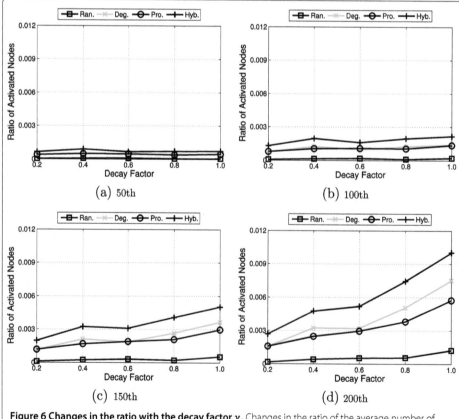

Figure 6 Changes in the ratio with the decay factor γ. Changes in the ratio of the average number of activated nodes to the total number of nodes in the network with the decay factor γ.

maximizing information diffusion. We have extended their work by introducing several parameters (*user propagation weight*, *decay factor*, and *content interestingness*) to provide a more general and practical information diffusion model.

We presented four neighbor selection schemes (`random`, `degree`, `propagation-weight`, and `hybrid` selection) and explored their feasibility. We compared these selection schemes by computing the ratio of the average number of activated nodes to the total number of nodes in the network. We discussed which selection methods are generally recommended under which conditions.

Our experimental results showed that the `hybrid` selection scheme produced the best results of maximizing information diffusion through intensive simulation. Even with a small k, the `hybrid` selection scheme outperformed the other selection schemes with a relatively large k. Since the `hybrid` selection scheme can use the information about the users' posts alone, we can efficiently spread the information without the information about the 'number of friends' each user has. Unlike the results based on synthetic parameters, the `degree` scheme is significantly better than the `propagation-weight` scheme.

As an extension to this work, we are considering a theoretical study to formally generalize and verify our results in order to consider a wide range of application environments (e.g., each of which will have different levels of content interestingness). We will also develop a more extended framework for information diffusion. We may consider not only a spreader with the knowledge about the user's neighbors but also a spreader with a partial knowledge of the network topology (e.g., a subset of users or neighbors of neighbors). For example, we will extend the concept of the `INS` problem by expanding the set of the initially activated nodes with the distance from the information spreader.

Another interesting problem is to consider a new problem in the opposite direction to prevent (or reduce) the spread of information (e.g., rumor) by carefully monitoring the (important) users with a high 'user propagation weight' and/or 'number of friends'.

Competing interests
The authors declare that they have no competing interests.

Authors' contributions
HK led the research project about the influential neighbors selection problem, conducted the experiments and wrote the manuscript; KB discussed the validity of the proposed model and participated in writing the manuscript; EY provided the Twitter dataset used in our experiments and participated in writing the manuscript. All authors read and approved the final manuscript.

Acknowledgements
This work was partly supported by the MSIP (Ministry of Science, ICT & Future Planning), Korea, under the ITRC (Information Technology Research Center) support program (NIPA-2014-H0301-14-1010) supervised by the NIPA (National IT Industry Promotion Agency) and was supported by the National Research Foundation of Korea (NRF) grant funded by the Korea government (No. 2014R1A1A1003707).

Author details
[1]Department of Computer Science and Engineering, Sungkyunkwan University, Suwon, Korea. [2]Department of Electrical and Computer Engineering, University of British Columbia, Vancouver, Canada. [3]Computer Laboratory, University of Cambridge, Cambridge, UK.

References
1. Brown, JJ, Reingen, PH: Social ties and word-of-mouth referral behavior. J. Consum. Res. **14**(3), 350–362 (1987)
2. Goldenberg, J, Libai, B, Muller, E: Talk of the network: a complex systems look at the underlying process of word-of-mouth. Marketing Letters. **12**(3), 211–223 (2001). http://link.springer.com/article/10.1023%2FA%3A1011122126881

3. Metaxas, PT, Mustafaraj, E, Gayo-Avello, D: How (not) to predict elections. In: Proceedings of the 3rd International Conference on Privacy, Security, Risk and Trust (PASSAT) and the 3rd International Conference on Social Computing (SocialCom), (2011)
4. Cao, Q, Sirivianos, M, Yang, X, Pregueiro, T: Aiding the detection of fake accounts in large scale social online services. In: Proceedings of the 9th USENIX Conference on Networked Systems Design and Implementation (NSDI), (2012)
5. Thomas, K, Grier, C, Paxson, V: Adapting social spam infrastructure for political censorship. In: Proceedings of the 5th USENIX Conference on Large-Scale Exploits and Emergent Threats (LEET), (2012)
6. Domingos, P, Richardson, M: Mining the network value of customers. In: Proceedings of the 7th ACM Conference on Knowledge Discovery and Data Mining (KDD), (2001)
7. Kempe, D, Kleinberg, J, Tardos, E: Maximizing the spread of influence through a social network. In: Proceedings of the 9th ACM Conference on Knowledge Discovery and Data Mining (KDD), (2003)
8. Kim, H, Yoneki, E: Influential neighbours selection for information diffusion in online social networks. In: Proceedings of the 21th International Conference on Computer Communication Networks (ICCCN), (2012)
9. Cha, M, Haddadi, H, Benevenuto, F, Gummadi, KP: Measuring user influence in twitter: the million follower fallacy. In: Proceedings of the 4th AAAI Conference on Weblogs and Social Media (ICWSM), (2010)
10. Kim, H: Don't count the number of friends when you are spreading information in social networks. In: Proceedings of the 8th International Conference on Ubiquitous Information Management and Communication (ICUIMC), (2014)
11. Gruhl, D, Guha, R, Liben-Nowell, D, Tomkins, A: Information diffusion through blogspace. In: Proceedings of the 13th International Conference on World Wide Web (WWW), (2004)
12. Leskovec, J, Krause, A, Guestrin, C, Faloutsos, C, VanBriesen, J, Glance, N: Cost-effective outbreak detection in networks. In: Proceedings of the 13th ACM Conference on Knowledge Discovery and Data Mining (KDD), (2007)
13. Chen, W, Wang, Y, Yang, S: Efficient influence maximization in social networks. In: Proceedings of the 15th ACM Conference on Knowledge Discovery and Data Mining (KDD), (2009)
14. Kimura, M, Saito, K: Tractable models for information diffusion in social networks. In: Proceedings of the 10th European Conference on Principle and Practice of Knowledge Discovery in Databases (PKDD), (2006)
15. Chen, W, Wang, C, Wang, Y: Scalable influence maximization for prevalent viral marketing in large-scale social networks. In: Proceedings of the 16th ACM Conference on Knowledge Discovery and Data Mining (KDD), (2010)
16. Wang, Y, Cong, G, Song, G, Xie, K: Community-based greedy algorithm for mining top-k influential nodes in mobile social networks. In: Proceedings of the 16th ACM Conference on Knowledge Discovery and Data Mining (KDD), (2010)
17. Kim, H, Beznosov, K, Yoneki, E: Finding influential neighbors to maximize information diffusion in twitter. In: Proceedings of the Companion Publication of the 23rd International Conference on World Wide Web Companion, pp. 701–706. WWW Companion '14, (2014)
18. Romero, DM, Galuba, W, Asur, S, Huberman, BA: Influence and passivity in social media. In: Proceedings of the 20th International Conference on World Wide Web (WWW), (2011)
19. Zhou, Z, Bandari, R, Kong, J, Qian, H, Roychowdhury, V: Information resonance on Twitter: watching Iran. In: Proceedings of the First ACM Workshop on Social Media Analytics (SOMA), (2010)
20. Hansen, LK, Arvidsson, A, Nielsen, FA, Colleoni, E, Etter, M: Good friends, bad news - affect and virality in Twitter. In: Future Information Technology. Communications in Computer and Information Science, pp. 34–43, (2011). http://link.springer.com/chapter/10.1007%2F978-3-642-22309-9_5
21. Kim, H, Tang, J, Anderson, R, Mascolo, C: Centrality prediction in dynamic human contact networks. Comput. Netw. **56**(3), 983–996 (2012)
22. Wehmuth, K, Ziviani, A: Daccer: Distributed assessment of the closeness centrality ranking in complex networks. Comput. Netw. **57**(13), 2536–2548 (2013)
23. Boutet, A, Kim, H, Yoneki, E: What's in Twitter, I know what parties are popular and who you are supporting now! Soc. Netw. Anal. Min. **3**(4), 1379–1391 (2013)

10

Influence-based community partition for social networks

Zaixin Lu[1*], Yuqing Zhu[2], Wei Li[1,3], Weili Wu[2] and Xiuzhen Cheng[4]

*Correspondence: luz@tsu.edu
[1] NSF Center for Research on Complex Networks, Texas Southern University, 3100 Cleburne Street, Houston, TX 77004, USA
Full list of author information is available at the end of the article

Abstract

Background/Purpose: Community partition is of great importance in sociology, biology and computer science. Due to the exponentially increasing amount of social network applications, a fast and accurate method is necessary for community partition in social networks. In view of this, we investigate the social community partition problem from the perspective of influence propagation, which is one of the most important features of social communication.

Methods: We formulate social community partition as a combinatorial optimization problem that aims at partitioning a social network into K disjoint communities such that the sum of influence propagation within each community is maximized. When $K = 2$ we develop an optimal algorithm that has a provable performance guarantee for a class of influence propagation models. For general K, we prove that it is $\mathcal{NP}$-hard to find a maximum partition for social networks in the well-known linear threshold and independent cascade models. To get near-optimal solutions, we develop a greedy algorithm based on the optimal algorithm. We also develop a heuristic algorithm with a low computational complexity for large social networks.

Results: To evaluate the practical efficiency of our algorithms, we do a simulation study based on real world scenarios. The experiments are conducted on three real-world social networks, and the experimental results show that more accurate partitions according to influence propagation can be obtained using our algorithms rather than using some classic community partition algorithms.

Conclusions: In this study, we investigate the community partition problem in social networks. It is formulated as an optimization problem and investigated both theoretically and practically. The results can be applied to find communities in social networks and are also useful for the influence propagation problem in social networks.

Keywords: Influence propagation; Community partition; $\mathcal{NP}$-hard

Background

Motivation

Social network is an interdisciplinary research area which has attracted a lot of attention in recent years. One important problem in social networks is community partition that provides the insight of the relationships and attributes of the users that a social network comprises. Generally, a social network can be modeled as a graph in which the nodes represent the users and the edges represent the relationships among the users. The objective of community partition is to cluster the users into groups according to their graph topology [1-8]. Another important problem in social networks is influence propagation. It is one of the most important features of social communication and plays a significant role in a variety of affairs such as diffusion of medical innovations and popularization of new technologies. For example, the influence maximization problem, with the objective of finding a small set of users in a social network as seeds to trigger a large influence propagation, has wide applications in viral marketing [9-13].

Due to the nondeterminacy of human behaviors, the influence propagation is mostly studied in probabilistic models such as the Linear Threshold (LT) model and Independent Cascade (IC) model [14-16], that is, the behaviors and decisions of users are uncertain and depend on the behaviors of others. For example, a user's adoption of a new product may have impacts on their friends, whose adoptions may further influence others. There-fore, probabilistic models are more suitable than deterministic models for simulating an influence propagation in social networks. Unfortunately, one important issue however is that the expected influence propagation through the entire social network is hard to esti-mate for most probabilistic models such as LT and IC [15,16]. Therefore, many works (e.g., [15-17]) construct a local area for each user and use the local influence propagation instead of the global one. But in some large social networks, there may be millions of users so that it is impossible to construct local areas for all the users.

There are also many works studying community-based algorithms for influence maxi-mization, assuming that influence propagates rarely across different communities. How-ever, based on our observation, there are few works done on community partition aiming specially at influence propagation in social networks. The performance of community-based algorithms cannot be guaranteed unless there exists an accurate influence-based community partition. In this paper, we investigate the problem inherent in the question that how to partition a social network into disjoint communities in terms of influence propagation. We believe this study is useful for the influence maximization problem and possibly activates further research and potential applications of community in social networks.

Related work

Community partition is of great importance not only for social networks but also for areas such as computer networks and biology networks. There are lots of works done on community partition in general networks (e.g., [6,8,18,19]), and much effort has been devoted to formalizing the intuition that a community is a set of nodes having more con-nections with each other while fewer connections with the remainder of the network. The first investigation for community partition were done by Weiss et al. [20]. For sub-sequent approaches, there are mainly four categories: hierarchy-based methods [1,2], spectrum-based methods [3,4], density-based methods [5] and modularity-based meth-ods [6-8,21-29]. Particularly, Newman's notion of modularity [6,8], which considers the internal connectivity with reference to a randomized model, has been a very popular mea-sure for community partition in general networks. In spite of the excellent performance on many real-world networks, this family of approaches usually has 'resolution limit' problems, i.e., modularity-based methods favor larger communities and fail to discover communities of small sizes [25,30]. Therefore some works investigate new methods for detecting communities, such as the self-reference methods and the comparative methods [18]. In addition, in [19], Hu et al. proposed an algorithm from the node's point of view to incorporate nodes into a community with the largest attractive force. In [31], Zhang et al. proposed an algorithm from the aspect of combinatorial optimization to partition nodes into disjoint parts. There are also many works which view communities from different perspectives. To learn more about the large body of works in community partition, please refer to [29,32-37].

Besides community partition, influence propagation is also an important issue in social networks. Domingos and Richardson in [13] and [12] first proposed general descriptive models for influence propagation in social networks. In [14], Kempe et al. formulated the influence propagation as an optimization problem, namely, influence maximization. They proved that the greedy algorithm has a provable performance guarantee for the LT and IC models. However, how to evaluate the expected influence propagation for selecting the nodes with the maximum marginal gain was left as an open problem, and the greedy algorithm in [14] was implemented by Monte Carlo (MC) simulation. After that many researchers started to investigate how to compute the influence propagation efficiently and a large volume of methods (e.g., [15,16,38]) have been proposed for the LT and IC models. Meanwhile, there are also many works investigating new influence propagation models (e.g., [39,40]) to approach the real-world scenarios.

Due to the nature of the communities, applying the research of community partition into influence propagation is promising. In [17], Wang et al. proposed a community-based greedy algorithm for mining the most influential nodes. In [41], Li et al. further proposed an algorithm for influence maximization in online social networks. They assume that each node's influence propagation is limited to the community it resides and thus they evaluate the influence propagation within each community to improve the computational efficiency. There are also many works for influence propagation or other social network applications taking the advantage of community structures (please see e.g., [42-45] for recent works).

Our contribution

Although there are a lot of works done on general community partition, based on our observation, there are few works done on community partition for influence propagation. In view of this, we investigate how to partition a social network into communities according to influence propagation. Our main contributions are as follows:

1. We formally define the influence-based community partition problem as a combinatorial optimization problem with the objective of partitioning a social network into K disjoint communities such that the sum of influence propagation within each community is maximized. We call the problem Maximum K-Community Partition (MKCP). The motivation is to keep as much influence propagation as possible after the partition and reduce the estimation errors caused using local influence propagation increased of the global one.

2. When $K = 2$, i.e., partition a social network into two disjoint parts, we develop an optimal algorithm for a class of influence propagation models. For general K, we prove there exists no polynomial time algorithm unless $\mathcal{P} = \mathcal{NP}$ for MKCP in the well-known LT and IC models, and a greedy algorithm based on the two partition algorithm is exhibited. We also develop a fast heuristic algorithm with a low computational complexity in case that the social network is very large.

3. We conduct simulation on real-world social networks to demonstrate the practical efficiency of the proposed algorithms. The influence propagation is based on the well-known LT and IC models, and the experimental results show that significantly better partitions can be obtained using our algorithms rather than using some community partition methods that are not specialized for influence propagation.

Paper organization

The rest of this paper is organized as follows. In 'Problem description' section, we give the background information, including the notation and problem definition. In 'Methods' section, we present our algorithms as well as the theoretical analysis of both the proposed algorithms and the $MKCP$ problem. In 'Results and discussion' section, we show the simulation results on some real-world social networks. In 'Conclusions' section, we conclude the paper.

Problem description

In this study, we formulate a social network as a simple directed graph without self-loops, where nodes represent users and edges represent relationships among the users. We first introduce some notations and then present the $MKCP$ problem based on the notations.

1. For a social network G, we denote by $V = \{1, 2, \ldots, n\}$ the set of nodes and $E = \{(i, j)\}$ the set of directed edges. A directed edge (i, j) denotes that there exists a chance of influence propagation between nodes i and j where i is the sender and j is the receiver. For each node $i \in V$, we denote by $p(i)$ $(0 \leq p(i) \leq 1)$ the probability that node i would produce an influence propagation or would share an idea with others through the social network. For example, in the Twitter social network, $p(i)$ should be related to the number of tweets i posts periodically. For each edge $(i, j) \in E$, we denote by $w(i, j)$ the influential degree from node i to node j, which depends on their closeness and the probability $p(i)$ for node i.

2. Let K denote the number of communities. We denote by $c_i \in \{1, 2, \ldots, K\}$ the community identifier of node i. We denote by $C_k = \{i | c_i = k\}$ the set of nodes with community identifier k $(1 \leq k \leq K)$. For each pair of nodes i and j in the same set C_k, we denote by $p_{C_k}(i, j)$ $(0 \leq p_{C_k}(i, j) \leq 1)$ the probability that node j receives the influence from node i through propagation within community C_k.

3. For a community C_k and a node $i \in C_k$, we denote by $\sigma_{C_k}(i)$ the influence propagation of node i within community C_k, i.e., $\sigma_{C_k}(i) = \sum_{j \in (C_k \setminus i)} p_{C_k}(i, j)$. For any nonempty subset $D \subseteq C_k$, we denote by $\sigma_{C_k}(D)$, the sum of influence propagation within community C_k for every node in D, i.e., $\sigma_{C_k}(D) = \sum_{i \in D} \sigma_{C_k}(i)$. For simplicity, we let $\sigma(X)$ denote $\sigma_X(X)$ for community X and in the rest of this paper we call $\sigma(\cdot)$ the influence propagation function for community '·'.

The probability that node j receives the influence from node i not only depends on the influential degree $w(i, j)$ but also depends on the network topology and the influence propagation model. For example, in the LT model, the sum of influence node j receives can be formulated as $\sum_{i \in N_{active}(j)} w(i, j)$ where $N_{active}(j)$ denotes the set of active nodes around j and $\sum_{i \in N_{active}(j)} w(i, j) \leq 1$. The influence propagation runs in discrete steps. At any time t, a node $j \in V$ becomes active when $\sum_{i \in N_{active}(j)} w(i, j) \geq \lambda(j)$ where $\lambda(j)$ is a threshold selected uniformly at random between 0 and 1. Therefore in the LT model, for any community C_k, $p_{C_k}(i,j)$ is the probability that j is eventually active when i is initially active. As an example shown in Figure 1, the numbers on the edges and nodes denote the influential degrees and random thresholds. Assume that all the nodes are in the same community and node u is a seed, then all the white nodes (including node y) can be activated by node u, because they can either be activated by u or by paths from u. All the black nodes (p, q and w) cannot be activated by node u, even though q is a direct outgoing neighbor of u. Therefore in the LT model, $p_{C_k}(i,j)$ not only depends on the influential degree $w(i,j)$. We next present the definitions of K-valid disjoint partition (K-VDP) and the MKCP problem.

Definition 1. (K-VDP). Given a graph $G(V,E)$ as a social network, a K-*valid disjoint partition* $\mathcal{P}$ is a collection of K sets $\{C_1, C_2, \ldots, C_K\}$ satisfying: (1) $\bigcup_{k=1}^{K}(C_k) = V$ and (2) $\forall i \neq j, C_i \cap C_j = \emptyset$.

Let K be an integer no less than 2. According to Definition 1, a K-VDP is a partition of V into K nonempty subsets such that each node is in exact one subset. We denote the influence propagation function for a K-VDP $\{C_1, C_2, \ldots, C_K\}$ by $f(C_1, C_2, \ldots, C_K) = \sum_{k=1}^{K} \sigma(C_k)$ and we want to maximize $f(C_1, C_2, \ldots, C_K)$. The formal definition of MKCP is given in Definition 2.

Definition 2. (MKCP). Given a graph G as a social network, an influence propagation model $\mathcal{I}$ (such as IC or LT) and an integer $K \geq 2$, Maximum K-Community Partition (MKCP) is the problem of finding a partition $\mathcal{P} = \{C_1, C_2, \ldots, C_K\}$ of K subsets of nodes,

$$\text{maximize} \quad f(C_1, C_2, \ldots, C_K) = \sum_{k=1}^{K} \sigma(C_k) \tag{1}$$

$$\text{subject to} \quad \{C_1, C_2, \ldots, C_K\} \text{ is a } K\text{-VDP for } G.$$

Consider the node set V as a single community, we have

$$f(\{V\}) = \sum_{i \in V} \sum_{j \in V \setminus \{i\}} p_V(i,j).$$

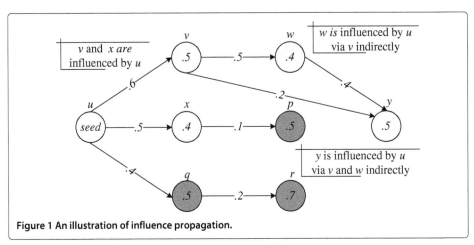

Figure 1 An illustration of influence propagation.

It is clear that when partitioning the social network into two or more communities, some pairs (i,j) will be separated and thus both $p_V(i,j)$ and $p_V(j,i)$ have to be removed in the sum of influence propagation. In addition, even though nodes i and j are partitioned into the same community X, $p_X(i,j)$ may be less than $p_V(i,j)$, and $p_X(j,i)$ may be less than $p_V(j,i)$ because X is a subset of V. Therefore, the influential propagation between any pair of nodes i and j is different for different community partitions no matter they are in the same community or not.

Methods

Optimal algorithm for M2CP

In this subsection, we present an optimal algorithm to M2CP for a class of influence propagation models. The algorithm is based on the Min Cut algorithm proposed in [46]. Before giving the formal algorithm and its theoretical analysis, we briefly discuss the difference between the Min Cut problem and the M2CP problem. A min cut of a graph G is a set of edges with the least number of elements (un-weighted case) or the least sum of weights (weighted case) that partitions G into two parts. On this basis, for M2CP, one may want to find a cut to minimize the influence propagation leaking out between the two parts. However, maximizing the sum of influence propagation within each community is not equivalent to minimizing the influence propagation crossing different communities. Figure 2 shows an example. There are eight nodes which are partitioned into two communities $C_1 = \{1,2,3,4\}$ and $C_2 = \{5,6,7,8\}$. Assume the gray-directed arcs are the possible influence propagation. Consider nodes 7, 5, and 1, respectively. It is clear that the influence received by nodes 7 and 5 will decrease after the partition because node 3 cannot influence node 7 and it cannot influence node 5 via node 7 indirectly. The influence received by node 1 also decreases because of the following: (1) node 5 cannot influence node 1, (2) node 7 cannot influence node 1 indirectly, and (3) node 3 cannot influence node 1 through the path $(3 \to 7 \to 5 \to 1)$. The first two kinds of influence propagation are between nodes in different communities, but the last one is between nodes in the same community. Therefore, maximizing the sum of influence propagation within each community is not just minimizing the influence propagation crossing different communities.

Given a social network as well as an influence propagation model, our algorithm iteratively finds $n-1$ partitions and selects the one with the maximum value as the final output.

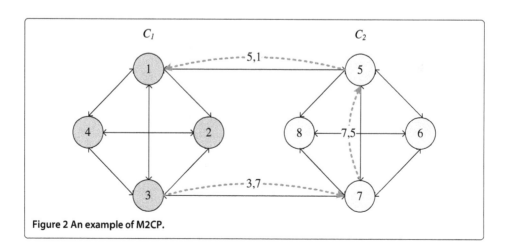

Figure 2 An example of M2CP.

In the beginning, we consider each node i as a single set and let $V = \{S_1, S_2, \ldots, S_n\}$ as the collection of all the sets where $S_i = \{i\}$. Select an arbitrary set $S_i \in V$ and let $A = \{S_i\}$. We then add the remainder sets one by one iteratively into A. Each time a set S_j with the maximum value of $\varsigma(A, S_j)$ is added, where $\varsigma(A, S_j) = \sigma(A \cup S_j) - \sigma(S_j)$. When there are only one set S_l left, $\{v(A), v(V \backslash A)\}$ are considered as the first partition where $v(X)$ is defined as the set of nodes in X. In addition, the last two sets not in A, say S_r and S_l, are merged as a single set $(S_r \cup S_l)$ for computing the next partition. The algorithm terminates when there are only one set in V. The pseudo-code is given in Algorithm 1.

Algorithm 1 Algorithm for M2CP (AM2CP)

Input: Given a graph G as a social network and an influence propagation model $\mathcal{I}$.

Output: a 2-VDP for G.

1: construct a collection V of n sets: $S_1, S_2, \ldots, S_n$, each of which contains a single node in graph G;

2: **while** $|V| > 1$ **do**

3:     let $A = \{\{i\}\}$ where $\{i\}$ is an arbitrary set in V;

4:     **while** $|V| - |A| > 1$ **do**

5:         let $S_j \leftarrow \text{argmax}_{S_z \in V \backslash A}(\varsigma(A, S_z))$;

6:         add S_j into A;

7:     **end while**

8:     let $\mathcal{P} \leftarrow (v(A), v(V \backslash A))$.

9:     let $\mathcal{P}_{\max}$ store the partition with the maximum objective value $f(v(A), v(V \backslash A))$;

10:    let $S_{r,l}$ to be the union of last two sets S_r and S_l in $(V \backslash A)$;

11:    delete S_r and S_l from V and add $S_{r,l}$ into V;

12: **end while**

13: return $\mathcal{P}_{\max}$;

The computational complexity of AM2CP (Algorithm 1) depends on the time complexity of computing $\sigma(\cdot)$, which further depends on the time complexity of computing the influence propagation $p_{C_k}(i, j)$ for community C_k and all the pairs (i, j) of nodes in it. In [15], Chen et al. prove that it is #$\mathcal{P}$-hard to compute the exact influence propagation in LT and IC models. Therefore, in this work, $p_{C_k}(i, j)$ is estimated by MC simulation. Assume we have a simulator to estimate $\sigma(\cdot)$ in τ time. Following Algorithm 1, we run steps (3 to 11) $n - 1$ times for the $n - 1$ partitions. For each partition, we add all the sets greedily into A that calls the function $\sigma(\cdot)$ $\mathcal{O}(n^2)$ times. Therefore, the overall running time of AM2CP is $\mathcal{O}(n^3 \tau)$.

We next show that AM2CP is an optimal solution for M2CP when the community influence propagation function $\sigma(\cdot)$ is super-modular. Let S be a finite set. A function $f : 2^S \rightarrow R$ is super-modular if for any $B \subset A \subset S$ and $u \notin A$,

$$\sigma(A \cup \{u\}) - \sigma(A) \geq \sigma(B \cup \{u\}) - \sigma(B), \tag{2}$$

or equivalently for any $B, A \subset S$,

$$\sigma(A \cup B) + \sigma(A \cap B) \geq \sigma(A) + \sigma(B). \tag{3}$$

Theorem 1. *If the influence propagation function $\sigma(\cdot)$ is super-modular, AM2CP is an optimal solution for M2CP.*

Proof. Based on AM2CP, each time we find a partition $\mathcal{P} = (v(\mathcal{A}), v(\mathcal{V} \backslash \mathcal{A}))$ that separates the last two sets S_r and S_l, and we merge the two sets for the next round. To show Theorem 1, it is sufficient to show that $\mathcal{P}$ has the maximum objective function value $\sigma(v(\mathcal{A})) + \sigma(v(\mathcal{V} \backslash \mathcal{A}))$ among all the partitions separating S_r and S_l, where $v(\mathcal{X})$ is the set of nodes in $\mathcal{X}$. We prove it by induction.

Without loss of generality, we assume the sets added into $\mathcal{A}$ are in the order: $S_{i_1}, S_{i_2}, \ldots, S_{i_{|\mathcal{V}|}}$ for round i and let $\mathcal{A}_{i_j}$ denote the collection of the first j sets added into $\mathcal{A}$ in round i. Then for any $S \subseteq \mathcal{A}_{i_1}$ and S_{i_j} with $j > 2$, we have $\sigma(v(\mathcal{A}_{i_2})) + \sigma(S_{i_j}) \geq \sigma(v(\mathcal{A}_{i_2} \backslash S)) + \sigma(S_{i_j} \cup v(S))$ because $v(S)$ is either S_{i_1} or $\emptyset$. Assume $\sigma(v(\mathcal{A}_{i_{k'}})) + \sigma(S_{i_j}) \geq \sigma(v(\mathcal{A}_{i_{k'}} \backslash S)) + \sigma(S_{i_j} \cup v(S))$ for any $2 \leq k' < k$, $S \subseteq \mathcal{A}_{i_{k'-1}}$ and S_{i_j} with $j > k'$. We next show that $\sigma(v(\mathcal{A}_{i_k})) + \sigma(S_{i_j}) \geq \sigma(v(\mathcal{A}_{i_k} \backslash S)) + \sigma(S_{i_j} \cup v(S))$ for any $S \subseteq \mathcal{A}_{i_{k-1}}$ and S_{i_j} with $j > k$.

Consider the following two cases: (1) $S_{i_{k-1}} \in S$ and (2) $S_{i_{k-1}} \notin S$. When $S_{i_{k-1}} \notin S$, we have $\sigma(v(\mathcal{A}_{i_{k-2}})) + \sigma(S_{i_j}) \geq \sigma(v(\mathcal{A}_{i_{k-2}} \backslash S)) + \sigma(S_{i_j} \cup v(S))$ due to the assumption. Therefore, $\sigma(v(\mathcal{A}_{i_k})) + \sigma(S_{i_j}) \geq \sigma(v(\mathcal{A}_{i_k} \backslash S)) + \sigma(S_{i_j} \cup v(S))$ because (1) $v(\mathcal{A}_{i_k}) = v(\mathcal{A}_{i_k} \backslash S) \cup v(\mathcal{A}_{i_{k-2}})$, (2) $v(\mathcal{A}_{i_{k-2}} \backslash S) = v(\mathcal{A}_{i_k} \backslash S) \cap v(\mathcal{A}_{i_{k-2}})$ and (3) $\sigma(\cdot)$ is super-modular.

When $S_{i_{k-1}} \in S$, we have $\sigma(v(\mathcal{A}_{i_{k-1}})) + \sigma(S_{i_k}) \geq \sigma(v(S)) + \sigma(S_{i_k} \cup v(\mathcal{A}_{i_{k-1}} \backslash S))$ due to the assumption in which $\sigma(v(S)) = \sigma(v(\mathcal{A}_{i_{k-1}}) \backslash v(\mathcal{A}_{i_{k-1}} \backslash S))$. Since $\sigma(\cdot)$ is super-modular, we have $\sigma(v(\mathcal{A}_{i_{k-1}}) \cup S_{i_j}) - \sigma(v(\mathcal{A}_{i_{k-1}})) \geq \sigma(v(S) \cup S_{i_j}) - \sigma(v(S))$. In sum, we have $\sigma(v(\mathcal{A}_{i_k} \backslash S)) + \sigma(S_{i_j} \cup v(S)) \leq \sigma(v(\mathcal{A}_{i_{k-1}}) \cup S_{i_j}) + \sigma(S_{i_k})$. In addition we have $\sigma(v(\mathcal{A}_{i_{k-1}}) \cup S_{i_j}) + \sigma(S_{i_k}) \leq \sigma(v(\mathcal{A}_{i_k})) + \sigma(S_{i_j})$ because in AM2CP, $S_{i_k} = \text{argmax}_{S_z \in \mathcal{V} \backslash \mathcal{A}_{i_{k-1}}}(\sigma(\mathcal{A}_{i_{k-1}} \cup S_z) - \sigma(S_z))$. Therefore in both cases, we have $\sigma(v(\mathcal{A}_{i_k})) + \sigma(S_{i_j}) \geq \sigma(v(\mathcal{A}_{i_k} \backslash S)) + \sigma(S_{i_j} \cup v(S))$. By induction, we have $\sigma(v(\mathcal{A}_{i_{|\mathcal{V}|-1}})) + \sigma(S_{i_{|\mathcal{V}|}}) > \sigma(v(\mathcal{A}_{i_{|\mathcal{V}|-1}} \backslash S)) + \sigma(S_{i_{|\mathcal{V}|}} \cup v(S))$ for any $S \subseteq \mathcal{A}_{i_{|\mathcal{V}|-2}}$. Therefore, the partition $\mathcal{P}$ of each round i in AM2CP has the maximum objective function value among all the partitions separating the last two sets. Each time we compare $\mathcal{P}$ with $\mathcal{P}_{\max}$ and merge the last two sets. Therefore $\mathcal{P}_{\max}$ is an optimal partition for the M2CP problem when the influence propagation function $\sigma(\cdot)$ is super-modular. $\square$

Since AM2CP is an optimal solution if $\sigma(\cdot)$ is super-modular, we are interested in the influence propagation models in which the influence propagation function $\sigma(\cdot)$ is super-modular. Note that $\sigma(\cdot)$, in this paper, is different from the influence function defined in [14]. In this paper $\sigma(X)$ is the sum of influence propagation within X for every node in X, i.e., $\sigma(X) = \sum_{i \in X} \sigma_X(i)$. In [14] $\sigma(X)$ is the influence propagation of seed set X in the entire social network. We show the following lemma.

Lemma 1. *When the influence propagation model is LT, for any two communities: $B \subset A$, and a node $u \notin A$, we have $\sigma(A \cup \{u\}) - \sigma(A) \geq \sigma(B \cup \{u\}) - \sigma(B)$.*

Proof. The influence propagation in the LT model, as shown in [14], can be simulated as a random process by flipping coins. Assume we have flipped all the coins in advance, then an edge is declared to be 'live' if the coin flip indicated an influence will be propagated successfully and it is declared blocked otherwise. A node j is influenced by a seed i if and only if there is a path of live edges from i to j. According to this principle, any simple path from i to j has a certain probability to be a live path. In [15], Chen et al. prove that for any node i, the influence propagation of i is equal to $\sum_{sp \in SP(i)} w(sp)$ where $SP(i)$ is the set of all the simple paths starting from i and $w(sp)$ is the probability that sp is a live path. Therefore, for a community X and a node $i \in X$, $\sigma_X(i) = \sum_{sp \in SP_X(i)} w(sp)$ where $SP_X(i)$ is the set of simple paths starting from i in community X, and $\sigma(X) = \sum_{i \in X} \sigma_X(i)$ is the sum of probabilities for all the simple paths in X. Since for any two communities, $B \subset A$, the set of simple paths in B is a subset of the set of simple paths in A, we have $\sigma(A) \geq \sigma(B)$. Similarly, we have $\sigma(A \cup \{u\}) - \sigma(A) \geq \sigma(B \cup \{u\}) - \sigma(B)$ because $\sigma(A \cup \{u\}) - \sigma(A)$ is the sum of probabilities of simple paths visit u exactly once in community $(A \cup \{u\})$, and $\sigma(B \cup \{u\}) - \sigma(B)$ is the sum of probabilities of simple paths visit u exactly once in community $(B \cup \{u\})$ which is a subset of the former. Therefore, the influence propagation function $\sigma(\cdot)$ in the LT model is super-modular.   □

Theorem 2. *AM2CP is an optimal solution for M2CP in the LT model.*

Proof. The theorem follows directly from Theorem 1 and Lemma 1.   □

By Lemma 1, we show that $\sigma(\cdot)$ is super-modular in the LT model. We next show that $\sigma(\cdot)$ in the IC model, however, is not super-modular. The description of IC model can be found in detail in [14]. Here we just give a counterexample. As an example shown in Figure 3, the weights are as follows: $w(1, 2) = w(1, 3) = w(1, 4) = 1$ and $w(2, 5) = w(3, 5) = w(4, 5) = 0.5$. According to the edges in Figure 3, nodes 2, 3, and 4 cannot influence each other and nodes 2, 3, 4, and 5 cannot influence node 1. Let community $A = \{1, 2, 3, 5\}$ and community $B = \{1, 2, 5\}$. So B is a subset of A. By direct computing, we have $\sigma(A \cup \{4\}) - \sigma(A) = 5.375 - 3.75 = 1.625$ and $\sigma(B \cup \{4\}) - \sigma(B) = 3.75 - 2 = 1.75$. Therefore, $\sigma(A \cup \{4\}) - \sigma(A) < \sigma(B \cup \{4\}) - \sigma(B)$ which implies $\sigma(\cdot)$ is not super-modular in the IC model.

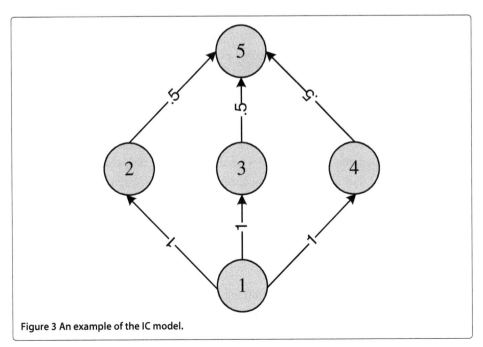

Figure 3 An example of the IC model.

Hardness

In this subsection, we study the hardness of MKCP. We show that the MKCP problem, with arbitrary K, is $\mathcal{NP}$-hard in the LT or IC model.

Theorem 3. *The MKCP problem is $\mathcal{NP}$-hard in the LT model for general K.*

Proof. To prove Theorem 3, we do a polynomial time reduction from the Minimum K-Cut problem. The input of Minimum K-Cut is a simple graph $G(V, E)$ without directions and an integer M. The objective is to find a set of at most M edges which when deleted, separate the graph into exactly K nonempty components. It is well known that the Minimum K-Cut problem is $\mathcal{NP}$-hard for general K.

Given a graph $G(V, E)$ for the Minimum K-Cut problem, we construct a social network $G'(V', E')$ as follows: (1) For each node $i \in V$, create a node i' in V'. (2) For each edge $(i, j) \in E$, create two edges (i', j') and (j', i') in E'. (3) Let Δ denote the maximum degree in G and n denote the number of nodes in G. Assign weight $w(i', j') = \frac{1}{(n\Delta)^2}$ for all the edges $(i', j') \in E'$.

It is clear that the reduction can be done in polynomial time. We next show that there is a K-Cut with M edges if and only if there is a K-VDP $\mathcal{P}$ with $f(\mathcal{P}) \geq \frac{2(|E|-M)}{(n\Delta)^2}$. Assume there is a K-Cut with M edges, then graph G can be partitioned into K communities with $|E| - M$ edges within the K communities. Consider the same partition in G'. The one-hop influence propagation is $\frac{2(|E|-M)}{(n\Delta)^2}$. Therefore, we have a K-VDP $\mathcal{P}$ with $f(\mathcal{P}) > \frac{2(|E|-M)}{(n\Delta)^2}$ for G'. Conversely, assume there is a K-VDP $\mathcal{P}$ for G' with $f(\mathcal{P}) \geq \frac{2(|E|-M)}{(n\Delta)^2}$. It has been shown in [16] that for any nodes $\forall i, j, l \in V$, the probability of influence propagation from i to j via node l is equal to $w(i, l)w(l, j)$ in the LT model. Therefore, a single two-hop influence propagation is $\frac{1}{(n\Delta)^4}$. The number of two-hop simple paths for any node $i' \in V'$ is no more than Δ^2. Therefore, the sum of two-hop influence propagation for every node in V' is no more than $\frac{n\Delta^2}{(n\Delta)^4} = \frac{1}{n^3\Delta^2}$. By direct computing, we have the sum of $(r + 1)$-hop influence propagation is less than the sum of r-hop influence propagation for any node i. Since the length of simple paths is no more than n, we have the sum of multi-hop influence propagation for every node in V' is less than $\frac{1}{(n\Delta)^2}$. This implies that $f(\mathcal{P}) \geq \frac{2(|E|-M)}{(n\Delta)^2}$ if and only if the one-hop influence propagation is no less than $\frac{2(|E|-M)}{(n\Delta)^2}$. Therefore, the same partition in G is a K-Cut with at most M edges. In sum, we prove Theorem 3. $\square$

Theorem 4. *The MKCP problem is $\mathcal{NP}$-hard in the IC model for general K.*

Proof. To prove Theorem 4, we can do the same reduction as the one in the proof of Theorem 3, i.e., assign uniform weight $\frac{1}{(n\Delta)^2}$ on all the edges. It can be shown by induction that the sum of $(r + 1)$-hop influence propagation a node i received is less than the sum of r-hop influence propagation it received for any node $i \in V'$ in the IC model. Therefore, by a similar argument, we have the sum of multi-hop influence propagation received for every node $i \in V'$ is less than the edge weight. Therefore, there exists a K-Cut with M edges if and only if there is a K-VDP $\mathcal{P}$ with $f(\mathcal{P}) \geq \frac{2(|E|-M)}{(n\Delta)^2}$. $\square$

The proofs of Theorems 3 and 4 are nothing but assign specific weights to make the multi-hop influence propagation negligible. It is intuitive that the general MKCP problem is even harder when multi-hop influence propagation is not negligible.

Heuristic algorithm for MKCP

In this subsection, we present two heuristic algorithms for MKCP. As mentioned in 'Related work' section in the literature, there are mainly four categories of methods for community partition: hierarchy-based methods, spectrum-based methods, density-based methods, and modularity-based methods. In our point of view, spectrum-based methods, density-based methods, and modularity-based methods are not suitable for MKCP. In spectrum-based methods, communities are partitioned by studying the adjacency matrix which cannot reflect the information of influence propagation. In density-based methods, communities are defined as areas of higher density than the remainder of the data set. Therefore, this category of methods requires the location knowledge of nodes which cannot be formulated in our MKCP problem. In modularity-based methods, the objective of community partition is only to maximize the global modularity score. Therefore, all the three categories of methods cannot be applied for MKCP and we focus on hierarchy-based methods.

Generally speaking, hierarchical community partition is a method to build a hierarchy of communities. There are two strategies for hierarchical partition. One is *split* and the other is *merge*. Split is a top down approach, i.e., all the nodes start within one community, and splits are performed on one of the communities recursively. Conversely, merge is a bottom up approach, i.e., each node starts in a distinct community, and pairs of communities are merged recursively as a new community. For typical hierarchical community partition problems, $n-1$ splits (or respectively merges) have to be done to build a hierarchy where n is the number of nodes. But for the MKCP problem, we need only $K-1$ splits or $n-K$ merges respectively to obtain a K-VDP. We will determine the splits and merges in a greedy manner. The Split algorithm runs by calling AM2CP recursively, and each time it partitions a community X into two communities X_1 and X_2 with the minimum value of $\sigma(X) - (\sigma(X_1) + \sigma(X_2))$. The pseudo-code is given in Algorithm 2. The Merge algorithm runs by randomly selecting a community X each time and finding another community Y to maximize the value of $\sigma(X \cup Y) - (\sigma(X) + \sigma(Y))$. The pseudo-code is given in Algorithm 3.

Algorithm 2 Split algorithm for MKCP (SAMKCP)

Input: Given a graph G as a social network, an influence propagation model $\mathcal{I}$ and an integer K.

Output: a K-VDP for G.

1: let $\mathcal{P} \leftarrow \{V\}$ (P holds the current communities);

2: **while** $|\mathcal{P}| < K$ **do**

3:    let C_{z_1} and $C_{z_2} \leftarrow \mathrm{argmin}_{C_z \in \mathcal{P}}(\sigma(C_z) - (\sigma(C_{z_1}) + \sigma(C_{z_2})))$ subject to $C_{z_1} \cap C_{z_2} = \emptyset$ and $C_{z_1} \cup C_{z_2} = C_z$;

4:    put C_{z_1} and C_{z_2} into $\mathcal{P}$ and delete C_z from $\mathcal{P}$;

5: **end while**

6: return $\mathcal{P}$;

In the general case, the running time of a split with an exhaustive search requires exponential time. However, when $\sigma(\cdot)$ is super-modular, we can apply AM2CP to determine C_{z_1} and C_{z_2} for each C_z which requires only $\mathcal{O}(|C_z|^3 \tau)$ time. Now let us consider the computational complexity of SAMKCP (Algorithm 2). To avoid duplicate computations, we can keep the optimal partition for each community in $\mathcal{P}$ and apply AM2CP on both C_{z_1} and C_{z_2} at step 4 to obtain their optimal partitions. Then the overall running time of SAMKCP is $\mathcal{O}(Kn^3\tau)$ when $\sigma(\cdot)$ is super-modular.

Algorithm 3 Merge algorithm for MKCP (MAMKCP)

Input: Given a graph G as a social network, an influence propagation model $\mathcal{I}$ and an
    integer K.

Output: a K-VDP for G.

  1: let $\mathcal{P} \leftarrow \{C_1, C_2, \ldots, C_n\}$ where each $C_i = \{i\}$ contains a single node in G;

  2: **while** $|\mathcal{P}| > K$ **do**

  3:     select a community $C_i \in \mathcal{P}$ randomly;

  4:     let $C_j \leftarrow \text{argmax}_{C_j \in \mathcal{P} \setminus C_i}(\sigma(C_i \cup C_j) - \sigma(C_i) - \sigma(C_j))$;

  5:     let $C_{i,j} \leftarrow C_i \cup C_j$;

  6:     put $C_{i,j}$ into $\mathcal{P}$ and delete C_i and C_j from $\mathcal{P}$;

  7: **end while**

  8: return $\mathcal{P}$;

In step 4 of MAMKCP (Algorithm 3), in order to maximize the marginal gain, we have to compute $\sigma(C_i \cup C_j)$ for all the communities $C_j \in \mathcal{P}$, thus, MAMKCP requires $\mathcal{O}(n^2\tau)$ time to obtain a K-VDP when n is large and K is small. The computational complexity of SAMKCP is even higher. Therefore, they may be not suitable for large social networks. To improve the running time performance, here we provide an alternative merge strategy for implementing MAMKCP. Instead of merging the communities with the maximum marginal gain, in step 4 we estimate the influence propagation of C_i through the entire graph, i.e., $\sigma_V(C_i)$, and then compute the average influence received by C_j from C_i, which is defined as $\frac{\sum_{l \in C_i} \sum_{r \in C_j} p_V(l,r)}{|C_j|}$, for all the communities $C_j \neq C_i$. This can be done by simply accumulating $p_V(l,r)$ for each community C_j when we computing $\sigma_V(C_i)$. Finally, we merge C_i with a community with the highest average received influence. In such a way, a merge can be done in $O(\tau)$ time. The overall running time of MAMKCP is only $\mathcal{O}(n\tau)$.

According to the complexity analysis, MAMKCP is better than SAMKCP in terms of the running time performance. For some large social networks, we can apply the simplified version of MAMKCP which requires only linear time. In terms of the partition quality, intuitively, SAMKCP is better than MAMKCP because it considers the global optimization (top-down approach) each time and MAMKCP considers the local optimization (bottom-up approach). We will demonstrate their performance through simulation in the next section.

Results and discussion

In this section, we carry out experiments over real-world social networks. The influence propagation is based on the well-known LT and IC models, and we run MC simulation to estimate the influential propagation function $\sigma(\cdot)$. We begin by describing the algorithms, data sets, and experimental settings in 'Algorithm', 'Data set', and 'Experiment setting' sections, respectively, and then discuss the experimental results in 'Experiment result' section.

Algorithm

In addition to the proposed algorithms, (SAMKCP, Algorithm 2) and (MAMKCP, Algorithm 3), we also implement two classic community partition algorithms for comparison purposes. One is a Modularity-based Algorithm (MODUA) proposed in [47] and the other is a Spectrum-based Algorithm (SPECA) proposed in [48]. Given a graph G, MODUA finds communities by optimizing the modularity score locally and it terminates until a maximal modularity score is obtained. Therefore, MODUA cannot partition G into a given number K of communities. While SPECA is flexible for the number K of communities, it partitions a graph iteratively into K communities by minimizing the general cut each time according to the adjacent matrix. To the best of our knowledge, we do not find any algorithm which is designed for disjoint community partition with the objective of maximizing the influence propagation within each community. In addition, we do not find any density-based algorithm that can be applied to our MKCP problem.

Data set

We conduct simulation on three real-world social networks as follow: (1) NetHEPT: taken from the co-authorship network in 'High Energy Physics (Theory)' section (from 1991 to 2003) of arXiv (http://arXiv.org). The nodes in NetHEPT denote the authors, and the edges represent the co-authorship. HetHEPT has 15,229 nodes and 31,376 edges. (2) NetEmail: taken from the email interchange network in University of Rovira i Virgili (Tarragona). The nodes in NetEmail denote the members in the university, and the edges represent email interchanges among the members (the data set is available at http://deim.urv.cat/~alephsys/data.php). NetEmail has 1,133 nodes and 10,902 edges. (3) NetCLUB: taken from the relationship network in Zachary's Karate club network, which is described by Wayne Zachary in [49]. NetCLUB has 34 nodes and 78 edges.

Experiment setting

In this study, we assume that the influential degree from nodes i to j depends on the closeness of their relationship and the probability $p(i)$ for node i where $p(i)$, as defined in Problem description' section, is the probability that node i would produce an influence propagation or would share knowledge with others. We apply the method proposed in [14] to estimate the closeness $c(i,j)$ between i and j. Let $\deg_{in}(j)$ denote the in-degree of node j, then $c(i,j) = e(i,j)/\deg_{in}(j)$, where $e(i,j)$ denotes the number of edges from i to j. Due to the lack of ground truth, we independently assign uniform random 0.1%, 1%, and 10% to sharing probabilities $p(i)$ for all the nodes i. Then we assume $\forall(i,j) \in E$, i has a chance of $w(i,j) = \frac{p(i)e(i,j)}{\deg_{in}(j)}$ to influence j.

Experiment result

We first evaluate the performance of our algorithms on NetCLUB. In algorithm SAMKCP or MAMKCP, $\sigma(\cdot)$ is computed by running MC simulation 1,000 times and get the average. Although AM2CP is not an optimal solution in the IC model, we still apply it in the splits in the simulation of IC model to improve the computational efficiency. Since MODUA is not flexible for the number of communities, we first apply MODUA to get a partition of NetCLUB and then apply our algorithms and SPECA to partition NetCLUB into the same number of communities. Figures 4 and 5 show the experimental results for the LT and IC models respectively. NetCLUB is partitioned into four communities. In

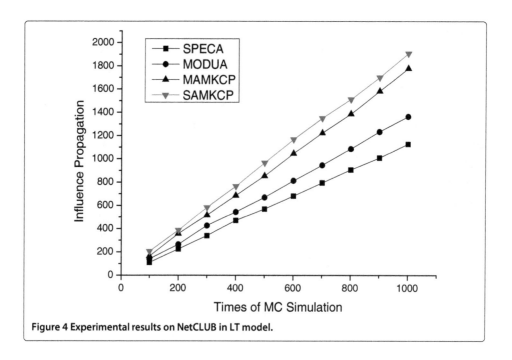

Figure 4 Experimental results on NetCLUB in LT model.

terms of influence propagation, both SAMKCP and MAMKCP are better than MODUA and SPECA. SAMKCP outperforms MODUA and SPECA by about 40% and 70% respectively. In addition, from Figures 4 and 5, we can see the influence propagation of each partition is increasing gradually and linearly when the times of simulation increase, which reflects the reliability of experimental results.

In the second experiment, we compare MAMKCP with MODUA and SPECA on NetEmail. SAMKCP is removed due to its high computational complexity. Figures 6 and 7 show the experimental results. The network is partitioned into 88 communities. MAMKCP has the maximum sum of influence propagation. The performance of SPECA

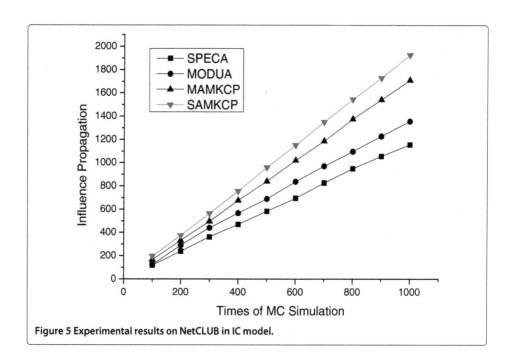

Figure 5 Experimental results on NetCLUB in IC model.

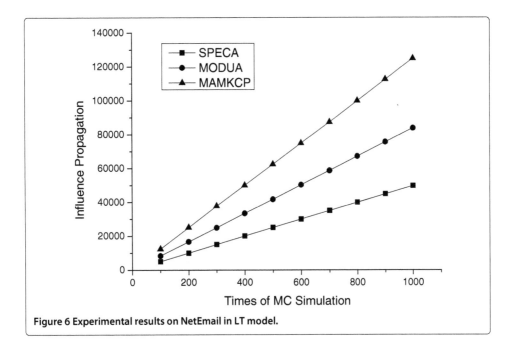

Figure 6 Experimental results on NetEmail in LT model.

is poor compared with MAMKCP and MODUA. The influence propagation within the partition of SPECA is about two times less than that of MAMKCP and about one time less than that of MODUA.

In the last experiment, we compare MAMKCP with MODUA and SPECA on NetHEPT. Since this network has 15,229 nodes and 31,376 edges, we use the simplified version of MAMKCP. Figures 8 and 9 show the experimental results. The network is partitioned into 1,820 communities. MAMKCP is still better than MODUA and SPECA, but the gap between MAMKCP and MODUA in this experiment is less than that in the second experiment. This agrees with our intuition in that simplified MAMKCP has a

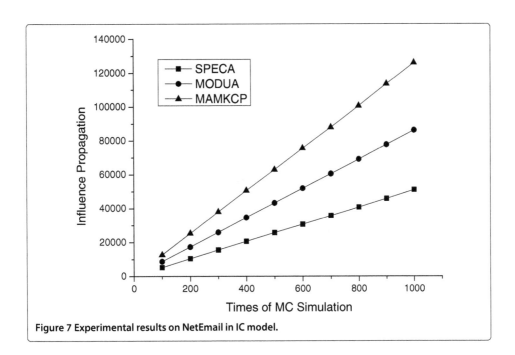

Figure 7 Experimental results on NetEmail in IC model.

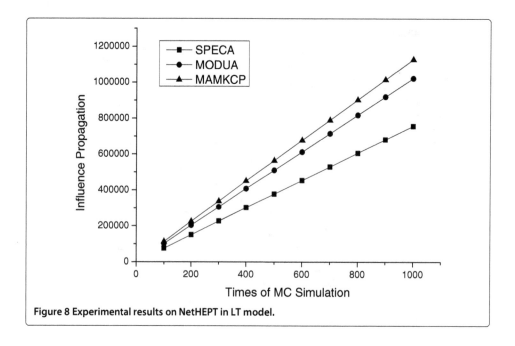

Figure 8 Experimental results on NetHEPT in LT model.

lower computational complexity but also has some loss in performance. According to the three experimental results, we can conclude that the proposed algorithms are better than modularity-based and spectrum-based methods for finding communities in terms of influence propagation.

Conclusions

Community partition and influence propagation are important problems in social networks. In this paper, we investigate the Maximum K-Community Partition (MKCP) problem to maximize the sum of influence propagation within each community. We analyze the problem both theoretically and practically. Especially we show that the M2CP

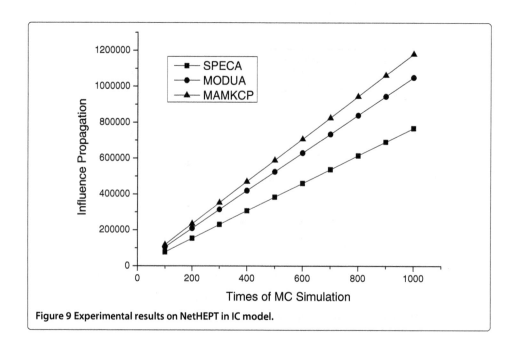

Figure 9 Experimental results on NetHEPT in IC model.

problem can be solved efficiently for a class of influence propagation models. In addition, we prove that the $MKCP$ problem is $\mathcal{NP}$-hard in the well-known LT and IC models for general K. We also develop two heuristic algorithms and demonstrate their efficiency through simulation on real-world social networks.

We believe this study is useful for the influence propagation problems. In future research, we plan to extend our work to the influence maximization problem to select the most influential nodes based on influence-based communities. Furthermore, we will study potential applications of influence-based communities in social networks.

Competing interests
The authors declare that they have no competing interests.

Authors' contributions
ZL and YZ formulated the problem and did the algorithm design and implementation. WL, WW, and XC contributed to the theoretical part of algorithm design and organized this research. All authors read and approved the final manuscript.

Acknowledgements
This research work is supported in part by National Science Foundation of USA under grants NSF 1137732 and NSF 1241626.

Author details
[1]NSF Center for Research on Complex Networks, Texas Southern University, 3100 Cleburne Street, Houston, TX 77004, USA. [2]Department of Computer Science, University of Texas at Dallas, 800 W. Campbell Road, Richardson, TX 75080, USA. [3]Department of Computer Science, Texas Southern University, 3100 Cleburne Street, Houston, TX 77004, USA. [4]Department of Computer Science, George Washington University, 2121 Eye Street NW, Washington DC 20052, USA.

References
1. Bollobas, B: Modern Graph Theory. Springer Verlag, New York (1998)
2. Girvan, M, Newman, MEJ: Community structure in social and biological networks. Proc. Natl. Acad. Sci. **99**(12), 7821–7826 (2002)
3. Luxburg, U: A tutorial on spectral clustering. Stat. Comput. **17**, 395–416 (2007)
4. Kannan, R, Vempala, S, Vetta, A: On clusterings: good, bad and spectral. J. ACM. **51**(3), 497–515 (2004)
5. Mancoridis, S, Mitchell, BS, Rorres, C: Using automatic clustering to produce high-level system organizations of source code. In: *Proceedings of the 6th International Workshop on Program Comprehension*, Ischia, Italy, 24–26 June 1998, pp. 45–53, (1998)
6. Newman, M, Girvan, M: Finding and evaluating community structure in networks. Phys. Rev. E. **69**, 026113 (2004)
7. White, S, Smyth, P: A spectral clustering approach to finding communities in graphs. In: *SDM'05: Proceedings of the 5th SIAM International Conference on Data Mining*, pp. 76–84, (2005)
8. Newman, M: Modularity and community structure in networks. Proc. Natl. Acad. Sci. USA. **103**(23), 8577–8582 (2006)
9. Brown, J, Reinegen, P: Social ties and word-of-mouth referral behavior. J. Consum. Res. **14**, 350–362 (1987)
10. Goldenberg, J, Libai, B, Muller, E: Using complex systems analysis to advance marketing theory development: modeling heterogeneity effects on new product growth through stochastic cellular automata. Acad. Market. Sci. Rev. **9**(3), 1–18 (2001)
11. Goldenberg, J, Libai, B, Muller, E: Talk of the network: a complex systems look at the underlying process of word-of-mouth. Market. Lett. **12**, 211–223 (2001)
12. Richardson, M, Domingos, V: Mining knowledge-sharing sites for viral marketing, Edmonton, Alberta, Canada, 23–26 July 2002, pp. 61–70. KDD (2002)
13. Domingos, P, Richardson, M: Mining the network value of customers, San Francisco, CA, USA, 26–29 August 2001, pp. 57–66. KDD (2001)
14. Kempe, D, Kleinberg, JM, Tardos, E: Maximizing the spread of influence through a social network. In: *Proceedings of the 9th ACM SIGKDD International Conference on Knowledge Discovery and Data Mining*, pp. 137–146. ACM, New York, (2003)
15. Chen, W, Yuan, Zhang, L: Scalable influence maximization in social networks under the linear threshold model. In: *Proceedings of the 10th IEEE International Conference on Data Mining*, Sydney, Australia, 14–17 December 2010, pp. 88–97, (2010)
16. Chen, W, Wang, C, Wang, Y: Scalable influence maximization for prevalent viral marketing in large-scale social networks. In: *Proceedings of the 16th ACM SIGKDD International Conference on Knowledge Discovery and Data Mining*, pp. 1029–1038. ACM, New York, (2010)
17. Wang, Y, Cong, G, Song, G, Xie, K: Community-based greedy algorithm for mining top-k influential nodes in mobile social networks. In: *Proceedings of the 16th ACM SIGKDD International Conference on Knowledge Discovery and Data Mining (KDD'10)*, pp. 1039–1048. ACM, New York, (2010)

18. Radicchi, F, Castellano, C, Cecconi, F, Loreto, V, Parisi, D: Defining and identifying communities in networks. Proc. Natl. Acad. Sci. USA. **101**(9), 2658–2663 (2004)

19. Hu, Y, Chen, H, Zhang, P, Zhang, P, Li, M, Di, Z, Fan, Y: Comparative definition of community and corresponding identifying algorithm. Phys. Rev. E. **78**, 026121 (2008)

20. Weiss, RS, Jacobson, E: A method for the analysis of the structure of complex organizations. Am. Sociol. Rev. **20**(6), 661–668 (1955)

21. Boettcher, S, Percus, AG: Extremal optimization for graph partitioning. Phys. Rev. E. **64**, 026114 (2001)

22. Clauset, A, Newman, MEJ, Moore, C: Finding community structure in very large networks. Phys. Rev. E. **70**(6), 066111 (2004)

23. Newman, MEJ: Fast algorithm for detecting community structure in networks. Phys. Rev. E. **69**, 066133 (2004)

24. Wakita, K, Tsurumi, T: Finding community structure in mega-scale social networks. In: *Proceedings of the 16th International Conference on World Wide Web, WWW'07*, pp. 1275–1276. ACM, New York, (2007)

25. Guimera, R, Pardo, MS, Amaral: LAN: modularity from fluctuations in random graphs and complex networks. Phys. Rev. E. **70**(2), 025101 (2004)

26. Massen, CP, Doye, JPK: Identifying communities within energy landscapes. **71**, 046101 (2005)

27. Duch, J, Arenas, A: Community detection in complex networks using extremal optimization. Phys. Rev. E. **72**(2), 027104 (2005)

28. Holland, JH: Adaptation in Natural and Artificial Systems. MIT, Cambridge (1992)

29. Pizzuti, C: Community detection in social networks with genetic algorithms. In: *Proceedings of the 10th Annual Conference on Genetic and Evolutionary Computation, GECCO'08*, pp. 1137–1138. ACM, New York, (2008)

30. Fortunato, S, Barthelemy, M: Resolution limit in community detection. Proc. Natl. Acad. Sci. USA. **104**(1), 36–41 (2007)

31. Zhang, X, Li, Z, Wang, R, Wang, Y: A combinatorial model and algorithm for globally searching community structure in complex networks. J. Combin. Optim. **23**(4), 425–442 (2010)

32. Fortunato, S: Community detection in graphs. Phys. Rep. **486**, 75–174 (2010)

33. Gaertler, M: Clustering. In: *Brandes, U, Erlebach, T (eds.) Network Analysis: Methodological Foundations*, pp. 178–215. Springer (2005)

34. Lancichinetti, A, Fortunato, S: Community detection algorithms: a comparative analysis. Phys. Rev. E. **80**, 056117 (2009)

35. Schaeffer, S: Graph clustering. Comput. Sci. Rev. **1**(1), 27–64 (2007)

36. Andersen, R, Chung, F, Lang, K: Local graph partitioning using PageRank vectors. In: *Proceedings of the 47th Annual IEEE Symposium on Foundations of Computer Science*, Berkeley, CA, USA, 21–24 October 2006, pp. 475–486 (2006)

37. Leicht, EA, Newman, MEJ: Community structure in directed networks. Phys. Rev. Lett. **100**(11), 118703 (2008)

38. Leskovec, J, Krause, A, Guestrin, C, Faloutsos, C, VanBriesen, J, Glance, N: Cost-effective outbreak detection in networks. In: *Proceedings of the 13th ACM SIGKDD International Conference on Knowledge Discovery and Data Mining*, San Jose, CA, USA, 12–15 August 2007, pp. 420–429, (2007)

39. Kimura, M, Saito, K: Tractable models for information diffusion in social networks, pp. 259–271, PKDD, (2006)

40. Kimura, M, Saito, K, Motoda, H: Efficient estimation of influence functions for SIS model on social networks. In: *Proceedings of the 21st International Joint Conference on Artificial Intelligence*, Pasadena, CA, USA, 11–17 July 2009, pp. 2046–2051, (2009)

41. Li, H, Bhowmick, S, Sun, A: CINEMA: conformity-aware greedy algorithm for influence maximization in online social networks, pp. 323–334. EDBT, (2013)

42. Galstyan, A, Musoyan, V, Cohen, P: Maximizing influence propagation in networks with community structure. Phys. Rev. E. **79**(5), 056102 (2009)

43. Nguyen, NP, Yan, G, Thai, MT, Eidenbenz, S: Containment of misinformation spread in online social networks. WebSci, pp. 213–222 (2012)

44. Dinh, TN, Xuan, Y, Thai, MT: Towards social-aware routing in dynamic communication networks. IPCCC, pp. 161–168 (2009)

45. Belak, V, Lam, S, Hayes, C: Targeting online communities to maximise information diffusion. In: *Proceedings of the WWW Workshop on Mining Social Networks Dynamics*, pp. 1153–1160. Lyon, France, (2012)

46. Stoer, M, Wagner, F: A simple min-cut algorithm. J. ACM. **44**(4), 585–591 (1997)

47. Blondel, V, Guillaume, J, Lambiotte, R, Lefebvre, E: Fast unfolding of communities in large networks. J. Stat. Mech. Theor. Exp (2008)

48. Dhillon, I, Guan, Y, Kulis, B: A fast kernel-based multilevel algorithm for graph clustering. In: *Proceedings of The 11th ACM SIGKDD*, Chicago, Illinois, USA, 21-24 August 2005, pp. 629–634, (2005)

49. Zachary, W: An information flow model for conflict and fission in small groups. J. Anthrop. Res. **33**, 452–73 (1977)

11

Power and loyalty defined by proximity to influential relations

Dror Fidler

Correspondence: d.fidler@ucl.ac.uk
The Bartlett, University College London, Tottenham Court Road, London, UK

Abstract

This paper examines a simple definition of power as a composite centrality being the composition of eigenvector centrality and edge betweeness. Various centralities related to the composition are compared on social and collaboration networks. A derived defection score for social fission scenarios is introduced and is demonstrated in Zachary's Karate club to predict the sole defection in terms of network measures rather than psychological factors. In a network of political power in Mexico across various periods, the two definitions of power serve to shed light on a political power transition between two groups.

Keywords: Composite centrality; Power; Loyalty; Eigenvector; Betweeness; Fission

Introduction

Networks are often modeled as a *graph*, which consists of set of nodes (V) and edges (E), such that $E \subseteq V \times V$. If E is a symmetric relation, then G is called an *undirected* graph. A *network centrality* is a function defined on V which assigns importance to nodes according to certain criteria.

Various feedback centralities have been introduced (Seeley [1], Hubbell [2], Katz [3], Bonacich [4]), which share the common objective of measuring a node's importance while taking into account the importance of its neighbors. The simplified form of a feedback centrality termed eigenvector centrality is based on the Perron-Frobenius theorem which ensures that for a strongly connected graph, the leading eigenvector of the adjacency matrix contains only real positive values ([5]). Let $X = (x_1 \ldots x_n)$ be the eigenvector of the largest eigenvalue of the adjacency matrix A_G of G, and λ_1 is the largest eigenvalue. Then, the eigenvector centrality of node i is $C_{EV}(i) = \frac{1}{\lambda_1} x_i$. Informally, C_{EV} will find a set of nodes which are more densely connected (clique-like) than other subsets of V. A node with a high C_{EV} score would have relatively more edges between its neighbors.

Betweeness centrality, which was introduced by Freeman in [6] and Anthonisse in [7], measures the proportion of shortest paths passing by a given node. Formally, let $\sigma_{s,t}$ be the number of shortest paths between nodes s,t, and $\sigma_{s,t}(v)$ be the number of shortest paths between s,t that pass through v; then, the betweeness of v is defined as $C_B(v) = \sum_{s \neq v} \sum_{t \neq v} \frac{\sigma_{s,t}(v)}{\sigma_{s,t}}$. In [7], betweeness is also defined for edges, for an edge $e \in E$, $C_{EB}(e) = \sum_{s \in v} \sum_{t \in v} \frac{\sigma_{s,t}(e)}{\sigma_{s,t}}$. In a social network, an edge with high betweeness would mean that the relation between the represented actors is important in the sense that it is expected to be used more by other actors in the network. Edge betweeness has also been used to detect community structure ([8]).

Definitions and properties

Composite centralities have been suggested based on statistical measures ([9]); here, the natural composition is taken. Let C_1 be a node centrality, and C_2 be an edge centrality whose values are non negative. The fact that C_1 is node based and C_2 is edge based suggests a natural function composition, define:

$$A_{C_2}[i,j] = \begin{cases} C_2((i,j)) & (i,j) \in E \\ 0 & (i,j) \notin E \end{cases} \tag{1}$$

And notate $C_1(C_2)(v)$ as the value for v when C_1 is computed on A_{C_2}. A matrix is said to be *irreducible* if its interpretation as a graph adjacency matrix produces a strongly connected graph. If G is an edge weighted graph, it may be that $C_{EB}(e) = 0$ for $e \in E$, while for non-weighted graphs, this is not the case; since every edge would be on the shortest path between its endpoints. Thus, for a weighted graph, using Equation 1 may produce a reducible matrix, since some edges may have zero betweeness.

Proposition 0.1. *Let G be an positive edge weighted undirected connected graph, then $A_{C_{EB}}$ is irreducible.*

Proof. Let $u, v \in V$, since G is connected, there exists at least one shortest path P_{uv} connecting u and v. From the definition of C_{EB}, for any edge $e \in P_{uv}$, $C_{EB}(e) > 0$. Therefore, in the graph defined by $A_{C_{EB}}$, there exists a positively weighted path connecting u and v. □

Notate $C_{EVB}(v) = C_{EV}(C_{EB})(v)$. From 0.1, C_{EVB} is well defined, as the Perron-Frobenius theorem holds the same way as for C_{EV}. In this case, it is assumed that high edge betweeness indicates a potentially important relation, and that an actor is more powerful if it participates in important relations, either directly, or its neighbors have important relations between themselves.

An artificial example

A simple example in Figure 1 demonstrates that C_{EVB} may differ from both C_{EV}, C_B or any linear combination of them. The example consists of two small complete graphs which are connected by one node (node 11) and another node (node 12) connected to node 11. Clearly, node 12 has zero C_B and low C_{EV}, but it has the second highest C_{EVB}. Node 12 is accessible only via node 11, the most powerful node in all three measures, so if we assume that all nodes are initially accessed at a similar rate, the relation between 11 and 12 will be the most used, while the nodes within the cliques would have many relations that are used only between the two endpoints (see Figure 1). This shows that C_{EVB} may detect a 'behind the scenes' player like node 12, while C_{EV} and C_B would assign it low scores.

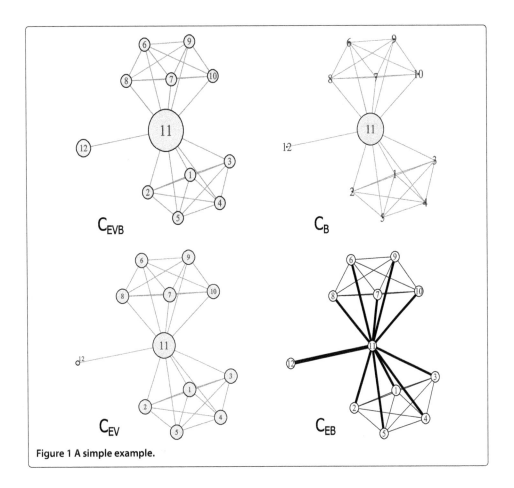

Figure 1 A simple example.

Eigenvectors in a weighted graph and scaling behaviour

The justification of using C_{EV} on an edge weighted network is, as explained by Newman in [10], if $X = (x_1 \ldots x_n)$ is the leading eigenvector, then

$$C_{EV}(i) = x_i = \frac{1}{\lambda_1} \sum_j A_{ij} x_j \tag{2}$$

hence multiplying the weight of an edge by a positive factor will adjust the contribution of the neighbour incident on that edge to the eigenvector centralities of its incident nodes by the same factor, i.e. if the weight of (v,u) is 3 then the contribution of u to $C_{EV}(v)$ is multiplied by a factor of 3. Thus, calculating the eigenvector centrality of an edge weighted network would score nodes according to the weighted density of their neighborhood.

An informal scaling argument regarding C_{EVB} is shown as follows. It is proven in [11] that for a graph $G = (V, E)$ and any node $v \in V$,

$$C_B(v) = \sum_{(u,v) \in E} C_{EB}((u, v)) - (n - 1) \tag{3}$$

Furthermore, it is numerically demonstrated in [12] that if G is a node degree scale free network with exponent between 2 and 3, then C_B follows a power law distribution with exponent approximately 2.2. So, if C_{EV} scales 'nicely' in relation to a node degree power law exponent, that would mean that the row sums of the original adjacency matrix are related to the scaling behaviour of C_{EV}. Since node betweeness is distributed as a power law as mentioned, then Equation 3 implies that C_{EVB} will scale in a similar way in relation to C_B, as the row sums in the edge betweeness weighted adjacency matrix are proportional to C_B. Indeed, visually inspecting the scatterplots of log-transformed C_B and C_{EVB} (Figure 2) demonstrates that for nodes that do have zero C_B may still have significant values of C_{EVB} in a similar way as in the artificial example; as for nodes that do not have zero C_B, there is a linear or 'cone'-shaped relation , which provides some evidence of a power scaling relation between C_B and C_{EVB}.

Predicting loyalty in a fission scenario

Let $V = S_1 \cup S_2$ be a disjoint partition of V. Assume w.l.o.g that $v \in S_1$. Let $X = (x_1, ..., x_n)$ be the leading eigenvector, then the contribution of S_2 to $C_{EVB}(v)$ is:

$$C_{EVB}^{S_2}(v) = \sum_{(v,v_i) \in E, v_i \in S_2} C_{EB}((v, v_i))x_i \tag{4}$$

By the definition of C_{EVB} as power, Equation 4 describes the proportion of power of v that comes from direct links to the opposing group members. In a social fission situation, it may be the case that members of one group defect to the other as in [13]. Motivated by defection prediction, define the *defection score* as:

$$D_{EVB}(v) = C_{EVB}^{S_2}(v) - C_{EVB}^{S_1}(v) \tag{5}$$

For a node v, $D_{EVB}(v)$ is simply the difference between the power of v that comes from links to the opposing group and the power that comes from links to its own group. It is hypothesized that a high positive D_{EVB} would mean a higher temptation to defect, while a more negative D_{EVB} would mean a greater tendency to stay put.

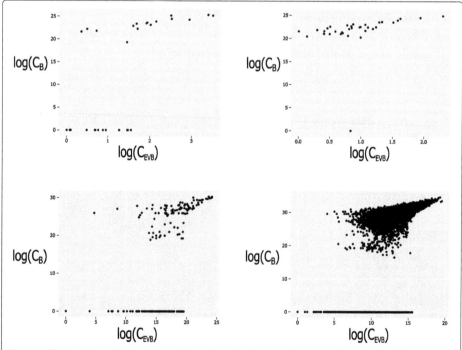

Figure 2 The Log/log relation of C_B and C_{EVB}. Clockwise from top left : Zachary's Karate club, Mexican political elite, Astrophysics collaboration and Newmans network science collaboration network. Negligible values were added to C_B to allow log of zero values. Both functions are translated to the origin $(0, 0)$.

Computational complexity

The complexity of computing a composite function as defined here is simply the sum of the complexities of the underlying functions. An algorithm of $O(|V||E|)$ for betweeness is described in [14]. Eigenvector centrality requires only the largest eigenvalue and the corresponding eigenvector. In practice, this is solvable in $O(|V| + |E|)$ using an ARPACK eigenvector solver. Thus, the expected overall time is the same as for edge betweeness. The computational complexity for $D_{EVB}(v)$ is $O(|V|)$ if $C_{EVB}(v)$ is already computed.

Case studies

Several social networks are examined, two 'friendship' networks: Zachary's Karate club ([13]) and a network of the Mexican political elite in the twentieth century. In addition, two larger collaboration networks are studied, a collaboration network of researchers in Network Science (NS) taken from [15] and the collaboration network of preprints on the astrophysics archive at www.arxiv.org, 1995-1999, as compiled by Newman [16]. As can be seen in Table 1, C_{EVB} and C_B are more correlated in the friendship networks than the collaboration networks.

A network describing social fission

Zachary's Karate club is one of the earliest social networks studied as a graph ([13]). The network consists of 34 actors whose common activity is a Karate club, edges are weighted by the level of acquaintance shared by actors beyond the club. The club underwent fission during the period of observation due to a long conflict between the club administrator and the Karate instructor. Zachary's original analysis was based on network flow and minimal cuts, where the edge weights represented capacity. In this case, the reciprocal of the weights are taken, as the edge weights represent distance and not flow capacity. As seen in Figure 3, C_{EVB} differs from C_{EV} and C_B with regard to key players; for instance, actor 34 is reduced in C_{EVB} in comparison to other actors, while actors 3 and 9 have a relative increase in C_{EVB}. By inspecting C_{EB} visually in Figure 3, it indeed seems that actors 3 and 9 are better located within the network regarding proximity to edges with high betweeness. Zachary's flow analysis managed to model and predict the group affiliation before and after the fissure with near perfection save one case.

Zachary's original explanation [13] was psychological, based on the temporal circumstance of individual 9:

'This can be explained by noting that he was only three weeks away from a test for black belt (master status) when the split in the club occurred. Had he joined the officers' club he would have had to give up his rank and begin again in a new style of karate with a white (beginner's) belt, since the officers had decided to change the style of karate practiced in their new club'.

Table 1 Spearman rank correlation scores compared for various networks

Network	$|V|$	$|E|$	$C_{EVB} \mid C_B$	$C_{EVB} \mid C_{EV}$	$C_B \mid C_{EV}$
Karate club	34	78	0.762	0.479	0.398
Mexican politicians	35	117	0.703	0.607	0.739
NS collaboration	374	914	0.427	0.504	0.049
Astro-ph	14,845	119,652	0.604	0.786	0.431

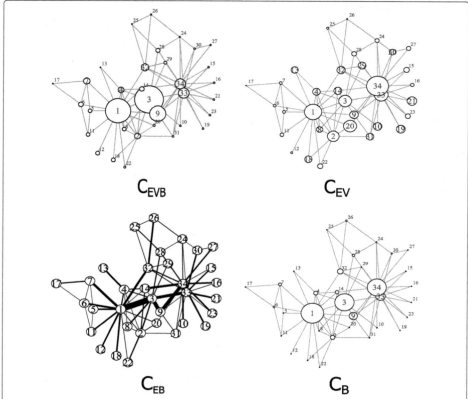

Figure 3 The Karate club. Four centralities in Zachary's network. Colors of nodes (blue or red) designate faction membership, while the larger the node is, the higher the centrality score. For edge betweeness (lower left), thicker edges have higher scores.

Here, an additional factor may be observed based on D_{EVB} scores. D_{EV} is defined in a similar way to D_{EVB}, using the adjacency matrix of G without computing edge betweeness, and as visible in Figure 4, D_{EV} predicts that actor 10 would have the highest incentive to defect while D_{EVB} predicts actor 9 for defection (as indeed took place). In addition, D_{EVB} predicts that actors 1 and 34, which are the leaders of the factions, would have the greatest tendency to stay put while D_{EV} makes no such prediction. Unfortunately, no data exists as to the possible dilemmas of other actors such as nodes 10 and 33.

Collaboration networks

The NS network constructed by Newman ([15]) consists of 1,589 nodes; here, the largest connected component is studied, consisting of 379 nodes. Edges are weighted by collaboration strength as defined in [16], so reciprocals are taken here to represent distance between collaborators. The three centralities are shown in Figure 5, in which the five nodes with the highest scores are identified by their ID (specific names are available in [15] for readers interested). The occasional 'local' nature of C_{EV} is apparent in Figure 5, nodes on one sole branch of the network receive the highest scores due to a higher density of edges. In this case, C_{EV} may show isolation rather than power, a group with many links between themselves on an isolated branch. Examining the differences between C_{EVB} and C_B, it is clear that actors 51, 52 and 95 score well in both measures, but actor 26 loses power in C_{EVB}, while actor 4 drops to the 19th place in the C_{EVB} scores.

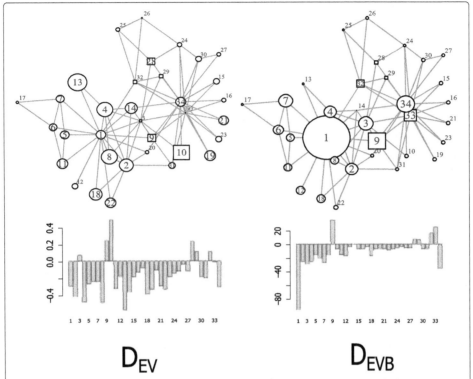

Figure 4 Loyalty or defection. Predicting the incentive to defect. Larger squares mean a higher positive defection score, while larger circles mean a more negative score, which represents the tendency to stay within the original group.

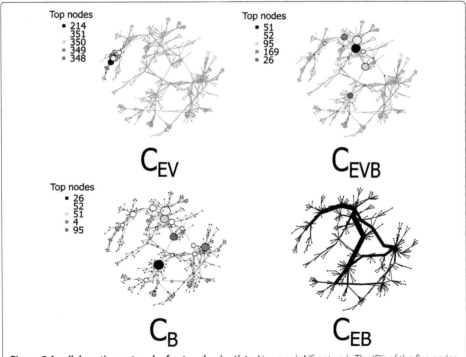

Figure 5 A collaboration network of network scientists. Newman's NS network. The ID's of the five nodes with the highest scores in each case are listed in descending order.

As with the Karate club, the reason why actor 4 loses power according to C_{EVB} is clearer by looking at Figure 5, the edges with higher betweeness form a path through the 'middle' while actor 4 is located on a lower scored subsidiary of the sub-network of edges with high betweeness. So, although actor 4 has high betweeness as a node centrality, C_{EVB} is reduced due to a lower scoring edge betweeness neighborhood.

A transition of political power

A network of the Mexican political elite was described in [17] and compiled in [18]. The network consists of the core of the political elite and their collaborators across a time period stretching from the early to late twentieth century. The edges of the network are unweighted and represent close ties. During the time period examined, the PRI (Partido Revolucionario Institucional) was continuously in power, however there was an internal struggle between two main groups within the party, politicians associated with the military against 'civilian' politicians. During the period, there was a transition of power from the former to the latter. In this context, since the network spans most of the twentieth century, C_{EV} would represent the amount of connections surrounding a politician during the height of his political activity but as already demonstrated in the NS network (Figure 5) that is not necessarily the same as a high C_{EVB} score. On the other hand, C_{EVB} would indicate the proximity of a politician to the relations that are expected to be significant throughout the era; therefore, C_{EVB} is interpreted as political power. The defection scores, in this context, are interpreted as the level of political collaboration with members of the other side. In Figure 6, C_{EV} and C_{EVB} are examined in order to understand if both perspectives can illuminate the power transition purely by examining the network. In Figure 6, it can be seen that node 12 has the highest C_{EVB} and C_{EV} score. Node 12 represents Miguel Alemán Valdés, the 46th Mexican president whose reign marked the transition from military associated power to more 'civilian' rule. Interestingly, he also has the highest D_{EVB} and D_{EV} scores, meaning that the most powerful politician in the network (highest C_{EVB} score) collaborated closely with 'civilian' politicians, both from a 'local' viewpoint (high D_{EV}) and from a 'global power' viewpoint (high D_{EVB}). Indeed, in 1952, he was succeeded by node 18, Adolfo Ruiz Cortines, a 'civilian' politician, which signified the beginning of the new era. A different observation from the D_{EVB} chart is that a high level of collaboration with the opposing side is more expressed than in D_{EV} when family ties are present. For instance, node 34 is Miguel Alemán Velasco who is the son of Miguel Alemán Valdés, and node 14 is Ramón Beteta who was the brother of node 13, major general Ignacio Beteta, a close associate of node 10, the powerful Lázaro Cárdenas, and both 34 and 14 score high on D_{EVB}. To conclude, the point of political power transition is visible in Figure 6, and the idea that family ties may precede group affiliation in political power sharing is visible in D_{EVB}.

Conclusions

The composition C_{EVB} was shown to be well defined, and it was shown to differ in several aspects from C_{EV} and C_B in case studies. A node defection score based on C_{EVB} and C_{EV} was defined for two-fission situations, and D_{EVB} was shown to better predict the sole defection in Zachary's study than a similar defection score based purely on C_{EV}. A significance threshold for D_{EVB} could be useful (scores below the threshold would mean no defection) and may be worthwhile of further research. The empirical analysis suggests

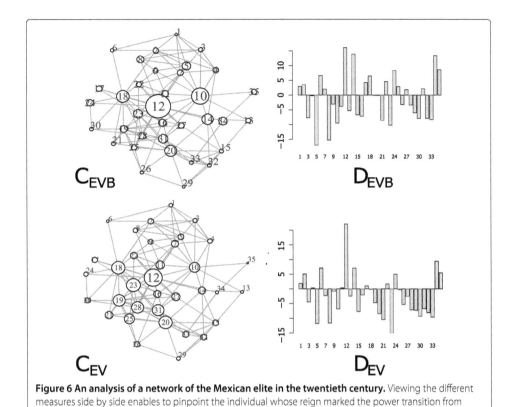

Figure 6 An analysis of a network of the Mexican elite in the twentieth century. Viewing the different measures side by side enables to pinpoint the individual whose reign marked the power transition from 'militarists' to 'civilians'.

that C_{EVB} balances the local properties of eigenvector centrality with the global properties of betweeness, giving a different perspective on power distribution. C_{EVB} in combination with C_{EV} and the defection scores were demonstrated to be useful tools in the analysis of the transition and sharing of power in twentieth century Mexican politics. Finally, the possibility of modeling k-fission scenarios (using a more general defection score) is a natural expansion but would need considerable supporting empirical data as to the behaviour of individuals in such situations.

Competing interests
The author declares that he has no competing interests.

Acknowledgments
This paper was produced from research funded from the EPSRC Platform grant awarded to the Space Group at the Bartlett, Faculty of the Built Environment, University College London (grant reference EP/G02619X/1).

References
1. Seeley, JR: The net of reciprocal influence. Can. J. Psychol. III. **4**, 234–240 (1949)
2. Hubbell, CH: In input-output approach to clique identification. Sociometry. **28**, 377–399 (1965)
3. Katz, L: A new status index derived from sociometric analysis. Psychometrika. **18**(1), 39–43 (1953)
4. Bonacich, P: Power and centrality: a family of measures. Am. J. Sociol. **92**(5), 1170–1182 (1987)
5. Brualdi, RA, Ryser, HJ: Combinatorial Matrix Theory. Cambridge University Press, Cambridge (1991). ISBN 9780521322652
6. Freeman, L: A set of measures of centrality based on betweenness. Sociometry. **40**, 35–41 (1977)
7. Anthonisse, JM: The rush in a directed graph. Technical, Report BN 9/71. Stichting Mathematisch Centrum, Amsterdam (1971)
8. Girvan, M, Newman, MEJ: Community structure in social and biological networks. PNAS. **99**(12), 7821–7826 (2002)
9. Joseph, AC, Chen, G: Composite centrality: a natural scale for complex evolving networks. Phys. D: Nonlinear Phenomena. **267**, 58–67 (2014)

10. Newman, MEJ: Analysis of weighted networks. Phys. Rev. E. **70**, 056131 (2004)
11. Brandes, U, Erlebach, T: Network Analysis: Methodological Foundations. Lecture Notes in Computer Science. Springer-Verlag New York, Inc., New York (2005)
12. Goh, K-I, Kahng, B, Kim, D: Universal behavior of load distribution in scale-free networks. Phys. Rev. Lett. **87**, 278701 (2001)
13. Zachary, WW: An information flow model for conflict and fission in small groups. J. Anthropol. Res. **33**, 452–473 (1977)
14. Brandes, U: A faster algorithm for betweenness centrality. J. Math. Sociol. **25**(2), 163–177 (2001)
15. Newman, MEJ: Finding community structure in networks using the eigenvectors of matrices. Phys. Rev. E. **74**, 036104 (2006)
16. Newman, MEJ: Scientific collaboration networks. II. Shortest paths, weighted networks, and centrality. Phys. Rev. E. **64**, 016132 (20016)
17. Mendieta, JG, Schmidt, S: The political network in Mexico. Soc. Netw. **18**(4), 355–381 (1996)
18. Nooy, W, Mrvar, A, Batagelj, V: Exploratory social network analysis with, Pajek, Chapter 12, Cambridge (2004)
19. Batagelj, V, Mrvar, A: Pajek datasets (2006). http://vlado.fmf.uni-lj.si/pub/networks/data/
20. Csardi, G: igraphdata: a collection of network data sets for the igraph package. R package version 0.1-1 (2013)

Permissions

List of Contributors

Wei Chen
Microsoft Research, No. 5 Danling Street, 100080 Beijing, China

Tian Lin
Institute for Advanced Study, Tsinghua University, No. 1 Tsinghua Yuan, 100084 Beijing, China

Cheng Yang
Department of Computer Science and Technology, Tsinghua University, No. 1 Tsinghua Yuan, 100084 Beijing, China

Amir Afrasiabi Rad and Paola Flocchini
School of Electrical Engineering and Computer Science, University of Ottawa, Ottawa, Ontario, Canada

Joanne Gaudet
Alpen Path Solutions Inc., Ottawa, Ontario, Canada

Pablo Aragón, Helena Gallego and Andreas Kaltenbrunner
Universitat Pompeu Fabra, Barcelona, Spain
Eurecat-Technology Centre of Catalonia, Avinguda Diagonal, 177, 08018 Barcelona, Spain

David Laniado and Yana Volkovich
Eurecat-Technology Centre of Catalonia, Avinguda Diagonal, 177, 08018 Barcelona, Spain

Konstantin E. Avrachenkov and Dmytro G. Rubanov
Inria Sophia Antipolis, 2004 Route des Lucioles, 06902 Valbonne, France
Higher School of Economics, 16 Soyuza Pechatnikov St., St. Petersburg 190121, Russia

Aleksei Y. Kondratev
Higher School of Economics, 16 Soyuza Pechatnikov St., St. Petersburg 190121, Russia
Institute of Applied Mathematical Research, Karelian Research Center, Russian Academy of Sciences, 11 Pushkinskaya St., Petrozavodsk 185910, Russia

Vladimir V. Mazalov
Institute of Applied Mathematical Research, Karelian Research Center, Russian Academy of Sciences, 11 Pushkinskaya St., Petrozavodsk 185910, Russia

Saint-Petersburg State University, 7/9 Universitetskaya Nab., St. Petersburg 199034, Russia

Vesa Kuikka
Finnish Defence Research Agency, Tykkikentäntie 1, 11311 Riihimäki, Finland

Zhenpeng Li, Benhui Chen, Jian Yang and Peng Su
Department of Applied Statistics, Dali University, Dali 671003, China

Xijin Tang
Academy of Mathematics and Systems Sciences, Chinese Academy of Sciences, Beijing 100190, China

Konstantin Avrachenkov and Jithin K. Sreedharan
INRIA Sophia Antipolis 2004, route des Lucioles - BP 93, 06902 Sophia Antipolis Cedex, France

Natalia M. Markovich
Institute of Control Sciences, Russian Academy of Sciences, Moscow, Russia

Demetris Antoniades
Department of Computer Science, University of Cyprus, Nicosia, Cyprus

Constantine Dovrolis
College of Computing, Georgia Institute of Technology, Atlanta, Georgia, USA

Hyoungshick Kim
Department of Computer Science and Engineering, Sungkyunkwan University, Suwon, Korea

Konstantin Beznosov
Department of Electrical and Computer Engineering, University of British Columbia, Vancouver, Canada

Eiko Yoneki
Computer Laboratory, University of Cambridge, Cambridge, UK

Zaixin Lu
NSF Center for Research on Complex Networks, Texas Southern University, 3100 Cleburne Street, Houston, TX 77004, USA

Yuqing Zhu and Weili Wu
Department of Computer Science, University of Texas at Dallas, 800 W. Campbell Road, Richardson, TX 75080, USA

Wei Li
NSF Center for Research on Complex Networks, Texas Southern University, 3100 Cleburne Street, Houston, TX 77004, USA
Department of Computer Science, Texas Southern University, 3100 Cleburne Street, Houston, TX 77004, USA

Xiuzhen Cheng
Department of Computer Science, George Washington University, 2121 Eye Street NW, Washington DC 20052, USA

Dror Fidler
The Bartlett, University College London, Tottenham Court Road, London, UK

Ming Jia, Hualiang Xu, Jingwen Wang, Yiqi Bai, Benyuan Liu and Jie Wang
Department of Computer Science, University of Massachusetts, Lowell, MA 01854, USA

Yingjie Wang and Xiangrong Tong
School of Computer and Control Engineering, Yantai University, Qingquan Road, Yantai 244005, China

Yang Gao
School of Mathematics and Information Science, Yantai University, Qingquan Road, Yantai 244005, China

Guisheng Yin and Qilong Han
College of Computer Science and Technology, Harbin Engineering University, Harbin 150001, China

Zhipeng Cai
College of Computer Science and Technology, Harbin Engineering University, Harbin 150001, China
Department of Computer Science, Georgia State University, Atlanta 30303, Georgia

Index

9 781639 892563